Artificial Intelligence and Computational Modeling in Heat Transfer and Fluid Dynamics

Scrivener Publishing
100 Cummings Center, Suite 541J
Beverly, MA 01915-6106

Publishers at Scrivener
Martin Scrivener (martin@scrivenerpublishing.com)
Phillip Carmical (pcarmical@scrivenerpublishing.com)

Artificial Intelligence and Computational Modeling in Heat Transfer and Fluid Dynamics

Edited by

Mukesh Kumar Awasthi

and

Reshu Gupta

Scrivener Publishing

WILEY

This edition first published 2026 by John Wiley & Sons, Inc., 111 River Street, Hoboken, NJ 07030, USA and Scrivener Publishing LLC, 100 Cummings Center, Suite 541J, Beverly, MA 01915, USA

For more information about Scrivener publications please visit www.scrivenerpublishing.com.

Wiley Global Headquarters
111 River Street, Hoboken, NJ 07030, USA

For details of our global editorial offices, customer services, and more information about Wiley products visit us at www.wiley.com.

The manufacturer's authorized representative according to the EU General Product Safety Regulation is Wiley-VCH GmbH, Boschstr. 12, 69469 Weinheim, Germany, e-mail: Product_Safety@wiley.com.

Library of Congress Cataloging-in-Publication Data

ISBN 9781394433575

Cover image: Generated with AI using Adobe Firefly
Cover design by Russell Richardson

Set in size of 11pt and Minion Pro by Manila Typesetting Company, Makati, Philippines

Printed in the USA

10 9 8 7 6 5 4 3 2 1

Contents

Preface

Artificial Intelligence (AI) and computational modeling have transformed the fields of heat transfer and fluid dynamics, offering innovative solutions for complex engineering challenges. This book *Artificial Intelligence and Computational Modeling in Heat Transfer and Fluid Dynamics* presents a comprehensive exploration of AI-driven techniques, their applications, and the advancements in computational modeling to enhance efficiency and accuracy in thermal and fluid systems. The chapters in this book provide a detailed examination of various methodologies, from machine learning applications to AI-enhanced simulations, making this an essential resource for researchers, engineers, and industry professionals.

Chapter 1 introduces the role of AI in heat transfer and fluid dynamics, highlighting its applications in aerodynamics, chemical processing, and power generation. **Chapter 2** delves into machine learning techniques for fluid mechanics, addressing flow prediction, turbulence modeling, and optimization. **Chapter 3** explores AI-driven computational fluid dynamics (CFD) to enhance simulation accuracy and reduce computation time. **Chapter 4** investigates the application of artificial neural networks in analyzing natural convection in hybrid nanofluids. **Chapter 5** presents an AI-based optimization framework for heat transfer in gyrotactic-nanofluid flow.

Chapter 6 discusses AI-driven techniques for optimizing heat exchanger design and performance. **Chapter 7** focuses on AI-powered energy optimization in HVAC systems using machine learning and game theory. **Chapter 8** applies artificial neural networks to radiative heat transfer in magnetized stenosed arteries. **Chapter 9** examines AI-driven flow optimization techniques in renewable energy systems. **Chapter 10** expands on AI's role in enhancing efficiency and reliability in renewable energy grids.

Chapter 11 investigates deep learning approaches for optimizing energy management in sustainable power systems. **Chapter 12** applies physics-informed neural networks to model exothermic reactions in porous media. **Chapter 13** compares artificial neural networks with traditional numerical methods for solving MHD hyperbolic tangent nanofluid flow. **Chapter 14** provides case studies showcasing AI applications in industrial thermal and fluid processes. **Chapter 15** explores AI-driven advancements in microfluidics and nanofluidics for precise flow control and diagnostics.

This book serves as a bridge between AI methodologies and practical applications in heat transfer and fluid dynamics, offering valuable insights into emerging trends, challenges, and future directions. By integrating AI with traditional computational techniques, the chapters collectively present a roadmap for developing next-generation solutions for complex thermal and fluid systems. We hope this book will inspire researchers and practitioners to explore AI-driven innovations that enhance efficiency, sustainability, and technological progress in engineering applications.

Mukesh Kumar Awasthi
Reshu Gupta

1

Artificial Intelligence in Heat Transfer and Fluid Dynamics: Innovations, Applications, and Future Directions

R. Sakthikala[1]* and R. Revathi[2]

[1]*P.S.G.R. Krishnammal College for Women, Coimbatore, TN, India*
[2]*Dr. N.G.P Arts & Science College, Coimbatore, TN, India*

Abstract

Artificial intelligence (AI) is a rapidly growing field in computer science that is changing the world by creating intelligent machines. It is already present in various aspects of our lives, from self-driving cars to music and art. Artificial intelligence systems analyze large amounts of data, identifying patterns and making predictions. In heat transfer and fluid dynamics, AI can optimize system design, predict and control temperature and flow rates, and analyze large data sets. This leads to improved efficiency, reduced costs, and enhanced safety. The AI techniques used in this field include neural networks, genetic algorithms, and machine learning. Applications of AI in heat transfer and fluid dynamics include aerodynamics, chemical processing, and power generation. Additionally, AI transforms aerodynamics by simulating complex fluid dynamics, predicting and controlling aerodynamic behavior, and optimizing aircraft and wind turbine design. This leads to improved aerodynamic efficiency, reduced fuel consumption, and enhanced safety. By applying AI in these fields, we can accelerate innovation and improve performance.

***Keywords*:** Artificial intelligence, heat transfer, fluid dynamics, neural networks, machine learning, optimization, turbulence modeling

**Corresponding author*: sakthikala09@gmail.com

Mukesh Kumar Awasthi and Reshu Gupta (eds.) Artificial Intelligence and Computational Modeling in Heat Transfer and Fluid Dynamics, (1–22) © 2026 Scrivener Publishing LLC

1.1 Introduction

Artificial intelligence (AI) is an important part of computer science, changing many businesses and creating new opportunities. It can look at large data sets, find patterns, and make predictions, which is useful in many areas, like self-driving cars and the arts. In engineering areas such as heat transfer and fluid dynamics, AI provides new methods to improve efficiency, safety, and performance.

Heat transfer and fluid dynamics are very important for systems that include industrial reactors and vehicles designed for aerodynamics (Figure 1.1). These fields deal with solving difficult equations, such as the Navier–Stokes equations (Figure 1.2) and Fourier's law of heat conduction, which require a lot of computing power. Traditional ways, like computational fluid dynamics (CFD), have improved a lot but still struggle with managing large amounts of data, real-time control, and optimization.

Artificial intelligence represents a new paradigm, allowing engineers to analyze massive datasets faster, predict system behavior more accurately, and iteratively design systems faster. The ability of AI to analyze large datasets, catch complex patterns, and produce correct predictions has proven invaluable when dealing with problems that are limited by traditional

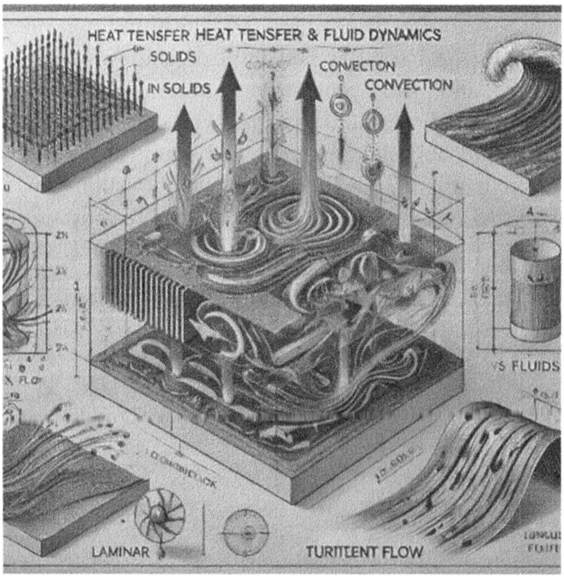

Figure 1.1 A diagram of key phenomena in heat transfer and fluid dynamics, including conduction, convection, turbulence, and flow separation.

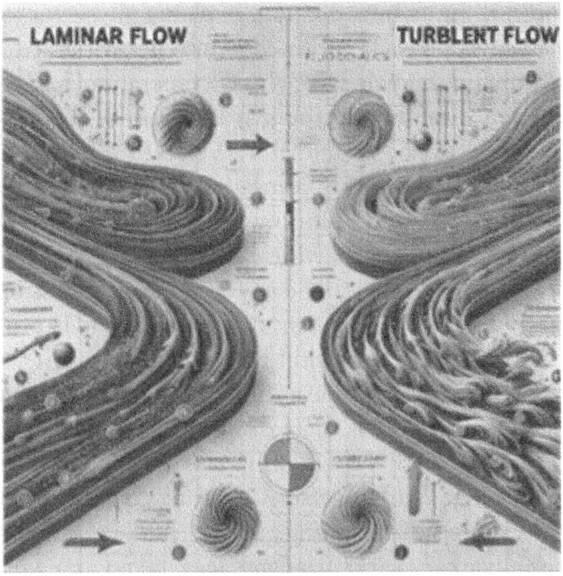

Figure 1.2 Flow visualization of Navier–Stokes solutions for laminar and turbulent regimes.

approaches. Tokenization: This paper explores the transformational potential of AI in these areas, examining its methods, applications, and future potential.

Brunton *et al.* [1] gave a wide perspective on applying machine learning (ML) techniques in fluid domains. It also discusses integrating ML algorithms into turbulence, control, and flow prediction. Moreover, it is proven that ML can be beneficial for solving complex fluid dynamics problems, usually solved using CFD, in terms of computation time and accuracy. The generalizability of ML is one of the biggest issues in the research domain, as it utilizes data from CFD. Furthermore, it provides an overview and detailed comparisons between traditional methods (such as Navier–Stokes simulations) and ML-based approaches, showing the benefits of ML in both computational and real-time profiles. Krzywanski [2] own a recent sense and structure on the great use of AI for the optimization of the heat exchangers' design and demonstrate an implementation of AI-type methods such as genetic algorithms or neural networks to enhance thermal efficiency, minimize energy usage, and obtain cheaper systems.

Physics-Informed Neural Networks PINNs: A Deep Learning Framework for Solving Forward and Inverse Problems Involving PDEs

Raissi, M. *et al.* [3], in its introduction, explains physics-informed neural networks. In essence, physics-informed neural networks are an ML model trained with domain knowledge, where constraints based on physical laws are integrated directly into the loss function of the neural network. According to Malalasekera, W., and H. K. Versteeg [4], this textbook offers a thorough introduction to CFD using the finite volume method. It discusses CFD's theoretical underpinnings, numerical techniques, and real-world applications. The book is widely considered a crucial resource for comprehending CFD principles and is written for professionals and students interested in fluid dynamics simulations. Each idea offers important new perspectives on the relationship between heat transfer, fluid dynamics, and AI. Even though they have different areas of emphasis, taken as a whole, they show how AI is increasingly being used to improve engineering procedures. These papers showcase cutting-edge methods that revolutionize the field, ranging from turbulence modeling and system optimization to directly integrating physics into ML models. Although each paper has advantages and disadvantages, taken as a whole, they provide a thorough framework for future study and advancement in this field. Artificial intelligence overcomes the drawbacks of conventional techniques like CFD by utilizing its capacity to process enormous datasets, model nonlinear systems, and optimize performance dynamically.

The purpose of this chapter is to:

- Introduce AI methods related to fluid dynamics and heat transfer.
- Examine industry use cases and practical applications.
- Talk about the difficulties and potential paths for incorporating AI into these domains.

1.2 Theoretical Foundations of Heat Transfer and Fluid Dynamics

- Heat transfer and fluid dynamics rely on foundational equations. These are essential in understanding the challenges AI can address.

1.2.1 Governing Equations

A. Navier–Stokes equations for fluid flow:

$$\rho\left(\frac{\partial v}{\partial t}+(v.\nabla)v\right)=-\nabla p+\mu\nabla^2 v+f$$

Where,

ρ: Fluid density; v: Velocity vector; p: Pressure; μ: Dynamic viscosity; f: external force

B. Fourier's law for heat conduction:

$$q=-k\nabla T$$

Where,

q: Heat flux; k: Thermal conductivity; T: Temperature

C. Energy equation for heat transfer:

$$\frac{\partial(\rho e)}{\partial t}+\nabla.(\rho ev)=\nabla.(k\nabla T)+\Phi$$

Where,

e is the internal energy, and Φ represents viscous dissipation.

1.3 Artificial Intelligence in Engineering: Methods and Techniques

1.3.1 Neural Networks

A key component of AI, neural networks are made to simulate and learn intricate nonlinear interactions occurring in engineering problems. Neural networks are especially good at solving problems like forecasting temperature fields, heat flux, and flow patterns in the context of heat transfer and fluid dynamics. An examination of two popular neural network architectures is provided below:

Neural networks model complex nonlinear interactions:

- **Feedforward neural networks (FNNs):** Used in heat flux prediction.

Due to their ability to approximate intricate nonlinear relationships between input variables and outputs, feedforward neural networks are frequently used in heat flux prediction. Regarding fluid dynamics and heat transfer:

- **Heat Flux Prediction:** To precisely forecast the heat flux, FNNs are trained on datasets that include input variables like temperature gradients, thermal conductivity, and material properties.
- **Uses for Convection and Conduction:** FNNs predict heat flow through materials by modeling the relationship governed by Fourier's law in the case of conduction. FNNs predict heat transfer rates on surfaces or within domains in convection scenarios by considering flow parameters (such as fluid temperature and velocity).
- **Simulation Enhancement:** By directly forecasting results based on input features, they save computational time when compared to solving conventional partial differential equations (PDEs), which makes them useful for real-time applications.

- **Convolutional Neural Networks (CNNs):** Analyze spatial data, such as temperature fields. Convolutional neural networks (CNNs) are especially well-suited for tasks involving temperature and velocity fields in fluid dynamics and heat transfer because of their superior ability to analyze spatially distributed data:
  a) **Thermodynamic Field Analysis:** CNNs analyze temperature distribution data to find anomalies, hotspots, or patterns. For instance, they can identify areas in a heat exchanger where heat dissipation is inefficient.
  b) **Visualization of Fluid Flow:** CNNs examine velocity fields in fluid dynamics to detect boundary layer behavior, turbulence zones, or flow separations. This aids in optimizing heating, ventilation, and air conditioning (HVAC) systems and airfoil designs.

c) **Boundary Layer and Thermal Gradients:** CNNs can investigate complex spatial gradients close to surfaces, including boundary layers where velocity or temperature abruptly changes, offering information on methods for improving heat transfer.
d) **Computational Fluid Dynamics Acceleration:** CNNs generate surrogate models that predict temperature and flow fields with high accuracy and significantly faster computation times by learning from high-fidelity simulation data.

- **Practical Integration**

Workflows for fluid dynamics and heat transfer are increasingly incorporating both CNNs and FNNs, including:

- **Design Optimization:** AI tools driven by these networks improve thermal and flow efficiency by optimizing the geometry of heat exchangers, turbines, or aerodynamic surfaces.
- **Real-Time Monitoring:** By using sensor data to identify faults or forecast system performance, these models can improve safety and maintenance during operations.
- **Research and Experimentation:** By identifying significant patterns in sizable datasets, these networks assist in the interpretation of experimental results.

Both FNNs and CNNs are advancing fluid dynamics and heat transfer predictive modeling, design, and operational efficiency by utilizing their respective advantages.

1.3.2 Reinforcement Learning

A sort of ML called reinforcement learning (RL) (Figure 1.3) teaches an agent to make choices by interacting with its surroundings to produce the best results. Reinforcement learning works especially well for optimizing dynamic systems whose parameters change frequently. Because of its adaptability, it can be used in engineering applications like heat exchanger performance optimization and fluid flow control. Dynamic systems are optimized by reinforcement learning, including:

- **Adjusting fluid flow rates**

    - **Dynamic Flow Regulation:** By continuously adjusting to shifting circumstances, RL can regulate fluid flow rates in pipelines and industrial systems. By reducing pressure losses and increasing efficiency, the RL agent discovers the ideal flow conditions. Application: The RL agent lowers energy costs while guaranteeing a sufficient supply in a water distribution system by adjusting valve positions to maintain a constant flow rate.
    - **Energy Optimization in Pumps:** RL systems control pump speeds and flow rates to attain the best possible energy consumption by analyzing real-time sensor feedback. For instance, RL can balance coolant flow rates in HVAC systems to minimize energy consumption and reach desired temperature levels.

    - **Mitigating Turbulence and Cavitation:** RL models forecast and modify flow dynamics to avoid cavitation and turbulence, which can harm machinery and lower productivity.

- **Controlling Heat Exchanger Performance**

    - **Dynamic Heat Transfer Management:** By regulating flow rates and inlet/outlet temperatures, RL maximizes heat exchanger performance. The system adapts operating parameters for optimal heat transfer efficiency by learning from both historical and current data.

Example: RL systems in power plants modify steam flow and pressure levels to optimize energy recovery.

- **Adaptive Temperature Control:** To reduce thermal stress on the heat exchanger's components, RL agents dynamically adjust the temperature gradient.

Applications: In chemical processing industries, where exact temperature control guarantees product quality and averts equipment failure, this is essential.

- **Energy Efficiency and Load Balancing:** RL algorithms ensure that the heat exchanger runs effectively under a range of loads by optimizing the energy input-output ratio.

Example: RL systems in industrial cooling systems adjust to changing demands while preserving ideal heat dissipation and preventing system overload.

Advantages of Reinforcement Learning in Dynamic Systems

1. **Self-Adaptive Behavior:** RL systems do not require manual recalibration because they constantly learn and adapt to new environmental conditions.
2. **Improved Efficiency:** RL improves overall system performance, minimizes waste, and lowers energy consumption by optimizing operational parameters.
3. **Scalability:** RL models are adaptable to a wide range of applications, ranging from small setups to massive industrial systems.
4. **Predictive Maintenance:** By analyzing system performance trends, RL agents can anticipate probable failures, enabling proactive maintenance and decreased downtime.

Figure 1.3 An illustration of reinforcement learning applications in dynamic systems, including fluid flow optimization and heat exchanger performance management.

1.3.3 Physics-Informed Neural Networks

Advanced AI models known as physics-informed neural networks (PINNs) (Figure 1.4) directly integrate physical laws like Navier–Stokes or heat equations into their architecture. The PINNs use data to increase accuracy while guaranteeing that their predictions adhere to governing principles by embedding these equations.

Key characteristics:

- Time and space variables are inputs.
- Physical quantities like temperature and velocity are predicted by outputs.
- Data loss (fit to known data) and physics loss (deviation from governing equations) are combined in loss functions.
- Heat transfer, fluid dynamics, and structural mechanics are a few examples of its applications.

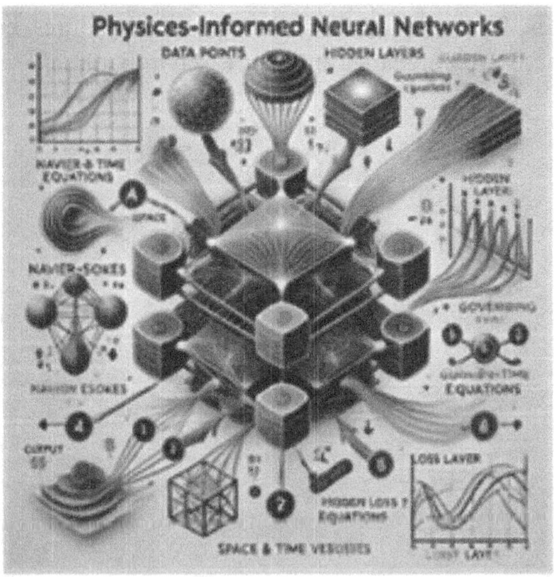

Figure 1.4 Physics-informed neural networks integrate physical laws and data for consistent predictions.

1.4 Artificial Intelligence Applications in Heat Transfer

1.4.1 Thermal System Optimization

Artificial intelligence improves the design and functionality of thermal systems by precisely forecasting temperature distributions and maximizing their performance. It lets engineers analyze a wide range of design configurations and determine the most effective ones through ML models and sophisticated simulations.

- **Temperature Distribution Prediction:** AI-based technologies forecast temperature profiles in intricate thermal systems using simulation data. By optimizing heat transfer pathways, designers can ensure uniform temperature distribution with the aid of these predictions.

For example, AI forecasts temperature and airflow changes in HVAC systems, enabling accurate fan speed and duct placement adjustments for optimal energy efficiency.

- **Improvements in Energy Efficiency:** AI models reduce energy waste by simulating thermal performance under various conditions. Artificial intelligence, for instance, optimizes cooling rates in industrial processes like metal casting to guarantee consistent properties while consuming less power.
- **Rapid Prototyping:** By evaluating heat transfer scenarios more quickly than conventional numerical techniques, AI shortens the design cycle and saves money and time on prototyping.

1.4.2 Real-Time Monitoring

Predictive AI systems transform thermal process monitoring through anomaly detection, failure prediction, and overheating prevention. These systems improve system longevity and operational safety.

- **Anomaly Detection:** AI systems examine thermal sensor data in real time to spot anomalies in temperature trends.

These systems can notify operators to take preventive action by identifying deviations early. For example, AI in electronics monitors data center processor temperatures and dynamically modifies cooling systems to avoid overheating-related hardware damage.

- **Dynamic Adaptation:** AI systems optimize heating and cooling procedures in real time by continuously learning and adapting to operational changes. Artificial intelligence, for example, modifies heat-dissipation systems in aerospace systems while in flight to safeguard delicate parts.
- **Predictive Maintenance:** By spotting patterns in thermal behavior, AI forecasts equipment failures, allowing for prompt maintenance and minimizing unscheduled downtime.

1.4.3 Material Discovery

To create high-conductivity materials, AI models investigate material properties. Artificial intelligence speeds up the search for novel materials with exceptional thermal characteristics, which are necessary for cutting-edge applications in electronics, aerospace engineering, and energy systems.

Exploring Material Properties: AI models forecast thermal conductivity, robustness, and material efficiency by analyzing simulation and experimental data. This makes it possible for researchers to quickly screen thousands of material combinations. For instance, high-conductivity and graphene-based materials for electronic device heat dissipation have been developed thanks to AI-assisted research.

Customized Material Development: AI creates material compositions for particular uses, like effective heat exchangers in power plants or lightweight thermal insulators for spacecraft.
Reducing Experimental Costs: AI reduces the need for extensive physical testing, saving time and money by simulating material behavior under various thermal conditions.

1.5 Artificial Intelligence in Fluid Dynamics

1.5.1 Turbulence Modeling

A crucial component of fluid dynamics is turbulence modeling, which focuses on the erratic and chaotic behavior of fluid motion. Due to their accuracy, traditional methods such as direct numerical simulations (DNS) and large eddy simulations (LES) are frequently employed; however, they are time-consuming and computationally demanding. Turbulence modeling powered by AI provides a ground-breaking solution that drastically cuts computation times without sacrificing accuracy.

Artificial Intelligence as a Replacement for Traditional Models

1. **Learning from Data:**

   - To forecast turbulence behavior, AI models, particularly neural networks, are trained on high-fidelity DNS or LES data.
   - These models do not require repeated large-scale simulations because, once trained, they generalize turbulence patterns across various scenarios.

2. **Direct integration with CFD:**

   - Artificial intelligence is integrated into CFD software, substituting AI-driven predictions for turbulence effects for sub-grid scale models.
   - As a result, simulations run more quickly without sacrificing accuracy.

Efficiency Gains with AI

1. **Speed:** For complex geometries, traditional LES and DNS can take weeks. Real-time or nearly real-time simulations are made possible with AI, which can cut computation times by up to 90%.
2. **Scalability:** Large-scale issues that would be impossible to solve with traditional techniques can be handled by AI models. Modeling atmospheric turbulence or optimizing designs for whole fleets of cars or airplanes are two examples.

Applications of AI in Turbulence Modeling

1. **Aerodynamics:** AI improves airflow around wind turbines, automobile bodies, and airplane wings. It improves overall performance, lowers drag, and increases fuel efficiency by precisely modeling turbulence. For instance, next-generation electric aircraft's aerodynamic designs were developed using AI-based turbulence models.
2. **Pipeline Transport:** AI optimizes flow rates and lowers energy losses by forecasting turbulence in gas and oil pipelines. This guarantees fluid transportation that is both safer and more economical.
3. **Environmental Studies:** AI helps forecast how pollutants may spread through the air or water. An example is simulating the spread of pollutants from industrial emissions to lessen environmental harm.
4. **Energy Systems:** By anticipating and managing turbulent flow to increase heat transfer rates, AI improves the design of cooling systems in power plants.

Advantages of AI in Turbulence Modeling

1. **Reduced Computational Cost:** AI does away with the high-performance computer resources that LES or DNS require.
2. **Improved Accuracy:** AI models frequently outperform conventional models in specific applications by learning from high-fidelity data.
3. **Adaptability:** AI's predictive powers are constantly being enhanced by its ability to adjust to new datasets and shifting circumstances.
4. **Wider Accessibility:** Smaller businesses and scholarly researchers can now use advanced turbulence modeling due to its lower computational requirements.

Thus, a paradigm shift in fluid dynamics is represented by AI-driven turbulence modeling. AI opens new design and analysis possibilities while cutting down on the time and expense of conventional methods by utilizing data and ML. Its potential to revolutionize various industries is demonstrated by its applications in energy systems, pipeline systems, environmental monitoring, and aerodynamics.

1.5.2 Aerodynamic Optimization

Refining designs to reduce drag, increase lift, and enhance overall performance is known as aerodynamic optimization. Conventional methods rely on computationally costly and time-consuming methods such as wind tunnel experiments, iterative simulations, and CFD. Artificial intelligence-driven solutions use data-driven models and ML to provide a revolutionary approach to aerodynamic optimization (Figure 1.5).

Artificial Intelligence Techniques in Aerodynamic Optimization

1. **Surrogate Modeling**

    - Artificial intelligence reduces the computational load by producing surrogate models that closely resemble CFD simulations.
    - By rapidly predicting aerodynamic parameters like lift and drag coefficients, these models allow for quicker design iterations.

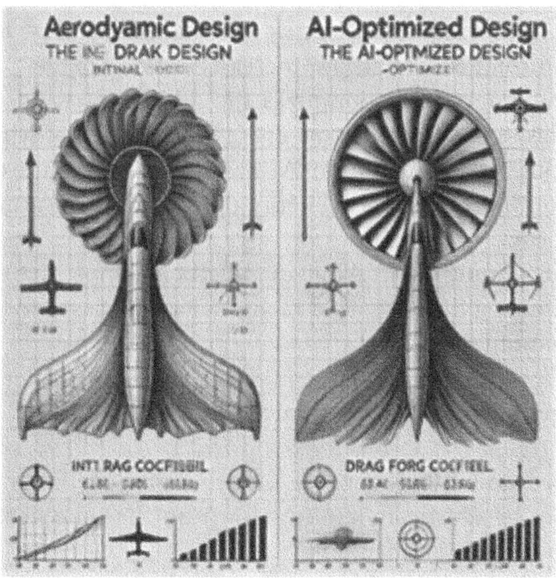

Figure 1.5 Artificial intelligence-driven design iterations for an aircraft wing profile.

2. **Reinforcement Learning**

- By using iterative feedback, reinforcement learning algorithms optimize aerodynamic shapes.
- Reinforcement learning agents, for example, modify wing profiles to attain the optimal balance between lift and drag.

3. **Neural Networks for Shape Prediction:**

- Deep learning models analyze existing aerodynamic designs and predict optimized shapes for given flow conditions.

Applications of AI in Aerodynamic Optimization

1. **Aircraft Design:** AI aids in designing propeller blades, wings, and fuselages to lower drag and increase fuel economy. For instance, AI-assisted designs for contemporary commercial aircraft can save up to 10% on operating fuel consumption.
2. **Automobile Industry:** AI optimizes vehicle bodies to minimize drag, improving stability and fuel efficiency at high speeds. For instance, electric car manufacturers use AI to optimize their designs for increased driving range.
3. **Wind Energy:** AI optimizes the designs of wind turbine blades to capture the most energy in a variety of wind conditions. As an illustration, AI-based blade curvature optimization increases yearly energy production by a number of percent.
4. **Sports Equipment:** AI gives athletes a competitive edge by optimizing the designs of racing suits, bicycles, and helmets to minimize drag.

Advantages of AI in Aerodynamic Optimization

1. **Speed and Efficiency:** AI models allow for faster design cycles by drastically cutting down on the time needed for aerodynamic simulations.
2. **Cost Reduction:** AI lowers the overall development cost by reducing the need for costly wind tunnel testing.

3. **Enhanced Performance:** AI improves aerodynamic performance by identifying creative design solutions that conventional approaches might miss.
4. **Real-Time Adaptation:** AI systems can make real-time design adjustments, such as modifying control surfaces for the best aerodynamics while in flight.

Challenges and Limitations

- **Data Dependency:** To train, AI models need sizable datasets of experimental or aerodynamic simulation data.
- **Computational Fluid Dynamics Integration:** It can be challenging to integrate AI with current CFD workflows and tools in a seamless manner.
- **Trust and Validation:** To guarantee that AI-generated designs satisfy performance and safety requirements, they must undergo thorough validation.

Fluid dynamics has advanced with AI-driven aerodynamic optimization. Industries can produce high-performance, faster, and more economical designs by fusing the accuracy of CFD with the predictive power of AI. Its uses in sports, automotive, aerospace, and renewable energy are transforming the way aerodynamic problems are solved.

1.6 Practical Implementations

Artificial intelligence is revolutionizing aerospace engineering by making design processes faster and more effective, especially with aerodynamic optimization. Designers can improve aircraft configurations and achieve notable performance gains with the aid of sophisticated AI-driven simulations.

1.6.1 Applications in Aerospace

Design cycles are accelerated by AI-driven aerodynamic simulations, which reduce drag by 15% to 20%.

- **Aerodynamic Simulations:** AI-based models expedite the simulation process by substituting quicker surrogate models for laborious CFD. Real-time feedback during the design

phase is made possible by these AI-driven tools that forecast lift and drag coefficients for different configurations.
- **Drag Reduction:** To reduce drag and increase fuel efficiency, AI optimizes fuselage designs, engine locations, and wing shapes. As an illustration, AI-powered modern commercial aircraft design reduces drag by 15% to 20%, greatly reducing carbon emissions and operating expenses.
- **Structural Health Monitoring:** AI systems examine flight data to identify structural irregularities, allowing for safer and more predictive maintenance.
- **Autonomous Flight:** By mimicking aerodynamic behavior and instantly adjusting to environmental changes, AI helps develop autonomous flight systems.

1.6.2 Power Generation

Artificial intelligence improves power plant cooling by maximizing flow rates and avoiding heat exchanger fouling. It increases the effectiveness of mechanical and thermal systems, especially by optimizing energy management and improving cooling mechanisms.

- **Cooling Optimization:** AI monitors power plant thermal loads and dynamically modifies cooling flow rates to guarantee steady operation. The AI models analyze temperature data to find inefficiencies and make real-time adjustment recommendations. As an illustration, AI lowers maintenance expenses and downtime by anticipating deposition patterns and modifying cleaning schedules to stop fouling and scaling in heat exchangers.
- **Energy Management:** AI optimizes turbine performance and minimizes waste by balancing energy input and output throughout the power generation system.
- **Predictive maintenance and fault detection:** AI systems analyze operational data to forecast component failures, enabling preventative measures to avoid unplanned outages.

1.6.3 Chemical Processing

Reactor designs are optimized by AI models, increasing energy efficiency and yield. Artificial intelligence transforms chemical processing by lowering energy consumption, increasing yields, and optimizing reactor designs.

It assists industries in creating sustainable and effective processes through sophisticated modeling.

- **Reactor Design Optimization:** AI-powered models identify the best reactor configurations and process parameters by simulating chemical reactions under various circumstances. As an illustration, petrochemical facilities employ AI to improve reaction efficiency, which raises yield and lowers raw material usage.
- **Energy Efficiency:** AI finds energy-use inefficiencies and suggests adjustments to cut waste. This is particularly important for procedures like catalytic reactions and distillation.
- **Product Quality Control:** AI models monitor the quality of the product in real-time, modifying process variables to satisfy exacting requirements.
- **Sustainability Initiatives:** By maximizing the use of renewable feedstocks and reducing emissions, AI aids in developing environmentally friendly processes.

Artificial intelligence fosters innovation in chemical processing, power generation, and aerospace by increasing productivity, cutting costs, and facilitating sustainable practices. Its use in cooling systems, chemical reactors, and aerodynamic simulations demonstrates its revolutionary potential in engineering.

1.7 Challenges and Future Directions

1.7.1 Data Scarcity

High-quality, domain-specific data is often lacking for AI applications in fluid dynamics and heat transfer. The intricacy of real-world phenomena, high expenses, and time constraints make it challenging to gather experimental data in these domains.

To overcome these obstacles:

- **Synthetic Data Generation:** Methods for producing synthetic datasets include CFD simulations. By simulating real-world situations, these datasets allow AI models to train efficiently even when experimental data is unavailable.

- **Transfer Learning:** To forecast heat transfer rates or fluid flow behaviors in particular applications, pre-trained models on engineering or general physics-based datasets can be refined.
- **Federated Learning:** By working together, industries and academic institutions can enable decentralized training that protects privacy while utilizing proprietary or sensitive data.

1.7.2 Model Interpretability

For engineers and scientists to accept AI models used to forecast fluid dynamics and heat transfer phenomena, they must be interpretable. Black-box models can impede comprehension and reduce their reliability in crucial applications such as thermal management, aerodynamics, and HVAC systems.

To make it easier to understand:

- **Post-Hoc Explanations:** AI predictions are influenced by important factors, such as material properties and boundary conditions, which can be found using tools like SHAP or LIME.
- **Physically Informed AI Models:** These models naturally correspond with domain expertise by incorporating physical laws and constraints (such as Navier–Stokes equations) into neural network architectures, guaranteeing increased accuracy and trust.
- **Visualization Techniques:** Practitioners can better understand the predictions of temperature distribution or fluid flow patterns by using techniques like heatmaps and vector field representations.

1.7.3 Integration with Quantum Computing

Heat transfer and fluid dynamics could see revolutionary breakthroughs thanks to quantum computing, especially in situations where solving computationally costly models is necessary.

- **Accelerated CFD Simulations:** Real-time analysis of complex systems, like power plants or airplane engines, is now possible thanks to quantum algorithms' exponential speedup of the solution of the governing equations of fluid flow and heat transfer.

- **System Design Optimization:** By more effectively examining large design spaces, quantum-inspired techniques can optimize thermal systems, like heat exchangers.
- **Quantum Machine Learning:** By using quantum superposition to process massive datasets, quantum ML can improve prediction accuracy for thermal conductivity analysis, convection heat transfer, and turbulence modeling.

Nevertheless, there are obstacles to integrating quantum computing into these fields:

- **Hardware Restrictions:** Large-scale CFD problems and heat transfer simulations are beyond the capabilities of current quantum devices.
- **Algorithmic Development:** Customized quantum algorithms for resolving equations, like energy equations or Fourier's law, are still in their infancy.
- **Interdisciplinary Collaboration:** To fully utilize quantum computing in these domains, physicists, computational engineers, and AI researchers must work closely together.

1.8 Conclusion

Artificial intelligence revolutionizes heat transfer and fluid dynamics, offering effective answers to challenging issues. It promotes sustainability and innovation by resolving computational issues and facilitating real-time optimizations. The impact of AI will be further enhanced by future research, pushing engineering to new heights.

References

1. Brunton, S.L., Noack, B.R., Koumoutsakos, P., Machine Learning for Fluid Mechanics. *Annu. Rev. Fluid Mech.*, *52*, 1, 477–508, 2020.
2. Krzywanski, J., A General Approach in Optimization of Heat Exchangers by Bio-Inspired Artificial Intelligence Methods. *Energies*, 12, 23, 4441, 2019.

3. Raissi, M., Perdikaris, P., Karniadakis, G.E., Physics-Informed Neural Networks: A Deep Learning Framework for Solving Forward and Inverse Problems Involving PDEs. *J. Comput. Phys.*, *378*, 686–707, 2019.
4. Malalasekera, W. and Versteeg, H.K., *An Introduction to Computational Fluid Dynamics: The Finite Volume Method*, Pearson Education, Limited Edinburgh Gate Harlow Essex CM20 2JE England, second edition published 2007.

2

Machine Learning Applications in Fluid Mechanics

A. Ahadi[1,2], P. Hosseini Baei[1] and M. Sheikholeslami[1,2*]

[1]Department of Mechanical Engineering, Babol Noshirvani University of Technology, Babol, Iran
[2]Renewable Energy Systems and Nanofluid Applications in Heat Transfer Laboratory, Babol Noshirvani University of Technology, Babol, Iran

Abstract

Machine learning (ML) has become a game-changing technique in fluid mechanics, providing fresh perspectives on analyzing and forecasting intricate phenomena. This chapter examines how ML may be integrated with fluid mechanics, emphasizing how it can transform tasks related to flow prediction, turbulence modeling, and optimization. An introduction to ML encompassing supervised, unsupervised, and semi-supervised learning techniques opens the chapter. The use of important algorithms in fluid mechanics is examined, including support vector machines, neural networks, and clustering approaches.

The topic then shifts to physics-informed ML, which combines data-driven models with physical rules. Examples show how these techniques improve simulation and comprehension of fluid dynamics in terms of efficiency and accuracy. The chapter also discusses turbulence modeling, going over conventional methods such as direct numerical simulation (DNS), Reynolds-averaged Navier–Stokes (RANS), and large eddy simulation (LES), emphasizing how ML may either replace or enhance them.

In addition to outlining prospects for further study, the concluding parts address the difficulties in integrating ML into fluid dynamics, including data scarcity, interpretability, and processing cost. To fully utilize ML in fluid mechanics, this chapter highlights the necessity of multidisciplinary cooperation.

***Keywords*:** Fluid mechanics, machine learning, CFD, turbulence modeling

**Corresponding author*: mohsen.sheikholeslami@nit.ac.ir

Mukesh Kumar Awasthi and Reshu Gupta (eds.) Artificial Intelligence and Computational Modeling in Heat Transfer and Fluid Dynamics, (23–50) © 2026 Scrivener Publishing LLC

2.1 Introduction

Large volumes of data from field observations, experiments, and extensive numerical simulations have historically been the focus of fluid mechanics. Indeed, due to developments in experimental measuring capabilities and high-performance computing architectures, big data has become a reality in fluid dynamics research in recent decades [1]. Many methods, from sophisticated data processing and compression algorithms to fluid mechanics databases, have been created over the last 50 years to deal with such data [2, 3]. However, statistical analysis, heuristic algorithms, and domain experience have been heavily dependent on fluid mechanics data processing. Data is expanding quickly in all scientific domains, opening up new avenues for study and commercial opportunities. A revived interest in ML, which draws information from this data, has resulted from the confluence of massive data quantities, advanced algorithms, open-source software, benchmark challenges, enhanced computer power, and industrial investment in data-driven problem resolution. This has led to several benchmark issues and open-source software issues. In fluid mechanics, ML is currently advancing quickly. Fluid mechanics problems such as reduced-order modeling, controlled flow, turbulence closure modeling, form optimization, and experimental data processing are addressed using ML techniques, which may be classified as supervised, semi-supervised, or unsupervised (Figure 2.1). As scientific research moves from basic

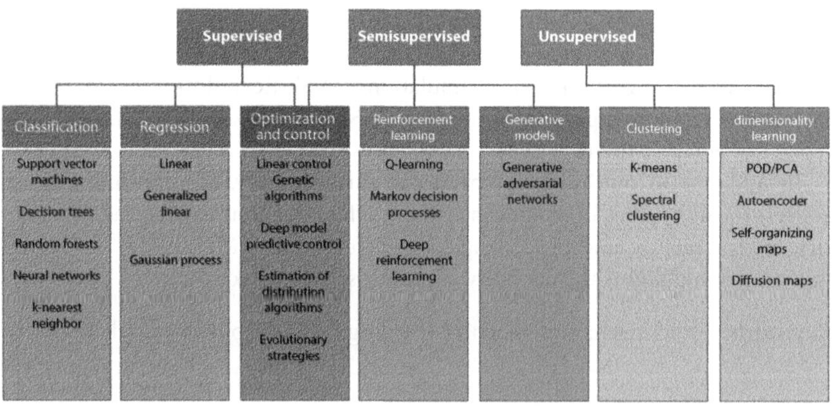

Figure 2.1 The kind and amount of information available for the learning process determines whether an ML algorithm is classified as supervised, unsupervised, or semi-supervised. The word 'POD' stands for appropriate orthogonal decomposition, and 'PCA' for principal component analysis.

principles to data-driven approaches, these methods provide a flexible and modular framework comparable to the evolution of numerical tools in the 1940s and 1950s. Learning algorithms can be advantageous for fluid mechanics, but they also pose obstacles that could help these algorithms become even more sophisticated to support engineering intuition and human comprehension.

Figure 2.2 summarizes the examined experimental techniques for each category and suggests possible applications of ML. A categorization of method difficulty is also included, which takes into account the experimental complexity, as well as difficulties in implementing the ML method and the experimental approach together. It should be noted that this classification is illustrative and related to the examples given in the text; as such, it is not intended to be a categorical statement about the merits of any experimental classification of all experimental applications in terms of their primary category, which is (red) estimation and control, (blue) experimental design and modeling, and (green) measurement techniques. Within each region, we display experimental methods or tasks in black, while the orange bubbles illustrate the overall advances that ML has made to those tasks. The potential flows between the categories are reflected in the arrow-shaped borders between them. As explained in further depth in the book, each case is ranked according to its ML and experimental complexity. Please note that this evaluation is intended to provide examples of potential uses and is not comprehensive.

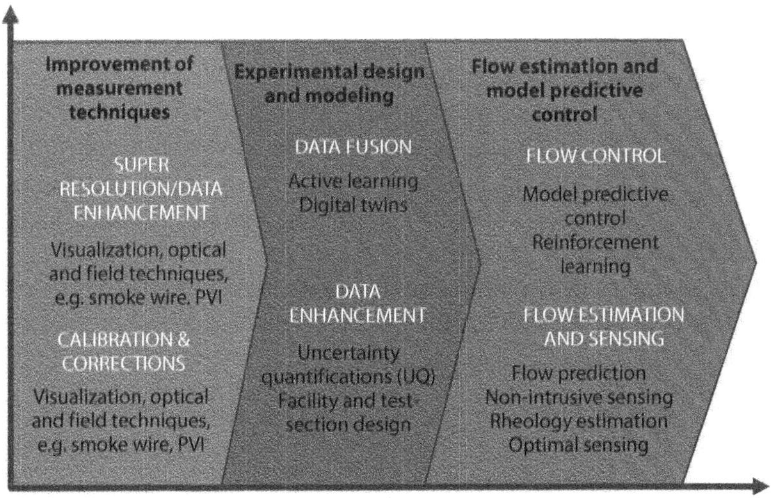

Figure 2.2 An overview of how ML affects experimental fluid mechanics.

Accurately modeling turbulent flow requires capturing the smallest scales of turbulence, which necessitates that the grid elements in the simulation be finer than these tiny eddies. This level of detail is essential for replicating the fluid's behavior at the smallest turbulence scales, highlighting the computational complexity involved in such simulations. This assumption often results in meshes with billions of elements, which are too expensive to utilize in calculations due to the time and technology involved. The computational fluid dynamics (CFD) simulations, for bigger (geometrically) challenges, are now feasible because of the advancements in computer computing power. The ability to perform computations across multiple processors, whether within a single machine or on dedicated computing clusters, greatly enhances the efficiency of CFD systems. This parallel processing capability allows for faster simulations and more complex analyses, making it a critical feature in modern CFD applications. Due to the requirement for constant communication between processors, it is not feasible to simulate arbitrarily huge domains with only more CPUs; instead, the reduction in computation time decreases with each additional core. There is an ideal number of processors for a certain issue, beyond which the computations get slower. Because of the drawbacks, efforts to use ML-based solutions to increase the precision and speed of CFD computations started in the 1980s. The fact that ML is used to solve a variety of scientific and engineering problems, including reliability assessment [4], nanotechnology [5], virology [6], immunology [7], bioinformatics [8], or post-processing CFD results [9], is another reason to investigate its viability in turbulence modeling.

2.2 The Basics of Machine Learning

The process of estimating relationships between a system's properties, outputs, and inputs using a small amount of data may be stated as the learning problem [10]. As shown in Figure 2.2, we differentiate between a learning model (LM), the system at issue, and a generator of samples. We stress that LMs' approximations are inherently stochastic, and that the minimization of a risk functional may be used to characterize their learning process:

$$R(w) = \int L\left[y, \phi(x, y, w)\right] p(x, y)\, dx\, dy \tag{2.1}$$

The LM is defined by the function φ (x, y, w), where the loss function L is designed to balance multiple objectives such as accuracy, simplicity, and smoothness. Here, w represents the model parameters, while x and y denote the input data and outputs, respectively, sampled from a probability distribution p. It is important to note that the risk functional is influenced by the probability distribution p (x,y), which imposes constraints on the LM's predictive capabilities.

2.2.1 Supervised Learning

Supervised learning relies on a supervisor to provide a comprehensive data set (x*, y*) for training purposes. This methodology is predominantly utilized in tasks such as regression and classification, where the primary objective is to establish a relationship between input variables and their corresponding outputs using labeled data. Classification tasks aim to assign categorical labels to data points. Practical applications include distinguishing emails as either "spam" or "non-spam" or utilizing image data to classify fluid dynamics phenomena such as "bubbly flow" or "turbulent flow." Conversely, regression tasks are concerned with modeling continuous data relationships. Examples include estimating eddy viscosity based on the gradient of mean flow velocity under turbulent conditions or predicting the market value of a vehicle using factors like its age and mileage. In recent years, applying ML algorithms for regression and classification has seen a significant rise in fluid dynamics research.

Examples of data-driven automated flow regime categorization are presented [11–13]. Surrogate model-based optimization [14], turbulence modeling [15], non-intrusive reduced order modeling [16, 17], aeroacoustic noise prediction [18], surrogate modeling [19, 20], and system identification for prediction and control [21–23] are examples of regression problems that may be more prevalent. Selecting a set of hypotheses that balances model complexity with available data and incorporating physical limitations into the learning process are the primary challenges in solving these tasks. The result is a predictive "surrogate" model, regardless of the application. These models can take many different forms. For instance, this work examines linear combinations of artificial neural networks (ANNs) [24], radial basis functions [25], and recursive expression trees, as in genetic programming [26]. Since these models have analytical representations, they can be differentiated analytically.

2.2.1.1 *Neural Networks*

The modular building component of NNs, the neuron, depicts the neurons found in the human brain and provides them with strength and flexibility. After using an activation function to process an input, each neuron generates an output. It is possible to combine many neurons to create distinct structures that communicate information about the circumstances and the kind of input. One of the most popular network topologies, feedforward networks employ the weighted output of one layer of neurons as the input for the subsequent layer. In NN designs, the data is received by an input layer, and predictions are made by an output layer. The network weights are determined using nonlinear optimization techniques like backpropagation [27] to reduce the error between the labeled training data and the predictions. A range of nonlinear activation functions and several layers are features of deep neural networks. Convolutional neural networks (CNNs) are powerful networks that excel in identifying patterns and images when activation functions are defined using convolutional kernels [28, 29].

2.2.1.2 *Random Forests and Support Vector Machines for Classification*

Classification is a supervised learning task that uses pre-labeled training data to categorize a set of measurements. The perceptron [30], which differentiated between two kinds of linearly separable input, was most likely the earliest learning technique. Two fundamental classification methods that have been widely applied in business are support vector machines [31] and random forests [32]. The following loss functional, which is given here for two classes, might be used to specify the problem:

$$L\left[y,\phi(x,y,w)\right]=\begin{cases}0, & \text{if} \;\; y=\phi(x,y,w)\\ 1, & \text{if} \;\; y\neq\phi(x,y,w)\end{cases} \tag{2.2}$$

2.2.2 Unsupervised Learning

Descriptive learning is another name for unsupervised learning. Finding patterns or distinguishing characteristics in the data is the aim. Therefore, the function that needs to be learned is f: X → X, which is from the input space to itself. Clustering and dimensionality reduction are the two primary issues in unsupervised learning. The goal of dimensionality reduction is to portray the data in a lower-dimensional manner. The fundamental premise is that the key information in the data is contained in a small number of features, also referred to as hidden or latent variables. For instance, a good face recognition algorithm builds a smaller collection of templates that encapsulates the key information needed for recognition by concentrating on visual patterns linked to age, gender, or pose [33].

2.2.2.1 Vector Quantization and Clustering

An unsupervised learning method called clustering finds related groupings in the data. K-means clustering, the most popular method, divides data into k clusters, which divide data space into Voronoi cells. An observation is a member of the cluster with the closest centroid. Data representative points that can be divided into a predefined number of clusters are found using vector quantizers. These points can then be used to estimate future samples in place of the complete data set. The data x and the cluster center coordinates are mapped using the vector quantizer φ (x, w). Finding the quantizer's parameters requires minimizing the loss function, which is frequently the squared distortion of the cluster centers' data.

$$L\left[\phi(x,w)\right] = \left\|x - \phi(x,w)\right\|^2 \tag{2.3}$$

2.2.3 Semi-Supervised Learning

With either a modest amount of labeled training data or additional ambient correction information, semi-supervised learning techniques function under partial supervision. Two methods in this area are reinforcement learning (RL) and generative adversarial networks (GANs).

Generative adversarial networks are recognized as complex algorithms in ML designed to develop models capable of generating data that closely resembles real-world data [34]. These networks utilize two distinct neural networks, the "generator" and the "discriminator," to process artificial data. In this system, the generator creates data that closely mimics real data, and the discriminator evaluates this data to detect the differences between real and artificial data.

In this process, the generator network is responsible for creating artificial data that closely resembles the real data in the training data set. The discriminator evaluates these generated data points and identifies differences and similarities. These two networks work interactively and complement each other, with each network continuously trying to outperform the other. This competitive interaction is a zero-sum game, meaning one side must win while the other loses. Generative adversarial networks are designed to generate data that seems indistinguishable from real-world data. These algorithms have found applications in various fields, including generating images, videos, texts, and even in some medical applications. One of the biggest advantages of using GANs is their ability to produce high-quality data nearly indistinguishable from real data. This capability is useful in simulations, ML, and data security applications. In the GAN system, the continuous optimization process takes place due to the competition between the generator and the discriminator networks. The generator produces new, more accurate data samples, while the discriminator evaluates and detects differences. This ongoing process leads to improving both networks' performance, enhancing the quality of the generated data.

Reinforcement learning is a mathematical approach to problem-solving that suggests an agent and its surroundings interact in a goal-directed manner [35]. In RL, the agent has a range of detecting states and actions. Semi-supervised learning is so named because, in contrast to supervised learning, the agent learns from its own experiences through inadequate and often sporadic rewards rather than having labeled knowledge about the right behaviors. Furthermore, the agent is focused on optimizing its long-term gains in addition to identifying patterns in its behavior or the surroundings. Since RL, a Markov decision process, interacts with the environment through trial and error and does not require a dynamic model like a Markov transition model, it is strongly connected to dynamic programming [36].

2.3 Fluid Mechanics Machine Learning Influenced by Physics

A few classical phases may be distinguished in applied ML, and each one offers the chance to incorporate existing physical knowledge:

(1) Selecting the issue to be modeled or the question to be addressed
(2) Selecting the training data
(3) Deciding on an ML architecture that would best model or represent the data
(4) Establishing loss functions to gauge success and guide the educational journey
(5) Minimizing the loss function over the training data by training the model using an optimization technique.

2.3.1 The Problem

Machine learning uses past data to build models that can provide real-time answers to queries, whereas data science uses data to answer questions. Choosing input data that will be easily accessible in the future and output data that accurately reflects the intended outcome are essential components of selecting the optimal modeling system. The ML model represents the functional relationship between input and output data. Depending on the goal and the outputs to be modeled, ML algorithms are classified into three categories: supervised, unsupervised, and reinforcement learning. In supervised learning, the ML system would model or predict expert labels in the training data. These output labels might be discrete, such as "Tiger" or "Leopard," when an input image is given; in that case, the job would be classification-based. Continuous labels, like the average lift or drag value for a certain airfoil layout, cause regression. Unsupervised learning is a difficult area of ML as it lacks expert labeling and requires that structure be recovered from the input data alone. This process is commonly known as data mining. Clustering is the work at hand, assuming the data's structure is discrete. Clusters can be utilized as proxy labels to categorize fresh data after they have been detected and described. The process is frequently called an embedding or dimensionality reduction effort, assuming the data structure is continuously changing. Finding a continuous and reduced-dimensional embedding is the goal of unsupervised learning tasks like principal component analysis and proper orthogonal decomposition [37]. A third and important area of ML research is RL, where an agent decides how to interact with its surroundings to learn how to respond to high-level concerns [38]. One example is learning to play Chess and Go [39, 40].

2.3.1.1 Examples Related to Fluid Mechanics

Machine learning is helping with several fluid mechanics and physical modeling problems [41, 42]. Turbulence closure modeling as an ML issue [43, 44] is the subject of a wide range of research, including Reynolds stress models [45, 46] and sub-grid-scale turbulence [47, 48]. Another significant method where previous physical information is included in turbulence closure modeling is through the design of valuable input characteristics [49–51]. The issue of enhancing CFD solvers has also lately drawn attention to ML [52, 53]. Super-resolution [54, 55], robust modal decompositions [56–58], network and cluster modeling [59, 60], control [61, 62], RL [63, 64], and experiment design in cyber-physical systems [65] are additional significant fluid mechanics topics that benefit from ML.

Significant advancements have been made in the vast connected discipline of aerodynamics thanks to data [66].

2.3.2 The Data

The foundation of ML is data, and the quality of the data that can be gathered or made available determines how well we can create models. This step cannot be separated from the selection of a problem above since, as previously mentioned, selecting data to inform a model is intimately tied to selecting what to model in the first place. The final ML model is directly impacted by the quantity and quality of the data. Since deep neural networks and other ML architectures are essentially complex interpolation engines, a variety of training data is necessary for these models to function well on unknown data. For instance, contemporary deep convolutional neural networks have gained notoriety for their unparalleled classification accuracy [67] on the ImageNet database [68], which offers a vast and diverse collection of training examples and comprises over 14 million annotated pictures with over 20,000 categories. Many people believe that the present deep learning era began with this combination of a large, labeled data set and a revolutionary deep learning architecture [69].

2.3.2.1 Examples Related to Fluid Mechanics

Individual flow field characterization sometimes requires millions of degrees of freedom, which makes fluid data notoriously high-dimensional and huge. Furthermore, these flow fields usually change with time, producing a time series with many snapshots. Because it is costly to examine numerous geometries, Reynolds numbers, computationally or experimentally, data is frequently quite sparse in parameter space, despite being enormous in spatial and/or temporal dimensions. As a result, several techniques have been developed for sparse and rich data. Additional considerations include watching the system evolve when it deviates from its typical condition and exciting transients. In situations like time-series data from force recordings on an experimental turbine or pressure measurements on the airfoil surface, fluid data may be scarce.

2.3.3 The Architecture

Following problem identification, data collection, and curation, an architecture for representing the ML model must be selected. Generally, a function that converts inputs into outputs is an ML model.

$$y = f(x;\theta) \tag{2.4}$$

where the values in θ parameterize this function, which frequently belongs to a certain family of functions. For example, this linear map, or matrix, would be parameterized using θ in a linear regression model, representing outputs as a linear function of inputs. It has been demonstrated that neural networks can approximate arbitrarily complicated functions given enough data and depth, making them an especially potent and adaptable class of models to depict functional connections between data [70, 71]. The human designer's creativity is the sole constraint on the vast array of possible neural network designs [37]. A straightforward feedforward network is the most often used design. Layers make up neural networks, with data entering at the input layer and going through several computational stages before arriving at the output layer. Each layer's weighted total data is merged and sent *via* a nonlinear activation function. The network weights, or weighted connectivity matrices, that represent the connections between nodes in neighboring layers are determined by the parameters θ. The architect or a meta-optimization determines the general network topology (i.e., the number of layers, size, activation function type, etc.), which in turn determines the family of functions that that class of network may mimic.

A lot of people have utilized genetic programming to develop flexible, human-interpretable data representations for control [61] and modeling [72, 73]. Time-series data modeling, particularly in fluids, continues to make extensive use of both traditional and modified linear regression. Dynamic mode decomposition [56, 74] improves this technique by applying linear regression under a low-rank constraint, which helps in detecting significant spatiotemporal patterns that evolve in a linear manner over time. The sparse identification of nonlinear dynamics (SINDy) approach [75] employs an advanced form of linear regression to develop a differential equation model with the fewest possible components while ensuring a precise fit to the data. This is achieved by incorporating either a loss function that encourages sparsity [76] or an optimization algorithm designed for sparse solutions [75, 77].

2.3.3.1 Examples Related to Fluid Mechanics

Numerous instances exist where physical solutions for fluid dynamics applications are enforced by bespoke neural network topologies. Ling *et al.* [45] proposed a novel neural network architecture designed to preserve

Galilean invariance when modeling Reynolds stress tensors. In parallel, the SINDy framework has been leveraged to create models for Reynolds stress, offering a data-driven approach to capturing complex fluid dynamics [78, 79]. For the analysis of intricate aeroelastic systems, researchers have adopted hybrid methodologies that merge the strengths of nonlinear neural networks with traditional linear system identification techniques [80]. Furthermore, a physics-informed neural network strategy has been utilized to encode the Navier–Stokes equations. This method is highly adaptable to various geometric configurations and boundary conditions, enabling precise predictions of flow fields even when working with sparse data sets. Airfoil pressure distributions have also been recovered using sparse sensing. A revolutionary operator network that can handle simulation modeling and super-resolution upscaling is the Fourier neural operator.

In modeling complex Fluid dynamical systems, dynamics-based equivariant convolutional networks have emerged as powerful tools for preserving symmetry in high-dimensional systems. These networks are widely used in scientific simulations to learn symmetric and invariant structures in complex data. At smaller sub-grid scales, neural networks have been specifically designed to accurately account for inherent physical invariances in scalar flow models [81].

In this context, researchers Lee and Carlberg [82] have incorporated deep convolutional autoencoders into reduced-order modeling frameworks. These methods not only enhance modeling accuracy but also optimize computations by reducing data dimensionality [83, 84]. For instance, deep autoencoders can extract key features from high-dimensional data, providing models with lower computational complexity, which is particularly beneficial for large-scale dynamical systems.

2.3.4 The Loss Function

A measure of the model's performance on several tasks is the loss function. The L2 error, a prevalent element of the loss function, quantifies the average deviation between the model's forecasts and the actual results inside the input data set. To enhance the optimization process, additional terms such as the L1 or L2 norm of the parameters θ may be incorporated to encourage simplicity and mitigate overfitting. So, the function of loss generally reconciles various conflicting objectives, including model correctness and complexity. In a neural network design, phrases that encourage a certain behavior across several sub-networks may also be included in the loss function. Crucially, the loss function will offer useful data for approximating the gradients needed to optimize the parameters.

2.3.4.1 Examples Related to Fluid Mechanics

Fluid mechanics extensively uses sparse nonlinear modeling, which uses sparsity-promoting loss terms to produce parsimonious models. SINDy provides reduced-order models of the flow development of dominating coherent structures for different configurations [85, 86]. In addition to having a special loss function that takes into account the boundedness of solutions—a critical factor for reduced-order fluid models—the SINDy modeling framework has been extended to produce compact closure models [87].

2.3.5 The Optimization Algorithm

To identify ideal parameters θ, which are frequently high-dimensional and non-convex, ML models are trained using optimization techniques. This creates difficult optimization landscapes with several local minima. In contrast to convex optimization problems, which have robust and all-encompassing approaches, non-convex optimization has few general guarantees for convergence or global optimality [88, 89]. Stochastic gradient descent techniques are necessary for modern deep neural networks because of their enormous training data sets and especially high-dimensional parameters (θ). Since the optimization technique drives ML, it is frequently separated from the decision-making process. However, research is being done on creating sophisticated optimization algorithms. When creating a new architecture or adding a unique loss term, it is frequently also required to take the optimization technique into explicit consideration.

2.3.5.1 Examples Related to Fluid Mechanics

Loiseau [85] demonstrated that by applying skew-symmetry restrictions to the quadratic terms of a SINDy model, conserving energy in incompressible fluid flows may be explicitly enforced. These limitations appear as equality restrictions on the SINDy model's sparse coefficients θ. At each stage of the regression process, these equality restrictions can be applied using the Karush–Kuhn–Tucker criteria, as the standard SINDy optimization method relies on a gradually thresholded least-squares strategy. To develop new techniques for training ML models with unique topologies or loss functions, the SR3 optimization program [77] attempts to broaden and extend optimization issues to more difficult restrictions and general optimization tasks.

2.4 Methods for Modeling Turbulence

In reality, three turbulence modeling techniques are used for the great majority of flow simulations. A direct numerical simulation, which employs a grid with cells the same size as the turbulence scale, is the first, most accurate, and least-used technique. The second-most-accurate technique is RANS, which uses turbulence models and low-resolution grids to evaluate the effects of invisible vortices. Large eddy simulation is the third technique, which is still commonly employed in the industry but is not as well-known as RANS. Because the meshes used in this approach are more precise than those used in RANS, the biggest turbulence can be fully resolved, producing more accurate results.

2.4.1 Direct Numerical Simulation

The whole range of turbulence sizes, from the lowest dissipative scales to the largest turbulence that directly draws energy from the mean flow, must be reproduced. The integral scale L, which is the ratio of grid cell size to this scale, represents the channel width or fluid body size, whereas the Kolmogorov scale η is used to determine the maximum size of grid components. There are several methods to describe the Kolmogorov scale, fluid's kinematic viscosity (v), and turbulent kinetic energy dissipation rate.

$$\eta = (\nu^3 / \varepsilon)^{\frac{1}{4}} \tag{2.5}$$

Grid cell widths should be sufficiently small to guarantee that each cell's Reynolds number is no more than 1, as the number of grid points is determined by the flow's Reynolds number. As a result, the grid's size grows quickly as the simulation domain and flow speed increase. Furthermore, to meet the Courant–Friedrichs–Lewy criterion, the grid cells' small size necessitates the usage of extremely tiny time-steps [90]. These two correlations demonstrate how the cube of the Reynolds number increases the amount of floating-point operations needed to replicate a particular flow. Compared to other CFD methods, these computations have the largest processing power and computation time requirements, yet they yield good accuracy in reality. These techniques' main uses are in research, the development of turbulence models, and the study of flow phenomena that are difficult to measure experimentally. They are frequently employed in engineering applications for difficult jobs, including wing profiles.

To speed up CFD calculations, Pathak *et al.* [91] combined deep learning with conventional partial differential equations [92], demonstrating how ML may be utilized to improve DNS computations. Iterations are only partially solved with perfect precision, with the remainder calculated on a less precise grid. By contrasting full and reduced accuracy results, the deep learning model was trained on a two-dimensional convection-induced flow issue. Before the outcomes from the less accurate grid are shown on the denser grid, the mistakes for intermediate iterations are corrected. In terms of inaccuracy on the same grid as the traditional simulation, ML with conventional partial differential equations outperformed the baseline simulation [91].

2.4.2 Reynolds Averaged Navier–Stokes

This simulation relies on solving the Navier–Stokes equation in its time-averaged form. The Reynolds decomposition [93], which is the basis for this approach, states that a given value that describes the flow at any given moment may be divided into two parts: to solve the closure problem in flow equations, Boussinesq put out the eddy viscosity hypothesis [94]. This theory, which is applied even when it appears to be physically incorrect, states that mean strain rate and Reynolds stress have a linear connection [95]. Closure coefficients, which are constants employed in equations with uncertain values because of the closure problem, are empirically demonstrated to be the average of values derived from contrasting test calculations with measurements of actual flows. According to the turbulence scale l and turbulence kinetic energy k, the k-epsilon model uses one such parameter, Cμ, to determine the turbulent dissipation rate epsilon. Cμ is set at 0.09 by default. Due to these limitations, RANS computations cannot be universal since the values of the coefficients offering the highest accuracy differ for every flow [96]. Furthermore, even the most appropriate coefficients may simply be a compromise that does not produce findings with high accuracy in complicated studies, since the flow characteristics in various regions of the computational domain may differ. The use of so-called turbulence models to compute Reynolds stress is one of the main characteristics of simulations employing RANS. The most significant of them are:

- The most often utilized in RANS-type CFD computations is k-epsilon (k-ε) [97]. Two formulas that compute k (turbulence kinetic energy) and ε (turbulence kinetic energy dispersion rate) form its foundation. This model is recommended for simulating exterior flows, such as vehicle aerodynamics, since it effectively handles flow away from barriers.
- Together with k-ε, k-omega (k-ω) [98] is the industry standard for the great majority of computations. The two equations that determine k and ω—the particular dispersion rate of turbulence kinetic energy—are its foundation. Systems with pipes, ducts, and small spaces are calculated using this model as it is most effective at modeling flows close to walls.
- The "best of both worlds" is k-omega SST [99], a unique variation of k-ω that alternates between k-ω and k-ε based on how far a particular grid point is from the closest wall.
- The Spalart–Allmaras model [100] is mostly utilized in the aerospace sector and is not appropriate for modeling ordinary "industrial" flows. Calculating the turbulent viscosity of vortices is based on a single equation.

There are a number of additional turbulence models, but they are not as widely used and have not been improved by ML [101].

Ling *et al.* [45] evaluated ML methods for determining Reynolds stress anisotropy and increasing the accuracy of RANS computations in 2016. They employed the traditional linear eddy viscosity model [102], multilevel perceptron [103], and tensor-based neural networks. The collection contained simulation results for nine different situations, such as duct and channel flows with different Reynolds numbers, flow around cylinders, constricting channels, and crossflow with jets. After the models were trained, the results were compared. Reynolds stress anisotropy was anticipated to be the worst by the most used linear eddy viscosity model and multi-level perceptron, but tensor-based neural networks consistently yielded good results in every test instance [101]. In a study by Singh *et al.* [104], discrepancies between air foil simulation results and experimental data were examined. The researchers employed machine learning to enhance the accuracy of simulations using the Spalart–Allmaras turbulence model. Artificial neural networks were utilized to correct the turbulence model equations based on the identified discrepancies. The refined model was then used for numerical computations, demonstrating significant improvement in alignment with experimental data. Airfoils and flow parameters that were not included during model learning also maintained the ensuing improvement in the accuracy of the findings [104]. One of the conclusions was that it was legitimate to examine inconsistencies by comparing simulation and experimental data. Duraisamy *et al.* [105] developed a novel method, combining RANS with DNS or LES simulations. The study revealed that while DNS is highly accurate, it is computationally expensive and time-consuming, making it feasible only for low Reynolds number values and small-scale problems. To address these limitations, the researchers introduced a novel approach called field inversion and machine learning. This method first identifies spatial discrepancies in the model through inverse modeling and then applies ML techniques to convert these discrepancies into corrective terms for the model. This innovative approach significantly enhanced the accuracy of turbulent flow simulations.

2.4.3 Large Eddy Simulation

Smagorinski [106] and Deardorff [107] created a method for simulating turbulent flow that ignores the smallest scale of turbulence and completely resolves only the largest, most important vortices. Although smaller vortices are eliminated by filtering, their impact on fluid dynamics cannot be disregarded. They are assessed using specialist models. The approach takes more time and requires less computing power than RANS but less than DNS. Because of its reduced needs compared to DNS, LES has the benefit of being able to directly simulate bigger turbulence and be utilized for engineering calculations. However, because it models smaller-scale turbulence, it has a lesser accuracy than DNS. More ML-based solutions have been created for the approach as a result of its broader variety of real-world applications.

Drawing inspiration from advancements in ML for enhancing noisy or unclear images, Maulik and San [108] proposed a blind deconvolution technique for turbulent flows in 2017, utilizing an ANN. This approach reconstructs turbulent flow at scales finer than the model's grid resolution by applying a convolution process with a blur kernel, which is derived from the interplay between high- and low-resolution flow fields [109]. In order to invert the kernel and generate a flow field with higher precision, the ANN aims to ascertain its parameters, which makes it more applicable to LES simulations [110]. They conducted their experiments using the output of three flow simulations: compressible stratified turbulence, 3D Kolmogorov, and 2D Kraichan. Compared to deconvolution carried out with knowledge of the filter kernel, the results achieved are comparable [111].

Turbulent Flow-Net (TF-Net) was introduced by Wang *et al.* [112] and combines ML with two traditional CFD techniques, RANS and LES. Combining the computational efficiency of RANS with LES's capacity to resolve turbulent flow results in a less time-consuming and simpler approach than traditional LES.

Contemporary methods for simulating turbulent flows utilize neural networks to split the velocity field into three primary components: average flow, resolved fluctuations, and unresolved modeled fluctuations. In CFD simulations, predefined filters are typically used for this decomposition. In a pioneering study, the TF-Net neural network utilized CNNs to process recorded images from Rayleigh–Bénard convection flow simulations [113, 114]. These networks can graphically represent each component of the decomposed velocity field and simulate the flow's evolution over time. This capability, which distinguishes TF-Net from earlier methods, allows the model to accurately calculate the kinetic energy of turbulence within the same computational domain. Results demonstrated that TF-Net's CNNs outperformed other neural networks used for comparison [112].

2.5 Machine Learning in Fluid Dynamics: Obstacles and Prospects

The problems faced by fluid dynamics differ from those faced by many ML applications, such as image identification and advertising. To evaluate fluid flows, it is frequently necessary to accurately characterize the underlying physical mechanisms. Moreover, fluid flows display intricate, multiscale phenomena that are still mostly unclear in terms of comprehension and management. Techniques for unsteady flow fields must handle nonlinearities and numerous spatiotemporal scales, which are sometimes absent from well-known ML techniques. Furthermore, a lot of well-known ML applications, like playing the game Go, depend on low-cost system assessments and a thorough classification of the process that must be taught. This is not the situation with fluids, where models could necessitate using massive supercomputers running for lengthy periods of time, and tests might be hard to replicate or automate.

Algorithms like RL are frequently employed in autonomous driving and flight, and ML has also become crucial in robotics. Even though many robots work in fluids, it does not seem like the nuances of fluid dynamics are currently a big factor in their design. Solutions that mimic natural shapes and processes are frequently the norm, harking back to the early days of flight. We think that when robotic systems' energy consumption and dependability in intricate flow conditions become issues, a better comprehension and application of fluid mechanics will be essential to their design.

In flow management, making predictions based on data from uncontrolled systems is inherently challenging. This is because the fundamental characteristics of the system can be significantly altered through active or passive modifications aimed at achieving specific engineering objectives. Such changes can impact the flow dynamics, making it difficult to rely on historical data for accurate forecasting. In certain aspects, such as geographic resolution, flow data may be sparse, while in other aspects, such as parametric studies, they may be large. Additionally, flow data might be very diverse, so selecting the right kind of LM requires extra caution. Furthermore, obtaining statistically convergent findings may be prohibitively costly, even for stationary flows, and many fluid systems are nonstationary.

The interpretability, explainability, and generalizability of ML solutions are crucial since fluid dynamics is fundamental to defense, health, and transportation systems. Furthermore, it is frequently required to offer performance guarantees, which are currently uncommon. In fact, a significant number of ML algorithms lack convergence findings, analysis, and assurances. Whether the model will be utilized for extrapolation, which is far more difficult, or for interpolation within a parameter regime should also be taken into account. Finally, we stress that to avoid overfitting in ML, cross-validation on concealed data sets is crucial.

2.6 Summary

Fluid mechanics is one of the many scientific fields where ML has emerged as a crucial facilitator. This chapter examines how ML techniques may address fluid mechanics difficulties and how they could progress the discipline. Introducing the basics of ML and classifying them into supervised, unsupervised, and semi-supervised learning paradigms is the first step in the conversation. For tasks like regression and classification, supervised learning is prioritized, and techniques like random forests, support vector machines, and neural networks are key components. Meanwhile, unsupervised learning techniques that can reveal hidden patterns in fluid flow data, such as clustering and vector quantization, are emphasized. A potential approach to use sparsely labeled data in massive data sets is semi-supervised learning, which combines aspects of both approaches.

The chapter shifts to physics-informed ML, which incorporates the Navier-Stokes equations and other fluid dynamics governing equations into ML models. By incorporating physical restrictions into data-driven predictions, this hybrid technique ensures adherence to accepted physical principles and provides improved performance. Practical examples from fluid mechanics are used to demonstrate the real-world applications of the issue formulation, data representation, architectural design, loss functions, and optimization approaches sections. These illustrations highlight advancements, including enhanced turbulence forecasts and the creation of reduced-order models.

Conventional turbulence modeling methods, such as RANS, LES, and DNS, are additionally addressed. The ML-driven techniques offer a potential substitute or supplement to these computationally intensive method ologies, allowing for quicker and maybe more accurate simulations. For example, neural networks do not require certain computationally demanding simulations since they may train turbulence closure models directly from data.

The chapter ends with a discussion of the prospects and difficulties in this new profession. Notwithstanding its potential, ML has several challenges, including the requirement for sizable, high-quality data sets, the interpretability of models, and the computing resources needed for training. But these difficulties also offer chances for creativity, such as creating more effective algorithms, utilizing transfer learning, and encouraging multidisciplinary cooperation between ML researchers and fluid mechanics specialists.

This thorough investigation highlights the revolutionary potential of ML in fluid mechanics while recognizing the multidisciplinary work needed to get beyond present obstacles and seize new opportunities.

References

1. Pollard, A., Castillo, L., Danaila, L., Glauser, M.N., Whither Turbulence and Big Data for the Twenty-First Century, in: *Whither Turbulence and Big Data in the 21st Century*, A. Pollard, L. Castillo, L. Danaila, M. Glauser, (eds.), Springer, Cham, 2017. https://doi.org/10.1007/978-3-319-41217-7_31
2. Perlman, E., Burns, R., Li, Y., Meneveau, C., Data exploration of turbulence simulations using a database cluster, in: *Proceedings of the 2007 ACM/IEEE Conference on Supercomputing*, 2007, November, pp. 1–11.
3. Wu, X. and Moin, P., A direct numerical simulation study on the mean velocity characteristics in turbulent pipe flow. *J. Fluid Mech.*, 608, 81–112, 2008.

4. Shafiq, A., Çolak, A.B., Sindhu, T.N., Reliability investigation of exponentiated Weibull distribution using IPL through numerical and artificial neural network modeling. *Qual. Reliab. Eng. Int.*, 38, 7, 3616–3631, 2022.
5. Colak, A.B., Experimental study for thermal conductivity of water-based zirconium oxide nanofluid: developing optimal artificial neural network and proposing new correlation. *Int. J. Energy Res.*, 45, 2, 2912–2930, 2021.
6. Shafiq, A., Çolak, A.B., Sindhu, T.N., Lone, S.A., Alsubie, A., Jarad, F., Comparative study of artificial neural network versus parametric method in COVID-19 data analysis. *Results Phys.*, 38, 105613, 2022.
7. Blazewicz, J., Borowski, M., Chaara, W., Kedziora, P., Klatzmann, D., Lukasiak, P., Wojciechowski, P., GeVaDSs–decision support system for novel Genetic Vaccine development process. *BMC Bioinf.*, 13, 1–16, 2012.
8. Błażewicz, J., Łukasiak, P., Wilk, S., New machine learning methods for prediction of protein secondary structures. *Control Cybern.*, 36, 1, 183–201, 2007.
9. Majchrzak, M., Jakubowski, M., Starosta, R., AI-based method of vortex core tracking as an alternative for Lambda2. *Vibr. Phys. Syst.*, 31, 3, 2020319-1–2020319-10, 2020.
10. Cherkassky, V. and Mulier, F.M., *Learning from data: concepts, theory, and methods*, 560 p., John Wiley & Sons, Wiley-IEEE Press, August 2007. ISBN: 978-0-471-68182-3
11. Majors, J.H., Machine learning identifies flow patterns faster and better with a combined analysis approach. *Scilight*, 2018, 3, 2018.
12. Hobold, G.M. and da Silva, A.K., Machine learning classification of boiling regimes with low speed, direct and indirect visualization. *Int. J. Heat Mass Transfer*, 125, 1296–1309, 2018.
13. Kang, M., Hwang, L.K., Kwon, B., Machine learning flow regime classification in three-dimensional printed tubes. *Phys. Rev. Fluids*, 5, 8, 081901, 2020.
14. Kim, S.H. and Boukouvala, F., Machine learning-based surrogate modeling for data-driven optimization: a comparison of subset selection for regression techniques. *Optim. Lett.*, 14, 4, 989–1010, 2020. https://doi.org/10.1063/1.5022254
15. Lefauve, A. and Couchman, M.M., Data-driven classification of sheared stratified turbulence from experimental shadowgraphs. *Phys. Rev. Fluids*, 9, 3, 034603, 2024.
16. Daniel, T., Casenave, F., Akkari, N., Ryckelynck, D., Model order reduction assisted by deep neural networks (ROM-net). *Adv. Model. Simul. Eng. Sci.*, 7, 1–27, 2020.
17. Hesthaven, J.S. and Ubbiali, S., Non-intrusive reduced order modeling of nonlinear problems using neural networks. *J. Comput. Phys.*, 363, 55–78, 2018.
18. Dominique, J., Christophe, J., Schram, C., Sandberg, R.D., Inferring empirical wall pressure spectral models with gene expression programming. *J. Sound Vib.*, 506, 116162, 2021.

19. Calado, A., Poletti, R., Koloszar, L.K., Mendez, M.A., A robust data-driven model for flapping aerodynamics under different hovering kinematics. *Phys. Fluids*, 35, 4, 2023. https://doi.org/10.1063/5.0139020
20. Gkimisis, L., Dias, B., Scoggins, J.B., Magin, T., Mendez, M.A., Turchi, A., Data-driven modeling of hypersonic reentry flow with heat and mass transfer. *AIAA J.*, 61, 8, 3269–3286, 2023.
21. Pan, S. and Duraisamy, K., Long-time predictive modeling of nonlinear dynamical systems using neural networks. *Complexity*, 2018, 1, 4801012, 2018.
22. Van den Hof, P.M., System identification-data-driven modelling of dynamic systems, Eindhoven University of Technology, 2012.
23. Huang, S.C. and Kim, J., Control and system identification of a separated flow. *Phys. Fluids*, 20, 10, 2008. https://doi.org/10.1063/1.3005860
24. Goodfellow, I., Bengio, Y., & Courville, A., Regularization for deep learning. *Deep Learning*, 1, 224–270, 2016.
25. Buhmann, M.D., Radial Basis Functions. *Acta Numerica*, 9, 1–38, 2003. doi:10.1017/S0962492900000015
26. Banzhaf, W., Nordin, P., Keller, R.E., Francone, F.D., *Genetic programming: an introduction: on the automatic evolution of computer programs and its applications*, Morgan Kaufmann Publishers Inc., San Francisco, CA, United States, 1998.
27. Rumelhart, D.E., Hinton, G.E., Williams, R.J., Learning representations by back-propagating errors. *Nature*, 323, 6088, 533–536, 1986.
28. Krizhevsky, A., Sutskever, I., Hinton, G.E., Imagenet classification with deep convolutional neural networks. *Advances in neural information processing systems*, vol. 25, 2012.
29. Grossberg, S., Nonlinear neural networks: Principles, mechanisms, and architectures. *Neural Netw.*, 1, 1, 17–61, 1988.
30. Rosenblatt, F., The perceptron: a probabilistic model for information storage and organization in the brain. *Psychol. Rev.*, 65, 6, 386, 1958.
31. Scholkopf, B. and Smola, A.J., *Learning with kernels: support vector machines, regularization, optimization, and beyond*, MIT Press, Cambridge, Massachusetts, London, England, 2018.
32. Breiman, L., Random forests. *Mach. Learn.*, 45, 5–32, 2001.
33. Swets, D.L. and Weng, J.J., Using discriminant eigenfeatures for image retrieval. *IEEE Trans. Pattern Anal. Mach. Intell.*, 18, 8, 831–836, 1996.
34. Goodfellow, I., Pouget-Abadie, J., Mirza, M., Xu, B., Warde-Farley, D., Ozair, S., Bengio, Y., Generative adversarial nets. *Adv. Neural Inf. Process. Syst.*, 27, 2014.
35. Sutton, R.S. and Barto, A.G., *Reinforcement learning: An introduction*, MIT Press, Cambridge, MA, 2018.
36. Bellman, R., On the theory of dynamic programming. *Proc. Natl. Acad. Sci.*, 38, 8, 716–719, 1952.

37. Brunton, S.L. and Kutz, J.N., *Data-driven science and engineering: Machine learning, dynamical systems, and control*, Cambridge University Press, 2022.
38. Sutton, R.S. and Barto, A.G., *Reinforcement Learning: An Introduction*, vol. 1, Cambridge University Press, 01 March 1999, Google Scholar Digital Library Digital Library.
39. Mnih, V., Kavukcuoglu, K., Silver, D., Rusu, A.A., Veness, J., Bellemare, M.G., Hassabis, D., Human-level control through deep reinforcement learning. *Nature*, 518, 7540, 529–533, 2015.
40. Silver, D., Schrittwieser, J., Simonyan, K., Antonoglou, I., Huang, A., Guez, A., Hassabis, D., Mastering the game of go without human knowledge. *Nature*, 550, 7676, 354–359, 2017.
41. Brunton, S.L., Noack, B.R., Koumoutsakos, P., Machine learning for fluid mechanics. *Annu. Rev. Fluid Mech.*, 52, 1, 477–508, 2020.
42. Brenner, M.P., Eldredge, J.D., Freund, J.B., Perspective on machine learning for advancing fluid mechanics. *Phys. Rev. Fluids*, 4, 10, 100501, 2019.
43. Duraisamy, K., Iaccarino, G., Xiao, H., Turbulence modeling in the age of data. *Annu. Rev. Fluid Mech.*, 51, 1, 357–377, 2019.
44. Ahmed, S.E., Pawar, S., San, O., Rasheed, A., Iliescu, T., Noack, B.R., On closures for reduced order models—A spectrum of first-principle to machine-learned avenues. *Phys. Fluids*, 33, 9, 2021. https://doi.org/10.1063/5.0061577
45. Ling, J., Kurzawski, A., Templeton, J., Reynolds averaged turbulence modelling using deep neural networks with embedded invariance. *J. Fluid Mech.*, 807, 155–166, 2016.
46. Kutz, J.N., Deep learning in fluid dynamics. *J. Fluid Mech.*, 814, 1–4, 2017.
47. Maulik, R., San, O., Rasheed, A., Vedula, P., Subgrid modelling for two-dimensional turbulence using neural networks. *J. Fluid Mech.*, 858, 122–144, 2019.
48. Novati, G., de Laroussilhe, H.L., Koumoutsakos, P., Automating turbulence modelling by multi-agent reinforcement learning. *Nat. Mach. Intell.*, 3, 1, 87–96, 2021.
49. Wang, J.X., Wu, J.L., Xiao, H., Physics-informed machine learning approach for reconstructing Reynolds stress modeling discrepancies based on DNS data. *Phys. Rev. Fluids*, 2, 3, 034603, 2017.
50. Zhu, L., Zhang, W., Kou, J., Liu, Y., Machine learning methods for turbulence modeling in subsonic flows around airfoils. *Phys. Fluids*, 31, 1, 2019. https://doi.org/10.1063/1.5061693
51. Zhu, L., Zhang, W., Sun, X., Liu, Y., Yuan, X., Turbulence closure for high Reynolds number airfoil flows by deep neural networks. *Aerosp. Sci. Technol.*, 110, 106452, 2021.
52. Wang, H., Cao, Y., Huang, Z., Liu, Y., Hu, P., Luo, X., Sun, Y., Recent advances on machine learning for computational fluid dynamics: A survey, *arXiv preprint arXiv:2408.12171*, 2024.
53. Thaler, S., Paehler, L., Adams, N.A., Sparse identification of truncation errors. *J. Comput. Phys.*, 397, 108851, 2019.

54. Erichson, N.B., Mathelin, L., Yao, Z., Brunton, S.L., Mahoney, M.W., Kutz, J.N., Shallow neural networks for fluid flow reconstruction with limited sensors. *Proc. R. Soc. A*, 476, 2238, 20200097, 2020.
55. Fukami, K., Fukagata, K., Taira, K., Super-resolution reconstruction of turbulent flows with machine learning. *J. Fluid Mech.*, 870, 106–120, 2019.
56. Taira, K., Brunton, S.L., Dawson, S.T., Rowley, C.W., Colonius, T., McKeon, B.J., Ukeiley, L.S., Modal analysis of fluid flows: An overview. *AIAA J.*, 55, 12, 4013–4041, 2017.
57. Taira, K., Hemati, M.S., Brunton, S.L., Sun, Y., Duraisamy, K., Bagheri, S., Yeh, C.A., Modal analysis of fluid flows: Applications and outlook. *AIAA J.*, 58, 3, 998–1022, 2020.
58. Scherl, I., Strom, B., Shang, J.K., Williams, O., Polagye, B.L., Brunton, S.L., Robust principal component analysis for particle image velocimetry. *Phys. Rev. Fluids*, 5, 054401, 10, 2020.
59. Nair, A.G. and Taira, K., Network-theoretic approach to sparsified discrete vortex dynamics. *J. Fluid Mech.*, 768, 549–571, 2015.
60. Kaiser, E., Noack, B.R., Cordier, L., Spohn, A., Segond, M., Abel, M., Niven, R.K., Cluster-based reduced-order modelling of a mixing layer. *J. Fluid Mech.*, 754, 365–414, 2014.
61. Zhou, Y., Fan, D., Zhang, B., Li, R., Noack, B.R., Artificial intelligence control of a turbulent jet. *J. Fluid Mech.*, 897, A27, 2020.
62. Maceda, G.Y.C., Li, Y., Lusseyran, F., Morzyński, M., Noack, B.R., Stabilization of the fluidic pinball with gradient-enriched machine learning control. *J. Fluid Mech.*, 917, A42, 2021. https://doi.org/10.1017/jfm.2021.301
63. Fan, D., Yang, L., Wang, Z., Triantafyllou, M.S., Karniadakis, G.E., Reinforcement learning for bluff body active flow control in experiments and simulations. *Proc. Natl. Acad. Sci.*, 117, 42, 26091–26098, 2020.
64. Verma, S., Novati, G., Koumoutsakos, P., Efficient collective swimming by harnessing vortices through deep reinforcement learning. *Proc. Natl. Acad. Sci.*, 115, 23, 5849–5854, 2018.
65. Fan, D., Jodin, G., Consi, T.R., Bonfiglio, L., Ma, Y., Keyes, L.R., Triantafyllou, M.S., A robotic intelligent towing tank for learning complex fluid-structure dynamics. *Sci. Rob.*, 4, 36, eaay5063, 2019.
66. Kou, J. and Zhang, W., Data-driven modeling for unsteady aerodynamics and aeroelasticity. *Prog. Aerosp. Sci.*, 125, 100725, 2021.
67. Bhat, S.S., Ananth, A., Venugopala, P.S., Design and Evolution of Deep Convolutional Neural Networks in Image Classification–A Review. *Int. J. Integr. Eng.*, 15, 1, 213–225, 2023.
68. Deng, J., Dong, W., Socher, R., Li, L.J., Li, K., Fei-Fei, L., Imagenet: A large-scale hierarchical image database, in: *2009 IEEE conference on computer vision and pattern recognition*, 2009, June, IEEE, pp. 248–255.
69. Sejnowski, T.J., *The deep learning revolution*, MIT Press, Cambridge, Massachusetts, London, England, 2018.

70. Hornik, K., Stinchcombe, M., White, H., Multilayer feedforward networks are universal approximators. *Neural Netw.*, 2, 5, 359–366, 1989.
71. Hornik, K., Approximation capabilities of multilayer feedforward networks. *Neural Netw.*, 4, 2, 251–257, 1991.
72. Schmidt, M. and Lipson, H., Distilling free-form natural laws from experimental data. *Science*, 324, 5923, 81–85, 2009.
73. Bongard, J. and Lipson, H., Automated reverse engineering of nonlinear dynamical systems. *Proc. Natl. Acad. Sci.*, 104, 24, 9943–9948, 2007.
74. Kutz, J.N., Brunton, S.L., Brunton, B.W., Proctor, J.L., *Dynamic mode decomposition: data-driven modeling of complex systems*, Society for Industrial and Applied Mathematics, Philadelphia, PA, USA, 2016.
75. Brunton, S.L., Proctor, J.L., Kutz, J.N., Discovering governing equations from data by sparse identification of nonlinear dynamical systems. *Proc. Natl. Acad. Sci.*, 113, 15, 3932–3937, 2016.
76. Tibshirani, R., Regression shrinkage and selection via the lasso. *J. R. Stat. Soc. Ser. B Stat. Methodol.*, 58, 1, 267–288, 1996.
77. Zheng, P., Askham, T., Brunton, S.L., Kutz, J.N., Aravkin, A.V., Sparse relaxed regularized regression: SR3. *Stat*, 1050, 18, 2018.
78. Beetham, S. and Capecelatro, J., Formulating turbulence closures using sparse regression with embedded form invariance. *Phys. Rev. Fluids*, 5, 8, 084611, 2020.
79. Beetham, S., Fox, R.O., Capecelatro, J., Sparse identification of multiphase turbulence closures for coupled fluid–particle flows. *J. Fluid Mech.*, 914, A11, 2021.
80. Kou, J. and Zhang, W., A hybrid reduced-order framework for complex aeroelastic simulations. *Aerosp. Sci. Technol.*, 84, 880–894, 2019.
81. Frezat, H., Balarac, G., Le Sommer, J., Fablet, R., Lguensat, R., Physical invariance in neural networks for subgrid-scale scalar flux modeling. *Phys. Rev. Fluids*, 6, 2, 024607, 2021.
82. Lee, K. and Carlberg, K.T., Model reduction of dynamical systems on nonlinear manifolds using deep convolutional autoencoders. *J. Comput. Phys.*, 404, 108973, 2020.
83. Noack, B.R., Afanasiev, K., Morzyński, M., Tadmor, G., Thiele, F., A hierarchy of low-dimensional models for the transient and post-transient cylinder wake. *J. Fluid Mech.*, 497, 335–363, 2003.
84. Benner, P., Gugercin, S., Willcox, K., A survey of projection-based model reduction methods for parametric dynamical systems. *SIAM Rev.*, 57, 4, 483–531, 2015.
85. Loiseau, J.C. and Brunton, S.L., Constrained sparse Galerkin regression. *J. Fluid Mech.*, 838, 42–67, 2018.
86. Erichson, N.B., Muehlebach, M., Mahoney, M.W., Physics-informed autoencoders for Lyapunov-stable fluid flow prediction, arXiv preprint arXiv:1905.10866, 2019.

87. Sun, L. and Wang, J.X., Physics-constrained bayesian neural network for fluid flow reconstruction with sparse and noisy data. *Theor. Appl. Mech. Lett.*, 10, 3, 161–169, 2020.
88. Grant, M., Boyd, S., Ye, Y., Disciplined convex programming, in: *Global Optimization. Nonconvex Optimization and Its Applications.* L. Liberti, N. Maculan, (eds.) , vol. 84, pp. 155–210, Springer, Boston, MA, 2006. https://doi.org/10.1007/0-387-30528-9_7
89. Boyd, S. and Vandenberghe, L., *Convex optimization*, Cambridge University Press, United Kingdom, 2004.
90. Courant, R., Friedrichs, K., Lewy, H., Über die partiellen Differenzengleichungen der mathematischen Physik. *Math. Ann.*, 100, 1, 32–74, 1928.
91. Pathak, J., Mustafa, M., Kashinath, K., Motheau, E., Kurth, T., Day, M., Using machine learning to augment coarse-grid computational fluid dynamics simulations, *arXiv preprint arXiv:2010.00072*, 2020.
92. Bar-Sinai, Y., Hoyer, S., Hickey, J., Brenner, M.P., Learning data-driven discretizations for partial differential equations. *Proc. Natl. Acad. Sci.*, 116, 31, 15344–15349, 2019.
93. Reynolds, O., IV. On the dynamical theory of incompressible viscous fluids and the determination of the criterion. *Philos. Trans. R. Soc. London (A)*, 186, 123–164, 1895.
94. Boussinesq, J., *Essai sur la théorie des eaux courantes*, Imprimerie Nationale in Paris, 1877.
95. Schmitt, F.G., About Boussinesq's turbulent viscosity hypothesis: historical remarks and a direct evaluation of its validity. *Comptes Rendus Mécanique*, 335, 9-10, 617–627, 2007.
96. Margheri, L., Meldi, M., Salvetti, M.V., Sagaut, P., Epistemic uncertainties in RANS model free coefficients. *Comput. Fluids*, 102, 315–335, 2014.
97. Hanjalić, K. and Launder, B.E., A Reynolds stress model of turbulence and its application to thin shear flows. *J. Fluid Mech.*, 52, 4, 609–638, 1972.
98. Wilcox, D.C., Formulation of the kw turbulence model revisited. *AIAA J.*, 46, 11, 2823–2838, 2008.
99. Menter, F.R., Two-equation eddy-viscosity turbulence models for engineering applications. *AIAA J.*, 32, 8, 1598–1605, 1994.
100. Spalart, P. and Allmaras, S., A one-equation turbulence model for aerodynamic flows, in: *30th aerospace sciences meeting and exhibit*, 1992, January, p. 439.
101. Tracey, B.D., Duraisamy, K., Alonso, J.J., A machine learning strategy to assist turbulence model development, in: *53rd AIAA aerospace sciences meeting*, p. 1287, 2015.
102. Ray, J., Lefantzi, S., Arunajatesan, S., Dechant, L., Learning an eddy viscosity model using shrinkage and Bayesian calibration: A jet-in-crossflow case study. *ASCE-ASME J. Risk Uncertainty Eng. Syst. Part B: Mech. Eng.*, 4, 1, 011001, 2018.

103. Rosenblatt, F., *Principles of Neurodynamics: Perceptrons and the Theory of Brain Mechanisms*, Washington, Spartan Books, 1962.
104. Singh, A.P., Medida, S., Duraisamy, K., Machine-learning-augmented predictive modeling of turbulent separated flows over airfoils. *AIAA J.*, 55, 7, 2215–2227, 2017.
105. Singh, A.P., Duraisamy, K., Zhang, Z.J., Augmentation of turbulence models using field inversion and machine learning, in: *55th AIAA Aerospace Sciences Meeting*, p. 0993, 2017.
106. Smagorinsky, J., General circulation experiments with the primitive equations: I. The basic experiment. *Mon. Weather Rev.*, 91, 3, 99–164, 1963.
107. Deardorff, J.W., A numerical study of three-dimensional turbulent channel flow at large Reynolds numbers. *J. Fluid Mech.*, 41, 2, 453–480, 1970.
108. Cichocki, A. and Amari, S.-i., *Adaptive Blind Signal and Image Processing: Learning Algorithms and Applications*, vol. 2, pp. 1129–1159, John Wiley & Sons Ltd, Google Scholar, 2 May 2002. Print ISBN:9780471607915 |Online ISBN:9780470845899 |DOI:10.1002/0470845899
109. Maulik, R. and San, O., A neural network approach for the blind deconvolution of turbulent flows. *J. Fluid Mech.*, 831, 151–181, 2017.
110. Stolz, S., Adams, N.A., Kleiser, L., The approximate deconvolution model for large-eddy simulations of compressible flows and its application to shock-turbulent-boundary-layer interaction. *Phys. Fluids*, 13, 10, 2985–3001, 2001.
111. Clark, R.A., Ferziger, J.H., Reynolds, W.C., Evaluation of subgrid-scale models using an accurately simulated turbulent flow. *J. Fluid Mech.*, 91, 1, 1–16, 1979.
112. Wang, R., Kashinath, K., Mustafa, M., Albert, A., Yu, R., Towards physics-informed deep learning for turbulent flow prediction, in: *Proceedings of the 26th ACM SIGKDD international conference on knowledge discovery & data mining*, 2020, August, pp. 1457–1466.
113. Bénard, H., Les tourbillons cellulaires dans une nappe liquide. *Rev. Gen. Sci. Pure Appl.*, 11, 1261–1271, 1900.
114. Rayleigh, L., LIX. On convection currents in a horizontal layer of fluid, when the higher temperature is on the under side. *Lond. Edinb. Dublin Philos. Mag. J. Sci.*, 32, 192, 529–546, 1916.

3

Artificial Intelligence-Enhanced Developments in Computational Fluid Dynamics

Tushar Sagar[1], Sachin Kumar[2*], Dinesh Kumar Patel[2], Gaurav Nandan[2] and Vipin Kumar Sharma[3]

[1]*Department of Aerospace Engineering, IIMT University, Meerut, India*
[2]*Department of Mechanical Engineering, IIMT Engineering College, Meerut, India*
[3]*Department of Mechanical Engineering, MIET, Meerut, India*

Abstract

This chapter looks into how artificial intelligence (AI) is being used together with computational fluid dynamics (CFD). It focuses on how this combination is improving the accuracy of simulations and making computations faster. The introduction points out the importance of CFD in different engineering areas, noting its role in predicting how fluids act and making better designs. It also shows how AI is becoming more important in recent studies for boosting old CFD methods. This study aims to identify key AI techniques that can advance turbulence modeling and speed up the simulation process. The literature review tracks the growth of CFD from its early stages using basic numerical methods to today's advanced techniques. It explores how AI and machine learning have moved forward, particularly in how they are applied to fluid dynamics. This section also goes over past research that shows successful uses of AI in CFD, setting the stage for this current study. The methodology section describes how data was gathered, emphasizing the importance of high-quality datasets to train AI models well. The paper outlines the AI methods used, including neural networks and reinforcement learning. It also explains the CFD simulation framework that tests these models. The results are shown through performance metrics that check the accuracy and efficiency of AI-enhanced simulations compared to usual methods. Case studies are given to show specific examples where AI has significantly improved predictions of turbulence and cut down computation times.

**Corresponding author*: sachin.dubey765@gmail.com

Mukesh Kumar Awasthi and Reshu Gupta (eds.) Artificial Intelligence and Computational Modeling in Heat Transfer and Fluid Dynamics, (51–92) © 2026 Scrivener Publishing LLC

***Keywords*:** Artificial intelligence, computational fluid dynamics, turbulence modeling, simulation, neural networks, reinforcement learning, machine learning

3.1 Introduction

Computational fluid dynamics (CFD) is an advanced numerical method by solving some differential equations using numerical methods, which models fluid behavior, heat transfer and other related processes. The applications of this technology are spread over many sectors, including food technology, aerospace engineering, and urban planning. Computational fluid dynamics enables obtaining in-depth views into finer physical processes by creating a virtual model that describes fluid behavior [1]. Computational fluid dynamics is used to tackle equations that govern fluid dynamics using the numerical methods rooted in the key conservation principles: mass, momentum, and energy. These are the main equations to be solved that include Navier–Stokes equation, which describe the movement of viscous fluids, continuity, ensure the conservation of mass, energy equation, which control the transfer of thermal energy, and Fourier's law, which are used to describe the movement of thermal energy in solid materials [2]. Computational fluid dynamics is a tool based on fluid dynamics. It allows you to model fluids' movement, transfer of heat, as well as their interaction with the environment. It helps scientists and engineers analyze fluid behavior in different situations that can be very difficult to experiment with in person [3].

There are many applications of it in various industries. Within the food industry, it is crucial for food processing, modeling, and optimization of thermal processes such as baking, frying, pasteurization, drying, and cooking [4]. Advances in CFD for food processing better analyze the heat and mass transfer involved during food processing to fine-tune process parameters as a result, thus improving food product quality and safety. It can also simulate heat transfer in baking and recommend optimum pasteurization times needed to ensure that the food is not too dangerous and maintain its quality [5]. Computational fluid dynamics is crucial in aerospace engineering to improve the aerodynamic performance of aircraft. Engineers can simulate airflow around planes and predict aerodynamic forces, which are important to design optimally various plane components [6, 7]. Computational fluid dynamics also benefits urban planning since it can model urban flooding and evaluate flood risks of urban situations by modeling complex flow patterns in cities. Additionally, CFD is utilized for studying subsurface drip irrigation, such as soil water movement and the unsaturated soil dynamics [8]. In the context of fuel cells, CFD is used to analyze hydrogen transport and electrochemical reactions, in particular in proton exchange membrane fuel cells [9]. Computational fluid dynamics is used in turbo machinery to simulate complex flow patterns and predict performance characteristics in components like axial compressors, which are necessary for effective thermal process design. Computational fluid dynamics can greatly impact the field of biomass combustion as an important category [10]. By modeling CFD solid fuels such as biomass, we can understand how solid fuels such as biomass burn in this industrial burner. This analysis enables us to find temperature distribution, emitted amounts, and heat production at this point, but it gives us some insight into how we can replace traditional fossil fuels, for example, by biomass, which is better for the environment [11].

Almost all flows in the real world are turbulent and so require turbulence modeling. In CFD, the turbulence models are used to calculate the influence of chaotic fluid motions. The most widely used approach is the Reynolds-averaged Navier–Stokes (RANS) model, which solves the averaged Navier–Stokes equations to simulate the steady or nearly steady turbulent flow. When it comes to computational efficiency, the RANS model, such as k-ε and k-ω, is efficient. However, they may not capture all the intricate details of turbulence [12]. A large eddy simulation (LES) is another way of doing it, in which only a larger turbulent structure is resolved, and sub-grid models are applied for the rest. An LES is computationally more expensive as it provides a more detailed insight into RANS. The last, direct numerical simulation (DNS) resolves the Navier–Stokes equations, solving them without any turbulence calculus, since it captures all scales of motion. While DNS is the most precise method we have available, it also consumes excessive resources. Therefore, it is usually used for fundamental research purposes [13]. Specifically, in terms of numerical methods, CFD solves the governing equations using several techniques. One popular method for heat and mass transport equations across different phases is the finite volume method (FVM), which breaks down space into small volume cells and solves the equations for each cell. One of the methods is the finite element method, in which solutions are approximated through interpolation, a method commonly used in structural mechanics and fluid dynamics. Next, the finite difference method (FDM) approximates derivatives by finite differences, therefore discretizing the problem domain, and is popular for solving basic heat transfer processes [1].

A recent trend in artificial intelligence (AI) is greatly improving research in CFD, with studies able to create more accurate, efficient, and more sophisticated simulations of fluid dynamics. This progress comes with the help of machine learning (ML), deep reinforcement learning, and neural network formulation using physics-informed neural networks (PINNs), together forming a more powerful and flexible CFD framework [14]. Deep reinforcement learning has one of the key applications in flow control and optimization by enhancing strategies aimed at regulating flow by automatic changes to the simulation in real-time. This field is still undergoing many efforts to solve some problems, like transfer learning and multi-agent systems, which increase the data efficiency and deal with turbulence in complex situations [15]. In particular, recently improved PINNs have reduced their bottleneck of simulating incompressible fluids. The advancements have enhanced convergence and accuracy when solving fluid dynamics challenges. Adaptive techniques, such as adaptive sampling and loss balancing, introduced new techniques to improve performance under different flow cases, making these models more powerful in handling complex fluid behaviors [16]. As the sophistication of AI incorporated into the smoothed particle hydrodynamics (SPH) emulators continues to advance, the learning of the SPH emulators is becoming smoother. The SPH researchers can, however, use AI for these SPH techniques to gain more precise simulations of dynamic free surface flows and apply these models also to situations beyond initial training data [17, 18]. Figure 3.1 presents a detailed analysis of the enhancement of CFD simulations with AI.

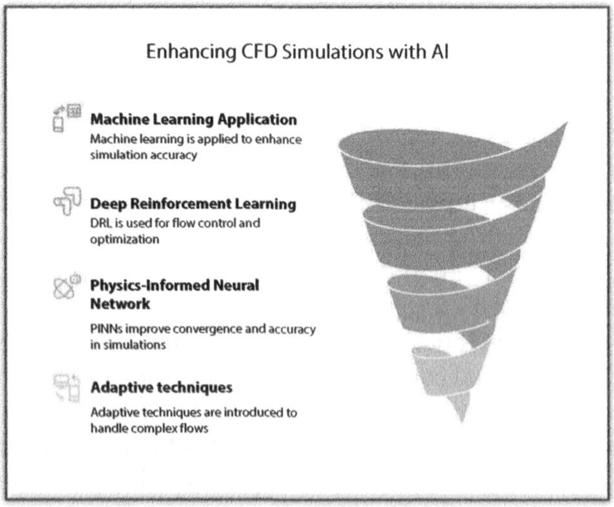

Figure 3.1 Enhancement of CFD simulations with AI.

The research is based on the use of AI for better simulations by lowering the number of errors, reducing the computational time, as well as making the design process much simpler. The level of these goals is also in line with emerging research trends, stressing the necessity of combining AI and ML to surmount the deficiencies of the basic CFD approaches. The study aims to increase the accuracy of the simulation. Using AI methods, in particular ML, can help researchers model the wetter fluid dynamics better, and thus gain better predictive abilities in cases of turbulent flows [19]. The research aims to reduce computational costs by utilizing AI technology to reduce CFD simulation time, which will consequently reduce analysis time and resources [20]. Using AI tools to analyze how a vehicle moves through the air causes designers to improve faster to reduce drag. They can quickly try out different ideas and determine what makes vehicles more efficient [21]. While the trend focuses on ML, engineering finds ways to use data to improve models and simulations [22]. This research is in accordance with current studies, aiming its AI application based on a solid scientific foundation. The use of AI in computational fluid dynamics has greatly advanced, but there are things yet to be negotiated, such as ensuring that AI models comply with the physical laws operating in fluid dynamics. Preserving accuracy and reliability calls for this adherence [23].

3.2 An Overview of Artificial Intelligence in Computational Fluid Dynamics

3.2.1 Evolution of Computational Fluid Dynamics

Progress in CFD has largely depended on the development of 'better' FDMs, which have received much attention and many milestones along the way. These methods have been decisive in making CFD an irreplaceable expertise for engineering and scientific purposes. Improvements in numerical analysis, computing capability, and knowledge of fluid behavior have led particularly to the advancement of FDMs [24].

When the partial derivatives were substituted by difference equations, FDM started giving the space finite difference cells. This was an important step in being able to numerically solve partial differential equations (PDEs) [25]. It was popular for solving the Navier–Stokes equations to understand fluid dynamics because of its effectiveness in managing intricate geometries and boundary conditions [26].

When electronic computers appeared in the middle of the 20th century, for the first time, such FDM could be successfully used in CFD. This is a breakthrough in technology that opened the way to more complicated simulations and an increase in different areas [27]. Large eddy simulations, as well as DNS, are commonly based on FDMs. Finally, these techniques demonstrate the flexibility and computational efficiency of the method in particular applications such as the high Reynolds number turbulent flows [28]. Figure 3.2 presents a detailed analysis of the evolution of CFD.

The FDM has also been used to cover the issues of weather forecasting and climate theory, and scientists, especially G.I. Marchuk, have made acclaimed progress in such domain. Their research has enabled them to improve precipitation and climatic patterns in models that predicted weather and climate trends [29].

With the rise of ML and AI, CFD may change so much that some of these apparent drawbacks of the FDMs could be overcome. As Tian [113] noted, in data center scenarios, fast fluid dynamics (FFD) shows almost the same predictions as traditional CFD simulations if the just as advection schemes, grids, and turbulence models are used. In particular, Djukić [114] presented a thorough validation of the lattice Boltzmann method (LBM) against CFD in simulating individual specific patients' complex vessels of the blood flow and demonstrated that it is an accurate and efficient method for doing so. A comparison of the CFD software FLUENT with the Varangian code LASAT is presented [115], comparing the two using

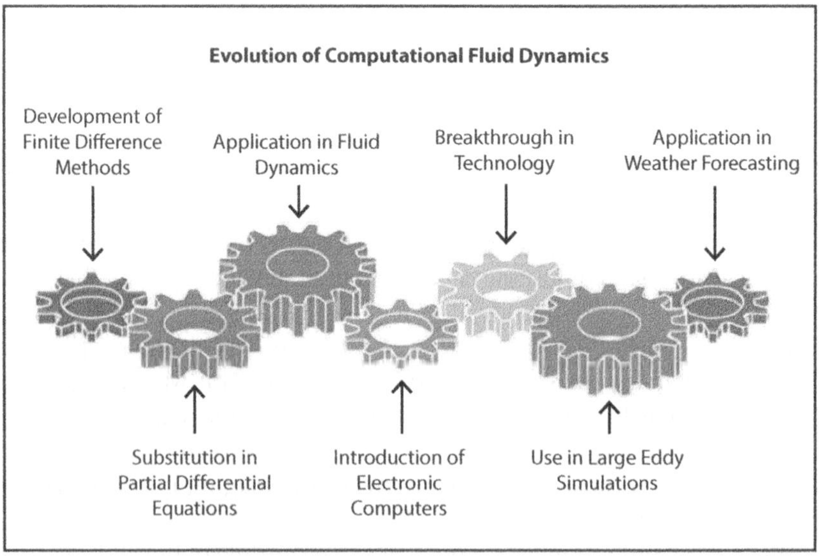

Figure 3.2 Evolution of CFD.

a simple single-source test case, which differs in their results. Pettersson and Rizzi [106] investigated the precision of different CFD techniques and turbulence models for the calculation of local boundary layer parameters in the process of their development, agreeing with discrepancies with data from wind tunnels. Below is a summary of Table 3.1 that brings together various CFD traditional methods and outlines their study objectives.

Table 3.2 brings together various AI Applications, outlining their contributions, results, and conclusions.

Table 3.1 Computational fluid dynamics' traditional methods and objectives.

Traditional methods	Study objectives	References
The FFD can yield results that are almost identical to those from traditional CFD when applied to data center scenarios.	• Create an FFD model that enhances the speed of CFD calculations for data center uses without sacrificing accuracy. • Analyze how well various turbulence models, including a basic algebraic model, can predict temperatures at the rack inlets in an actual data center.	[103]
The LBM has been proven to be an effective alternative to conventional CFD techniques for simulating blood flow in intricate, patient-specific arteries.	• Validate the accuracy of LBM for simulating blood flow in complex patient-specific arteries. • Compare the results of LBM to traditional CFD methods.	[104]
Computational fluid dynamics and Lagrangian dispersion methods using a simple test case to identify differences that need to be considered before using higher-level simulation methods.	• Compare the results of the CFD code FLUENT and the Lagrangian code LASAT using a simple, single-source test case. • Identify differences between the two methods that need to be considered before using higher-level simulation methods to model airport local air quality.	[105]

(*Continued*)

Table 3.1 Computational fluid dynamics' traditional methods and objectives. (*Continued*)

Traditional methods	Study objectives	References
Accuracy of different CFD methods in computing local boundary layer properties compared to wind tunnel measurements.	• Investigate the accuracy of CFD methods in computing local boundary layer properties, compared to wind tunnel measurements. • Determine whether CFD methods can consistently compute local boundary layer properties across a wide range of Reynolds numbers, which are not achievable in wind tunnels.	[106]
The Navier–Stokes method and LBM for aerodynamic and aeroacoustics applications, highlighting their trade-offs in accuracy and computational cost.	• To compare the LBM and Navier–Stokes methods in terms of their accuracy and computational cost for aerodynamic and aeroacoustics applications. • To provide a fair and unbiased comparison of the core capabilities of the two numerical methods, focusing on practical relevance • To consider the time-to-solution metric when assessing the suitability of the two numerical methods	[107]
Computational fluid dynamics techniques, including DNS, LES, and RANS, in terms of computational demands, accuracy, and suitability for different fluid flow scenarios.	• Examine recent advancements in CFD simulation techniques • Compare CFD techniques (e.g., DNS, LES, RANS, hybrid methods) in terms of computational demands, accuracy, and suitability for different fluid flow scenarios • Highlight effective validation methods (e.g., wind tunnel testing, analytical solutions, field measurements) for ensuring simulation reliability and aligning models with experimental data	[108]

(*Continued*)

Table 3.1 Computational fluid dynamics' traditional methods and objectives. (*Continued*)

Traditional methods	Study objectives	References
A hybrid CFD method using deep neural networks can accelerate urban-scale simulations by 30% compared to traditional CFD.	• Develop a hybrid methodology that combines CFD simulations and deep neural networks to accelerate fluid dynamics simulations. • Demonstrate that this hybrid approach can reduce the time-to-solution by 30% in an urban-scale case study and enable the generation of massive datasets at a lower cost compared to traditional CFD simulations.	[109]
Computational fluid dynamics results against benchmark experiments to validate CFD codes for mine face ventilation.	• To validate the use of CFD tools for analyzing and designing mine face ventilation systems. • To compare CFD results against mining-related benchmark experiments	[110]

Table 3.2 Literature review on the evolution of CFD.

Contributions	Applications	Results	Conclusions	References
1. Development of open-source CFD software with high precision and high performance. 2. Validation and verification of test cases for supersonic and hypersonic compressible turbulence.	1. Direct numerical simulation of compressible wall-bounded turbulence. 2. Validation case of Mach 2.9 compression ramp.	1. OpenCFD-SCU software achieves acceleration by a factor of more than 200 compared to CPU software. 2. OpenCFD-SCU with 512 GPUs is faster than CPU software with 130,000 CPUs.	1. OpenCFD-SCU software accelerates simulation speed and saves computational cost. 2. OpenCFD-SCU achieves 98.7% parallel weak scalability with 24,576 GPUs.	[30]

(*Continued*)

Table 3.2 Literature review on the evolution of CFD. (*Continued*)

Contributions	Applications	Results	Conclusions	References
1. Algorithms for the numerical solution of differential equations. 2. Successful modeling of phase separation and surface tension.	1. Modeling phase separation in binary immiscible fluid mixtures. 2. Simulating surface tension effects in fluid dynamics.	1. Successful modeling of phase separation in fluids. 2. Accurate representation of surface tension in mixtures.	1. The Groot–Warren method is recommended for dissipative particle dynamics (DPD) simulations due to precision. 2. Gear-3 algorithm is a stable second choice despite energy conservation issues.	[31]
1. Fourth-order finite difference method for Boussinesq equations. 2. Efficient Poisson solvers using FFT for computations.	1. Lorenz flow example for accuracy verification. 2. Differentially heated cavity problem simulations.	1. Full fourth-order accuracy checked with the Lorenz flow example. 2. Benchmark simulations of the differentially heated cavity problem are presented.	1. The fourth-order method efficiently solves Boussinesq equations. 2. Accurate simulations for shear flow and cavity problems.	[32]
1. A direct evaluation of the dynamic-permeability convolution is presented. 2. Memory terms match discretization points for waveform coverage.	-	1. Scheme confirmed accuracy *via* numerical and analytic result comparison. 2. Convolution enhances stability, allowing larger time steps.	1. Time-domain scheme solves Biot's equations across all frequencies. 2. Convolution modeling enhances the stability and accuracy of Darcy flow.	[33]

(*Continued*)

Table 3.2 Literature review on the evolution of CFD. (*Continued*)

Contributions	Applications	Results	Conclusions	References
1. Discusses a model for fine particle dispersion. 2. Proposes a new efficient difference scheme.	1. Longitudinal dispersion of suspended particles in turbulent flow. 2. Settling particle dispersion from elevated sources.	1. Non-negativity of numerical concentration is proved. 2. Computational experiments illustrate scheme properties.	1. Constructed a fitted finite volume difference scheme for particle dispersion. 2. Demonstrated numerical scheme conserves non-negativity of continuous solution.	[34]
1. Formulated a 3D finite-difference method using discontinuous grids. 2. Reduced computational requirements significantly without loss of accuracy.	1. A 3D wave propagation simulation in earthquake studies. 2. Reducing grid spacing near free surfaces and fault planes.	1. Significant reduction in computational requirements, typically one-fifth to one-tenth. 2. Maintained accuracy with discontinuous grids adapted to velocity structure.	1. Discontinuous grids significantly reduce computational requirements. 2. Accuracy is maintained despite coarser grid spacing.	[35]
1. Proposed a rational high-order compact FDM. 2. Validated method with various numerical experiments and flow problems.	1. Lid-driven cavity flow problem 2. Backward-facing step flow problem	1. Validated method through numerical experiments on various problems. 2. Solutions for the driven cavity problem compared with literature results.	1. The proposed RHOC method effectively solves the Navier–Stokes equations. 2. Numerical results validate the method against analytical solutions.	[36]

(*Continued*)

Table 3.2 Literature review on the evolution of CFD. (*Continued*)

Contributions	Applications	Results	Conclusions	References
1. Investigates numerical models for nonlinear reaction-diffusion equations. 2. Establishes a center manifold approach for consistent finite difference models.	1. Modeling linear dynamics with FDMs. 2. Solving nonlinear PDEs effectively.	1. The center manifold approach models linear dynamics consistently. 2. Advection-diffusion equation stably modeled for all grid spacings.	1. Center manifold theory generates effective finite difference models. 2. Higher-order consistency needs further research on odd derivatives.	[37]
1. Designed time-space finite difference schemes ensuring energy and mass conservation. 2. Developed split methods for computational stability and efficiency.	1. Solving dynamical equations of a compressible fluid. 2. Integrating meteorological primitive equations.	1. Developed energy and mass-conserving finite difference schemes. 2. Achieved computational stability and economic solution methods.	1. Energy and mass conservation are perfectly guaranteed. 2. Computational stability and economy are achieved effectively.	[38]
1. Constructs finite-difference schemes for coupled ordinary differential equations (ODEs). 2. Ensures correct linear stability for all step sizes.	1. Biological sciences applications discussed. 2. Engineering applications mentioned.	1. Constructed finite-difference schemes for coupled ODEs. 2. Ensured correct linear stability for all step-sizes.	1. Finite-difference schemes ensure correct stability for all step sizes. 2. Absence of numerical instabilities in differential equation modeling.	[39]

3.2.2 Artificial Intelligence and Machine Learning Advances

In recent years, the use of ML and CFD has become trendy in enhancing the precision and speed of simulations. Combining these two fields means that researchers hope to make CFD simulations faster and more accurate, as well as to predict in real-time [40]. This collaboration is set to revolutionize how simulations are conducted, making them more efficient overall.

By using data approaches like improvements in deep learning, reinforcement learning, and data science, CFD models can employ methods of ML. These methods can specify certain features in fluid dynamics, as well as efficiencies in solving [41]. A related type of shape optimization is performed through data-driven surrogate models that connect shape characteristics of airfoils and hulls to popular and important metrics such as drag and lift. Once trained using CFD data, such models can be quickly tested with varied design options, and they can be incorporated in optimization processes [42]. Scientific machine learning, often referred to as SciML, is a new area of research that merges traditional physics-based models with data-driven approaches to solve differential problems more effectively [43]. Physics-based models are what this field takes advantage of, but then still takes the speed and efficiencies from data-driven techniques to improve numerical approximations [44]. Figure 3.3 presents a detailed comparison of the CPU time and wall-clock time utilized in the computing process for both CFD simulations and the ML model.

Physics-informed ML solves a very important challenge that ensures any ML model obeys the physical principles that determine fluid dynamics. The ML framework with physical constraints embedded into it brings

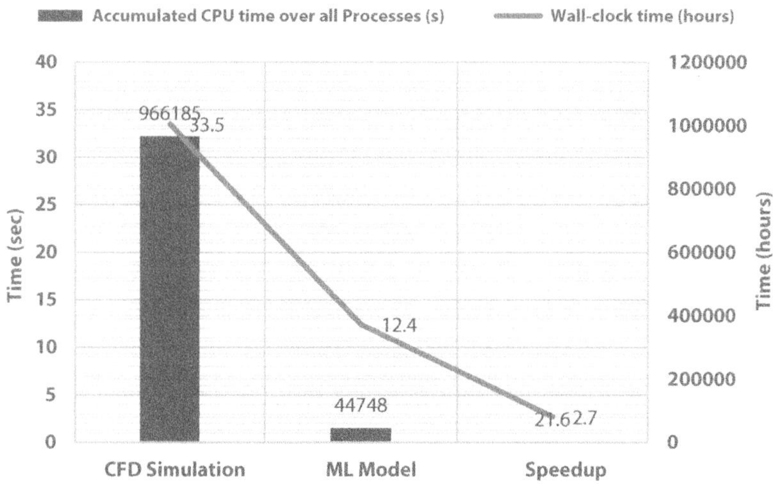

Figure 3.3 Comparison of the CPU time and wall-clock time utilized in the computing process for both CFD simulations and the ML model.

more real-world phenomena into a more accurate representation [45]. If we use physics-based knowledge integration, physics-informed ML can greatly enhance the accuracy of predictions in a wide range of areas, e.g., mineral processing. For example, when mass balance is added in the loss functions of ML models, it performs better than those that have only data as part of the loss functions without considering physical laws [46].

It also enables the improvement of the established turbulence models, RANS and LES. More precise predictions of Reynolds stress are possible when compared to the traditional methods because of the data analyzed by ML models [47]. However, ML can be used to replace some CFD numerical solvers to bridge the gap between efficiency, accuracy, and the ability to generalize for different cases.

Nowadays, ML is used very much in science, engineering, and CFD. As these techniques apply to such a wide variety of fields, including aerodynamics, combustion, atmospheric and ocean sciences, biology, plasma studies, symbolic regression, and reduced order modeling, they tend to infiltrate these areas [48]. Figure 3.4 presents a detailed comparison of the ML and CFD integration outcomes.

Machine learning models play a role in surrogate modeling, which takes advantage of the fact that it can replace the CFD solvers with large decreases in time for running simulations. Regarding the ML models

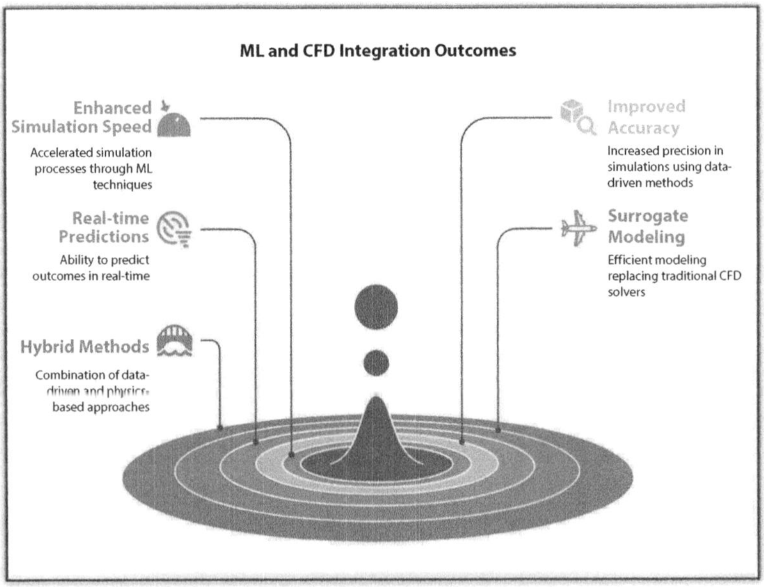

Figure 3.4 Machine learning and CFD integration outcomes.

choice of CFD, random forest, and support vector machine are currently the popular supervised learning techniques, neural networks, and deep learning models are among the options, as well [49]. The real choice is model-dependent, though: It depends whether the problem in question is making predictions, optimizing a process, or speeding up a simulation. New hybrid methods that combine data-driven and physics-based approaches are developed to advance research in multiphase flow [50].

The research shows that combining ML with CFD is an exciting and rapidly developing area. This integration holds great promise for improving fluid dynamics simulations and tackling intricate engineering problems.

3.2.3 Past Research on Artificial Intelligence in Computational Fluid Dynamics

Nowadays, the speed-up of simulations or an insider view into the CFD is provided thanks to the application of AI to CFD. Artificial intelligence algorithms can either enhance or substitute some parts of the CFD model based on several simulated input-output datasets. Unsurprisingly, these are known as AI-based emulators [51].

There are several ways to use AI in CFD. Physics-informed neural networks lead to physically accurate solutions that do not need a training database and can solve flow equations directly. The downside to this, though, is that computing a PDE with AI is quite resource-intensive [52]. Figure 3.5 presents a detailed analysis of AI applications in CFD.

Another approach is a convolutional layer, just like what is done in AI models for image recognition. This is followed by these layers, which need a structured input, just like pixels in an image [53]. Related to memory consumption, graph neural networks utilize the CFD computational mesh and link between nearby cells to infer flow conditions, but they might suffer from issues of training. Finally, the transformer can also approximate flows in 3D, frictional, and compressible, as in compressors, which makes it possible to handle complex CFD setups as input [54].

Using such an ML model, AI models are capable of learning from past CFD simulations and using that knowledge for new parameterized optimization. An AI model will be able to approximate the CFD process by mapping 3D geometries and boundary conditions to the resulting 3D flow [55].

Machine learning models can more accurately model the complex and unpredictable nature of flow fields when high-fidelity turbulence data, such as DNS, is used as opposed to the provided measured data from the root database. There are many possibilities to develop fluid dynamics simulations

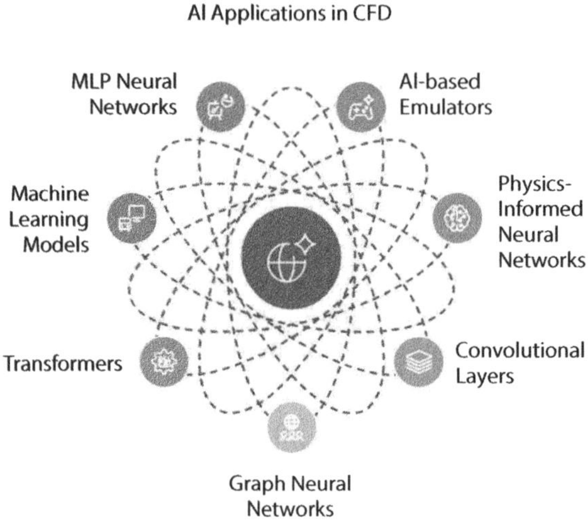

Figure 3.5 Artificial intelligence applications in CFD.

by combining AI and CFD. Artificial intelligence can be used as a surrogate model, expanding the geometric design space and improving the accuracy and efficiency of the model. The issues tackled in this integration and the solutions proposed are innovative [56, 57]. In one study, CFD databases of the comprehensive thermal and fluid dynamic behavior of a cooling fin are used to create surrogate models using ML algorithms for the prediction of the thermal and fluid dynamic behavior of a cooling fin from its geometric coordinates. The MLP neural network models perform well consistently, and hence the MLP architecture is particularly suitable in characterizing micro-enhanced surfaces and holds great promise for future use as a surrogate CFD model in the context of geometry optimization efforts [58].

The discussion and references offer insights into how AI is applied in CFD. Below is a summary of Table 3.3, which brings together various AI methods, outlining their features, benefits, and drawbacks.

3.3 Methodology of Artificial Intelligence-Driven Enhancement in Computational Fluid Dynamics

3.3.1 Data Collection

To create a proper method that utilizes AI to gather data in CFD simulations, one has to remember a few important things to fully utilize

Table 3.3 Literature review of past research on CFD.

Technique	Description	Advantages	Limitations	References
AI-Based Emulators	Artificial intelligence models are trained on simulated data to mimic and replace traditional CFD models.	Enhanced performance, new levels of analysis, and efficient simulation of large-scale problems.	Requires rigorous validation.	[59]
Physics-Informed Neural Networks	Artificial intelligence models that directly solve flow equations.	No training database needed, physically accurate solutions	Computationally expensive, limited complexity of AI structures.	[60]
Convolutional Layers	Artificial intelligence models use image recognition techniques with convolutional layers.	Effective for ordered input data.	Requires ordered input data, not suitable for irregular meshes.	[61]
Graph Neural Networks	AI models that use the computational mesh of CFD simulations and relationships between adjacent cells.	Successful in determining flow quantities in 2D and 3D.	Limited by memory requirements during training.	[62]

(Continued)

Table 3.3 Literature review of past research on CFD. (*Continued*)

Technique	Description	Advantages	Limitations	References
Transformer Architecture	Artificial intelligence models that approximate 3D, frictional, and compressible flow.	Can use high-dimensional input, reflects changes in geometry and boundary conditions.	-	[63]
Machine Learning-Enhanced Turbulence Models	Machine learning models combined with traditional turbulence models (RANS, LES).	Improved accuracy and computational efficiency.	Challenges include overfitting, limited data accessibility, and interpretability of black-box ML models.	[64]
Surrogate Models	Machine learning algorithms learn surrogate models to predict thermal and fluid dynamic behavior from geometric coordinates.	-	-	[65]

(*Continued*)

Table 3.3 Literature review of past research on CFD. (*Continued*)

Technique	Description	Advantages	Limitations	References
AI-Driven Adaptive Mesh	An AI model to achieve adaptive intelligent mesh refinement in the fluid domain of a numerical reactor core.	Effectively improves mesh quality while preserving the boundaries of the initial channel mesh model; Enhances simulation accuracy and efficiency.	-	[66]
Finite Volume Method	Discretizes the control volume into cells, variables are solved at the cell centroids, the flux term needs face centroid values, which are interpolated from the cell centroids.	-	-	[67]

this method. The factors come into play in building ML methods, building effective structures on how to clone our data, and finding the correct blend between data-based and physical principles-based approaches.

This is first accomplished using neural networks, which can handle equations like the pressure Poisson equation. This approach also runs calculations faster while keeping the results accurate [68]. Moreover, AI-based reduced-order models can rapidly estimate outcomes for complicated flow scenarios and indicate how fast the process of data gathering can become simplified through ML [69].

Table 3.4 Data collection with their methods, objectives, and research gaps.

Methods used	Practical implications	Objectives	Research gap	References
1. Data-driven neural network-MPS method 2. Fully connected artificial neural network for the pressure Poisson equation	1. Accelerates pressure calculation while maintaining accuracy and stability. 2. Suitable for GPU parallelization, edge computing, and real-time simulations.	1. Address the computing performance of the moving particle semi-implicit method. 2. Accelerate pressure calculation while maintaining accuracy and stability.	-	[68]
1. Customizable user-interface components for data annotation. 2. Automated annotator qualification and saved reusable pipelines.	1. Reduces overhead in data annotation processes. 2. Improves reproducibility in data collection workflows.	1. Minimize overhead in data annotation processes. 2. Improve the reproducibility of data collection projects.	1. Limited adaptability and extensibility of existing annotation UIs. 2. Overhead training and filtering annotators remain a challenge.	[70]
1. Domain decomposition approach for large domain predictions. 2. Neural network training for subdomain predictions.	1. Enables accurate predictions for large multiphase flow domains. 2. Reduces computational time for high-resolution CFD models.	1. Develop an AI-based reduced-order model for multiphase flow. 2. Enable predictions for larger domains than the training data.	-	[69]

(*Continued*)

Table 3.4 Data collection with their methods, objectives, and research gaps. (*Continued*)

Methods used	Practical implications	Objectives	Research gap	References
1. Physics-based modeling 2. Machine learning approaches	1. Revolutionize CFD with combined physics and ML insight. 2. Break barriers in shape optimization, flow control, and uncertainty quantification.	1. Survey recent developments in data-driven modeling in CFD. 2. Explore integration of physics-based and ML strategies.	1. Many open problems with data-driven modeling remain unaddressed. 2. Grand challenges in turbulent flow modeling await solutions.	[71]
1. Descriptor learning with convolutional neural networks (CNNs) for fluid region similarity encoding 2. Deformation limiting patch advection for tracking deformable fluid regions	1. Efficient synthesis of high-resolution smoke flow simulations. 2. Non-dissipative small-scale details integrated into flow motions.	1. Synthesize high-resolution flow simulations efficiently. 2. Encode fluid region similarities using CNN-based descriptors.	-	[72]
1. Integration definition for functional modeling (IDEF)-based approach for input data identification and collection. 2. Methodological approach for documenting simulation projects.	1. Accelerates the data identification and collection process. 2. Encourages effective documentation of simulation projects.	1. Accelerate input data identification and collection. 2. Provide a methodology for project documentation.	-	[73]

An important thing is naming strong data collection frameworks for their research. Problems like reproducibility and training efficient annotators can be tackled through tools like CROWDAQ that ease the user to annotate and collect data. It is important because it brings structural consistency to data collection and creates high-value, massive datasets needed for training successful AI models for CFD [70].

Data-driven methods joined with core physics concepts can yield a large improvement in CFD simulations. The best features from both sides are used in a hybrid approach to give the best accuracy in models and more efficient computations [71]. Thus, using both physics-based and ML approaches is important, and we see a need to bridge that gap.

Above is Table 3.4, a summary that brings together various AI methods, outlining their practical implications, objectives, and research gaps.

3.3.2 Artificial Intelligence Techniques

The CFD applications are becoming more oriented to apply AI methods to achieve good results in precision, as well as simulation efficiency. In many areas of CFD, turbulence modeling, surrogate modeling, geometry, and mesh automation, ML (a branch of AI) is essential [74]. For instance, neural networks are particularly suited for learning complex flow patterns, which can be used in making a better turbulence closure model. Additionally, ML algorithms can simplify intricate geometry or meshing processes, which reduces the need for manual labor and simplifies work as a whole [75]. Deep learning, including GAN, can create realistic and meet certain design requirements with geometries using techniques. On top of that, ML techniques support the real-time flow control and optimization by analyzing simulation data and changing the demanded control strategies to fit the desired flow characteristics using reinforcement learning algorithms, learning the parameters to reach the desired flow conditions [76]. Training effective AI models, such as neural networks and reinforcement learning systems, requires high-quality datasets. Usually, these datasets in CFD fields correspond to different parameters related to velocity fields, pressure distribution, temperature profile, and turbulence characteristics. Although there are ML-based approaches to CFD simulation improvement, the datasets being used for this purpose should be accurate because they not only include real physical phenomena that would reflect the physical aspects of the real system, but they also represent highly reliable sources [52]. They also need to be diverse with respect to a wide range of flow scenarios, shapes, and boundary conditions to ensure the model's applicability to all situations. Moreover, the datasets should be well-resolved. It must capture details of the complexity, in particular in the challenging case of turbulence. Thirdly, the data should be free of any errors or noise that could hamper the model's learning process [111]. Probably, the researchers picked data from advanced CFD simulations like DNS or LES. Since these methods require large computations, they provide highly detailed and accurate information about fluid flow. Direct numerical simulations cover all turbulence scales without modeling, and LES tracks the larger turbulent scales, which means both are excellent approaches for producing high-quality training data [112].

Simulations could have been additional to experimental data, coming from a wind tunnel or a fluid flow test, for validation. Although this type of data does not provide the same level of detail as the simulation data, nor is it likely to be the main source of information [113] since it covers a smaller range. Many important steps are involved in preprocessing that guarantees that the data used in simulations or experiments holds good. Second, when cleaning the data that noise or inconsistency will not come in that gives the results in an err way. Following that, normalization and scaling are carried out to translate values such as velocity or pressure to a common scope, which is crucial to giving networks to learn well, as it both promotes convergence and generally enhances learning [114].

Data augmentation techniques are often applied to widen the diversity in the dataset. That could comprise creating some small boundary conditions or flow parameter changes that generate synthetic data for some simulations. An AI model can generalize better by such methods to different scenarios, improving the accuracy of the simulations. Furthermore, feature engineering also becomes important, in which key features like statistical quantities are chosen or derived instead of using raw data, e.g., statistical quantities like Reynolds stresses for the turbulence modeling. It simplifies the data that the AI focuses on the most relevant physical information [115].

Despite the fact that it is typically prepared using tensors or grids when it comes to structuring the data for AI models, it is typically organized in the spatial character of CFD data: 3D flow fields. For instance, in reinforcement learning, the data is framed as state-action pairs, which define the simulation environment and control parameters, such as flow optimization. The dataset is usually split into training, validation, and test sets, and finally, it is a common practice to evaluate the model's accuracy and efficiency using the dataset [116].

Artificial intelligence-based methods can identify irregularities in CFD simulations and correct mistakes to improve their reliability and strength [77]. One approach involves using PINNs, which follow the fundamental equations and boundary conditions [78]. For instance, researchers are investigating ML solutions as possible alternatives to the Navier–Stokes equations in CFD. In scenarios involving incompressible flows, ML surrogate models can support flow solvers, increasing processing speed and minimizing resource use.

These strategies work together to boost the precision of CFD simulations by more effectively capturing intricate flow dynamics, automating lengthy tasks, and allowing for real-time optimization and control [79]. The combination of AI, ML, and deep learning tackles existing challenges while opening up new avenues for improving simulation accuracy, efficiency, and automation [80].

3.3.3 Computational Fluid Dynamics Simulation Framework

To build a simulation framework based on CFD, in which the AI would help resolve both accuracy and efficiency, a lot of thought needs to be carried out. The combination of AI with CFD can contribute to the evaluation of water quality on which informed decisions amount to, protecting the ecosystems and water resources sustainably as pollution rises [81]. Traditional approaches can often be complicated and not very precise, highlighting the need for better modeling techniques. The goal of this integration is to overcome the shortcomings of current methods by utilizing the strengths of deep learning alongside fluid dynamics simulations, ultimately leading to better predictions and improved efficiency. Below is Figure 3.6, bringing together various simulation frameworks and AI techniques.

Data preprocessing is an important phase that will create good quality meshes, form grids, and open fluid domains. Firstly, will get started with the import and cleaning of the geometry to ensure that it is solid and then ready for meshing. Dividing shapes into smaller components, the generation of mesh and grid formation, plays a major role in determining the accuracy and speed of simulations [82]. The most crucial thing is that the turbulence models selected for the model selection and training can play a huge role in second-guessing the precision of a CFD simulation. In certain situations, the response surface methodology (RSM) performs better. In addition, neural networks can be trained based on simulation data to understand the physical phenomena [83].

Integrating AI techniques involves the use of both neural networks and genetic algorithms for modeling a multiphysics system. We can develop AI-driven surrogate models to estimate the performance of different configurations without much analysis involved, and thus streamline the process. Validation and verification are considered critical steps where the

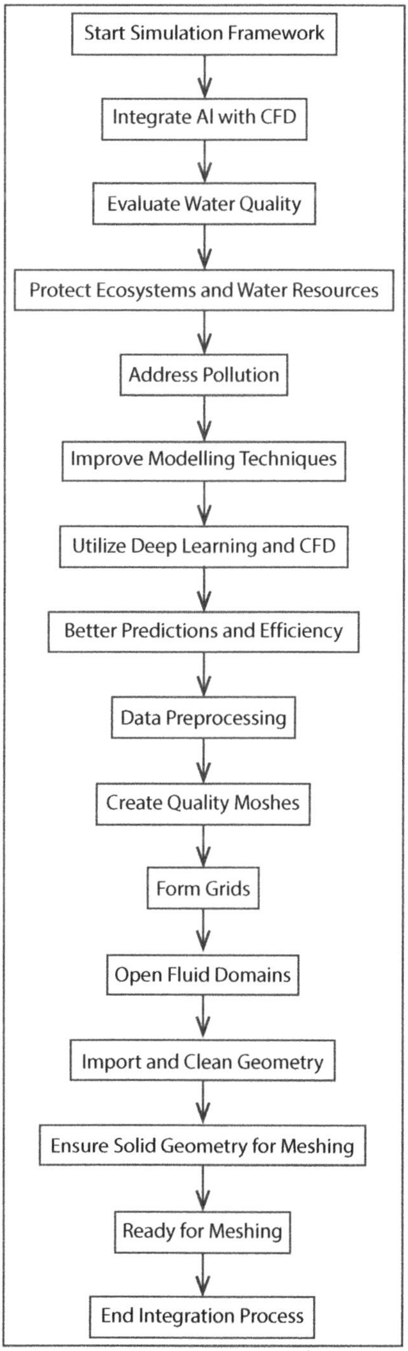

(**a**)

Figure 3.6 (a) A schematic diagram of a simulation framework. *(Continued)*

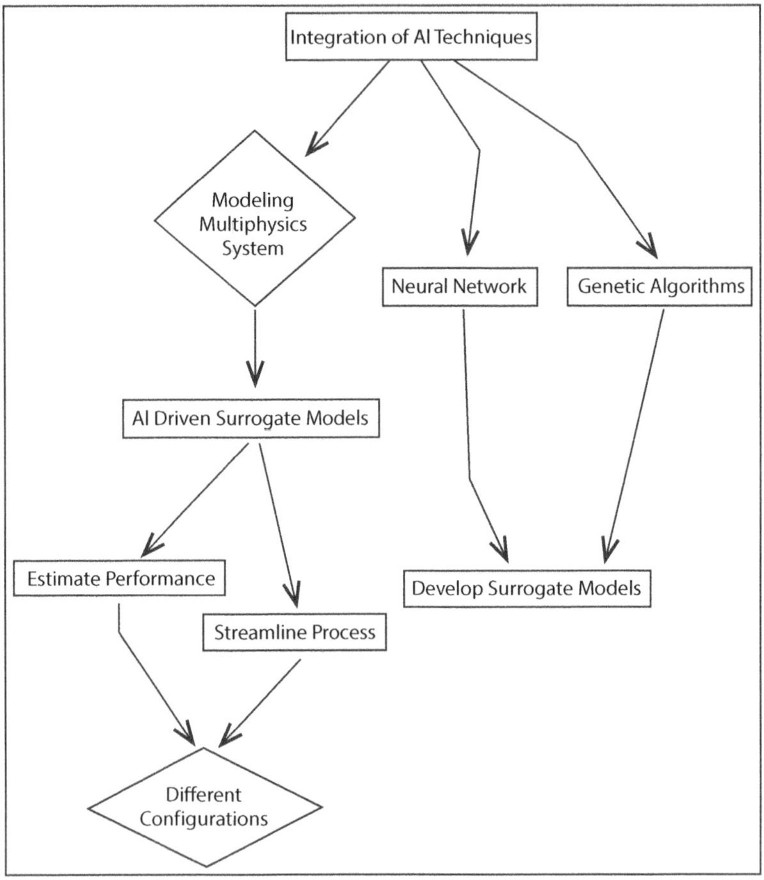

(b)

Figure 3.6 (Continued) (b) Systematic diagram of integrating AI techniques.

prediction from the ML models is compared with 3D CFD simulation results to ensure the prediction model accuracy under different operational conditions [84].

The computational resources and time required by RSM simulations are often higher, if not higher than other models. Such selection of models and setups of simulations should balance accuracy and computational cost. Thirdly, domain and mesh configuration are critical because the computational grid must be fine enough to resolve the scales of interest but not so fine as to add too much extra computational time [85]. Using polyhedral cells can provide a high-quality mesh with a lower cell count, making it ideal for complex geometries.

3.4 Discussion

3.4.1 Performance Metrics

A few important performance indicators can be used to measure the impact of AI improvements on CFD simulations. There are some efficiencies in which computations are done, precision in the result, how well the model can add knowledge to new situations, and how easily the model can be understood. They combine to provide a fine assessment of how AI impacts CFD.

3.4.1.1 Computational Efficiency

- **Speedup in Inference:** Improving the speed of AI models also improves how quickly simulations run. For example, research indicates that running the processes on GPUs can be 2.4 times slower than using a pipeline execution on CPUs [86].
- **Resource Optimization:** AI methods, such as adaptive grid refinement, help to concentrate computing power on areas with high errors, which ultimately lowers the total computational expenses. By directing resources where they are most needed, these techniques make the process more efficient and cost-effective [87].

3.4.1.2 Accuracy

- **Error Metrics:** When evaluating the performance of AI-enhanced models, one key factor to consider is accuracy, which is typically measured by looking at error rates in their predictions. For instance, research has shown that some basic models can have prediction errors reaching up to 300% in specific CFD scenarios [88].
- **Model Validation:** Utilizing reference simulations like LES is essential for confirming the precision of AI-optimized closure coefficients in RANS simulations [89].

3.4.1.3 Generalization Ability

The effectiveness of AI models is often measured by how well they can adapt to new data without needing to be retrained. This skill is particularly important for real-world uses in CFD, where models must perform accurately on previously unseen scenarios [90].

3.4.1.4 *Performance Formula*

The performance formula is a combination of linear prediction and explainability metrics to ease the assessment of how well a model performs in CFD applications. Through these attempts, the decision of this model is more integrated and considered than the effectiveness and clarity of the model decisions, and thus, more adequately evaluated for its usefulness [91]. Figure 3.7 presents a detailed analysis of performance indicators for AI in CFD simulations.

Highly accurate CFD simulations can now be achieved with the help of AI advancements; however, challenges still exist to keep the accuracy of the models and apply them correctly across different scenarios. Below is Table 3.5, summarizing various limitations and results.

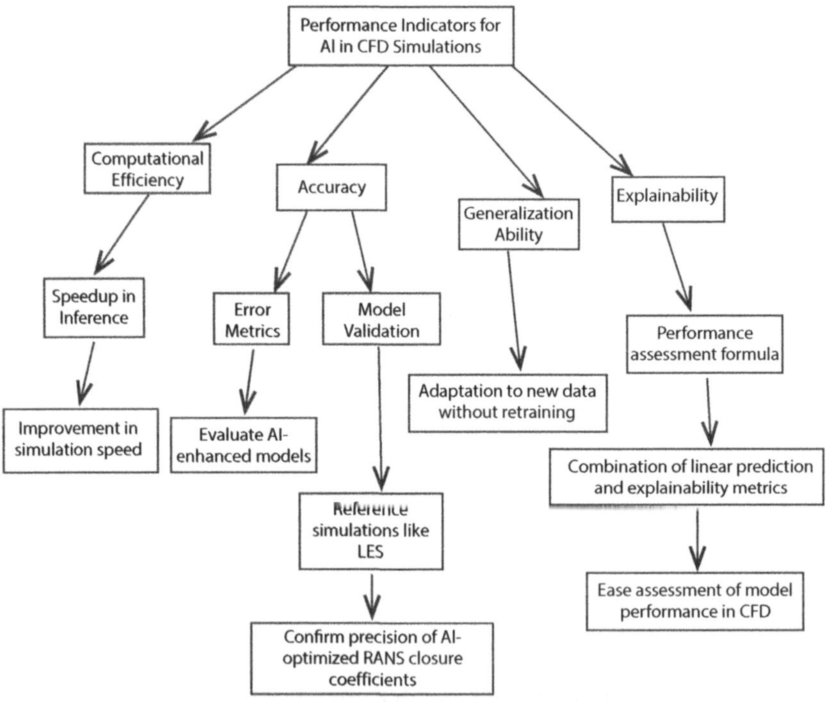

Figure 3.7 Performance indicators for AI in CFD simulations.

Table 3.5 Discussions with their limitation and results.

Limitations	Problem statement	Results	References
1. Lack of accuracy guarantees with convolutional neural network (CNN) solutions. 2. Potential for inaccuracies and unstable simulations.	1. Poisson equation resolution is computationally intensive for fluid solvers. 2. Convolutional neural networks reduce inference time but lack accuracy guarantees.	1. Hybrid strategy ensures accuracy and stability in simulations. 2. Convolutional neural networks provide solutions 1 to 10^{-25} times faster than traditional solvers.	[92]
1. Metrics assume linear, Gaussian errors, incomplete, and interdependent. 2. Metrics cannot directly quantify uncertainty, unlike error modeling.	1. Conventional metrics fail to quantify uncertainty effectively. 2. Error models provide a clearer understanding of error structure.	1. The authors argue that a correct error model should be an alternative to performance metrics. 2. Conventional metrics are inappropriate for nonlinear error models.	[93]
-	1. Need for fast automotive aerodynamic evaluation. 2. Reducing design cycles using an AI-based simulation model.	1. Average mean absolute error of optimal model: 5.249% 2. Average calculation time of single example: 1.2968s	[94]
1. Expense of evaluating CFD simulations 2. Need for reduced-order or surrogate models	1. Computational fluid dynamics simulations are expensive for design optimization. 2. Need for accelerated convergence in fluid simulations.	1. CFDNet outperforms the domain-specific physics solver by 1.9 - 7.4X on steady laminar and turbulent flows. 2. CFDNet meets the convergence constraints and provides significant speedups over traditional models.	[95]

(*Continued*)

Table 3.5 Discussions with their limitation and results. (*Continued*)

Limitations	Problem statement	Results	References
-	1. Assessing accuracy, sensitivity, and robustness in CFD simulations. 2. Evaluating uncertainty in computational parameters and inputs.	1. Enhanced insight into factors influencing physics simulations. 2. Improved accuracy and reliability in turbulent channel flow simulations.	[96]
1. Expensive hyper-reduction strategies for nonlinear terms. 2. Difficulties in fluid-structure interactions.	1. High-fidelity models are slow for real-time fluid simulations. 2. Reduced order models face challenges with nonlinear terms and fluid-structure interactions.	1. Accurate results in almost real-time for fluid flows. 2. Successful applications in various fluid dynamics scenarios.	[97]
1. A CFD solver may not respond correctly to design changes. 2. Physically invalid design points are automatically removed during optimization.	1. Computational fluid dynamics solver inaccurately responds to design changes under batch mode. 2. Physically invalid design points not addressed during the optimization process.	1. Physically invalid design points removed from the optimization process. 2. An intelligent CFD solver is used for accurate simulation results.	[98]

3.5 Case Study

Both the efficiency and accuracy improvement of CFD modeling using AI have been very promising. There are many case studies that show the use of AI-based methods to efficiently improve the CFD processes, decrease the computation time, and increase prediction capabilities. With the use of a deep-learning-driven computer-aided design (CAD) and computer-aided engineering (CAE) system, it is easier to create 3D CAD models and predictions from CAE outcomes to quickly iterate on design in engineering. This method quickly gives instant insights into the engineering performance, greatly shortening the overall design process [99]. The forecasting of fluid flow properties in nanofluids has been successfully filled in using the missing CFD data with the use of AI techniques like particle swarm optimization combined with a fuzzy inference system [100].

- Application of data-driven methods can lead to significant improvement in model reduction within CFD when it is applied to bifurcating solutions in fluid dynamics. A recent study illustrates how taking the proper orthogonal decomposition together with the neural network methodology can yield better simulations with reduced computational performance. Not only does this approach improve the modeling efficiency, but it also provides a better opportunity to describe detailed fluid system behaviors [101].
- The use of AI and ML in multiphase flow modeling has seen great results in smart proxy modeling. These technologies enable the simulation times to be cut down from several hours to a few minutes, while maintaining excellent accuracy. This gives a clear indication that AI can be used to solve some of the toughest problems of complex fluid dynamics [102]. While AI-powered advancement offers a huge benefit, it is still faced with many obstacles in ensuring these models can be trusted and applied in some situations. These issues need to be tackled with more studies and even fully utilize all the potential of AI in computational fluid dynamics.

3.6 Conclusion

- The combination of AI techniques with customary CFD methods gives better prospects for turbulence modeling. For a number of engineering sectors, one of which is turbo machinery and biomass combustion, where accurate prediction of fluid behavior is essential to a successful case, this improvement is particularly meaningful. Additionally, neural network and reinforcement learning-based AI approaches have cut down the required time for simulation manifold. This increased efficiency is of key importance for real-time applications and for computational demands such as simulations that would usually require significant amounts of computational power.

- To achieve the best performance of AI-optimized models using reference simulations like LES must be used. The validation process thus verifies that simulations with added AI are as accurate, or more accurate, than the ones presented with old methods.
- It researches that CNNs can reach computation speed, which is "1 to 10^{-25} faster" than traditional solvers. The 10^{-25} will likely be a mistake or a stretch of exaggeration, but the fact is that the computation time is substantially decreased. It speaks more realistically about a huge speedup, for example, several times larger. We have significantly reduced the time that is necessary for calculations (reduced by about 99%) compared to traditional solvers by implementing an AI-based approach using CNNs. Hence, these methods make it possible for us to come up with the answers at a much faster pace than before.
- The results indicate that the CFDNet model is 1.9 to 7.4 times faster than the traditional solvers for steady laminar and turbulent flows. Computation time reductions of about 47% to 86% are obtained.
- This average MAE of 5.249 % is what the AI model has. Nevertheless, the research does not inform the depth of error in standard CFD approaches, so it is somewhat misleading to know whether the AI model does significantly better. This can be achieved using PINNs, allowing an AI to provide 'physically accurate solutions,' and also help with turbulence modeling. Although it does not provide specific figures or percentage improvement in accuracy for some of the claims.
- A study on a CAD/CAE system based on deep learning technology identifies how AI has been utilized to speedily implement design changes using deep learning technology. It is this form of innovation that greatly reduces simulation time from several hours to just a few minutes.
- A case study also provides insights about how such integration of AI into CAD/CAE can greatly transform the design process. Quickly using deep learning allows designers to

iterate their ideas faster, so the productivity and efficiency of the whole workflow are enhanced.

- The literature review in the paper stresses the advancing CFD and AI fields that are developing continuously, with future improvements of AI by improving the technology might further enhance the turbulence modeling and computational speed.
- To conclude, CFD combined with AI holds great potential to increase the accuracy and efficiency of the simulations, and though these are promising, there are challenges to be met for the broader application.

References

1. Szpicer, A., Bińkowska, W., Stelmasiak, A., Zalewska, M., Wojtasik-Kalinowska, I., Piwowarski, K., Piepiórka-Stepuk, J., Półtorak, A., Computational Fluid Dynamics Simulation of Thermal Processes in Food Technology and Their Applications in the Food Industry. *Appl. Sci.*, *15*, 1, 424, 2025, https://doi.org/10.3390/app15010424.
2. Park, H. and Yoon, W., Computational Fluid Dynamics (CFD) Modelling and Application for Sterilization of Foods: A Review. *Processes*, *6*, 6, 62, 2018, https://doi.org/10.3390/pr6060062.
3. Zhang, T. and Barakos, G., Assessment of implicit adaptive mesh-free CFD modelling. *Int. J. Numer. Methods Fluids*, 96, 670–700, 2024, https://doi.org/10.1002/fld.5266.
4. Hanspal, N. and Cryer, S., The Use of Computational Fluid Dynamics (CFD) within the Agricultural Industry to Address General and Manufacturing Problems. *Fluids*, 2024, https://doi.org/10.3390/fluids9080186.
5. Szpicer, A., Bińkowska, W., Stelmasiak, A., Zalewska, M., Wojtasik-Kalinowska, I., Piwowarski, K., Półtorak, A., Innovative Implementation of Computational Fluid Dynamics in Proteins Denaturation Process Prediction in Goose Breast Meat and Heat Treatment Processes Optimization. *Appl. Sci.*, 2024, https://doi.org/10.3390/app14135567.
6. Immordino, G., Vaiuso, A., Da Ronch, A., Righi, M., Predicting transonic flowfields in non–homogeneous unstructured grids using autoencoder graph convolutional networks. *J. Comput. Phys.*, *524*, 113708, 2025, https://doi.org/10.1016/j.jcp.2024.113708.
7. Shen, Y., Needels, J., Alonso, J., VortexNet: A Graph Neural Network-Based Multi-Fidelity Surrogate Model for Field Predictions VortexNet: A Graph Neural Network-Based Multi-Fidelity Surrogate Model for Field Predictions, https://doi.org/10.2514/6.2025-0494, 2025.

8. Zhang, H. and Wu, B., Computational fluid dynamics investigation of subsurface drip irrigation in sandy loam soil. *Comput. Electron. Agric.*, *231*, 109934, 2025, https://doi.org/10.1016/j.compag.2025.109934.
9. Samris, A. and Mounir, H., Three-dimensional computational fluid dynamics (3D-CFD) simulation of hydrogen transport to investigate the effect of output voltage and inlet anode velocity on proton exchange membrane fuel cell performances. *Results Chem.*, *13*, 101929, 2025, doi: 10.1016/j.rechem.2024.101929.
10. He, X. and Klausmann, F., RANS Capabilities for Transonic Axial Compressor: A Perspective From GPPS Computational Fluid Dynamics Workshop. *J. Turbomach.*, *147*, 2, 2024, https://doi.org/10.1115/1.4066431.
11. Chaiyo, R., Wongwiwat, J., Sukjai, Y., Thermal and economic evaluation of replacing pulverized coal with torrefied biomass in a small industrial burner in Thailand using computational fluid dynamics. *Cleaner Eng. Technol.*, *24*, 100898, 2025, https://doi.org/10.1016/j.clet.2025.100898.
12. Gorle, J.M.R., Terjesen, B.F., Summerfelt, S.T., Hydrodynamics of Atlantic salmon culture tank: Effect of inlet nozzle angle on the velocity field. *Comput. Electron. Agric.*, *158*, 79–91, 2019, https://doi.org/10.1016/j.compag.2019.01.046.
13. Jałowiecka, M. and Makowsk, L., Computational fluid dynamics modelling of short time bottle filling process. *Chem. Process Eng.*, 2023, https://doi.org/10.24425/cpe.2020.132537.
14. Wang, H., Cao, Y., Huang, Z., Liu, Y., Hu, P., Luo, X., Song, Z., Zhao, W., Liu, J., Sun, J., Zhang, S., Wei, L., Wang, Y., Wu, T., Ma, Z.-M., Sun, Y., Recent Advances on Machine Learning for Computational Fluid Dynamics: A Survey, ArXiv (Cornell University), https://doi.org/10.48550/arxiv.2408.12171, 2024.
15. Kim, I., Jeon, Y., Chae, J., You, D., Deep Reinforcement Learning for Fluid Mechanics: Control, Optimization, and Automation. *Fluids*, *9*, 9, 216, 2024, https://doi.org/10.3390/fluids9090216.
16. Zhou, W., Miwa, S., Okamoto, K., Advancing fluid dynamics simulations: A comprehensive approach to optimizing physics-informed neural networks. *Phys. Fluids*, 2024, https://doi.org/10.1063/5.0180770.
17. Amato, E., Zago, V., Del Negro, C., A physically consistent AI-based SPH emulator for computational fluid dynamics. *Nonlinear Eng.*, 2024, https://doi.org/10.1515/nleng-2022-0359.
18. Sun, X., Cao, W., Shan, X., Liu, Y., Zhang, W., A Generalized Framework for Integrating Machine Learning into Computational Fluid Dynamics. *J. Comput. Sci.*, *82*, 102404, 2024, https://doi.org/10.1016/j.jocs.2024.102404.
19. Rahman, M.S., Hazra, S., Chowdhury, I.A., Advancing Computational Fluid Dynamics through Machine Learning: A Review of Data-Driven Innovations and Applications. *J. Fluid Mech. Mech. Des.*, *6*, 2, 42–51, 2024, https://doi.org/10.46610/jfmmd.2024.v06i02.005.
20. Jeon, J., Lee, J., Vinuesa, R., Kim, S.J., Residual-based physics-informed transfer learning: A hybrid method for accelerating long-term CFD simulations

via deep learning. *Int. J. Heat Mass Transfer*, 2023, https://doi.org/10.1016/j.ijheatmasstransfer.2023.124900.
21. Bijjala, S., AIML Enabled Rapid Vehicle Aerodynamics Design Improvements, SAE Technical Paper Series, https://doi.org/10.4271/2024-28-0007, 2024.
22. Liu, B., Gou, M., Sun, X., Du, H., Application of Artificial intelligence in Computational fluid dynamics. *Front. Comput. Intell. Syst.*, *1*, 3, 57–60, 2022, https://doi.org/10.54097/fcis.v1i3.2072.
23. Rahman, M.S., Hazra, S., Chowdhury, I.A., Advancing Computational Fluid Dynamics through Machine Learning: A Review of Data-Driven Innovations and Applications. *J. Fluid Mech. Mech. Des.*, 6, 2, 42–51, 2024, https://doi.org/10.46610/jfmmd.2024.v06i02.005.
24. Tominaga, Y., Sato, Y., Sadohara, S., CFD simulations of the effect of evaporative cooling from water bodies in a micro-scale urban environment: Validation and application studies. *Sustain. Cities Soc.*, 19, 259–270, 2015, https://doi.org/10.1016/J.SCS.2015.03.011.
25. Montazeri, H., Blocken, B., Hensen, J., Evaporative cooling by water spray systems: CFD simulation, experimental validation and sensitivity analysis. *Build. Environ.*, 83, 129–141, 2015, https://doi.org/10.1016/J.BUILDENV.2014.03.022.
26. Malekjani, N. and Jafari, S., Simulation of food drying processes by Computational Fluid Dynamics (CFD); recent advances and approaches. *Trends Food Sci. Technol.*, 2018, https://doi.org/10.1016/J.TIFS.2018.06.006.
27. Bhutta, M., Hayat, N., Bashir, M., Khan, A., Ahmad, K., Khan, S., CFD applications in various heat exchangers design: A review. *Appl. Therm. Eng.*, 32, 1–12, 2012, https://doi.org/10.1016/J.APPLTHERMALENG.2011.09.001.
28. Nielsen, P., Fifty years of CFD for room air distribution. *Build. Environ.*, 91, 78–90, 2015, https://doi.org/10.1016/J.BUILDENV.2015.02.035.
29. Alizadehdakhel, A., Rahimi, M., Alsairafi, A., CFD modeling of flow and heat transfer in a thermosyphon. *Int. Commun. Heat Mass Transfer*, 37, 312–318, 2010, https://doi.org/10.1016/J.ICHEATMASSTRANSFER.2009.09.002.
30. Dang, G., Liu, S., Guo, T., Duan, J., Li, X., Direct numerical simulation of compressible turbulence accelerated by graphics processing unit: An open-source high accuracy accelerated computational fluid dynamic software. *Phys. Fluids*, *34*, 12, 126106, 2022, https://doi.org/10.1063/5.0127684.
31. Novik, K.E. and Coveney, P.V., Finite-difference methods for simulation models incorporating nonconservative forces. *J. Chem. Phys.*, *109*, 18, 7667–7677, 1998, https://doi.org/10.1063/1.477413.
32. Liu, J.-G., Wang, C., Johnston, H., A Fourth Order Scheme for Incompressible Boussinesq Equations. *J. Sci. Comput.*, *18*, 2, 253–285, 2003, https://doi.org/10.1023/A:1021168924020.
33. Masson, Y.J. and Pride, S.R., Finite-difference modeling of Biot'sporoelastic equations across all frequencies. *Geophysics*, *75*, 2, 2010, https://doi.org/10.1190/1.3332589.

34. Chernogorova, T.P. and Vulkov, L.G., A finite volume difference scheme for a model of settling particle dispersion from an elevated source in an open-channel flow. *Comput. Math. Appl.*, *67*, 12, 2099–2111, 2014, https://doi.org/10.1016/J.CAMWA.2014.03.012.
35. Aoi, S. and Fujiwara, H., 3D finite-difference method using discontinuous grids. *Bull. Seismol. Soc. Am.*, *89*, 4, 918–930, 1999, https://doi.org/10.1785/BSSA0890040918.
36. Yu, P.X., Tian, Z.F., Zhang, H., A rational high-order compact difference method for the steady-state stream functionvorticity formulation of the NavierStokes equations. *Comput. Math. Appl.*, *73*, 7, 1461–1484, 2017, https://doi.org/10.1016/J.CAMWA.2017.01.024.
37. Roberts, A.J., A holistic finite difference approach models linear dynamics consistently. *Math. Comput.*, *72*, 241, 247–262, 2003, https://doi.org/10.1090/S0025-5718-02-01448-5.
38. Zeng, Q. and Zhang, X., Perfectly energy-conservative time-space finite difference schemes and the consistent split method to solve the dynamical equations of compressible fluid. *Sci. China Chem.*, *25*, 8, 866–880, 1982, https://doi.org/10.1360/YB1982-25-8-866.
39. Mickens, R.E. and Ramadhani, I., Finite-difference schemes having the correct linear stability properties for all finite step-sizes III. *Comput. Math. Appl.*, *27*, 4, 77–84, 1994, https://doi.org/10.1016/0898-1221(94)90056-6.
40. Quarteroni, A., Gervasio, P., Regazzoni, F., Combining physics–based and data–driven models: advancing the frontiers of research with Scientific Machine Learning. *Math. Models Methods Appl. Sci.*, 2025, https://doi.org/10.1142/s0218202525500125.
41. Koutsoupakis, J. and Giagopoulos, D., AI-Based Surrogate Models for Multibody Dynamics Systems. *J. Phys. Conf. Ser.*, 2647, 2024, https://doi.org/10.1088/1742-6596/2647/2/022002.
42. Csala, H., Scott, Arzani, A., Comparing different nonlinear dimensionality reduction techniques for data-driven unsteady fluid flow modeling. *Phys. Fluids*, *34*, 11, 2022, https://doi.org/10.1063/5.0127284.
43. Wang, H., Cao, Y., Huang, Z., Liu, Y., Hu, P., Luo, X., Sun, Y., Recent advances on machine learning for computational fluid dynamics: A survey, *arXiv preprint arXiv:2408.12171*, 2024, https://arxiv.org/abs/2408.12171.
44. Shateri, A., Yang, Z., Liu, Y., Xie, J., Data-driven optimization of turbulent kinetic energy and tumble-y in combustion engines: A comparative study of machine learning models. *Fuel*, *389*, 134590, 2025, https://doi.org/10.1016/j.fuel.2025.134590.
45. Basha, N., Arcucci, R., Angeli, P., Anastasiou, C., Abadie, T., Casas, C.Q., Machine learning and physics-driven modelling and simulation of multiphase systems. *Int. J. Multiphase Flow*, *179*, 104936, 2024, https://doi.org/10.1016/j.ijmultiphaseflow.2024.104936.
46. Jane, R., Rose, S., James, C., Advancing Artificial Intelligence (AI) and Machine Learning (ML) Based Soft Sensors for In-Cylinder Predictions with

a Real-Time Simulator and a Crank Angle Resolved Engine Model. *Energies*, 2024, https://doi.org/10.3390/en17112731.

47. Chen, L., Xia, C., Zhao, Z., Fu, H., Chen, Y., AI-Driven Sensing Technology: Review. *Sensors (Basel, Switzerland)*, 24, 2024, https://doi.org/10.3390/s24102958.
48. Etukudoh, E., Hamdan, A., Ibekwe, K., Umoh, A., Ilojianya, V., AI and machine learning in climate change research: A review of predictive models and environmental impact. *World J. Adv. Res. Rev.*, 2024, https://doi.org/10.30574/wjarr.2024.21.1.0257.
49. Rana, S., Exploring the Advancements and Ramifications of Artificial Intelligence. *J. Artif. Intell. Gen. Sci. (JAIGS)*, 2024, ISSN:3006-4023. https://doi.org/10.60087/jaigs.v2i1.p35.
50. Zuccarini, C., Ramachandran, K., Jayaseelan, D., Material discovery and modeling acceleration *via* machine learning. *APL Mater.*, 2024, https://doi.org/10.1063/5.0230677.
51. Amato, E., Zago, V., Del Negro, C., A physically consistent AI-based SPH emulator for computational fluid dynamics. *Nonlinear Eng.*, *13*, 1, 2024, https://doi.org/10.1515/nleng-2022-0359.
52. Aulich, M., Goinis, G., Voß, C., Data-Driven AI Model for Turbomachinery Compressor Aerodynamics Enabling Rapid Approximation of 3D Flow Solutions. *Aerospace*, *11*, 9, 723, 2024, https://doi.org/10.3390/aerospace11090723.
53. Koutsoupakis, J. and Giagopoulos, D., AI-Based Surrogate Models for Multibody Dynamics Systems. *J. Phys. Conf. Ser.*, *2647*, 2, 022002, 2024, https://doi.org/10.1088/1742-6596/2647/2/022002.
54. Larrañaga, A., Brunton, S.L., J Martínez, Chapela, S., Porteiro, J., Data-driven prediction of the performance of enhanced surfaces from an extensive CFD-generated parametric search space. *Mach. Learn. Sci. Technol.*, *4*, 2, 025012–025012, 2023, https://doi.org/10.1088/2632-2153/acca60.
55. Naseem, A., Naseem, S., Fatima, S., Khan, N., Abidin, S.U., Niaz, A., Machine Learning Integration in Computational Fluid Dynamics for Turbulence Modeling. *Eur. J. Appl. Sci. Eng. Technol.*, *3*, 1, 17–29, 2025, https://doi.org/10.59324/ejaset.2025.3(1).02.
56. Shams Taleghani, A. and Torabi, F., Editorial: Recent developments in aerodynamics. *Front. Mech. Eng.*, *10*, 2025, https://doi.org/10.3389/fmech.2024.1537383.
57. Ren, S., Miao, X., Li, H., Dong, L., Chen, D., Ai-Driven Adaptive Mesh Refinement for Thermal-Hydraulic Simulations in Nuclear Reactors, http://dx.doi.org/10.2139/ssrn.5093725.
58. Fertahi, S.E.-D., Rehman, S., Benini, E., Lahrech, K., Samaouali, A., Arbaoui, A., Insights from the Last Decade in Computational Fluid Dynamics (CFD) Design and Performance Enhancement of Darrieus Wind Turbines. *Processes*, *13*, 2, 370–370, 2025, https://doi.org/10.3390/pr13020370.

59. Cattaneo, M., Kenett, R.S., Luciano, E., Adversarial AI in insurance: an overview. *Eur. Actuarial J.*, *14*, 1, 297–306, 2023, https://doi.org/10.1007/s13385-023-00365-1.
60. Aghaee, A. and Khan, M.O., Pinning down the accuracy of physics-informed neural networks under laminar and turbulent-like aortic blood flow conditions. *Comput. Biol. Med.*, *185*, 109528–109528, 2024, https://doi.org/10.1016/j.compbiomed.2024.109528.
61. Xie, Z.-C., Xu, Z.-D., Gai, P.-P., Xia, Z.-H., Xu, Y.-S., A deep learning–based surrogate model for spatial-temporal temperature field prediction in subway tunnel fires *via* CFD simulation. *J. Dyn. Disasters*, *1*, 1, 100002–100002, 2024, https://doi.org/10.1016/j.jdd.2024.100002.
62. Hashemi, A. and Izadkhah, A., A Graph Neural Network Simulation of Dispersed Systems. *Mach. Learn. Sci. Technol.*, 2025, https://doi.org/10.1088/2632-2153/adb0a0.
63. Fang, M., Zhang, F., Zhu, D., Xiao, R., Tao, R., Machine learning modeling based on informer for predicting complex unsteady flow fields to reduce consumption of computational fluid dynamics simulation. *Eng. Appl. Comput. Fluid Mech.*, *19*, 1, 2024, https://doi.org/10.1080/19942060.2024.2443118.
64. Piu, L., Péquin, A., Freitas, R.S.M., Iavarone, S., Pitsch, H., Parente, A., A Data-Driven Approach to Refine the Partially Stirred Reactor Closure for Turbulent Premixed Flames. *Flow Turbul. Combust.*, 2025, https://doi.org/10.1007/s10494-024-00626-3.
65. Li, X., Sun, W., Qin, C., Yan, Y., Zhang, L., Tu, J., Evaluation of supervised machine learning regression models for CFD-based surrogate modelling in indoor airflow field reconstruction. *Build. Environ.*, *267*, 112173, 2025, https://doi.org/10.1016/j.buildenv.2024.112173.
66. Gbadago, D.Q., Go, S., Hwang, S., A leap forward in chemical process design: Introducing an automated framework for integrated AI and CFD simulations. *Comput. Chem. Eng.*, *192*, 108906, 2025, https://doi.org/10.1016/j.compchemeng.2024.108906.
67. Rodrigues, G. and Srivastava, N., Comparative study between finite volume method and analytical method to analyse thermal efficiency of double-pipe heat exchanger. *Case Stud. Therm. Eng.*, *66*, 105713, 2025, https://doi.org/10.1016/j.csite.2024.105713.
68. Yao, Q., Wang, Z., Zhang, Y., Li, Z., Jiang, J., Towards real-time fluid dynamics simulation: a data-driven NN-MPS method and its implementation. *Math. Comput. Modell. Dyn. Syst.*, *29*, 1, 95–115, 2023, https://doi.org/10.1080/13873954.2023.2184835.
69. Heaney, C., Wolffs, Z., T'omasson, J.A., Kahouadji, L., Salinas, P., Nicolle, A., Matar, O., Navon, I.M., Srinil, N., Pain, C.C., An AI-based Domain-Decomposition Non-Intrusive Reduced-Order Model for Extended Domains applied to Multiphase Flow in Pipes. *Phys. Fluids*, abs/2202.06170(5), 055111, 2022, https://doi.org/10.1063/5.0088070.

70. Ning, Q., Wu, H., Dasigi, P., Dua, D., Gardner, M., Logan, R.L., Marasović, A., Nie, Z., Easy, Reproducible and Quality-Controlled Data Collection with CROWDAQ. *Empirical Methods in Natural Language Processing*, pp. 127–134, 2020, https://doi.org/10.18653/V1/2020.EMNLP-DEMOS.17.
71. Bergmann, M., Cordier, L., Iliescu, T., Editorial: Data-driven modeling and optimization in fluid dynamics: From physics-based to machine learning approaches. *Front. Phys.*, *10*, 2022, https://doi.org/10.3389/fphy.2022.1072691.
72. Chu, M. and Thuerey, N., Data-driven synthesis of smoke flows with CNN-based feature descriptors. *ACM Trans. Graphics*, *36*, 4, 1–14, 2017, https://doi.org/10.1145/3072959.3073643.
73. Liyanage, D.N.H.P., Methodologies for Data Collection and Model Documentation in Computer Simulation. *Int. J. Comput. Internet Manage.*, *13*, 2, 4, 2005, https://dialnet.unirioja.es/servlet/articulo?codigo=5823327.
74. Patil, U.S., Optimization of Traffic Flow Using Computational Fluid Dynamics and AI Algorithms. *Adv. Nonlinear Var. Inequal.*, *27*, 4, 113–130, 2024, https://doi.org/10.52783/anvi.v27.1496.
75. Kodman, J.B., Singh, B., Murugaiah, M., A Comprehensive Survey of Open-Source Tools for Computational Fluid Dynamics Analyses. *J. Adv. Res. Fluid Mech. Therm. Sci.*, *119*, 2, 123–148, 2024, https://doi.org/10.37934/arfmts.119.2.123148.
76. Ye, B. and Zhou, W., Efficiency increment of CFD modeling by using ANFIS artificial intelligence for thermal-based separation modeling. *Case Stud. Therm. Eng.*, *60*, 104820, 2024, https://doi.org/10.1016/j.csite.2024.104820.
77. Chowdhury, I.A., State-of-the-Art CFD Simulation: A Review of Techniques, Validation Methods, and Application Scenarios. *J. Recent Trends Mech.*, *9*, 2, 45–53, 2024, https://doi.org/10.46610/jortm.2024.v09i02.005.
78. Abdollahi, S.A., Basem, A., Alizadeh, A., Jasim, D.J., Ahmed, M., Sultan, A.J., Ranjbar, S.F., Maleki, H., Combining artificial intelligence and computational fluid dynamics for optimal design of laterally perforated finned heat sinks. *Results Eng.*, *21*, 102002–102002, 2024, https://doi.org/10.1016/j.rineng.2024.102002.
79. Sousa, P., Rodrigues, C.V., Afonso, A., Enhancing CFD solver with Machine Learning techniques. *Comput. Methods Appl. Mech. Eng.*, *429*, 117133, 2024, https://doi.org/10.1016/j.cma.2024.117133.
80. Liu, Y., Zhang, J., Yang, S., Li, J., Liu, Q., Prospective on applying machine learning in computational fluid dynamics (CFD) simulation of metallurgical reactors. *Ironmaking Steelmaking Process. Prod. Appl.*, 2024, https://doi.org/10.1177/03019233241278460.
81. Alfwzan, W.F., Selim, M.M., Almalki, A.S., Alharbi, I.S., Water quality assessment using Bi-LSTM and computational fluid dynamics (CFD) techniques. *Alexandria Eng. J.*, *97*, 346–359, 2024, https://doi.org/10.1016/j.aej.2024.04.030.

82. Singer, G., Pinsker, R., Stelzer, M., Aggarwal, M., Pertl, P., Trattner, A., Ejector validation in proton exchange membrane fuel cells: A comparison of turbulence models in computational fluid dynamics (CFD) with experiment. *Int. J. Hydrogen Energy*, *61*, 1405–1416, 2024, https://doi.org/10.1016/j.ijhydene.2024.02.365.
83. Peksen, M.M., CFD and Artificial Intelligence-Based Machine Learning Synergy for the Assessment of Syngas-Utilizing Pre-Reformer in r-SOC Technology Advancement. *Appl. Sci.*, *14*, 22, 10181, 2024, https://doi.org/10.3390/app142210181.
84. Karali, H., Inalhan, G., Tsourdos, A., AI-Driven Multidisciplinary Conceptual Design of Unmanned Aerial Vehicles. *AIAA SCITECH 2024 Forum*, 2024, https://doi.org/10.2514/6.2024-1708.
85. Wijesooriya, K., Mohotti, D., Lee, C.-K., Mendis, P., A technical review of computational fluid dynamics (CFD) applications on wind design of tall buildings and structures: Past, present and future. *J. Build. Eng.*, 74, 106828–106828, 2023, https://doi.org/10.1016/j.jobe.2023.106828.
86. Rojek, K. and Wyrzykowski, R., Performance and Scalability Analysis of AI-Accelerated CFD Simulations Across Various Computing Platforms, in: *Lecture Notes in Computer Science,* pp. 223–234, 2023, https://doi.org/10.1007/978-3-031-31209-0_17.
87. Yuan, W., Wang, Z., Chen, H., Fan, K., Numerical analyses of aerodynamic characteristics of integrated L-shaped high-rise building. *Adv. Eng. Softw.*, 114, 144–153, 2017.
88. Okwuwe, J. and Oladayo Emmanuel, O.-H., AI-Augmented Finite Difference Methods for Solving PDES: Advancing Numerical Solutions in Mathematical Modeling. *Asian Journal of Mathematics and Computer Research*, *31*, 4, 56–67, 2024, https://doi.org/10.56557/ajomcor/2024/v31i4 8985.
89. Luo, Y., Chen, Y., Zhang, Z., CFDBench: A Comprehensive Benchmark for Machine Learning Methods in Fluid Dynamics, *ArXiv* (Cornell University), https://doi.org/10.48550/arxiv.2310.05963, 2023.
90. Zhou, W., Miwa, S., Okamoto, K., Advancing fluid dynamics simulations: A comprehensive approach to optimizing physics-informed neural networks. *Phys. Fluids*, *36*, 1, 2024, https://doi.org/10.1063/5.0180770.
91. Wu, L., Xu, J., Tong, W., PERform: assessing model performance with predictivity and explainability readiness formula. *J. Environ. Sci. Health Part C*, *42*, 4, 298–313, 2024, https://doi.org/10.1080/26896583.2024.2340391.
92. Illarramendi, E., Bauerheim, M., Cuenot, B., Performance and accuracy assessments of an incompressible fluid solver coupled with a deep Convolutional Neural Network. *arXiv: Fluid Dyn.*, 2021, https://doi.org/10.48550/arXiv.2109.09363.
93. Tian, Y., Nearing, G., Peters-Lidard, C.D., Harrison, K.W., Tang, L., Performance Metrics, Error Modeling, and Uncertainty Quantification. *Mon. Weather Rev.*, *144*, 2, 607–613, 2016, https://doi.org/10.1175/MWR-D-15-0087.1.

94. Cao, X., Wang, Q., Li, H., Ma, H., Research on Fast CFD Simulation of Automobile Flow Field Based on Artificial Intelligence. *J. Phys.*, *2441*, 1, 012011, 2023, https://doi.org/10.1088/1742-6596/2441/1/012011.
95. Obiols-Sales, O., Vishnu, A., Malaya, N., Chandramowliswharan, A., CFDNet: a deep learning-based accelerator for fluid simulations. *International Conference on Supercomputing*, 2020, https://doi.org/10.1145/3392717.3392772.
96. Rezaeiravesh, S., Vinuesa, R., Schlatter, P., An Uncertainty-Quantification Framework for Assessing Accuracy, Sensitivity, and Robustness in Computational Fluid Dynamics. *J. Comput. Sci.*, 62, 101688, 2022, ISSN 1877-7503, https://doi.org/10.1016/j.jocs.2022.101688.
97. Fresca, S. and Manzoni, A., Real-time simulation of parameter-dependent fluid flows through deep learning-based reduced order models. *Fluids*, 6, 7, 259, 2021, https://doi.org/10.3390/fluids6070259.
98. Li, L., Cheng, Z., Lange, C.F., CFD-Based Optimization of Fluid Flow Product Aided by Artificial Intelligence and Design Space Validation. *Math. Probl. Eng.*, *2018*, 1–14, 2018, https://doi.org/10.1155/2018/8465020.
99. Yoo, S., Lee, S., Kim, S., Hwang, K.H., Park, J.H., Kang, N., Integrating Deep Learning into CAD/CAE System: generative design and evaluation of 3D conceptual wheel. *Struct. Multidiscip. Optim.*, 64, 4, 2725–2747, Oct 2021, https://doi.org/10.1007/s00158-021-02953-9.
100. Syah, R., Elveny, M., Nasution, M.K.M., Ponkratov, V.V., Kuznetsova, M.Y., Poltarykhin, A., Babanezhad, M., Numerical investigation of nanofluid flow using CFD and fuzzy-based particle swarm optimization. *Sci. Rep.*, *11*, 1, 20973, 2021, https://doi.org/10.1038/S41598-021-00279-6.
101. Data-Driven Enhanced Model Reduction for Bifurcating Models in Computational Fluid Dynamics, 2022, https://doi.org/10.48550/arxiv.2202.09250.
102. Ansari, A.H., Hosseini Boosari, S.S., Mohaghegh, S.D., Successful Implementation of Artificial Intelligence and Machine Learning in Multiphase Flow Smart Proxy Modeling: Two Case Studies of Gas-Liquid and Gas-Solid CFD Models. *J. Pet. Environ. Biotechnol.*, *11*, 1, 1–8, 2020.
103. Tian, W., VanGilder, J., Condor, M., Han, X., Zuo, W., An Accurate Fast Fluid Dynamics Model for Data Center Applications. OSTI OAI (U.S. Department of Energy Office of Scientific and Technical Information, pp. 1275–1281, 2019, https://doi.org/10.1109/itherm.2019.8757336.
104. Djukic, T., Topalovic, M., Filipovic, N., Validation of lattice Boltzmann based software for blood flow simulations in complex patient-specific arteries against traditional CFD methods. *Math. Comput. Simul*, *203*, 957–976, 2023, https://doi.org/10.1016/j.matcom.2022.07.027.
105. Aloysius, S., Pearce, D., Wrobel, L., ALAQS comparison of CFD and lagrangian dispersion methods – simple scenario, 2007.

106. Pettersson, K. and Rizzi, A., Comparing Different CFD Methods Accuracy in Computing Local Boundary Layer Properties. *Eng. Appl. Comput. Fluid Mech.*, *3*, 1, 98–108, 2009, https://doi.org/10.1080/19942060.2009.11015257.
107. Suss, A., Mary, I., Garrec, T.L., Marié, S., Comprehensive comparison between the lattice Boltzmann and Navier–Stokes methods for aerodynamic and aeroacoustic applications. *Comput. Fluids*, *257*, 105881–105881, 2023, https://doi.org/10.1016/j.compfluid.2023.105881.
108. Chowdhury, I.A., State-of-the-Art CFD Simulation: A Review of Techniques, Validation Methods, and Application Scenarios. *J. Recent Trends Mech.*, *9*, 2, 45–53, 2024, https://doi.org/10.46610/jortm.2024.v09i02.005.
109. Iserte, S., Macías, A., Martıńez-Cuenca, R., Chiva, S., Paredes, R., Quintana-OrtíE., S., Accelerating urban scale simulations leveraging local spatial 3D structure. *J. Comput. Sci.*, *62*, 101741–101741, 2022, https://doi.org/10.1016/j.jocs.2022.101741.
110. Yi, H., Kim, M., Lee, D., Park, J., Applications of Computational Fluid Dynamics for Mine Ventilation in Mineral Development. *Energies*, *15*, 22, 8405, 2022, https://doi.org/10.3390/en15228405.
111. Babanezhad, M., Behroyan, I., Nakhjiri, A., Marjani, A., Shirazian, S., Computational Modeling of Transport in Porous Media Using an Adaptive Network-Based Fuzzy Inference System. *ACS Omega*, 5, 30826–30835, 2020, https://doi.org/10.1021/acsomega.0c04497.
112. Whang, S., Roh, Y., Song, H., Lee, J., Data collection and quality challenges in deep learning: a data-centric AI perspective. *VLDB J.*, 32, 791–813, 2021, https://doi.org/10.1007/s00778-022-00775-9.
113. Towne, A., Dawson, S., Brès, G., Lozano-Dur'an, A., Saxton-Fox, T., Parthasarathy, A., Jones, A., Biler, H., Yeh, C., Patel, H., Taira, K., A Database for Reduced-Complexity Modeling of Fluid Flows. *AIAA J.*, 2022, https://doi.org/10.2514/1.j062203.
114. Gerretzen, J., Szymańska, E., Jansen, J., Bart, J., Van Manen, H., Van Den Heuvel, E., Buydens, L., Simple and Effective Way for Data Preprocessing Selection Based on Design of Experiments. *Anal. Chem.*, 87, 24, 12096–103, 2015, https://doi.org/10.1021/acs.analchem.5b02832.
115. Gil, A., Quartulli, M., Olaizola, I., Sierra, B., Learning Optimal Time Series Combination and Pre-Processing by Smart Joins. *Appl. Sci.*, 2020, https://doi.org/10.3390/app10186346.
116. Felix, E. and Lee, S., Systematic literature review of preprocessing techniques for imbalanced data. *IET Software*, 13, 479–496, 2019, https://doi.org/10.1049/IET-SEN.2018.5193.

4

Artificial Neural Network-Based Analysis of Natural Convection in *Ag-TiO_2/H_2O* Hybrid Nanoliquids

Madhavarao Kulkarni[1,2]

[1]*P. G. Department Studies in Mathematics, Basaveshwar Science College, Bagalkot, India*
[2]*P. G. Department Studies in Mathematics, Bharat Ratna Prof. C.N. Rao Research Centre, Basaveshwar Science College, Bagalkot, India*

Abstract

In this chapter, artificial intelligence and machine learning approaches, such as artificial neural networks and numerical simulations, are employed with a hybrid nanofluid flow amid vertical plates. This paper also examines the transfer of heat through convection, utilizing thermo-physical properties of hybrid nanofluids, and an external magnetic field as a novel methodology with analytical solutions and artificial neural networks. The complex fluid flow governing partial differential equations changed into ordinary differential equations *via* similarity variables. The obtained data from the simulation is transformed into one of the artificial neural networks, such as the Levenberg–Marquardt neural network, and is divided into training, testing, and validation. The study also includes the analysis of skin friction coefficient and heat transfer rate. The analytical study with Laplace transformation is employed to simulate graphs and tables that effectively depict many physical factors in fluid flow and the transfer of heat. Amalgating hybrid nanoparticles into a regular fluid yields superior heat transfer compared to both nanofluid and working fluid alone. Better heat transfer is obtained when hybrid nanoparticles are included in the base liquid as opposed to the base fluid and nanofluid alone, according to simulations for different physical parameters in the model. Greater values of the velocity ratio and combination of convection parameters result in a rise in the hybrid nanofluid's velocity. As the magnetic parameter

Email: mgkmaths@gmail.com; ORCID: https://orcid.org/0000-0002-9442-9507

Mukesh Kumar Awasthi and Reshu Gupta (eds.) Artificial Intelligence and Computational Modeling in Heat Transfer and Fluid Dynamics, (93–116) © 2026 Scrivener Publishing LLC

and volume fraction of $Ag\text{-}TiO_2$ grow, the temperature of the hybrid nanofluid rises sharply.

Keywords: Analytical study, convection, heat transfer, hybrid nanofluid, Laplace transformation

4.1 Introduction

Artificial intelligence and machine learning are distinct disciplines in computer science that focus on the examination and advancement of systems that can execute tasks with a predetermined goal. The tasks encompass problem-solving, adapting to diverse environments, decision-making, learning, and communication. Artificial intelligence and machine learning have been implemented in a variety of applications, including medical image computing, computer vision robotics, information retrieval, natural language processing, pattern recognition, image processing, data mining, and knowledge representation. The importance of this component is deemed critical while dealing with a variety of issues in the field of physical engineering. As a result, it is commonly used with maximum efficiency in a variety of mechanical systems, including internal combustion engines, refrigeration systems, and heating devices. First, the effect of temperature, particle concentration, and nanoparticle size on thermal conductivity was examined. However, the recently created artificial neural network (ANN) model is used to evaluate it. Researchers and scientists today use neural networks to simulate fluid flow as a result of these phenomena. Alzahrani *et al.* [1] implemented an ANN model with a numerical approach to understand features of the flow of electrically conductive Williamson fluid traveling across a stretched surface. The Galerkin approach is used to estimate the data set used for the ANN model, whereas the Levenberg–Marquard algorithm is employed for prediction. Miandoab *et al.* [2] investigated the transfer of heat and pressure drop in a horizontal tube filled with graphene oxide and water nanofluid, respectively. According to findings, a flow of nanofluid was investigated by examining the various volume ratios. The findings provided evidence that the ANN model can make accurate predictions regarding output values. The Darcy–Forchheimer model embraces flow in a non-linear graded liquid optimized by Shafiq *et al.* [3], exploited by ANN. This was accomplished under convective conditions. Further inquiries into AI with fluids have been studied [4–6].

There are numerous real-world scenarios these days where we need to deal with various kinds of nanoparticles. These nanoparticles play a crucial role in controlling the different thermophysical properties of the several fluids involved. Most everyday fluids, such as water, kerosene oil, ethylene glycol, and motor oil, are poor heat conductors. Lower levels of thermal conductivity and other thermal properties are among the primary causes of this. Researchers include nanoparticles in the basic fluids to solve this problem and enhance the fluids' thermal properties. To get a more detailed understanding of these nanoparticle-based nanofluids, several researchers investigated and put forward different models. Choi *et al.* [7] were pioneers in introducing a novel type of fluid known as nanofluid containing submicronic solid particles ranging in length from 1 to 100 nm during their research on innovative coolants and cooling technologies. During an experiment, Eastman *et al.* [8] found that adding 5% CuO nanoparticles to water makes the heat conductivity of conventional fluid rise to 60%. Khanafer and Vafai [9] investigated the steady and compressible flow of nanofluid within a cutting tool. The findings indicated that incorporating Al2O3 nanoparticles led to a reduction in the temperature of the cutting tool. Pavithra *et al.* [10] investigated water-based and ethylene glycol-based nanofluids on inclined plates, finding that zirconium nanofluids showed the highest temperature enhancement. More recently, hybrid nanofluid has surpassed nanofluid in terms of thermal conductivity, making it the preferred working fluid in convection devices [11–14]. Mixtures of two or more distinct nanoparticles distributed in monoconventional liquid constitute hybrid nanofluids. There are many extensive uses of hybrid nanofluids when it comes to thermal efficiency, in transportation, medicinal fields, refrigeration, heat exchanges, channels, and energy storage systems. Innovative research has been carried out with a variety of hybrid nanofluids in the present technology. Alhajaj *et al.* [15] studied nanofluids and hybrid fluids *via* porous channels using computational and experimental methods. The authors [16] discussed the consequences of a mixture of nanoliquid on a tin container. Batmunkh *et al.* [17] have produced Ag–TiO_2 nanoparticles through the application of a magnetic stirring technique.

The flow and heat transmission between two vertical parallel plates will be examined in the current work. Several researchers conducted parallel plate works, including Sheikholeslami *et al.* [18], Tarakaramu and Narayana [19], Sheikholeslami and Ganji [20], and Hatami *et al.* [21]. Furthermore, a buoyancy-driven flow with a heat source and sink is more apparent in explaining this type of model. Alzwayi and Paul investigated a free-convection flow between two parallel plates with a heat source and sink as part of the current inventive trend. [22] Bhargava *et al.* [23], Ali *et al.* [24], Nasr and Al-Ghamdi [25], Sheikholeslami and Ganji [26], Hajizadeh *et al.* [27], Narahari *et al.* [28], Dib *et al.* [29], and Esfe *et al.* [30].

Hayat *et al.* [31] and Salehi *et al.* [32] studied the unsteady squeezing flow between two parallel walls in the presence of a magnetic field.

In view of this, the objective of this work is to investigate the heat transfer and flow of a hybrid nanofluid being transferred between two vertical parallel plates while being exposed to thermal radiation, a magnetic field, and a temperature-dependent heat source or sink. Through Laplace transforms, the dimensionless equations can be resolved analytically.

4.2 Mathematical Modeling

A nanoliquid combination flows between two vertical plates. The x-axis is expected to run to the left, while the y-axis should be parallel to the plates. The letter "d" represents the distance between the plates. When confronting thermal radiation and a changeable heat source or sink, a magnetic field is applied in the direction perpendicular to the surfaces. Figure 4.1 presents a mathematical model. Here, T_l is the temperature at which the plates and the nanofluid mixture that circulates are maintained at the very beginning of the experiment. T_c, the temperature of the right plate, is increased to a higher temperature, T_h, when t is greater than 0. They are in a state of thermal equilibrium with one another since the conventional fluid and nanoparticles have been traced for a certain amount of time. No sliding condition between them is also taken into consideration. Supposedly, the hybrid nanofluid will maintain thermal and physical properties throughout its lifetime. Table 4.1 shows the thermo physical properties of liquid and nanoparticles [11–17].

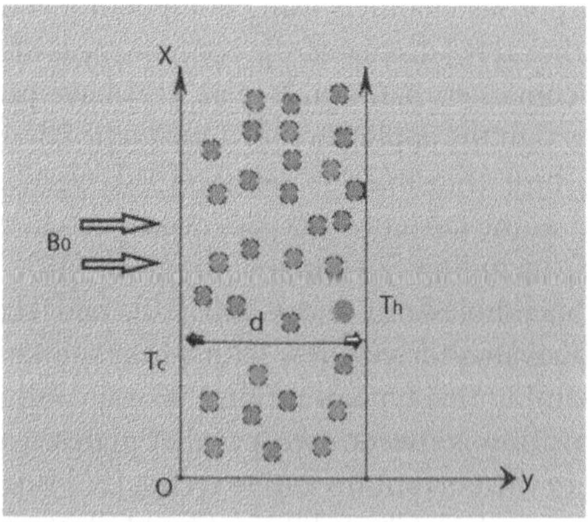

Figure 4.1 Geometrical configuration.

Table 4.1 Thermophysical properties of liquid and nanoparticles.

Properties	Water	Ag	TiO_2
$\rho(kg/m^3)$	997.1	10,500	4250
$C_p(J/kgK)$	4179	235	686.2
$k(W/mK)$	0.613	429	8.953
$\beta(1/k)\times10^{-5}$	21	1.89	0.9
$\sigma(s/m)$	5.5×10^{-6}	2.3×10^{6}	3.5×10^{6}

The governing equations are as follows:

$$\frac{\partial u}{\partial t}=\frac{\rho_{hnf}}{\rho_{hnf}}\frac{\partial^2 u}{\partial y^2}+\frac{(\rho\beta)_{hnf}}{\rho_{hnf}}g(T-T_\infty)-\frac{\sigma_{hnf}B_0^2}{\rho_{hnf}}u \tag{4.1}$$

$$\frac{\partial T}{\partial t}=\alpha_{hnf}\frac{\partial^2 T}{\partial y^2}-\frac{1}{(\rho C_p)_{hnf}}\frac{\partial q_r}{\partial y}+\frac{Q_0}{(\rho C_p)_{hnf}}(T-T_\infty) \tag{4.2}$$

$$\left.\begin{array}{l} t\le 0: u=0, T=T_c,\ 0<y<d,\\ t>0: u=0, T=T_c,\ y=0,\\ u=0, T=T_h,\ y=d. \end{array}\right\} \tag{4.3}$$

The rheological characteristics of nanofluids and hybrid nanofluids:

- Density

$$\begin{aligned} \rho_{nf}&=(1-\phi_1)\rho_f+\phi_1\rho_{s_1}\\ \rho_{hnf}&=(1-\phi_2)\left[(1-\phi_1)\rho_f+\phi_1\rho_{s_1}\right]+\phi_2\rho_{s_2} \end{aligned} \tag{4.4}$$

- Dynamic viscosity: $\mu_{nf}=\dfrac{\mu_f}{(1-\phi_1)^{2.5}}$

$$\mu_{hnf}=\frac{\mu_f}{(1-\phi_1)^{2.5}(1-\phi_2)^{2.5}}$$

- Heat capacity
$$\begin{cases} (\rho c_p)_{nf} = (1-\phi_1)(\rho c_p)_f + \phi_1(\rho c_p)_{s_1} \\ (\rho c_p)_{hnf} = (1-\phi_2)\left[(1-\phi_1)(\rho c_p)_f + \phi_1(\rho c_p)_{s_1}\right] + \phi_2(\rho c_p)_{s_2} \end{cases}$$

- Thermal expansion coefficient
$$(\rho\beta)_{nf} = (1-\phi_1)(\rho\beta)_f + \phi_1(\rho\beta)_{s_1}$$
$$(\rho\beta)_{hnf} = (1-\phi_2)\left[(1-\phi_1)(\rho\beta)_f + \phi_1(\rho\beta)_{s_1}\right] + \phi_2(\rho\beta)_{s_2}$$

- The electrical conductivity:

$$\sigma_{nf} = \frac{\sigma_{s_1} + 2\sigma_f - 2\phi_1(\sigma_f - \sigma_{s_1})}{\sigma_{s1} + 2\sigma_f + \phi_1(\sigma_f - \sigma_{s_1})}\sigma_f$$
$$\sigma_{hnf} = \frac{\sigma_{s_2} + 2\sigma_{nf} - 2\phi_2(\sigma_{nf} - \sigma_{s_2})}{\sigma_{s_2} + 2\sigma_{nf} + \phi_2(\sigma_{nf} - \sigma_{s_2})}\sigma_{nf}; \sigma_{nf} = \frac{\sigma_{s_1} + 2\sigma_f - 2\phi_1(\sigma_f - \sigma_{s_1})}{\sigma_{s1} + 2\sigma_f + \phi_1(\sigma_f - \sigma_{s_1})}\sigma_f$$

- The thermal conductivity

$$k_{nf} = \frac{k_{s_1} + (s-1)k_f - (s-1)\phi_1\left(k_f - k_{s_1}\right)}{k_{s1} + (s-1)k_f + \phi_1\left(k_f - k_{s_1}\right)}k_f$$
$$k_{hnf} = \frac{k_{s_2} + (s-1)k_{nf} - (s-1)\phi_2\left(k_{nf} - k_{s_2}\right)}{k_{s_2} + (s-1)k_{nf} + \phi_2\left(k_{nf} - k_{s_2}\right)}k_{nf};$$
$$k_{nf} = \frac{k_{s_1} + (s-1)k_f - (s-1)\phi_1\left(k_f - k_{s_1}\right)}{k_{s1} + (s-1)k_f + \phi_1\left(k_f - k_{s_1}\right)}k_f$$

Non-dimensional quantities:

$$u = \frac{du}{\nu_f},\ \theta = \frac{T - T_c}{T_h - T_c}, y = \frac{y}{d'} t = \frac{\nu_f t}{d^2} \tag{4.5}$$

Substitute Equation 4.5 into Equations 4.1, 4.2, and 4.4, and we have

$$\frac{\partial u}{\partial t}=\frac{A_1}{A_2}\frac{\partial^2 u}{\partial y^2}+A_3\theta-A_4 u \tag{4.6}$$

$$\frac{\partial \theta}{\partial t}=\frac{1}{Pr}\frac{1}{A_6}\left(A_5+\frac{4}{3}R\right)\frac{\partial^2\theta}{\partial y^2}+\frac{h_s}{A_6}\theta. \tag{4.7}$$

The boundary restrictions of Equation 4.3 become

$$\left.\begin{array}{ll} t\le 0: u=0, \theta=0, & 0<y<1, \\ t>0: u=0, \theta=0, & y=0, \\ u=0, \quad \theta=1, & y=1. \end{array}\right\} \tag{4.8}$$

The parameters defined in the above expressions are

$$Pr=\frac{\mu_f (Cp)_f}{k_f}; h_s=\frac{Q_0 d^2 (T_w-T_\infty)}{\nu_f (Cp)_f}; A_1=\frac{\mu_{hnf}}{\mu_f}; A_2=\frac{\rho_{hnf}}{\rho_f};$$
$$A_3=\frac{(\rho\beta)_{hnf}}{(\rho\beta)_f}\frac{\rho_f}{\rho_{hnf}}; M=\frac{\sigma_f B_0^2 d^2}{\mu_f}; A_4=M\frac{(\sigma)_{hnf}}{(\sigma)_f}\frac{\rho_f}{\rho_{hnf}};$$
$$A_5=\frac{k_{hnf}}{k_f}; A_6=\frac{(\rho Cp)_{hnf}}{(\rho Cp)_f}; A_7=\frac{h_s}{A_6}; R=\frac{4\sigma^* T_\infty^3}{kk_f}. \tag{4.9}$$

4.3 Methods of Solution

Laplace transforms are utilized to solve Equations 4.6 and 4.7 analytically, with boundary conditions (4.8). The following scenarios are taken into consideration when deriving the solutions:

i) For $h_s \neq 0, and\ M \neq 0$:

$$\frac{A_1}{A_2}\frac{d^2u}{dy^2}U((s,y))-(s+A_4)U(s,y)+A_3\theta(s,y)=0 \tag{4.10}$$

$$\frac{1}{Pr}\frac{1}{A_6}(A_3+4/3R)\frac{d^2}{dy^2}(\theta(s,y))-(s-A_7)\theta(s,y)=0 \tag{4.11}$$

Simplifying Equations 4.10 and 4.11, we obtain

$$U(s,y)=c_1e^{(m_1\sqrt{(s+A_4)}y)}+c_2e^{(-m_1\sqrt{(s+A_4)}y)}$$
$$+\frac{(m_1^2A_3)}{((m_1^2-m_2^2)s+m_1^2A_4+m_2^2A_7)}(c_3e^{(m_2\sqrt{(s-A_7)}y)}+c_4e^{(m_2\sqrt{(s-A_7)}y)}) \tag{4.12}$$

$$\theta(s,y)=c_3e^{(m_1\sqrt{(s-A_7)}y)}+c_4e^{(m_2\sqrt{(s-A_7)}y)}, \tag{4.13}$$

Where

$$m_1=(A_1/A_2)^{(1/2)}, m_2=\{PrA_6(A_5+4/3R)^{-1}\}^{(1/2)}.$$

Taking the Laplace transform to the boundary conditions and Equation 4.8 becomes

$$U(s,0)=0,\quad \theta(s,0)=0,\quad U(s,1)=0,\ \theta(s,1)=1/s, \tag{4.14}$$

By Equations 4.13 and 4.14, we have

$$\theta(s,y)=\frac{Sinh(m_2\sqrt{s-A_7}\,y)}{s.Sinh(m_2\sqrt{s-A_7})} \tag{4.15}$$

Taking the inverse Laplace to Equation 4.15, we have

$$\theta = \frac{Sin(m_2\sqrt{(A_7)}y)}{(Sin(m_2\sqrt{(A_7)}))} + \sum_{n=1}^{\infty}(-1)^n \frac{2n\pi}{(m_2^2\sigma_1)} e^{(-\sigma_1 t)} Sin(n\pi y) \quad (4.16)$$

Here, $\sigma_1 = (n^2\pi^2)/(m_2^2 - A_7)$.

Similarly, taking Equations 4.12 and 4.14–4.16 and applying the inverse Laplace transform, we get

$$u = \frac{(A_3 m_1^2)}{(A_4 m_1^2)}\left[\frac{Sin(m_2\sqrt{(A_7)}y)}{Sin(m_2\sqrt{(A_7)}} - \frac{Sinh(m_2\sqrt{s - A_4}\,y)}{Sinh(m_2\sqrt{s - A_4})}\right] + \sum_{n=1}^{\infty}\frac{2(-1)^n A_3 m_1^2 n\pi}{A_8}\left(\frac{1}{\sigma_2}e^{\sigma_2 t} - \frac{1}{\sigma_1}e^{\sigma_1 t}\right)Sin(n\pi y)$$

$$\sigma_2 = (n^2\pi^2)/(m_1^2 + A_4)\ A_8 = (m_1^2 - m_2^2)n^2\pi^2 - m_1^2 m_2^2(A_4 + A_7). \quad (4.17)$$

(ii) $h_s = 0.0$ and $M \neq 0.0$:

$$\theta = y + \sum_{n=1}^{\infty}(-1)^n \frac{2}{n\pi} e^{(-\sigma_{1s} t)} Sin(n\pi y), \quad (4.18)$$

$$u = \frac{A_3}{A_4}\left[y - \frac{Sinh(m_1\sqrt{s - A_4}\,y)}{Sinh(m_1\sqrt{s - A_4})}\right] + \sum_{n=1}^{\infty}\frac{2(-1)^n A_3 m_1^2 n\pi}{A_8 s}\left(\frac{1}{\sigma_2}e^{\sigma_2 t} - \frac{1}{\sigma_{1s}}e^{\sigma_{1s} t}\right)Sin(n\pi y) \quad (4.19)$$

Here, $\sigma_{1s} = (n^2\pi^2)/m_1^2\ \ A_{8s} = (m_1^2 - m_2^2)n^2\pi^2 - m_1^2 m_2^2 A_4$

(iii) $h_s \neq 0.0$ and $M = 0.0$:

$$\theta = y + \sum_{n=1}^{\infty} (-1)^n \frac{2}{n\pi} e^{(-\sigma_1 st)} Sin(n\pi y),$$

$$u = \frac{A_3 m_1^2}{A_4 m_2^2}\left[\frac{Sin(m_1\sqrt{s-A_4}\,y)}{Sin(m_1\sqrt{s-A_4})} - y\right]$$

$$+\sum_{n=1}^{\infty} \frac{2(-1)^n A_3 m_1^2 n\pi}{A_8 m}\left(\frac{1}{\sigma_{2m}} e^{\sigma_{2mt}} - \frac{1}{\sigma_1} e^{\sigma_{1t}}\right) Sin(n\pi y) \quad (4.20)$$

Here, $\sigma_{2m} = (n^2\pi^2)/m_1^2 \;\; A_{8m} = (m_1^2 - m_2^2)n^2\pi^2 - m_1^2 m_2^2 A_7$

(iv) $h_s = 0.0$ and $M = 0.0$:

$$\theta = y + \sum_{n=1}^{\infty} (-1)^n \frac{2}{n\pi} e^{-\sigma_{2t}} Sin(n\pi y), \quad (4.21)$$

$$u = \frac{1}{6} A_3 m_1^2 y(1-y^2) + \sum_{n=1}^{\infty} \frac{2(-1)^n A_3 m_1^2 n\pi}{(m_1^2 - m_2^2)n^4\pi^3}\left(m_1^2 e^{-\sigma_{2mt}} - m_2^2 e^{-\sigma_{1st}}\right) Sin(n\pi y)$$

(4.22)

Garadients at the wall:
shear stress, and rate of heat transferis given as

$$\tau = \mu_{hnf}\left(\frac{\partial u}{\partial y}\right)_{y=0,d} \qquad q = \left(k_{hnf} + \frac{16\sigma^* T_\infty^3}{3k^*}\right)\left(\frac{\partial T}{\partial y}\right)_{y=0,d} \quad (4.23)$$

Using the definitions of (4.5) into (4.23),we find

$$\tau = \frac{\mu_{hnf}}{\mu_f}\left(\frac{\partial u}{\partial y}\right)_{y=0,1} \qquad q = \left(\frac{k_{hnf}}{k_f} + \frac{4}{3}R\right)\left(\frac{\partial T}{\partial y}\right)_{y=0,1} \quad (4.24)$$

To determine the dimensionless shear stress, τ, and rate of heat transfer, q, use Equations (4.16–4.22) are i) $h_s \neq 0$ and $M \neq 0$:

$$\frac{\partial u}{\partial y} = \frac{A_3 m_1^2}{A_4 m_1^2 + A_7 m_2^2}\left[\frac{m_2\sqrt{A_7}Cos(m_2\sqrt{A_7}\,y)}{Sin(m_2\sqrt{A_7}\,y)} - \frac{m_1\sqrt{A_4}Cosh(m_1\sqrt{A_4}\,y)}{Sinh(m_1\sqrt{A_4})}\right]$$
$$+\sum_{n=1}^{\infty}\frac{2(-1)^n A_3 m_1^2 n^2\pi^2}{A_8}\left(\frac{1}{\sigma_2}e^{-\sigma_{2t}} - \frac{1}{\sigma_1}e^{-\sigma_{1t}}\right)Cos(n\pi\,y)$$

ii) $h_s \neq 0$ and $M \neq 0.0$:

$$\frac{\partial u}{\partial y} = \frac{A_3}{A_4}\left[1 - \frac{m_1\sqrt{A_4}Cosh(m_1\sqrt{A_4}\,y)}{Sinh(m_1\sqrt{A_4})}\right]$$
$$+\sum_{n=1}^{\infty}\frac{2(-1)^n A_3 m_1^2 n^2\pi^2}{A_{8s}}\left(\frac{1}{\sigma_2}e^{-\sigma_{2t}} - \frac{1}{\sigma_{1s}}e^{-\sigma_{1st}}\right)Cos(n\pi\,y)$$

iii) $h_s \neq 0.0$ and $M = 0.0$:

$$\frac{\partial u}{\partial y} = \frac{A_3 m_1^2}{A_4 m_2^2}\left[\frac{m_2\sqrt{A_7}Cos(m_2\sqrt{A_7}\,y)}{Sin(m_2\sqrt{A_7}\,y)} - 1\right]$$
$$+\sum_{n=1}^{\infty}\frac{2(-1)^n A_3 m_1^2 n^2\pi^2}{A_{8m}}\left(\frac{1}{\sigma_{2m}}e^{-\sigma_{2mt}} - \frac{1}{\sigma_{1t}}e^{-\sigma_{1t}}\right)Cos(n\pi\,y)$$

iv) $h_s = 0.0$ and $M = 0.0$:

$$\frac{\partial u}{\partial y} = \frac{1}{6}A_3 m_1^2(1 - 3y^2)$$
$$+\sum_{n=1}^{\infty}\frac{2(-1)^n A_3 m_1^2}{(m_1^2 - m_2^2)n^3\pi^2}\left(m_1^2 e^{-\sigma_{2mt}} - m_2^2 e^{-\sigma_{1st}}\right)Cos(n\pi\,y)$$

v) $h_s \neq 0, M \neq 0,$

$$\frac{\partial\theta}{\partial y} = 1 + \left[\frac{m_2\sqrt{A_7}Cos(m_2\sqrt{A_7}\,y)}{Sin(m_2\sqrt{A_7}\,y)}\right] + \sum_{n=1}^{\infty}\frac{2(-1)^n n^2\pi^2}{m_2^2\sigma_1}e^{-\sigma_{1t}}Cos(n\pi\,y)$$

vi) $h_s = 0, M \neq 0,$

$$\frac{\partial\theta}{\partial y} = 1 + \sum_{n=1}^{\infty}2(-1)^n e^{-\sigma_{1st}}\,Cos(n\pi\,y)$$

vii) $h_s = 0, M = 0,$

$$\frac{\partial\theta}{\partial y} = 1 + \sum_{n=1}^{\infty}2(-1)^n e^{-\sigma_{3t}}\,Cos(n\pi\,y)$$

4.4 Results and Discussion

At different times, the temperature and velocity gradients with the ordinate y are shown in Figures 4.2(a) and 4.2(b). The data demonstrated that both temperature and velocity rose with time. It suggests that, over time, flow and thermal variations have been gradually altering. This allows us to determine how long it will take for temperature and velocity to stabilize between two parallel plates. Furthermore, the time necessary to achieve a stable state is found to be dependent on the controlling factors. This is why both profiles have been changed.

The figures show how the volume fraction of silver nanoparticles, ϕ_1, affects velocity and temperature. In Figures 4.3(a) and 4.3(b), elevated ϕ_1 results in decreasing velocity and temperature. It is worth noting that the density declines. The effect of the volume fraction of silver anoparticle, ϕ_1, on the velocity and temperature is illustrated in Figures 4.3(a) and 4.3(b), where higher ϕ_1, velocity, and temperature are found to decline. It should be noted that the density is found to be decreasing.

Figures 4.4(a) and 4.4(b) display the impact of the volume fraction of multiwall carbon nanotube particles ϕ_2 on velocity, and the temperature distribution is shown with the rise of ϕ_2 greater levels of velocity,

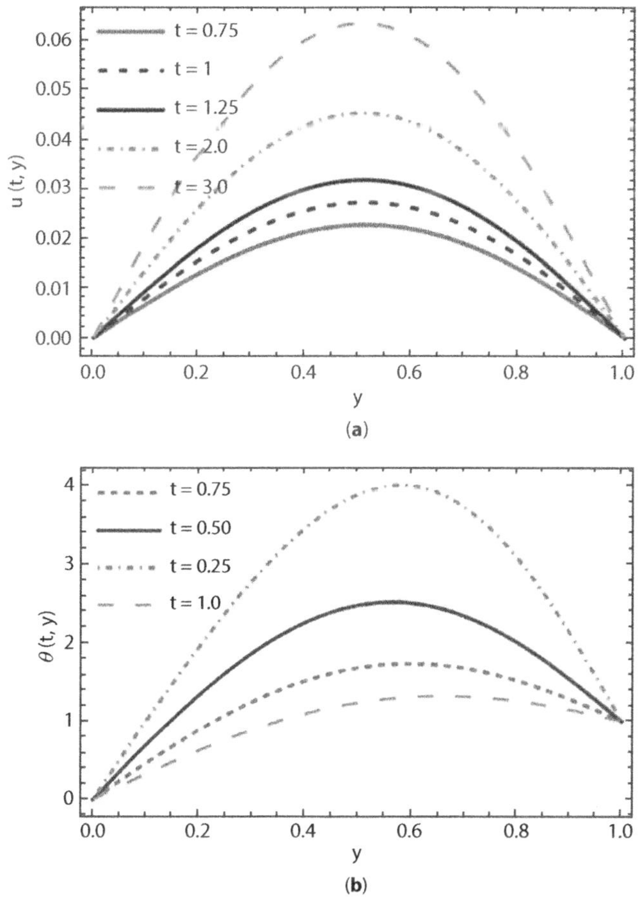

Figure 4.2 (a) Velocity profiles for varying t, (b) temperature profiles for varying t.

and temperature strength is declining. The density of ϕ_2 shrinks due to nanoparticle bombardment at the surface, while the concentration of hybrid nanoliquid upsurges with greater ρ_{hnf} value and volume fraction of titanium dioxide particles. As a result, the hybrid nanoliquid becomes heavier.

Figures 4.5(a) and 4.5(b) illustrate how the volume percentage of ϕ_2 affects the temperature and velocity; larger values result in a noteworthy reduction in both. Regular silver-water nanofluid is heavier than the titanium oxide nanoparticles once they are mixed in. Consequently, the temperature and velocity decline as ϕ_2 rises.

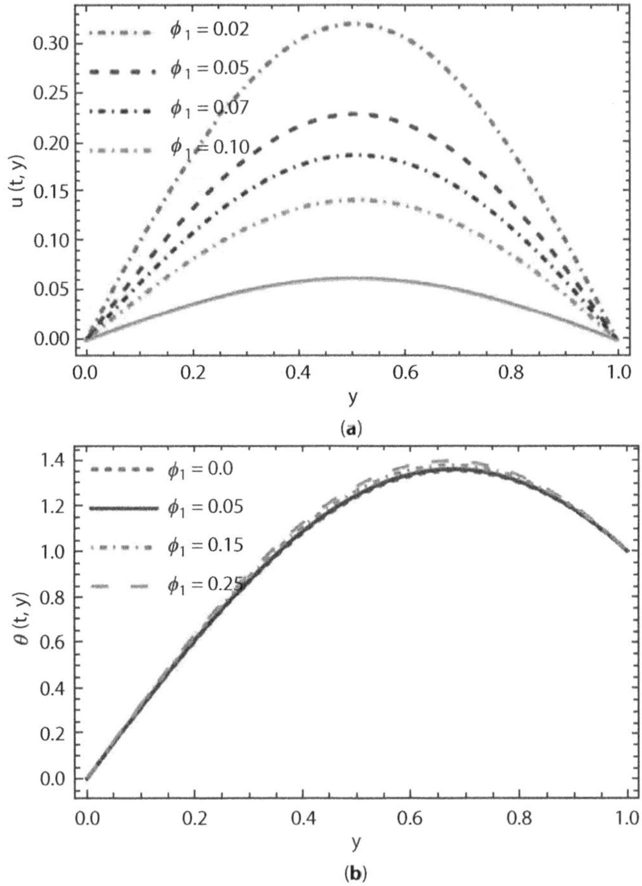

Figure 4.3 (a) Velocity profiles for ϕ_1, (b) temperature profiles for ϕ_1.

The impact of temperature and velocity on h_s values is seen in Figures 4.6(a) and 4.6(b). The temperature and velocity both sharply increase as h_s rises. Once h_s is increased from -0.2 to 0.9, velocity and temperature profiles appear to upsurge. As h_s grows, these values tend to converge at $y=1$. Between the heat source and sink, the temperature fluctuation is almost linear. At zero, the temperature profiles are always lower in the case of a heat sink. On the other hand, the heat source's temperature profiles are consistently higher and nearer the warming wall. It shows that greater amount of heat source generates additional energy in the hybrid nanofluid *via* temperature production.

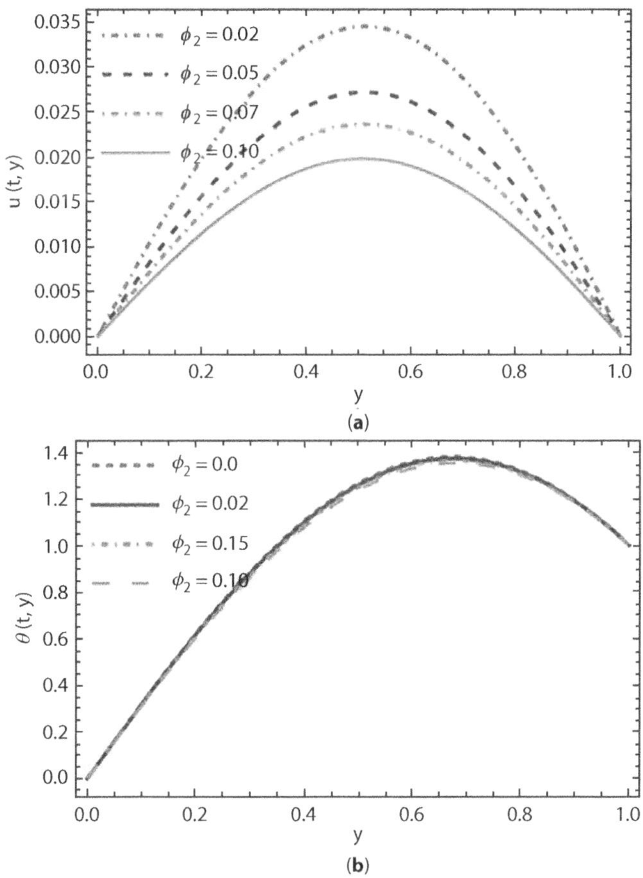

Figure 4.4 (a) Velocity profiles for ϕ_2. (b) Temperature profiles for ϕ_2.

Figure 4.7 displays the impacts of velocity on the magnetic characteristic. The fastest speed increases according to the velocity of motion. It is evident that for larger objects, the steady-state velocity must be raised to keep magnetic, buoyancy, and viscous forces balanced. In other words, when a magnetic field is applied, the highest speed increases, thus boosting the fluid's rate.

4.4.1 Artificial Neural Network Modeling Graphs

The surface friction coefficient and heat transfer rate results from the training, validation, and test sets of the ANN model are displayed in Figures 4.8(a) and 4.8(b). Artificial neural network models include the necessary

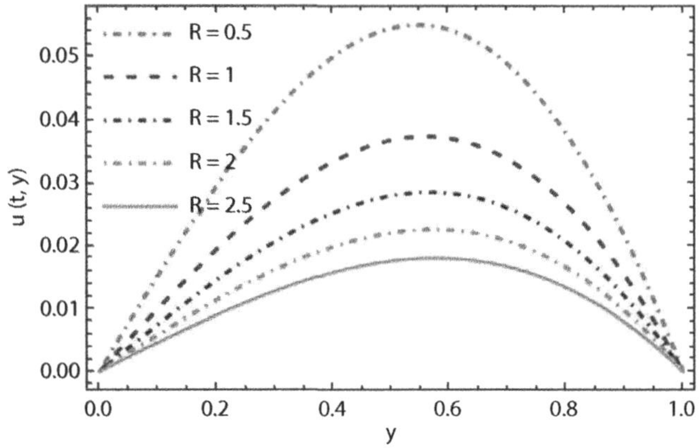

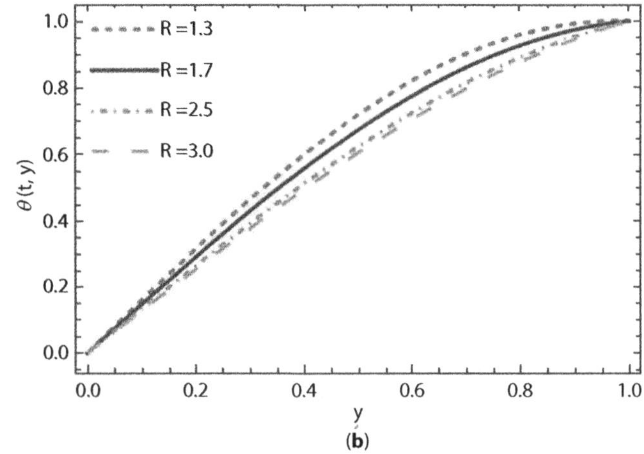

Figure 4.5 (a) Velocity profiles for *R*, (b) temperature profiles for *R*.

parts to replicate complex relationships between input and output variables, thanks to the bits provided. Comparing the ANN model's results with the computation-derived data reveals a high degree of conformance. As a result of network training, the MSE decreases, peaking between epochs 211 and 619. Something that can be seen is this. The enhanced iteration performance (MSE) of 0.1119E-4 and 8.00023E-10 is achieved at 211 and 619 epochs, respectively, for the skin friction and heat transfer rate.

Figures 4.9(a) and 4.9(b) illustrate a histogram of errors from the friction coefficient and Nusselt number, respectively. These graphs show the inconsistencies discovered in the ANN's aims when compared to its results.

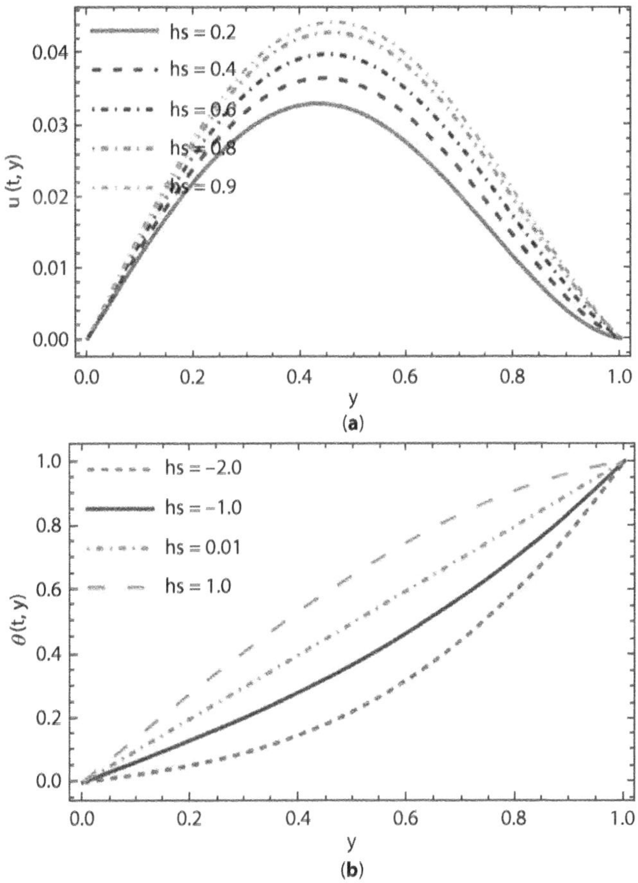

Figure 4.6 (a) Varying h_s on velocity profile, (b) varying h_s on temperature profiles.

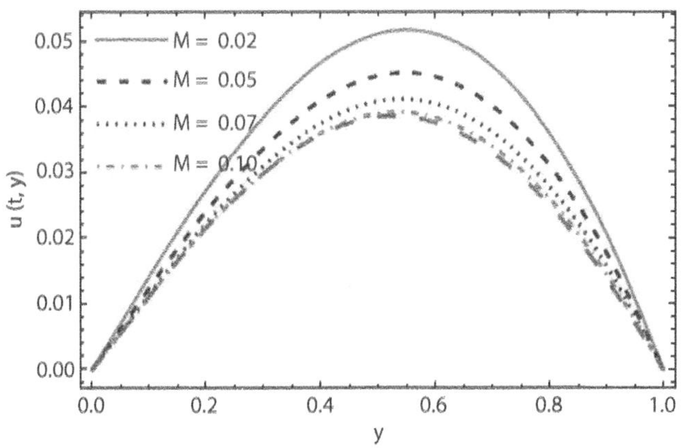

Figure 4.7 Impact of M on velocity distribution.

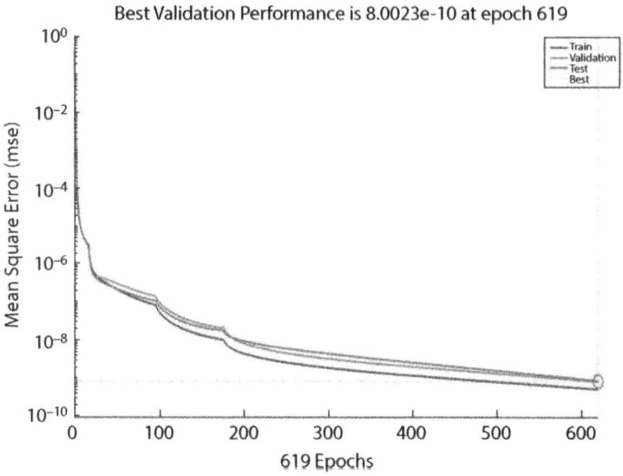

(a)

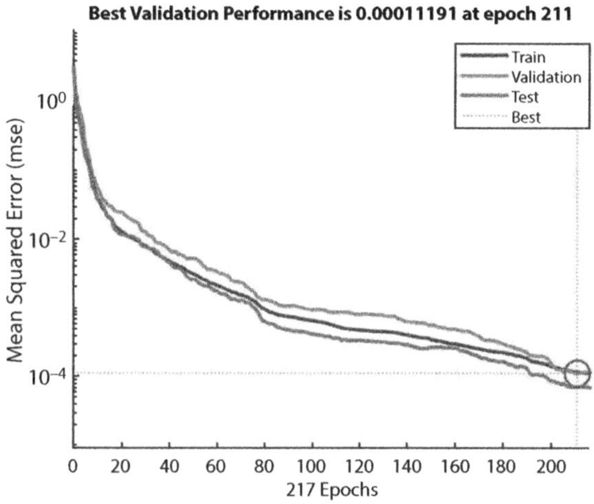

(b)

Figure 4.8 (a) and (b) Provide MSE performance graphs for the skinfriction coefficient and heat transfer rate.

When the error values along the x-axis of this histogram are considered, it becomes evident that these statistics are inconsequential. The data histogram was thoroughly reviewed, and the results revealed that the bulk of errors occurred at the yellow line, which represents the threshold for zero errors. The error counts in the histogram represent three independent data sets. Without a doubt, examining the error histogram reveals that the training phase of the ANN model was completed, as evidenced by the very low error frequency that it experienced.

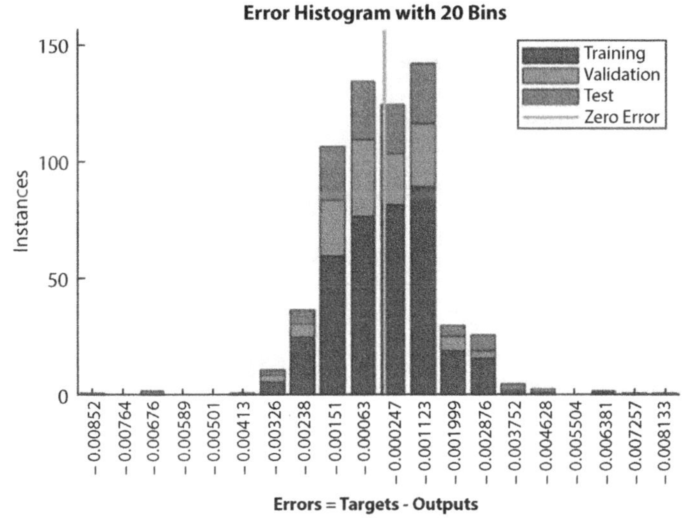

(a)

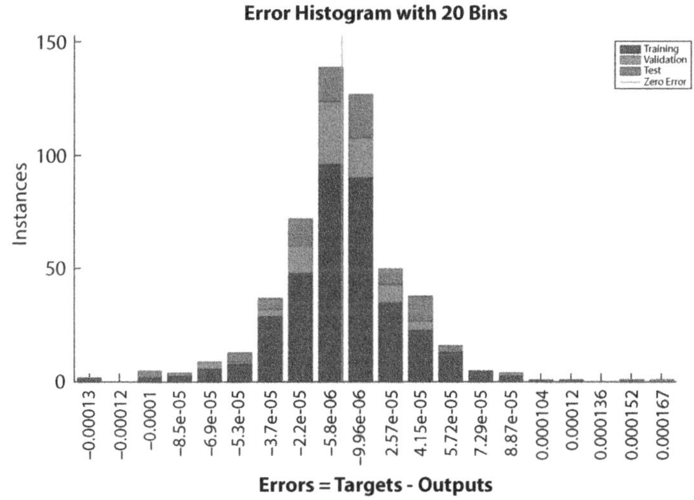

(b)

Figure 4.9 (a) and (b) For the error histogram of skin friction coefficient and heat transfer rate.

The findings of the skin frictional coefficient and heat transfer rate in the ANN model's training, validation, test, and validation sets are displayed in Figures 4.10(a) and 4.10(b). The fitting function is near the equation y = x, as seen by the four figures' excellent correlation between expected

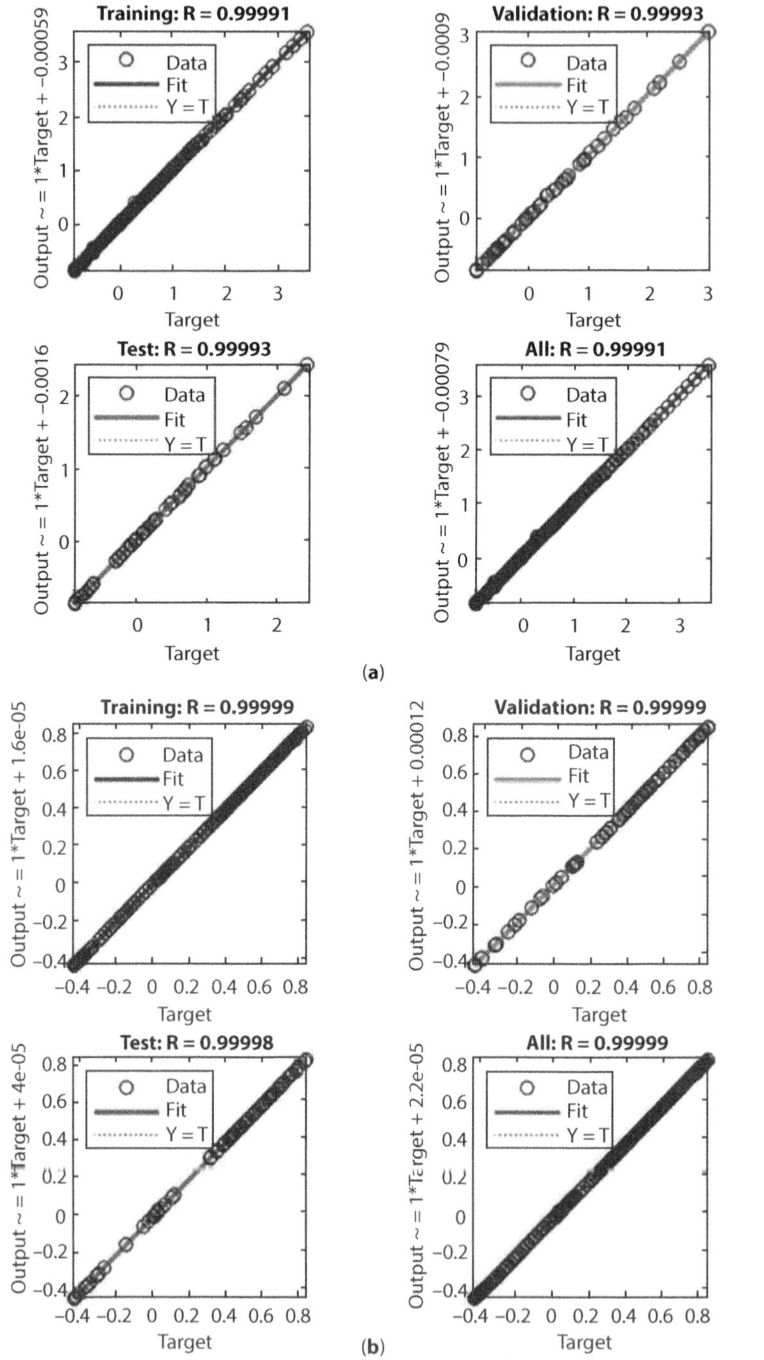

Figure 4.10 (a) and (b) Numerical and ANN model for the skinfriction factor and heat transfer rate.

and desired values. There is only one correlation coefficient per subplot. The effectiveness of the LMNN-BPA is established by the fact that the correlation coefficient, also referred to as the R-value, is equal to one over the whole trained regression graph between the computational model and numerical data.

4.5 Conclusions

The transient buoyancy-driven hybrid nanoliquid flow between two plates is investigated using ANNs, with consideration given to impact radiation, a magnetic field, and a changing heat source or sink. The modeled equations are resolved using the Laplace transformation, and some results will be drawn from the current study, which are:

- Rise of nanoparticle volume fraction results in a drop in temperature and velocity curves.
- Velocity declines as a boost in the magnetic parameter.
- Higher values of h_s rise in temperature and velocity are observed.
- Heat transfer grows with the collective nanoparticle volume fraction, resulting in shear stress as the plates drop.
- Enhancing the heat source or sink parameter improves temperature transfer through the left plate while lessening it through the right plate.
- An increase in the radiation parameter accelerates the rate of heat transfer.

References

1. Alzahrani, F. and Ijaz Khan, M.I., Entropy generation and Joule heating applications for Darcy Forchheimer flow of Ree-Eyring nanofluid due to double rotating disks with artificial neural network. *Alexandria Eng. J.*, 61, 3679–3689, 2022, DOI: 10.1016/j.aej.2021.08.071.
2. Rezaei Miandoab, A., Bagherzadeh, S.A., Meghdadi Isfahani, A.H., Numerical study of the effects of twisted-tape inserts on heat transfer parameters and pressure drop across a tube carrying Graphene Oxide nanofluid: An optimization by implementation of Artificial Neural Network and Genetic Algorithm. *Eng. Anal. Boundary Elem.*, 140, 1–11, 2022, DOI: 10.1016/j.enganabound.2022.04.006.

3. Shafiq, A., Çolak, A.B., Sindhu, T.N., Muhammad, T., Optimization of Darcy-Forchheimer squeezing flow in nonlinear stratified fluid under convective conditions with artificial neural network. *Heat Transfer Res.*, 3, 53, 2022.
4. Shafiq, A., Çolak, A.B., Naz Sindhu, T.N., Designing artificial neural network of nanoparticle diameter and solid–fluid interfacial layer on single-walled carbon nanotubes/ethylene glycol nanofluid flow on thin slandering needles. *Int. J. Numer. Methods Fluids*, 93, 3384–3404, 2021, DOI: 10.1002/fld.5038.
5. Shafiq, A., Çolak, A.B., Sindhu, T.N., Al-Mdallal, Q.M., Abdeljawad, T., Estimation of unsteady hydromagnetic Williamson fluid flow in a radiative surface through numerical and artificial neural network modeling. *Sci. Rep.*, 11, 14509, 2021, DOI: 10.1038/s41598-021-93790-9, PubMed: 34267255.
6. Shilpa, B. and Leela, V., LTNE effect on non-linear radiative MHD mixed convective flow in an annular porous medium: Intelligent Computing Paradigm. *Int. J. Ambient Energy*, 44, 1602–1617, 2023, DOI: 10.1080/01430750.2023.2180536.
7. Choi, S.U.S., Choi, Hrishikesh E., P., Heat transfer in nanofluids - a review. *Heat Tranfer Eng.*, 27, 3–19, 2006.
8. Eastman, J., Choi, S., Li, S., Thompson, L., Lee, S., Enhanced thermal conductivity through the development of nanofluids, in: *Fall Meeting of the Materials Research Society (MRS)*, Boston, USA, 1996.
9. Khanafer, K. and Vafai, K., Analysis of turbulent two-phase flow and heat transfer using nanofluid. *Int. Commun. Heat Mass Transfer*, 124, 105219, 2021, https://doi.org/10.1016/j.icheatmasstransfer.2021.105219.
10. Pavithra, K.M., Srilatha, P., Hanumagowda, B.N., Varma, S.V.K., Verma, A., Alkarni, S., *et al.*, A free convective two-phase fow of optically thick radiative ternary hybrid nanofuid in an inclined symmetrical channel through a porous medium. *Symmetry*, 15, 1615, 2023.
11. Das, P.K., A review based on the effect and mechanism of thermal conductivity of normal nanofluids and hybrid nanofluids. *J. Mol. Liq.*, 240, 420–446, 2017, https://doi.org/10.1016/J.MOLLIQ.2017.05.071.
12. Leong, K.Y., Ahmad, K.K., Ong, H.C., Ghazali, M.J., Baharum, A., Synthesis and thermal conductivity characteristic of hybrid nanofluids–a review. *Renew. Sustain. Energy Rev.*, 75, 868–878, 2017, https://doi.org/10.1016/j.rser.2016.11.068.
13. Toghraie, D., Chaharsoghi, V.A., Afrand, M., Measurement of thermal conductivity of ZnO–TiO 2/EG hybrid nanofluid. *J. Therm. Anal. Calorim.*, 125, 1, 527–535, 2016, https://doi.org/10.1007/s10973-016-5436-4.
14. Ahmadi, M.H., Mirlohi, A., Nazari, M.A., Ghasempour, R., A review of thermal conductivity of various nanofluids. *J. Mol. Liq.*, 265, 181–188, 2018, https://doi.org/10.1016/j.molliq.2018.05.124.
15. Alhajaj, Z., Bayomy, A.M., Saghir, M.Z., Rahman, M.M., Flow of Nanofluid and Hybrid fluid in Porous channels: Experimental and Numerical Approach. *Int. J. Thermofluids*, 1, 100016, 2020.

16. Madhukesh, J.K., Ramesh, G.K., Alsulami, M.D., Prasannakumara, B.C., Characteristic of thermophoretic effect and convective thermal conditions on flow of hybrid nanofluid over a moving thin needle. *Waves Random Complex Medium*, 34, 6, 5773–5795, 1–23, 2021, https://doi.org/10.1080/17455030.2021.2012303.
17. Batmunkh, M., Tanshen, M.R., Nine, M.J., Myekhlai, M., Choi, H., Chung, H., Jeong, H., Thermal conductivity of TiO_2 nanoparticles based aqueous nanofluids with an addition of a modified silver particle. *Ind. Eng. Chem. Res.*, 53, 8445–8451, 2014.
18. Sheikholeslami, M., Rashidi, M.M., Al Saad, D.M., Firouzi, F., Rokni, H.B., Domairry, G., Steady nanofluid flow between parallel plates considering thermophoresis and Brownian effects. *J. King Saud Univ. Sci.*, 28, 380–389, 2016.
19. Tarakaramu, N. and Narayana, P.V.S., Chemical reaction effects on bioconvectionnanofluid flow between two parallel plates in rotating system with variable viscosity: A numerical study. *J. Appl. Comput. Mech.*, 5, 4, 791–803, 2019.
20. Sheikholeslami, M. and Ganji, D.D., Nanofluid flow and heat transfer between parallel plates considering Brownian motion using DTM. *Comput. Methods Appl. Mech. Eng.*, 283, 651–663, 2015.
21. Hatami, M., Jing, D., Song, D., Sheikholeslami, M., Ganji, D.D., Heat transfer and flow analysis of nanofluid flow between parallel plates in presence of variable magnetic field using HPM. *J. Magn. Magn. Mater.*, 396, 275–282, 2015.
22. Alzwayi, A.S. and Paul, M.C., Transition of free convection flow between two isothermal vertical plates. *Int. J. Heat Mass Transfer*, 76, 307–316, 2014.
23. Bhargava, R., Kumar, L., Takhar, H.S., Numerical solution of free convection MHD micropolar fluid flow between two parallel porous vertical plates. *Int. J. Eng. Sci.*, 41, 123–136, 2003.
24. Ali, G., Ali, F., Khan, A., Ganie, A.H., Khan, I., A generalized magnetohydrodynamic two-phase free convection flow of dusty Casson fluid between parallel plates. *Case Stud. Therm. Eng.*, 29, 101657, 2022.
25. Nasr, A. and Al-Ghamdi, A.S., Numerical study of evaporation of falling liquid film on one of two vertical plates covered with a thin porous layer by free convection. *Int. J. Therm. Sci.*, 112, 335–344, 2017.
26. Sheikholeslami, M. and Ganji, D.D., Heat transfer of Cu-water nanofluid flow between parallel plates. *Powder Technol.*, 235, 873–879, 2013.
27. Hajizadeh, A., Shah, N.A., Shah, S.I.A., Animasaun, I.L., Rahimi-Gorji, M., Alarifi, I.M., Free convection flow of nanofluids between two vertical plates with damped thermal flux. *J. Mol. Liq.*, 289, 110964, 2019.
28. Narahari, M., Alaparthi, N., Pop, I., Exact analysis of the transient free convection flow of nanofluids between two vertical parallel plates in the presence of radiation. *Can. J. Chem. Eng.*, 95, 11, 2186–2198, 2017.

29. Dib, A., Haiahem, A., Bou-said, B., Approximate analytical solution of squeezing unsteady nanofluid flow. *Powder Technol.*, 269, 193–199, 2015.
30. Esfe, M.H., Arani, A.A.A., Azizi, T., Mousavi, S.H., Wongwises, S., Numerical study of laminar-forced convection of Al2O3-water nanofluids between two parallel plates. *J. Mech. Sci. Technol.*, 31, 785–796, 2017.
31. Hayat, T., Muhammad, T., Qayyum, A., Alsaedi, A., Mustafa, M., On squeezing flow of nanofluid in the presence of magnetic field effects. *J. Mol. Liq.*, 213, 179–185, 2016.
32. Salehi, S., Nori, A., Hosseinzadeh, K., Ganji, D.D., Hydrothermal analysis of MHD squeezing mixture fluid suspended by hybrid nanoparticles between two parallel plates. *Case Stud. Therm. Eng.*, 21, 100650, 2020.

5

Artificial Intelligence-Based Optimization of Heat Transfer in Gyrotactic-Nanofluid Flow

Priyanka Chandra[1] **and Raja Das**[2*]

[1]*Department of Mathematics, SR University, Warangal, Telangana, India*
[2]*Department of Mathematics, School of Advanced Sciences, Vellore Institute of Technology (VIT), Vellore, India*

Abstract

This chapter presents a central composite factorial design (CCFD)-based artificial neural network (ANN) model to optimize the heat transfer rates in a two-dimensional, steady, laminar-boundary layer flow for a nanofluid consisting of gyrotactic microorganisms on a nonlinear stretching plate. The base fluid, water, is selected to facilitate fluid flow stimulation. This flow problem occurs in various industrial and engineering applications, such as aerodynamic heating and polymer processing. Appropriate similarity transformations are employed to translate the governing partial differential equations with boundary conditions into nonlinear third-order ordinary differential equations for numerical computations. The Runge–Kutta fourth-order method is employed for simulating transformed highly nonlinear ordinary differential equations. The influence of physical parameters on the temperature, velocity, concentration, and microbe density profiles is examined through visual representations. A unique neural network is designed to optimize the Nusselt number with the numerical data displayed in both graphical and tabular formats. This research is pivotal for industrial and engineering applications, enabling the precise control of heat transfer rates through the optimization of critical parameters.

Keywords**:** Bio-nanofluids, artificial neural network, central composite factorial design, heat transfer

**Corresponding author*: rajadasrkl@gmail.com

Mukesh Kumar Awasthi and Reshu Gupta (eds.) Artificial Intelligence and Computational Modeling in Heat Transfer and Fluid Dynamics, (117–140) © 2026 Scrivener Publishing LLC

5.1 Introduction

Heat and mass transmission in diverse thermal systems has a huge potential when nanofluids and microorganisms are combined. To enhance energy transfer within the flow system, various types of fluids are now employed. Nonetheless, it is often seen that the final product is considerably affected by temperature fluctuations resulting from insufficient thermal conductivity. Consequently, the enhancement of the effectiveness of metallic flakes combined with base fluids, referred to as "nanofluid," was proclaimed by Buongiorno. The term "nanofluid" was initially introduced by Choi [1] in the context of thermophoresis and the limitations of Brownian motion. The impact of non-Newtonian nanofluids on an extended surface was investigated by Khan and Gorla [2]. Noghrehabadadi *et al.* [3] examined the heat transfer of nanofluids over a stretched subsurface, assuming thermally convective boundary conditions and partial slip. Rahman *et al.* [4] illustrated heat transfer *via* an inclined permeable plate in a micropolar fluid with variable fluid properties. Kuznetsov and Avramenko [5] illustrated the bioconvection of nanoparticles influenced by gyrotactic bacteria on a convectively heated horizontal panel.

The term bioconvection was first employed in a publication by James Henry Platt [6] to highlight the mechanics of the streaming formations observed in impenetrable patterns of free-floating microorganisms. The phenomenon results from the ascension of microorganisms in a fluid that is thicker than the underlying fluid. It is a mesoscale phenomenon wherein the locomotion of microorganisms generates macroscopic motion. The primary cause of up-swimming, possibly attributed to oxygen consumption, gravitational force, and other factors, is intricately linked to the sorts of microorganisms involved. Kuznetsov [7] examined bioconvection occurring across a horizontally oriented, thermally active surface influenced by gyrotactic bacteria. The flow of bioconvective nanofluid with various thermophysical parameters was investigated by Begum *et al.* [8].

Numerous researchers have demonstrated considerable interest in diverse numerical and analytical techniques for examining numerous coupled boundary layer fluid dynamics systems, including the finite element method [9, 10], homotopy analysis method [11], finite difference method [12], and differential transform method [13], among others. The existing solutions for these problems in the literature rely solely on established deterministic numerical and analytical techniques; hence, it is essential to explore stochastic computing methods grounded in numerical intelligence approaches.

Thus, in this chapter, we introduce a central composite factorial design (CCFD)-based artificial neural network (ANN) model to optimize heat transfer rates in the two-dimensional, steady, laminar boundary layer flow of a water-based nanofluid containing gyrotactic microorganisms over a nonlinear stretching plate. The coupled partial differential equations are converted into third-order ordinary differential equations. The transformed nonlinear ordinary differential equations are resolved by the Runge–Kutta fourth-order technique. We present graphical representations of the effects of various flow parameters on fluid velocity (f'), temperature (θ), nanoparticle volume fraction (ϕ), and density of motile microorganisms (χ). The optimization of the Nusselt number *via* the CCFD-ANN model is demonstrated through 3D surface plots. The model's accuracy and effectiveness are validated using mean squared error (MSE)-based fitness plots, residual plots, regression analysis, and error histograms. The proposed fluid flow problem occurs in various engineering and industrial applications, including biomedical and automotive cooling, biomedicine, nanodrug delivery, and pharmacy.

5.2 Mathematical Modeling

The research examines a two-dimensional steady mixed convection of incompressible, laminar boundary layer flow of nanofluid including gyrotactic microorganisms across an extending vertical surface inclined at an angle φ within porous media. Water is chosen as the foundation fluid to enhance fluid flow stimulation. The plate is raised vertically along its axis with a velocity $U_w = ax^n$, where a and n are arbitrary constants. Considering the concentration C_w, temperature T_w, and microbe density M_w of the plate surface is greater than the ambient concentration C_∞, temperature T_∞, and microbe density M_∞, respectively. The equations for continuity, momentum, nanoparticle concentration, and microorganism density are formulated as:

$$\frac{\partial u}{\partial x} + \frac{\partial v}{\partial y} = 0 \tag{5.1}$$

$$\left(u\frac{\partial u}{\partial x} + v\frac{\partial u}{\partial y}\right)\rho_f - \frac{\partial^2 u}{\partial y^2}\mu^* + \frac{u\mu^*}{K^*} - g\begin{bmatrix}\rho_f V_f (1 - C_\infty)(T - T_\infty) - (\rho_n - \rho_f)(C - C_\infty) \\ -\vartheta(\rho_m - \rho_f)(M - M_\infty)\end{bmatrix}\cos(\varphi) = 0 \tag{5.2}$$

$$u\frac{\partial T}{\partial x}+v\frac{\partial T}{\partial y}=\left[\frac{\partial T}{\partial y}\frac{\partial C}{\partial y}D_B+\left(\frac{\partial T}{\partial y}\right)^2\frac{D_T}{T_\infty}\right]\tau+\alpha_f\frac{\partial^2 T}{\partial y^2} \tag{5.3}$$

$$u\frac{\partial C}{\partial x}+v\frac{\partial C}{\partial y}=\frac{\partial^2 C}{\partial y^2}D_B+\frac{\partial^2 T}{\partial y^2}\frac{D_T}{T_\infty} \tag{5.4}$$

$$u\frac{\partial M}{\partial x}+v\frac{\partial M}{\partial y}=\frac{\partial^2 M}{\partial y^2}D_n-\frac{b_c W_C}{(C_w-C_\infty)}\frac{\partial}{\partial y}\left(M\frac{\partial C}{\partial y}\right) \tag{5.5}$$

with boundary conditions

$$\begin{cases} at\ y=0; \quad u=ax^n,\ v=0,\ \ T=T_w,\ \ C=C_w,\ \ M=M_w \\ as\ y\to\infty;\ u\to 0,\ \ v\to 0,\ \ T\to T_\infty,\ \ C\to C_\infty,\ \ M\to M_\infty \end{cases} \tag{5.6}$$

To render the governing equations and boundary conditions dimensionless, we construct a stream function $\psi(x;y)$ that satisfies $u|=\partial\Psi/\partial y$ and $v=-\partial\Psi/\partial x$, with the similarity variables defined as follows:

$$\eta=\sqrt{\frac{U_w(n+1)}{2xv}}y,\psi=a\sqrt{\frac{2xvU_w}{n+1}}f(\eta),\ \theta(\eta)=\frac{T-T_\infty}{T_w-T_\infty},\phi(\eta)$$
$$=\frac{C-C_\infty}{C_w-C_\infty},\chi(\eta)=\frac{M-M_\infty}{M_w-M_\infty} \tag{5.7}$$

Substituting Equation (5.7) into Equations (5.2–5.5):

$$f'''+ff''-\lambda f'-\frac{2n}{n+1}(f')^2+\cos(\varphi)\frac{2Ri}{n+1}\left[\theta-Nr\phi-Rb\chi\right]=0 \tag{5.8}$$

$$\theta''+\Pr\left[f\theta'+Nb\phi'\theta'+Nt(\theta')^2\right]=0 \tag{5.9}$$

$$Nb\left[\phi'' + Lef\varphi'\right] + Nt\theta'' = 0 \tag{5.10}$$

$$\chi'' + Lb\Pr f\chi' - Pe\phi''\left[\chi + \chi'\right] - \sigma Pe\phi' = 0 \tag{5.11}$$

Along with boundary conditions:

$$\begin{cases} f = 0, \quad f' = 1, \quad \theta = 1, \quad \phi = 1, \ \chi = 1, & at\ \eta = 0, \\ f' \to 0, \quad \theta \to 0, \quad \phi \to 0, \quad \chi \to 0 & as\ \eta \to \infty \end{cases} \tag{5.12}$$

In the above equations, Pe represents the Peclet number, Le is the Lewis number, Nb is the Brownian motion parameter, and Nt stands for the thermophoresis parameter. λ is the porosity parameter, Nr is the buoyancy ratio parameter, Ri is the Richardson number, Rb is the bio-convection Rayleigh number, σ is the motile parameter, and Pr is the Prandtl number.

$$Nr = \frac{(\rho_n - \rho_\infty)\Delta C}{\rho_\infty V_f (1 - C_\infty)\Delta T}, Ri = \frac{Gr_x}{\mathrm{Re}_x{}^2} = \frac{V_f l^2 g \Delta T}{x U_0^2},$$

$$Rb = \frac{\vartheta(\rho_m - \rho_\infty)\Delta M}{\rho_\infty V_f (1 - C_\infty)\Delta T}, \lambda = \frac{v}{aK^* x^{n-1}},$$

$$Le = \frac{v}{D_B \Delta C}, \ \Pr = \frac{v}{\alpha}, \ Nt = \frac{\tau D_T \Delta T}{v T_\infty}, Nb = \frac{\tau D_B \Delta C}{v T_\infty}, Lb = \frac{D_B}{D_n},$$

$$\sigma = \frac{M_\infty}{M_w - M_\infty}$$

The skin friction coefficient Cf_x, local Nusselt number Nu_x, local Sherwood number Sh_x, and the microbes-density number Mn_x are defined as follows:

$$Cf = \frac{2\tau_w}{U_w^2 \rho}, \ Nu = \frac{q_s x}{k\Delta T}, \ Sh = \frac{q_h x}{D_B \Delta C}, \ Mn = \frac{q_n x}{D_n \Delta M}$$

Here, τ_w, q_s, q_h *and* q_n are the mass flux, shear stress, heat flux, and microbes flux of the surface, respectively, given by:

$$\tau_w = -\mu\left(\frac{\partial u}{\partial y}\right)_{y=a}, q_s = -k\left(\frac{\partial T}{\partial y}\right)_{y=a}, q_h = -D_B\left(\frac{\partial C}{\partial y}\right)_{y=a},$$
$$q_n = -D_n\left(\frac{\partial M}{\partial y}\right)_{y=a}$$

By applying similarity transformations, the aforementioned equation is transformed to:

$$\frac{Cf_x\sqrt{\mathrm{Re}_x}}{2} = -f''(0), \frac{Nu_x}{\sqrt{\mathrm{Re}_x}} = -\theta'(0), \frac{Sh_x}{\sqrt{\mathrm{Re}_x}} = -\varphi'(0),$$
$$\frac{Mn_x}{\sqrt{\mathrm{Re}_x}} = -\chi'(0)$$

Here, $Re_x = U_0 x^2 / vl$ is the local Reynolds number.

5.3 Numerical Method

The nonlinear differential Equations (5.8–5.13) are converted into a simultaneous system of first-order ordinary differential equations by a linearity technique.

$$z_1 = f, z_2 = f', z_3 = f'', z_4 = \theta, \ z_5 = \theta', z_6 = \phi, z_7 = \phi', \ z_8 = \chi, \text{ and } z_9 = \chi'.$$

$$z_1' = z_2, \quad z_2' = z_3,$$
$$z_3' = -ff'' + \lambda f' + \frac{2n}{n+1}(f')^2 - \cos(\varphi)\frac{2Ri}{n+1}\left[\theta - Nr\phi - Rb\gamma\right],$$
$$z_4' = z_5, z_5' = -\Pr\left[f\theta' + Nb\phi'\theta' + Nt(\theta')^2\right],$$
$$z_6' = z_7, z_7' = (-Nt\theta'' - NbLef\varphi')/Nb,$$
$$z_8' = z_9, z_9' = -Lb\Pr f\chi' + Pe\phi''\left[\chi + \chi'\right] + \sigma Pe\phi' \quad (5.13)$$

With the initial conditions

$$Z_1(0)=0, Z_2(0)=0, Z_3(0)=s_1, Z_4(0)=1, Z_5(0)=s_2, Z_6(0)=1, Z_7(0) \\ = s_3, Z_8(0)=1, \ Z_9(0)=s_4 \tag{5.14}$$

Where s_1, s_2, s_3, s_4 are random parameters to be ascertained. The system of Equation (5.13) and initial conditions (5.14) is resolved by employing the fourth-order Runge–Kutta method in conjunction with the shooting method utilizing the Mathematica program. The program verifies the error to meet the subsequent final requirements.

$$Z_2(\infty)=0, \ Z_4(\infty)=0, Z_6(\infty)=0, Z_8(\infty)=0 \tag{5.15}$$

5.4 Results and Discussions

This section has been devoted to presenting the numerical results of the proposed problem, Equations (5.8–5.12), and optimizing the heat and mass transfer rates. The problem was solved with the Runge–Kutta fourth-order approach in conjunction with the target acquisition methodology, and the calculated values are displayed in Figures 5.1–5.6. Later, the optimization process is conducted using a CCFD-based ANN, which was discussed in Sections 5.4.1 and 5.4.2. We utilized the subsequent default values to produce graphs and tables: $R_b=0.1$, $Le=3$, $Ri=0.1$, $Nr=0.3$, $\alpha=\frac{\pi}{6}$, $\sigma=0.2$, $L_b=0.5$, $\lambda=0.5$, $Pr=5$, $Pe=0.1$, $n=1$, $N_b=0.5$, and $Nt=0.2$.

The effect of Brownian motion (Nb) on temperature $\theta(\eta)$ and concentration $\phi(\eta)$ are shown in Figures 5.1 and 5.2. The Nb parameter quantifies the degree of irregular movement of suspended nanoparticles inside the nanofluid. The data indicate that an increase in the Nb parameter results in an inflation of $\theta(\eta)$ whereas $\phi(\eta)$ declines. Raising the temperature enhances the energy of particles, resulting in increased random motion and accelerated collisions, hence intensifying Brownian motion. As concentration increases, the accessible space for particle movement diminishes, thereby decreasing the probability of a collision.

Figure 5.3 illustrates the impact of the thermophoresis parameter (Nt) on the fluid temperature. It indicates that $\theta(\eta)$ increases with greater values of Nt. Increasing the temperature of the fluid elevates the thermal gradient, which in turn enhances the intermediate force. Figure 5.4 illustrates

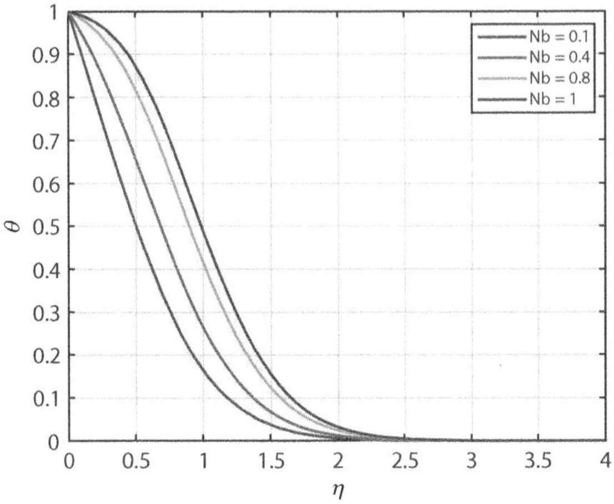

Figure 5.1 Impact of *Nb* on $\theta(\eta)$.

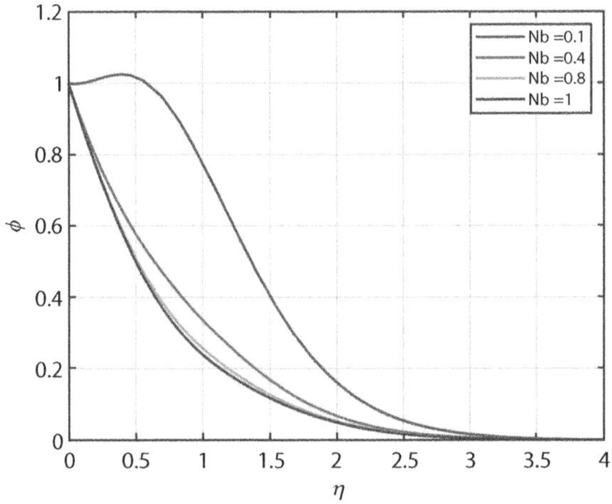

Figure 5.2 Impact of *Nb* on $\phi(\eta)$.

the influence of the Lewis number (*Le*) on the concentration of nanoparticle $\phi(\eta)$. The thermal diffusivity is evaluated relative to the mass diffusivity through the dimensionless Lewis number. From the illustration, it is evident that $\phi(\eta)$ decreases as *Le* values increase.

Figures 5.5 and 5.6 illustrate the influence of the Prandtl number (*Pr*) on temperature $\theta(\eta)$ and the density of microorganisms $\chi(\eta)$. It demonstrates that both $\theta(\eta)$ and $\chi(\eta)$ significantly decrease with increasing

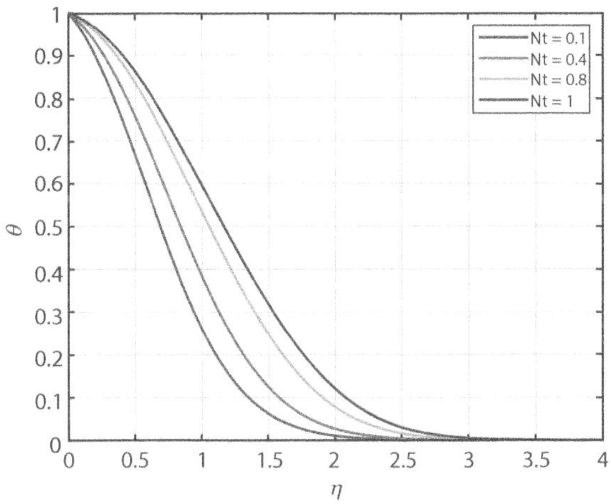

Figure 5.3 *Nt* versus $\theta(\eta)$.

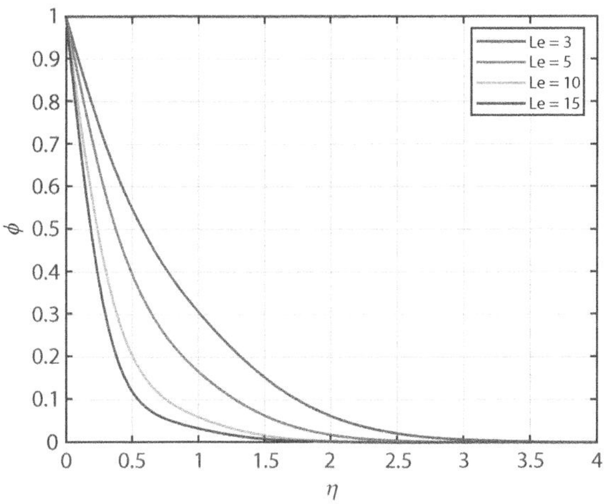

Figure 5.4 *Le* versus $\phi(\eta)$.

values of the *Pr*. The relationship between heat diffusivity and momentum diffusivity is characterized by the dimensionless Prandtl number. This value compares the effects of thermal conductivity against those of fluid viscosity. The value of the Prandtl number can determine the type of fluid being analyzed.

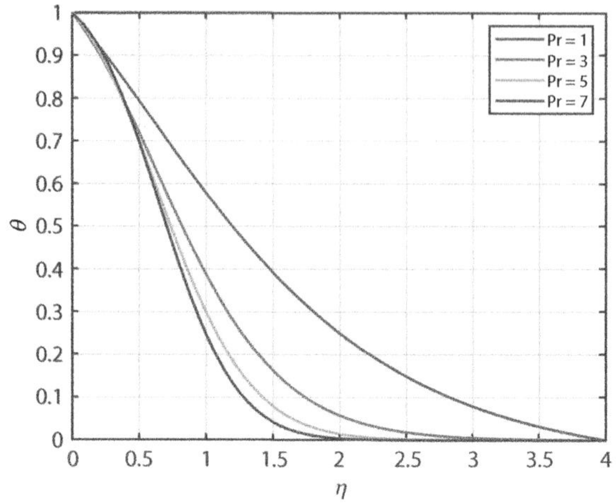

Figure 5.5 *Pr* versus $\theta(\eta)$.

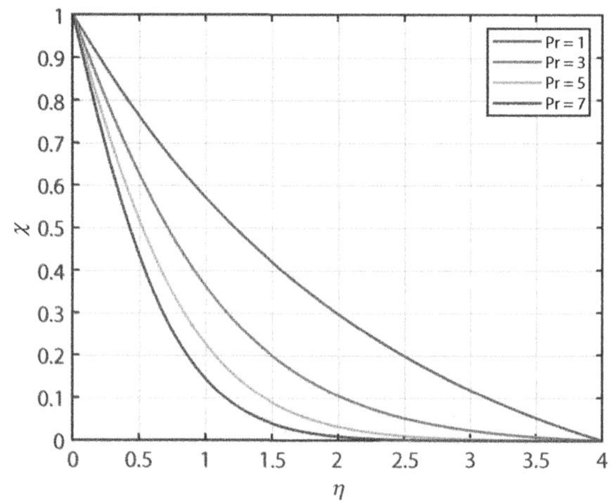

Figure 5.6 *Pr* versus $\chi(\eta)$.

5.4.1 Optimization Process

An ANN is an effective instrument for delineating a wide array of factors, utilizing limited resources, quantitative data, and requisite experimental design. The phases involved in an ANN are as follows:

1. Before training the neural network, the input and target data undergo normalization. Normalization guarantees that the

input and target values are adjusted to the range [0, 1], hence enhancing the stability and efficiency of the training process.
2. The dataset will be partitioned into three subsets: 70% for training, 15% for validation, and 15% for testing.
3. The loss function will be established by employing the target output and the projected output.
4. The weights and biases are updated, and the loss function is minimized *via* the Levenberg–Marquardt (LM) algorithm as described below:

5.4.1.1 Levenberg–Marquardt Algorithm

The LM approach was created to attain second-order training efficiency without the need to compute the Hessian matrix. When the performance value is represented as a sum of squares, a common practice in developing feedforward networks, the Hessian matrix could be estimated as $H = J^T J$, and the gradient can also be approximated as $g^* = J^T e$. Here, J represents the Jacobian matrix comprising the initial derivatives of the network errors, which concern the weights and biases, whereas e is an array of network errors. The calculation of the Jacobian matrix is simpler than that of the Hessian matrix and may be done with a standard backpropagation approach.

The LM algorithm employs this estimate of the Hessian matrix in the subsequent Newton-like update:

$$x_{k+1} = x_k - [J^T J + \mu I]^{-1} - J^T e$$

When μ = 0, this aligns with Newton's methodology employing the approximate Hessian matrix. When μ is significant, this converts into gradient descent with a small step size. Newton's approach exhibits superior speed and accuracy in proximity to an error minimum; thus, the objective is to transition to Newton's method expeditiously. Consequently, μ decreases after each completed step (down in the performance function) and increases only when a proposed step will improve the performance function. As a result, the performance function is consistently reduced at every stage of the technique.

The introductory explanation of the LM algorithm is presented [14]. The utilization of the LM algorithm for neural network training is detailed [15] and can be read from pages 12 to 19 [16]. This algorithm seems to be the most efficient approach for training moderately sized feedforward neural networks (up to several hundred weights).

5.4.2 Optimization Analysis by the Central Composite Factorial Design and Artificial Neural Network, Central Composite Factorial Design

The relationship between the responding variable and factor variables was analyzed using a face-CCFD. We used CCFD as it decreases the needed experiments to assess an ANN model relative to a full factorial design, hence enhancing cost and time efficiency. Table 5.1 outlines the included criteria and the corresponding levels.

The continuous ANN output for heat transfer rate (Nu_x) is given by:

$$\begin{aligned} Nu_x(Nb,\Pr,n) = {} & \delta_1\left(\frac{2}{1+e^{-(\alpha_1 Nb+\beta_1 \Pr+\omega_1 n+\kappa_1)}}-1\right) \\ & +\delta_2\left(\frac{2}{1+e^{-(\alpha_2 Nb+\beta_2 \Pr+\omega_2 n+\kappa_2)}}-1\right)+\cdots \\ & +\delta_m\left(\frac{2}{1+e^{-(\alpha_m Nb+\beta_m \Pr+\omega_m n+\kappa_m)}}-1\right)+\aleph \end{aligned} \tag{5.16}$$

Here, $\alpha_i, \beta_i, \omega_i, \delta_i, \kappa_i$ and $\aleph$ are the weights and biases of the neural network. The m represents the number of hidden layer neurons. The tanh function or hyperbolic tangent function is used in the hidden layer of the designed neural network.

Table 5.1 Parameters and their corresponding levels for Nu_x.

	Level		
Parameters	-1	0	1
Nb	0.1	1.25	2.4
Pr	0.1	1.25	2.4
n	0.1	3.5	6.9

5.4.2.1 *Designing an Artificial Neural Network Model for $Nu_x(0)$ Against Nb, Pr, and n*

The present section analyzed the response of the three variables ***Nb***, ***Pr***, and ***n***. The optimal model is established, and a sensitivity analysis of the significant factors on $\boldsymbol{Nu_x(0)}$ is conducted. Table 5.2 illustrates the values of the output function at 27 distinct positions, which are obtained by using the RK4 method.

To construct an optimal model, a thorough analysis has been performed to investigate the impact of altering the number of neurons in the neural network's hidden layer. The analysis specifically explores the impact of utilizing between 1 and 30 neurons. Correlation coefficient values, mean absolute errors, and root mean square errors were calculated for the training, testing, and validation datasets. The calculated values for configurations with 1 to 10 hidden neurons are presented in Table 5.3. Table 5.3 demonstrates that the best results are obtained with two neurons in the hidden layer. Consequently, we have implemented a network with two hidden neurons (h_1 and h_2). The ANN architecture that has been designed is shown in Figure 5.7. The training process will terminate upon reaching any of the stopping criteria outlined in Table 5.4.

In the single-layer ANN utilizing backpropagation with the LM algorithm, 70% of the data was randomly designated for training, while 15% was assigned to each testing and validation. The training data was employed to derive an approximate solution utilizing the MSE metric. Testing data was employed to assess performance on impartial inputs, while validation data was used to optimize the neural networks.

The evaluation of artificial computer performance utilizing the MSE is depicted in Figure 5.8, while the gradient values are illustrated in Figure 5.9. The estimated MSE value reached its minimum at 1.9089×10^{-05} after 17 epochs. Figures 5.8 and 5.9 indicate that the gradient value achieved is 4.2992×10^{-08}, suggesting the optimal performance should be at 21 epochs. However, from the validation plot shown in Figure 5.10, it can be observed that the MSE increases continuously four times for the validation dataset values. As a result, the training process was halted at 17 epochs instead of

Table 5.2 Experimental design and responses.

Runs	Coded values			Responses of $Nu_x = -\theta'(0)$
	Nb	*Pr*	*N*	
1	-1	-1	-1	0.27757
2	-1	-1	0	0.27255
3	-1	-1	1	0.27200
4	-1	0	-1	0.56673
5	-1	0	0	0.52790
6	-1	0	1	0.52345
7	-1	1	-1	0.75360
8	-1	1	0	0.71213
9	-1	1	1	0.70727
10	0	-1	-1	0.25198
11	0	-1	0	0.24771
12	0	-1	1	0.24725
13	0	0	-1	0.19996
14	0	0	0	0.18427
15	0	0	1	0.18247
16	0	1	-1	0.11823
17	0	1	0	0.11035
18	0	1	1	0.10940
19	1	-1	-1	0.22852
20	1	-1	0	0.22493
21	1	-1	1	0.22456
22	1	0	-1	0.06181
23	1	0	0	0.05666
24	1	0	1	0.05607
25	1	1	-1	0.01249
26	1	1	0	0.01158
27	1	1	1	0.01147

Table 5.3 Evaluation of an ANN model performance with varying quantities of hidden layer neurons (m).

m	Correlation coefficient (r)				Mean absolute error (MSE)				Root mean square error (RMSE)			
	Train.	**Test.**	**Val.**	**All**	**Train.**	**Test.**	**Val.**	**All**	**Train.**	**Test.**	**Val.**	**All**
1	0.784985	0.777447	0.49634	0.747841	0.080609	0.167032	0.220586	0.11415	0.107155	0.199814	0.254351	0.153555
2	**0.999742**	**0.999864**	**0.999936**	**0.999427**	**0.003261**	**0.003491**	**0.009275**	**0.004186**	**0.004954**	**0.004369**	**0.015934**	**0.007597**
3	0.999934	0.999936	0.997837	0.999283	0.001506	0.00366	0.015428	0.003888	0.002329	0.004121	0.020984	0.00846
4	0.998116	0.978937	0.99632	0.991941	0.011668	0.033571	0.056305	0.021526	0.013696	0.041655	0.060892	0.030633
5	0.996966	0.999251	0.989147	0.994485	0.02031	0.022429	0.024738	0.02128	0.026576	0.024208	0.031067	0.02696
6	0.999336	0.995832	0.996795	0.996958	0.006115	0.037158	0.01356	0.011817	0.0093	0.038831	0.013897	0.017688
7	0.981772	0.961251	0.827347	0.939479	0.028268	0.053155	0.134473	0.047689	0.047608	0.084345	0.144824	0.075869
8	0.871315	0.89839	0.847338	0.86751	0.092496	0.067475	0.086239	0.087862	0.126283	0.081252	0.097033	0.116598
9	0.882651	0.830464	0.805945	0.836564	0.079916	0.044338	0.168283	0.087737	0.101383	0.055697	0.229072	0.124364
10	0.999973	0.995392	0.995719	0.99793	0.001862	0.031195	0.018634	0.008692	0.002235	0.03209	0.02124	0.01493

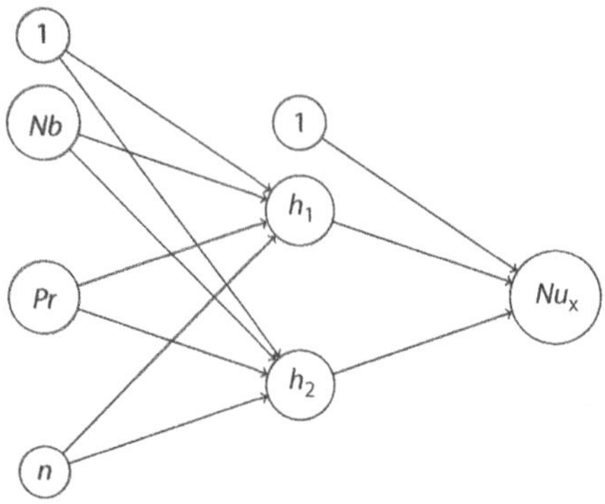

Figure 5.7 Structural layout of an ANN.

Table 5.4 Termination criteria for training the ANN model.

Unit	Initial value	Current value	Target value
Epoch	0	21	1000
Performance	0.413	2.45E-05	0
Gradient	0.649	4.30E-08	1.00E-07
Validation Checks	0	4	6

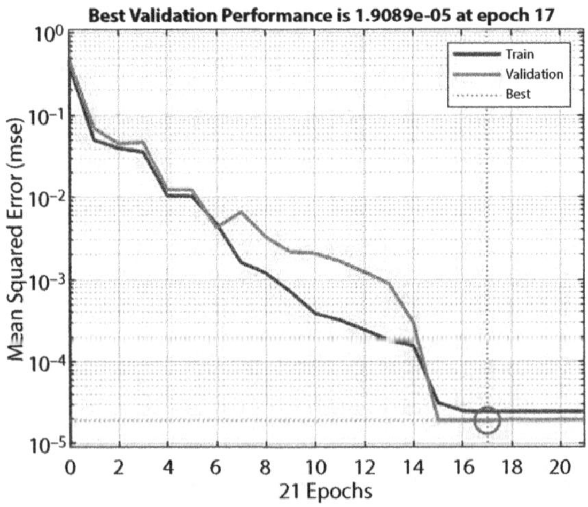

Figure 5.8 Mean squared error.

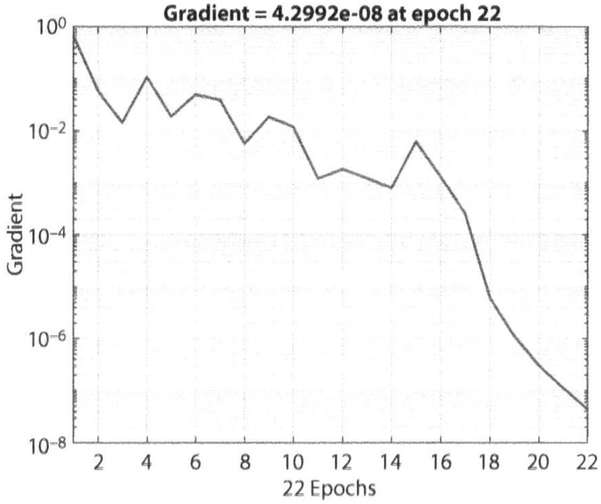

Figure 5.9 Gradient plot.

21 epochs. Consequently, the final ANN model was prepared using the MSE values of 1.9089×10^{-05} at 17 epochs. The finalized ANN model with optimized weights and biases is presented as follows:

$$Nu_x(Nb,\Pr,n) = -0.3244\left(\frac{2}{1+e^{-(1.194217Nb+1.811956\Pr+0.131342n-0.47641)}}-1\right) - 0.86819\left(\frac{2}{1+e^{-(2.382441Nb-1.56186\Pr+0.0136n+2.495117)}}-1\right) + 0.189811 \tag{5.17}$$

To validate the designed ANN model defined in Equation (5.17), error histograms, residual plots, and regression analyses were employed. Figure 5.11 uses error histograms to elucidate the error analysis for Nu_x. The bins approximate the target zero-line range of -3.4×10^{-04}. The residual plot is provided in Figure 5.12. The discrepancy found between the scatter plot and the expected y-value in the residual plot is referred to as the residual. The figure indicates that the majority of residuals lie around the zero line. Figure 5.13 displays the outcomes of the regression analysis. In all three datasets—validation, training, and testing—the correlation coefficient (R) is roughly 1, indicating optimal modeling accuracy. These confirm the accuracy and effectiveness of the proposed CCFD-based ANN model.

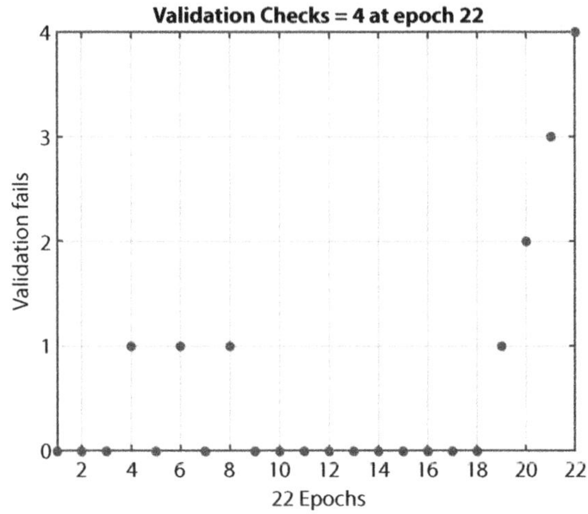

Figure 5.10 Validation plot.

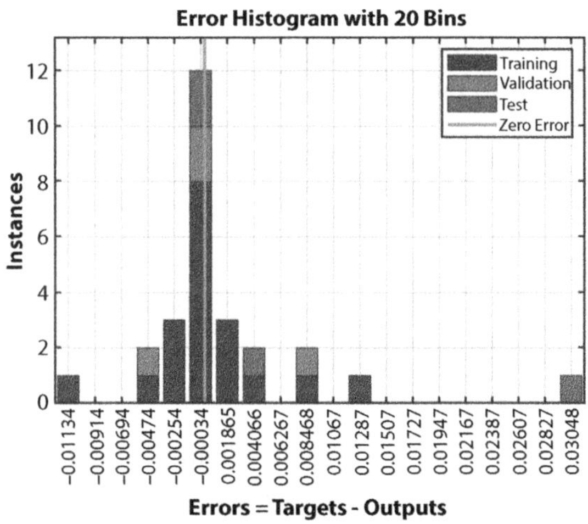

Figure 5.11 Error histogram plot.

The designed CCFD-ANN model is used to optimize the heat transfer rate (Nu_x). The effects of the Brownian motion parameter (Nb), the power index (n), and the Prandtl number (Pr) on the heat transfer rate (Nu_x) are discussed. Given the complexity of visualizing the effects of three parameters on Nu_x simultaneously, 3D surface plots were considered. These plots show the effects of two parameters at a time on Nu_x while keeping the third parameter constant. We have taken the 0th level value as the default

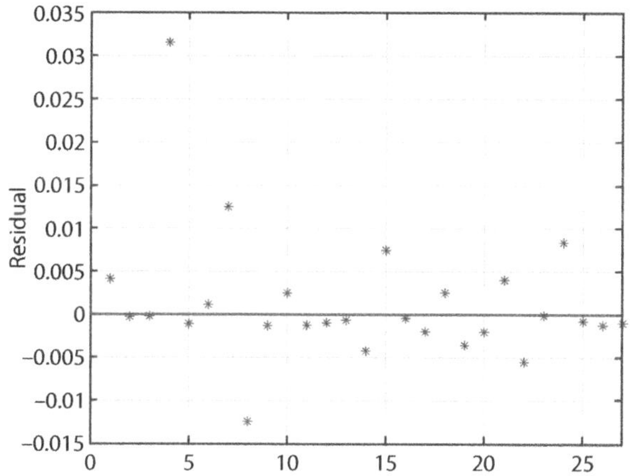

Figure 5.12 Residual plot.

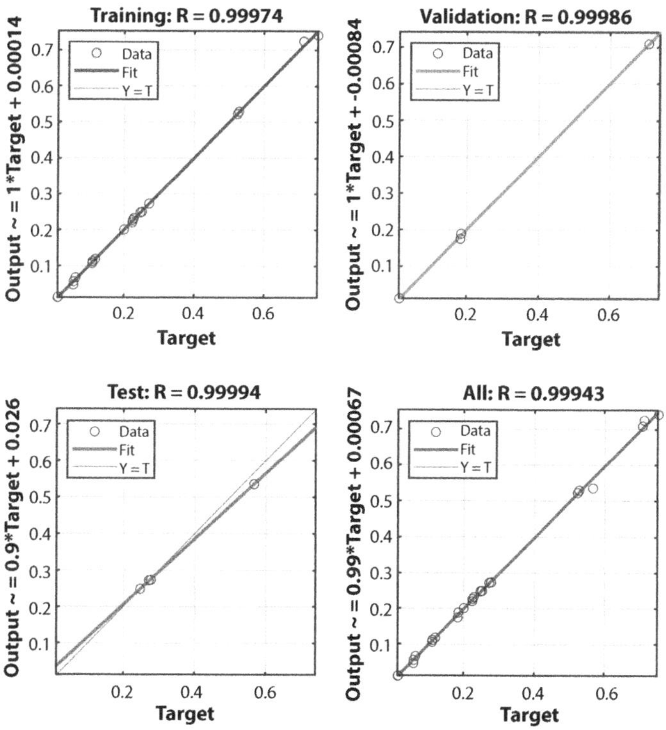

Figure 5.13 Regression analysis plot.

value for all constant parameters when drawing the 3D plots. Figure 5.14 illustrates the effect of the Brownian motion parameter (*Nb*) and the Prandtl number (*Pr*) on the heat transfer rate (Nu_x), with the power index (n) held constant. The surface plot shows that Nu_x is higher for larger values of *Nb* and *Pr*. Brownian motion refers to the stochastic movement of particles dispersed in a fluid medium. A higher value of *Nb* signifies an increased intensity of random motion. The augmented mobility facilitates the mixing of fluid particles, hence enhancing heat transmission *via* convection. The heightened activity results in a more effective transfer of heat energy between the fluid and the surface. The Prandtl number is the ratio of momentum diffusivity (viscosity) to thermal diffusivity. It quantifies the relative thickness of the velocity boundary layer in comparison to the thermal boundary layer. A higher *Pr* value indicates that the fluid possesses increased viscosity and less thermal diffusivity. Fluids with elevated Prandtl numbers have thicker velocity boundary layers and narrower thermal boundary layers. This leads to enhanced convective heat transfer as thermal energy is maintained at the surface and does not dissipate rapidly. The relationship between *n* and *Nb* on heat transfer rate is illustrated in Figure 5.15. Higher heat transfer rates are observed at lower n values, regardless of *Nb*. Similarly, Figure 5.16 depicts the influence of *Prand non* Nu_x. The peak Nu_x values are noted at reduced *n* values, independent of *Pr*.

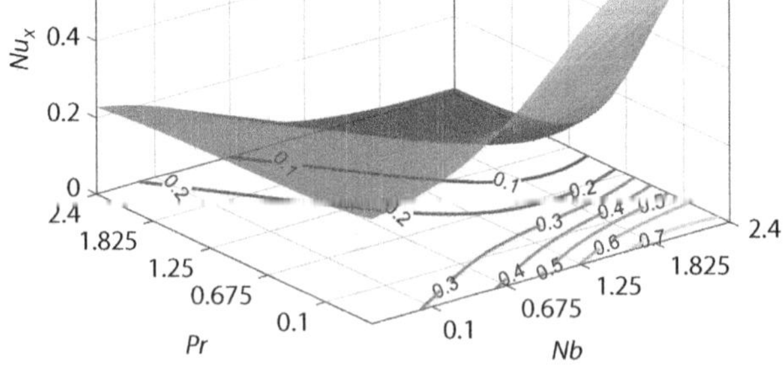

Figure 5.14 The effect of *Nb* and *Pr* on Nu_x.

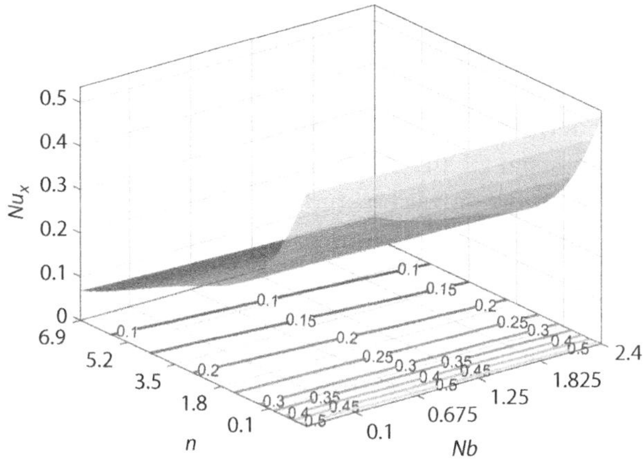

Figure 5.15 The effect of n and Nb on Nu_x.

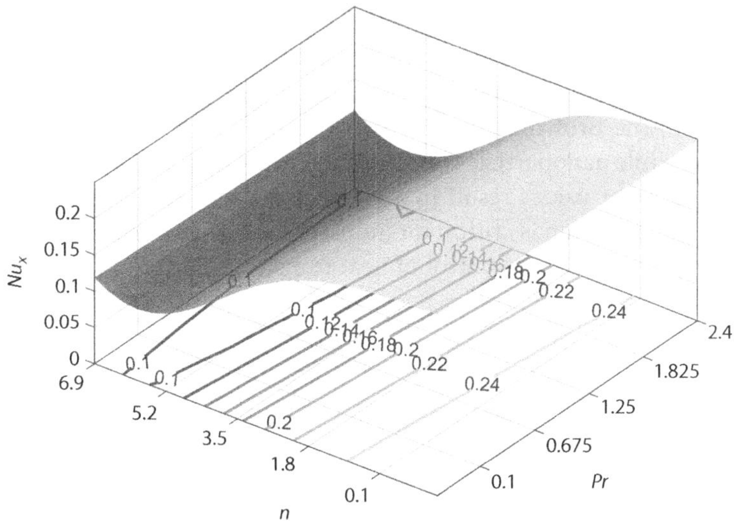

Figure 5.16 The effect of n and Nb on Nu_x.

5.5 Conclusions

This chapter introduces a CCFD-based ANN model aimed at optimizing heat transfer rates in the laminar, two-dimensional, steady, boundary layer flow of a water-based fluid consisting of gyrotactic microbes and nanoparticles over a nonlinear stretching plate. A unique neural network with CCFD is developed to optimize the heat transfer rate, with numerical data displayed in surface plots. The CCFD investigates both the center and the outer boundaries of the design space, guaranteeing a comprehensive understanding of the response behavior throughout the whole spectrum of interest. The proposed CCFD-ANN method represents an advanced iteration of ANN-based optimization studies, leveraging CCFD to encompass all possible combinations of various parameters. This approach allows for the approximation of solutions with greater precision due to the extensive array of data combinations considered. Additionally, unlike traditional ANN-based approaches that treat parameters as constants, this method introduces the parameters as variables, thereby enhancing the flexibility and accuracy of the optimization process. The Runge–Kutta fourth-order method is used to generate the reference dataset for the CCFD-ANN model. The main advantages of Runge–Kutta techniques include their ease of implementation, high stability, and self-starting nature, meaning that, in contrast to multi-step methods, the initial steps of a single-step integration method do not require special treatment. The influence of physical parameters on velocity, temperature, concentration, and microbe density profiles is examined through visual representations. The results indicate that an increase in the Brownian motion parameter leads to a rise in fluid temperature, while nanoparticle concentration decreases. Furthermore, higher Prandtl number values result in a significant decrease in microorganism density. This research is critical for industrial and engineering applications, as it enables the precise control of heat transfer rates through the optimization of key parameters.

References

1. Choi, S.U.S., Enhancing thermal conductivity of fluids with nanoparticles. *Am. Soc. Mech. Eng. Fluids Eng. Div. FED*, 231, 99–105, 1995.
2. Khan, W.A. and Gorla, R.S.R., Heat and mass transfer in non-Newtonian nanofluids over a non-isothermal stretching wall. *Proc. Inst. Mech. Eng., Part N: J. Nanoeng. Nanosyst.*, 225, 155–63, 2011, https://doi.org/10.1177/1740349912440680.
3. Pourrajab, R. and Noghrehabadi, A., Bioconvection of Nanofluid Past Stretching Sheet in a Porous Medium in Presence of Gyrotactic Microorganisms with Newtonian Heating. *MATEC Web Conf.*, 220, 01004, 2018.
4. Rahman, M.M., Aziz, A., Al-Lawatia, M.A., Heat transfer in micropolar fluid along an inclined permeable plate with variable fluid properties. *Int. J. Therm. Sci.*, 49, 993–1002, 2010, https://doi.org/10.1016/j.ijthermalsci.2010.01.002.

5. Kuznetsov, A.V. and Avramenko, A.A., Effect of small particles on this stability of bioconvection in a suspension of gyrotactic microorganisms in a layer of finite depth. *Int. Commun. Heat Mass Transfer*, 31, 1–10, 2004, https://doi.org/10.1016/S0735-1933(03)00196-9.
6. Platt, J.R., "Bioconvection patterns" in cultures of free-swimming organisms. *Science (80-)*, 133, 1766–7, 1961, https://doi.org/10.1126/science.133.3466.1766.
7. Kuznetsov, A.V., The onset of nanofluid bioconvection in a suspension containing both nanoparticles and gyrotactic microorganisms. *Int. Commun. Heat Mass Transfer*, 37, 1421–5, 2010, https://doi.org/10.1016/j.icheatmasstransfer.2010.08.015.
8. Begum, N., Siddiqa, S., Hossain, M.A., Nanofluid bioconvection with variable thermophysical properties. *J. Mol. Liq.*, 231, 325–32, 2017, https://doi.org/10.1016/j.molliq.2017.02.016.
9. Rana, P., Bè, R., Bég, O.A., Numerical solution for mixed convection boundary layer flow of a nanofluid along an inclined plate embedded in a porous medium. *Comput. Math. Appl.*, 64, 2816–32, 2012, https://doi.org/10.1016/j.camwa.2012.04.014.
10. Chandra, P. and Das, R., A hybrid machine learning algorithm for studying magnetized nanofluid flow containing gyrotactic microorganisms *via* a vertically inclined stretching surface. *Int. J. Numer. Method Biomed. Eng.*, 40, 1, e3780, 2023, https://doi.org/10.1002/CNM.3780.
11. Khan, A., Alyami, M.A., Alghamdi, W., Alqarni, M.M., Yassen, M.F., Tag Eldin, E., Thermal examination for the micropolar gold–blood nanofluid flow through a permeable channel subject to gyrotactic microorganisms. *Front. Energy Res.*, 10, 993247, 2022, https://doi.org/10.3389/fenrg.2022.993247.
12. Bég, O.A., Khan, M.S., Karim, I., Alam, M.M., Ferdows, M., Explicit numerical study of unsteady hydromagnetic mixed convective nanofluid flow from an exponentially stretching sheet in porous media. *Appl. Nanosci.*, 4, 943–57, 2014, https://doi.org/10.1007/s13204-013-0275-0.
13. Gireesha, B.J. and Sowmya, G., Heat transfer analysis of an inclined porous fin using Differential Transform Method. *Int. J. Ambient Energy*, 43, 3189–95, 2022, https://doi.org/10.1080/01430750.2020.1818619.
14. Marquardt, D.W., An Algorithm for Least-Squares Estimation of Nonlinear Parameters. *J. Soc. Ind. Appl. Math.*, 11, 431–41, 1963, https://doi.org/10.1137/0111030.
15. Hagan, M.T. and Menhaj, M.B., Training Feedforward Networks with the Marquardt Algorithm. *IEEE Trans. Neural Netw.*, 5, 989–93, 1994, https://doi.org/10.1109/72.329697.
16. Sabir, Z., Manzar, M.A., Raja, M.A.Z., Sheraz, M., Wazwaz, A.M., Neuro-heuristics for nonlinear singular Thomas-Fermi systems. *Appl. Soft Comput. J.*, 65, 152–69, 2018, https://doi.org/10.1016/j.asoc.2018.01.009.

6

Artificial Intelligence-Based Heat Exchanger Design and Optimization

Sachin Mishra[1*], Raj Kumar[1], Shailendra Singh Rathore[1], Sakshi Saxena[2], Pushpendra Sharma[1], Shubhra Khare[1] and Kuldeep Chauhan[1]

[1]*Department of Applied Sciences and Humanities, Invertis University Bareilly, Uttar Pradesh, India*
[2]*Institute of Applied Science, Mangalayatan University, Beswan, Aligarh, India*

Abstract
Artificial intelligence (AI) is important in minimizing costs, pressure drop, and the heat transfer area. This chapter uses AI techniques to forecast the application and performance of heat transfer coefficient, material thermal properties, and efficiencies with high accuracy according to the given parameters like geometry, properties, and operating conditions. This chapter explores how AI techniques contribute to computational fluid dynamics simulations by enhancing design accuracy, analyzing experimental data, and improving efficiency. This chapter contains machine learning (ML) methodologies and optimization algorithms that show the real world. In this chapter, we use AI techniques like ML, ANNs, and deep learning models that can be used to model complex, nonlinear relationships between design parameters and performance metrics. In this chapter, AI provides powerful tools to enhance the design and optimization of heat exchangers, offering greater efficiency and precision in the process. This chapter contains the working method and procedure of ML, optimization algorithms, and hybrid techniques while showcasing real-world applications and future trends in the field.

***Keywords*:** Artificial intelligence, computational fluid dynamics, trade credit, machine learning, pressure drop

**Corresponding author*: sachinmishra427@gmail.com; ORCID: 0009-0002-8088-4039
Raj Kumar: ORCID: 0009-0008-0653-3859
Shailendra Singh Rathore: ORCID: 0009-0001-9845-1306
Sakshi Saxena: ORCID: 0000-0003-3182-9156
Pushpendra Sharma: ORCID: 0000-0002-5525-6658
Shubhra Khare: ORCID: 0000-0003-3331-6602
Kuldeep Chauhan: ORCID: 0009-0001-6065-0078

Mukesh Kumar Awasthi and Reshu Gupta (eds.) Artificial Intelligence and Computational Modeling in Heat Transfer and Fluid Dynamics, (141–176) © 2026 Scrivener Publishing LLC

6.1 Introduction

Nowadays, artificial intelligence (AI) has an important role in science and technology. Artificial intelligence is transforming the design and optimization of heat exchangers by facilitating data-driven solutions and sophisticated prediction models. While AI offers quicker, more precise insights, traditional approaches frequently rely on laborious simulations and empirical connections. By utilizing machine learning (ML) techniques, designers may maximize thermal performance, save material costs, and increase energy efficiency. The following paragraphs give some background and motivation for the AI-based heat-exchanger design and optimization.

The global energy review states that energy demand exceeded pre-COVID-19 levels in 2021, increasing by 4.6% [4]. If primary energy consumption continues to expand at its current rate, it will rise by 75% between 2019 and 2050 [14]. Switching to decarbonized and renewable energy is the best strategy to meet the world's expanding energy needs while reducing the catastrophic environmental effects of fossil fuels [1]. Assessing the production of renewable energy for net-zero energy applications is essential when considering the strategic potential of multi-energy systems for the Sustainable Development Goals [2] of carbon neutrality with sustainable economic growth [3]. Space heating and cooling accounts for around 25% of Europe's energy consumption [8]. Even though the use of renewable energy has increased recently, only 21% of it is used for heating and cooling [17]. Consequently, increasing the sustainability and effectiveness of both cooling and heating will increase energy security, reduce costs for businesses, and individuals, and help the EU meet its greenhouse gas emission reduction goals [15].

In heat exchanger technology, AI has significantly advanced performance optimization and cost reduction. Deep learning (DL), expert, and ML techniques in AI systems offer notable improvements in predictive maintenance, performance optimization, and diagnostics. Machine learning provides flexibility through data analysis, but DL excels at identifying complex patterns. Expert systems generate recommendations based on domain knowledge but might not be as adaptable as data-driven approaches. Artificial intelligence can potentially revolutionize heat exchanger technology by improving efficiency and sustainability. Ongoing design advancements, materials, and AI techniques will drive future innovations, providing increasingly intricate answers to meet evolving performance and environmental standards. Heat exchangers are crucial parts of many industrial processes.

6.2 Artificial Intelligence-Based Heat Exchanger Design and Optimization

Including electricity manufacturing, heating, venting, and air conditioning (HVAC) systems, refrigeration, and chemical processing, they primarily transmit heat between two or more fluids, which may be liquids or gases [6]. A heat exchanger's design process is a complicated and intricate undertaking. This is particularly pertinent in adsorption cooling technology, which is regarded as a crucial technique for the efficient utilization of the smallest heat energy [7, 10, 13, 21]. A well-designed heat exchanger is essential for enhancing the efficiency of adsorption chillers because sorption units are essentially thermodynamic devices [12, 20]. The heat flow is a thermal device that allows heat to be exchanged between fluids [9, 16]. The double-pipe flow of heat, one of the different types of flow rate, is widely used in engineering procedures, energy conversion systems, and industries. Increasing (i) the rate of heat transfer between hot and cold fluid, (ii) the heat exchanger's effectiveness, (iii) its exact control, (iv) lowering the rate of fouling formation, etc., were the primary goals of researchers working in the field of heat exchangers. Fuzzy logic is one of the many AI approaches being used in significant research [18], neural network (NN) [5], saving, and monitoring the performance of the rate of heat flow. For sporadic data, a generalized regression neural network (GRNN) always employs a unity permit to enhance the rule and regulation of education with a highly equal policy for monitoring or forecasting; a GRNN model can handle any noise in the input datasets and predict results in as little as 6570 ms. A GRNN model can be created using just a basic backpropagation algorithm and a user who knows the basics of programming [19].

In short, AI-based flow of heat and maximization give the advantages in efficiency and sustainability. Engineers can get peak performance with less work and resources by utilizing sophisticated algorithms and data-driven insights [21]. This revolutionary method opens the door to more creative and intelligent thermal engineering solutions.

6.3 Principles of Heat Exchangers

Types and applications: Due to their ability to efficiently transfer heat between two or more fluids, heat exchangers are crucial parts of many commercial and industrial systems [22]. They come in a variety of configurations, each suitable for a certain set of applications and operational conditions.

Selecting the appropriate heat exchanger for a given process requires an understanding of these types and their applications [23].

6.3.1 Coaxial Heat Exchangers

One of the most frequently used types is the coaxial heat exchanger. They consist of a large cylindrical shell containing several tubes. While one fluid circulates within the shell outside the tubes, the other fluid flows through the tubes. The tube walls allow heat to be transmitted between fluids [24].

Uses: Because of their versatility and dependability, shell and tube heat exchangers are used in many different industries, such as:

- **Power generation:** In power plants, steam is cooled after being used in turbines using coaxial heat exchangers.
- **Chemical processing:** They can handle hot and corrosive fluids, so they are ideal for chemical reactors and heat recovery systems [25]. Oil and gas are used in refineries to heat or cool fluids and in the extraction and processing of crude oil.
- **Heating, venting, and air conditioning systems:** Tube and shell exchangers in ventilation, heating, and air conditioning systems carry out temperature control and heat recovery [26]. Their ability to tolerate large pressure and temperature fluctuations makes them suitable for demanding applications.

6.3.2 Plate Heat Exchangers

These exchangers consist of several thin, flat plates arranged one on top of the other to provide channels through which fluids can flow [27]. The plates are arranged to minimize the overall footprint and optimize the surface area available for heat transmission.

Applications: Plate heat exchangers are utilized because of their small size and high thermal efficiency.

- **Food processing:** They are used for tasks like pasteurizing and dairy products, chilling drinks, and other food items when efficiency and hygienic conditions are crucial.
- **Pharmaceutical manufacturing:** Due to their compact size and ease of cleaning, they are suitable for pharmaceutical processes requiring precise temperature control.

- **District heating:** Through the transport of heat between centralized heating systems and individual buildings or facilities, district heating ensures the efficient distribution of thermal energy.

6.3.3 Cooled by Air Heat Exchangers

In their construction and functioning, heat exchangers of air-cooled exchangers employ ambient air to chill the fluid [28]. They are typically composed of fin-equipped tubes and fans. As the hot fluid travels through the tubes, the fans push air over the fins to release heat [29].

Applications: Places with restricted water sources or water use regulations are ideal for these exchangers.

- **Power plants:** They are commonly used in power plants, where they freeze expanded steam, especially in areas with limited water supplies.
- **Refineries:** Air-cooled exchangers are used in refineries to cool various process fluids.
- **Refrigeration:** Refrigerator systems used during the water-cooling process in refrigeration are impractical or not economical.

6.4 Two-Pipe Heat Exchangers

A concentric tube setup, where one pipe conveys hot fluid and the other cold fluid, makes up a double-pipe heat exchanger [30]. Heat is transferred from the wall of the inner pipe to the fluid in the outer pipe.

Applications: These exchangers are commonly used in smaller-scale settings because of their simple construction. Typical uses include:

- **Laboratory operations:** Experiments and operations requiring precise temperature control are conducted in labs using them.
- **Compact-scale heating and cooling:** Suitable for low flow rates and constrained spaces in small-scale commercial and industrial applications [31].

6.5 Performance and Optimization Metrics

To maximize heat exchanger performance, several crucial metrics must be comprehended, and efficiency-enhancing strategies must be implemented.

- **Heat transfer rate:** This statistic quantifies the efficiency of heat transfer from one fluid to another and is affected by design parameters, flow configuration, and fluid attributes. of the heat exchanger [32]. A higher rate of heat transfer can lead to more efficient systems and less energy use.
- **Flow resistance:** As the flow circulates within the heat exchanger, its pressure decreases. A significant pressure drop indicates increased fluid flow resistance, which raises the energy required for pumping [33]. Design elements like flow arrangement and material selection play a major role in minimizing pressure drop.
- **Thermal effectiveness:** This gauges how well a heat exchanger performs in comparison to its theoretical optimal performance. It is influenced by the fluid temperature differential, the heat transfer region, and the design configuration. Finding a balance between these factors is necessary to optimize thermal effectiveness and achieve the desired performance.
- **Optimization strategies:** Two common methods for heat exchanger optimization are iterative design changes and empirical testing. However, advancements in modeling techniques and computational tools have made it feasible to optimize more precisely, simulating complex fluid dynamics and heat transfer situations to enhance overall performance [34]. Building reliable and efficient systems requires accurate measurements, performance, optimization strategies, and a deep understanding of the many types of heat exchangers and their applications. As technology advances, new findings and methods will further improve the capacity and efficiency of heat exchangers across a range of sectors [35].

6.6 Worldwide Market for Heat Exchangers

This graph (Figure 6.1) displays data from the 2022–2030 [77] global heat exchanger market.

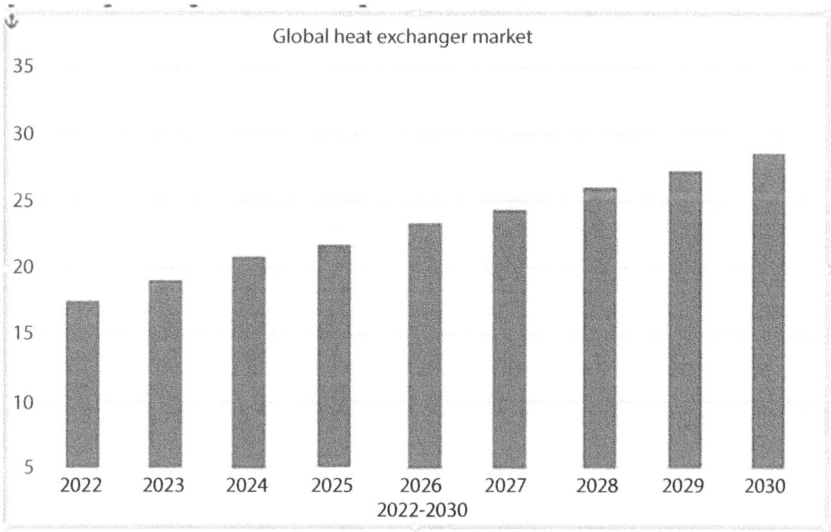

Figure 6.1 Data from the worldwide heat exchanger industry for 2022–2030 [77].

6.7 Basic Equation of Heat Transfer

A complete wall separates the cold and hot fluids in most heat transfer difficulties. The method of heat transfer in this case, from the heated fluid to the cold fluid, can be categorized into three steps:

- Convection transfers heat from the hot fluid to the wall;
- Conduction transfers heat through the wall; and
- Heat is transferred to the cold fluid by convection from the wall.

A schematic of heat transmission between two fluids is displayed in Figure 6.2 [78]. As is evident, heat resistance (R) exists throughout the transfer process. A thermal (physical) property called thermal resistance shows how resistant a material is to heat transfer caused by temperature variations, and it can be computed [36].

$$R = \frac{L}{AK}, \textit{for conduction} \tag{6.1}$$

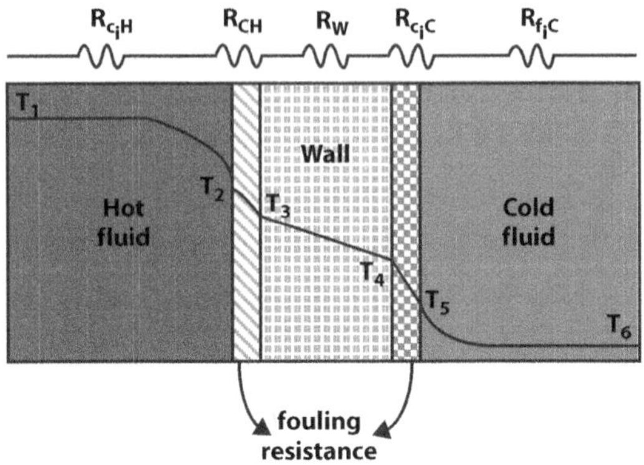

Figure 6.2 A diagrammatic representation showing a heat exchanger's heat transfer diagram [78].

$$R = \frac{1}{AK}, \textit{for convection} \tag{6.2}$$

Where A, L, K, and h are represented by the cross-sectional area, the wall's thickness, conduction, and convection heat transfer coefficients, respectively. The following formula can be used to explain the transfer of heat (Q) at each stage [37].

$$Q = \frac{\Delta T}{R} \tag{6.3}$$

Where, ΔT = Temperature difference
R= Resistance
Therefore, the equation of Q for Figure 6.2 [78] can be written as,

$$Q_1 = \frac{T_1 - T_2}{R_{c_iH}} \tag{6.4}$$

$$Q_2 = \frac{T_2 - T_3}{R_{f_iH}} \tag{6.5}$$

$$Q_3 = \frac{T_3 - T_4}{R_W} \tag{6.6}$$

$$Q_4 = \frac{T_4 - T_5}{R_{f_iC}} \tag{6.7}$$

$$Q_5 = \frac{T_5 - T_6}{R_{c_iC}} \tag{6.8}$$

From Equations 6.4–6.8, heat transfer (Q) is equivalent to each other. Therefore, Q can be written as,

$$Q_1 = Q_2 = Q_3 = Q_4 = Q_5 = Q \tag{6.9}$$

Where,
R_{c_iH} = The hot side's thermal resistance to convection.
R_{f_iH} = Fouling resistance of the hot side.
R_W = Resistance is denoted by the wall.
R_{f_iC} = the cold side's fouling resistance.
R_{c_iC} = Convection on the cold side, and it stands for thermal resistance.

The $R_{f,H}$ of the most often used fluids in heat exchangers. Equation 6.2 yields the overall heat transfer coefficient as follows [37]:

$$Q = \frac{T_1 - T_6}{R_{c_iH} + R_{f_iH} + R_W + R_{f_iC} + R_{c_iC}} \tag{6.10}$$

or

$$Q = \frac{T_1 - T_6}{\frac{1}{A_C H_C} + \frac{1}{h_H A_H} + \frac{r_w}{A_C} + \frac{r_{f_iC}}{A_C} + \frac{r_{f_iH}}{A_H}} \tag{6.11}$$

Where,
h_C and h_H = The cold and hot sides' respective convective heat transfer coefficients.
A_C and A_H = The cold and hot sides' surface areas of the wall.
Equations 6.12 and 6.13 can be used to determine the r_w for cylindrical and flat walls, respectively.

$$r_w = \frac{d_w}{AK}, \textit{ for flat wall} \tag{6.12}$$

$$r_w = \frac{\ln\left(\frac{r_0}{r_i}\right)}{2\pi KL}, \textit{ for cylindrical wall} \tag{6.13}$$

Where, r_0 and r_i stand for the wall's outside and inside diameters, respectively, and d_w for the wall's thickness.
The formula for total thermal resistance [38]:

$$R_t = \frac{T_1 - T_6}{\frac{1}{A_C H_C} + \frac{1}{h_H A_H} + \frac{r_w}{A_C} + \frac{r_{f_i C}}{A_C} + \frac{r_{f_i H}}{A_H}} \tag{6.14}$$

The equation of Q can be calculated using

$$Q = UA\Delta T \tag{6.15}$$

Where, U = the total heat transfer coefficient.

$$U = \frac{1}{h_c \frac{\frac{1}{A_C}}{A_{ref}} + \frac{\frac{r_{fiC}}{A_C}}{A_{ref}} + h_H \frac{\frac{1}{A_H}}{A_{ref}} + \frac{\frac{r_{fiH}}{A_H}}{A_{ref}} + \frac{\frac{r_W}{A_H}}{A_{ref}}} \tag{6.16}$$

A_{ref} serves as a reference point. When heat transfer occurs through a pipe, the surface areas of the pipe's interior and outside are not the same. Therefore, the A_{ref}, the pipes' outer surface is often chosen and needs to be ascertained.

6.8 Designing Heat Exchangers Thermally

Several ways are available to design the thermal heat exchanger. The effectiveness-number of transfer units (ε-NTU) and log-mean temperature difference (LMTD) are the most widely employed techniques [39]. The ε-NTUand LMTD are known as the effectiveness-number of transfer units and log-mean temperature difference. Heat transfer was calculated using the LMTD when fluid intake and exit temperatures were known. A trial-and-error method can be used to determine LMTD when there is uncertainty about the heat exchanger's various input and/or output temperatures. In this instance, the ε-NTU approach is frequently employed [26].

- **Log-mean temperature difference method:** As previously stated, the quantity of heat transfer can be computed from Equation 6.10 by calculating the temperature differential between hot and cool fluids. The heat exchanger itself can alter, as can the temperature differential between hot and cold fluids. In a heat exchanger design, the terminal temperatures of the hot and cold fluids ($T_{H,\ out,}$ and $T_{C,out}$) are highly significant variables. For countercurrent flow, a temperature approach happens if $T_{C,out}$ is less than $T_{H,out}$.

On the other hand, a temperature cross occurs if $T_{C,out}$ is greater than $T_{H,out}$ for countercurrent flow [19–40]. However, if $T_{C,out}$ equals $T_{H,out}$, a temperature meet occurs. For heat exchangers with a co-current flow design, temperature crossover is impossible according to the second rule of thermodynamics [41]. Wales [42] presented a parameter G in 1981 that can be used to calculate the heat exchangers' temperature conditions. The G parameters, which can range from -1 to 1, are defined by Equation 6.17.

$$G = \frac{T_{H,\text{out}} - T_{\text{c,out}}}{T_{H,in} - T_{c,in}} \tag{6.17}$$

$G < 0$, for the cross temperature
$G > 0$, for the approch temperature
$G = 0$, for the meet temperature

As the heat exchanger operates, it alters the temperature difference between the hot and cold fluids. The crucial question is which specific temperature variation should be used to calculate the heat transfer rate.

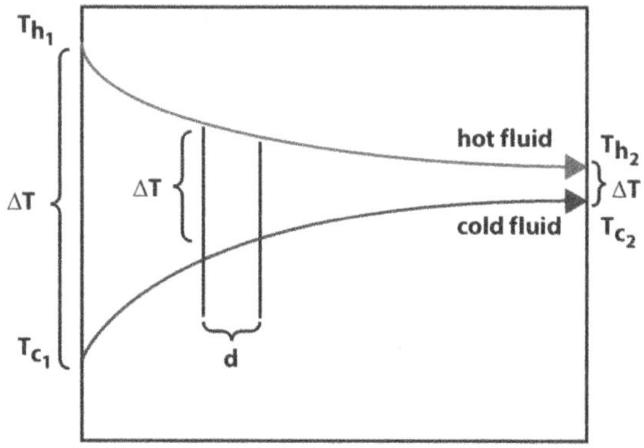

Figure 6.3 Thermal energy transfer between the fluids that are parallel and co-current [19, 78].

Figure 6.3 [78] shows heat transmission between two parallel fluids and co-current which can be used to address this question. Figure 6.3 allows us to write the heat transfer for the designated heat transfer area as follows:

$$dQ = U\Delta T dA \tag{6.18}$$

Effectiveness-number of transfer units: LMTD can be computed using a trial-and-error method when more than one of the heat exchanger's input and exit temperatures are unknown. Additionally, the ε-NTU strategy can be adopted to determine the rate of heat transmission. With $C_{p\,min}$ being the lowest value between the heat capacities of cold fluid ($C_{p,C}$) and hot fluid ($C_{p,H}$), the ε-NTU can be computed using Equation 6.19. The ratio of the actual heat transfer rate (q) to the highest feasible heat transfer rate (q_{max}) is the efficacy (ε), as per Equation 6.20.

$$NTU = \frac{UA_m}{Cp_{\min}} \tag{6.19}$$

$$\varepsilon = \frac{q}{q_m} \tag{6.20}$$

6.9 Issue with Thermal Design of Heat Exchanger

Heat exchanger thermal design. There are several heat exchanger thermal design issues from the perspective of quantitative analysis. The grading and sizing concerns are considered to be two of the most basic (and significant) issues.

- **Rating Problem:** The rating problem is to find out how well an existing exchanger, or an already-sized exchanger, performs in terms of heat transfer and pressure drop. The complete information about the surface geometries and materials is explained by the pressure drop characteristics and non-dimensional heat transfer. The rating issue is influenced by the fluid flow rates, inlet temperatures, fouling variables, and the design, flow configuration, and total size of the heat exchanger. Pressure drops on either side of the exchanger, fluid outlet temperatures, and the overall heat transfer rate are then determined by the rating issue. The performance or simulation problem is another name for the rating problem.
- **Size Issue:** The design of a new heat exchanger generally refers to the materials used for the tube/plate and fins, the flow arrangement, the kind of exchanger construction, and the physical size of the exchanger. But when it comes to a lengthy surface exchanger sizing issue, we will ascertain the physical dimensions of an exchanger (height, length, width, and areas of surface). We will assume that the materials, flow configuration, and exchanger construction type were predetermined using some of the selection criteria. The selection of gasket type, pass arrangements, number of plates, plate type, size, and other factors are all considered sizing problems for a plate exchanger.

6.10 The Need for Artificial Intelligence in Heat Exchanger Design and Optimization

Heat exchangers play a vital role in a wide range of industrial applications, including energy generation, chemical processing, HVAC systems, and manufacturing. Designing and optimizing these systems is a complex endeavor, requiring careful consideration of factors such as heat transfer performance, pressure drop, cost-effectiveness, and material compatibility. Traditional design approaches often rely on heuristics, manual calculations, and iterative trial-and-error methods, which can be both time-intensive and less effective. However, AI provides powerful tools to enhance the design and optimization of heat exchangers, offering greater efficiency and precision in the process.

6.10.1 Complexity of Heat Exchanger Design

Heat exchangers need to meet various performance criteria, including:

- **Heat transfer efficiency:** Maximizing the transfer of heat between fluids.
- **Pressure drop:** Minimizing the pressure drop to reduce energy losses.
- **Material selection:** Choosing materials that withstand temperature, pressure, and chemical environments.
- **Compactness:** Designing for space constraints while maintaining performance.
- **Cost-effectiveness:** Optimizing design within budget limits.

Given these complexities, AI can assist by modeling and analyzing design parameters, making it possible to explore a wider range of possibilities and identify the optimal solution faster than traditional methods [43].

6.11 Artificial Intelligence in Heat Exchanger Design

Technologies like ML and DL, genetic algorithms (GAs), and ANNs are increasingly applied to heat exchanger design to automate tasks, improve performance predictions, and optimize design parameters.

- **Machine learning for performance prediction**: ML algorithms can be trained on historical data of heat exchangers to predict the performance of new designs, including heat transfer rates and pressure drops. These models can improve over time, providing more accurate predictions as new data becomes available [44].
- **Optimization algorithms**: Optimization methods powered by AI, including GAs, particle swarm optimization, and simulated annealing, can search large design spaces more

efficiently than traditional methods. These algorithms can quickly find the best combination of parameters, such as flow arrangement, heat transfer area, and material properties, to achieve the desired performance [45]

- **Intelligent systems and layered learning**: ANNs and DL models can be used to model complex, nonlinear relationships between design parameters and performance metrics. These AI models can be trained on experimental data, simulating real-world conditions to predict performance in various scenarios. They can also be used for fault detection and predictive maintenance by analyzing sensor data from operational systems [46].
- **Surrogate modeling**: In heat exchanger design, the computational cost of simulating fluid flow and heat transfer can be high. Surrogate models, which are simpler mathematical models created with the help of AI techniques, can reduce the time and cost of simulations. These models can approximate the behavior of complex systems and guide the design process [47].

6.12 Benefits of Artificial Intelligence in Heat Exchanger Design and Optimization

- **Speed and efficiency**: AI can accelerate the design process by automating optimization and decision-making. This reduces the time taken to develop new designs and makes the process more agile [48].
- **Improved design performance**: AI can explore more design alternatives and identify configurations that optimize performance across multiple parameters simultaneously. For instance, it can suggest the ideal fluid flow pattern or determine the ideal adjustment between energy transfer and fluid resistance [49].
- **Cost reduction**: By optimizing designs for both performance and material usage, AI can help reduce operational and production costs. It can also help in predicting maintenance needs and preventing expensive breakdowns or inefficiencies in heat exchanger systems [50].

- **Customization**: AI-driven optimization allows the tailoring of heat exchanger designs to specific needs, such as unique operating conditions, space constraints, or environmental factors, ensuring maximum efficiency [51].

6.13 Artificial Intelligence Applications in Different Types of Heat Exchangers

Artificial intelligence can be applied to different types of heat exchangers, including:

- **Shell-and-tube heat exchangers**: AI algorithms can optimize the design by adjusting parameters such as the tube arrangement, shell diameter, and baffle configuration [52].
- **Plate heat exchangers**: AI can help optimize the number of plates, plate material, and arrangement for heat transfer efficiency and reduced pressure drop [53].
- **Air-cooled heat exchangers**: AI models can assist in selecting the optimal fan configuration and heat exchanger fin design to maximize performance while minimizing energy consumption [54].

6.13.1 Future Directions and Challenges

While AI has shown significant potential, its widespread application in heat exchanger design and optimization still faces some challenges:

- **Data availability**: High-quality, large datasets are necessary to train AI models effectively. In many industries, such data may be limited [55].
- **Integration with traditional methods**: Integrating AI with established engineering design processes can be complex and may require significant changes to existing workflows.

Despite these challenges, AI is poised to transform heat exchanger design and optimization by providing more efficient, cost-effective, and high-performance solutions.

6.14 Significance of Artificial Intelligence in Heat Exchanger Design

Artificial intelligence is revolutionizing engineering and manufacturing, particularly in the design of heat exchangers. These devices are essential in industries such as power generation, chemical processing, HVAC systems, automotive applications, and refrigeration. Conventional heat exchanger design methods typically depend on empirical data, heuristics, and experimental approaches. However, the integration of AI, especially ML and DL techniques, has significantly enhanced the speed, accuracy, and efficiency of the design process.

6.15 Key Aspects of Artificial Intelligence in Heat Exchanger Design

6.15.1 Optimization of Heat Transfer Performance

Artificial intelligence enables the optimization of heat transfer rates in heat exchangers. By utilizing ML algorithms, engineers can identify the best material properties, geometric designs, and fluid flow parameters to achieve maximum heat transfer efficiency while reducing energy consumption. Advanced AI methods such as GAs, particle swarm optimization, and simulated annealing are especially effective in addressing complex, multi-objective optimization challenges in the design of heat exchangers [56].

6.15.2 Enhanced Simulation and Modeling

Artificial intelligence can improve the accuracy of thermal-fluid simulations. Traditional methods of modeling heat exchanger performance often require simplifying assumptions, leading to approximations. Artificial intelligence can enhance models by incorporating a greater level of detail and accurately predicting the behavior of fluids, heat transfer rates, and pressure drops in various configurations. Machine learning models can be trained on vast datasets from real-world operations to provide more accurate simulations, reducing reliance on time-consuming and expensive experimental work.

6.15.3 Design Space Exploration

Heat exchangers come in various designs, such as shell-and-tube, plate, and air-cooled exchangers. The design space is vast, and AI can assist in exploring this space more efficiently. Artificial intelligence techniques can evaluate a wide variety of design options and identify configurations that meet specific performance requirements (such as thermal efficiency, cost, and reliability) more effectively than traditional methods. This helps in selecting the best designs faster.

6.15.4 Predictive Maintenance and Fault Detection

Artificial intelligence can also enhance the reliability and longevity of heat exchangers by predicting potential failures or maintenance needs. Through the use of AI-driven predictive analytics, engineers can monitor the operational parameters of heat exchangers (temperature, pressure, flow rates) in real-time and predict any anomalies that may indicate the onset of failure, such as fouling or leaks [57]. This proactive approach to maintenance can minimize downtime and reduce repair costs.

6.15.5 Customization and Personalization

In industries where custom heat exchanger designs are required, AI offers the ability to tailor designs to meet specific customer needs. By utilizing AI algorithms, engineers can consider various operational conditions and constraints to create heat exchangers that are optimized for particular use cases. This is especially valuable in industries like aerospace and chemical processing, where operating conditions vary greatly.

6.15.6 Sustainability and Energy Efficiency

Artificial intelligence plays a key role in enhancing the energy efficiency of heat exchangers. By analyzing operational data, AI can suggest improvements that reduce energy consumption, lower operational costs, and minimize the carbon footprint. For example, AI can recommend design adjustments that make better use of renewable energy sources or suggest more sustainable materials for heat exchangers [58].

6.15.7 Automation of the Design Process

The use of AI can automate the iterative design process, which typically involves trying different combinations of materials, geometries, and flow configurations. With AI, the design process becomes faster and more precise, with algorithms capable of evaluating thousands of possible configurations in a fraction of the time it would take a human engineer. This leads to faster time-to-market for new products and more cost-effective designs [59].

6.16 Applications of Artificial Intelligence in Heat Exchanger Design

Smart heat exchanger networks: AI can help in designing and managing heat exchanger networks in large systems, such as industrial plants or district heating systems, by optimizing the flow of heat between various exchangers to maximize efficiency and reduce energy consumption.

6.16.1 Energy Recovery Systems

Artificial intelligence is utilized to design heat exchangers that recover waste heat from industrial processes, improving overall system efficiency and sustainability.

6.16.2 Real-Time Performance Monitoring

Artificial intelligence-driven systems can track the performance of heat exchangers in real-time, identifying issues before they lead to costly failures or performance degradation.

6.16.3 Heat Exchangers

A heat exchanger is a type of device that causes the transference of heat (thermal heat) between two fluid systems at different temperatures [60–63]. In these systems, a special type of surface is used to prevent mixing. Therefore, these are used for various applications such as heating and cooling systems, refrigeration, textile-related chemicals, automobile, waste heat recovery, food industries, and renewable energy systems [61]. Various heat exchangers, such as plate heat exchangers, air-cooling heat exchangers, and pipe heat exchangers, are used for particular purposes to meet regulatory standards [63]. However, the major components of these exchangers are streams, enter and exit points, and surfaces for the transfer of heat [64, 65]. Besides the major components, some other components are tank, pipe, baffle, and fin, which are employed based on the design of the heat exchangers. The most important factor that makes them important for thermal purposes is the absence of moving components in the design of heat exchangers. The performance of a heat exchanger can be evaluated by applying the first and second laws of thermodynamics using experimental, mathematical, and systematic techniques, but the problem with experimental techniques is that these are very costly, while theoretical and mathematical approaches mostly depend on postulates and complex equations. Therefore, to overcome the above problems, an alternative method, i.e., AI, comes out as an emerging solution for enhancing the performance of thermal systems using different types of models, optimization techniques, and efficiency estimation methods [61]. These techniques are particularly employed to explain the thermal heat transfer properties of fluid and the related performance of thermal devices. Therefore, in this chapter, we will explain the upcoming developments of AI-based heat exchangers.

6.17 Upcoming Developments and Trends

This section deals with the upcoming developments in the field of heat exchangers. In this section, we will discuss cutting-edge technology that enhances the performance and efficiency of heat exchangers.

6.17.1 Cutting-Edge Materials

Advancements in material science have found a pivotal role in the transformation of the design and performance of heat exchangers, enabling superior efficiency, durability, and sustainability. Cutting-edge materials are employed to enhance the performance and usefulness of the heat exchanger, with the main focus on enhancing conductivity, efficiency of heat transformation, and corrosion resistance. Among these innovations, graphene and carbon nanotubes stand out as good choice materials due to their exceptional thermal conductivity and strength-to-weight ratio, which permit the enlargement of compact and efficient heat exchangers. The various types of materials used for this purpose, along with innovations, are as follows:

6.17.2 Nanomaterials

The materials in the nanomaterial range are called nanomaterials. These materials, due to their exceptionally unique thermal conductivity and mechanical properties, are most widely used for the development of heat exchangers. In addition to this, these materials have high surface areas, fouling, corrosion resistance properties, high efficiency, as well as sustainability. Among these nanomaterials, graphene and carbon nanotubes are most widely used for particular applications.

Artificial intelligence accelerates the discovery of new nanomaterials and their integration into heat exchangers, reducing reliance on trial-and-error approaches and experimental costs. Artificial intelligence is increasingly being employed to accelerate the adoption of nanomaterials in heat exchangers. Machine learning models enable the prediction of nanomaterial behavior under various operational scenarios, reducing the need for extensive experimentation. Thus, these materials result in a high rate of heat transfer [63, 66, 67].

6.17.3 Composite Materials

These are the amalgamation of two ingredients with different properties (both chemical and physical). These materials are most widely used in the design of heat exchangers due to their lightweight structure, high thermal conductivity, corrosion resistance, and mechanical strength. When these materials are used with AI, they offer transformative potential in designing efficient, sustainable, and highly optimized heat exchangers. Among various composite materials, carbon fiber-reinforced composites and graphene composites are among the most widely used.

6.17.4 Advanced Coating

Coating is generally applied to prevent corrosion using various coating materials such as Carbon fiber-reinforced composites. Advanced coatings are most widely used in augmenting the presentation, durability, and productivity of heat exchangers by addressing challenges such as fouling, corrosion, scaling, and thermal resistance. These coatings are designed to alter the surface characteristics of heat exchanger parts, facilitating better heat transfer, enhancing durability, and lowering maintenance expenses. Integrating AI greatly speeds up the creation, implementation, and refinement of advanced coatings, revolutionizing the conventional design and functioning of heat exchangers. Thus, by reducing maintenance needs, these coatings contribute to the efficiency of heat exchangers and extend their lifespan. These materials are most widely used in power generation, such as turbines, nuclear reactors, and chemical manufacturing.

6.18 Heat Exchange Design

Heat exchange equipment is most widely used in any industry for the transfer of heat, and its design also plays an important role in finding new technologies [68].

Various methods, such as LMTD and ε-NTU, are used for the thermal design of heat exchange, whereas the optimization can be performed using conventional and non-conventional methods.

6.18.1 Log-Mean Temperature Difference Method

The LMTD method evaluates the rate of transfer of heat by evaluating hot and cold fluid temperatures. These temperature differences changed along with the heat exchangers. Figure 6.4 [78] exhibited the transfer of heat within different fluids. In this system, the terminal temperatures play and decide the heat transfer within the system. If t_H is the temperature of the terminal side of the hot fluid and t_c is the temperature of the terminal side of the cold fluid then the following possibilities arise:

1. If $t_c < t_H$ for the countercurrent flow temperature approach occurs.
2. If $t_c > t_H$ for countercurrent flow= temperature cross happens.
3. If $t_c = t_H =$ emperature encounter takes place.

But according to the law of thermodynamics (2nd law), the cross temperature condition is not possible in the case of a heat exchanger; therefore,

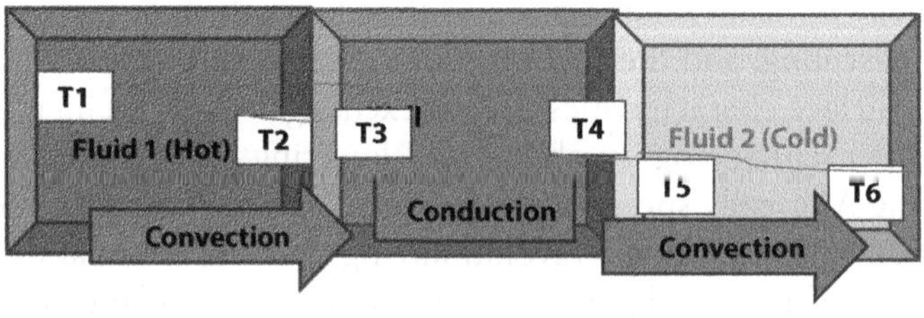

Figure 6.4 General diagram of heat exchanger (*heat transfer takes place from hot to cold fluid *via* a wall) [78].

a new term G is proposed by Wales, which explains the temperature conditions within the heat exchangers using the following formulas:

$$G = \frac{t_{\mathrm{H,out}} - t_{\mathrm{c,out}}}{t_{\mathrm{H,in}} - t_{c,in}}$$

If $G > 0$ = Approaches towards temperature
$G < 0$ = Cross Temperature
$G = 0$ Temperature meet

The straightforwardness of this method finds its importance in the heat exchanger design by the incorporation of a new factor, F, which is transferred between two non-dimensional parameters; P and R are thermal effectiveness and heat capacity ratio, respectively; P and R can be premeditated using the resulting equation [60, 69, 70]:

$$P = \frac{t_{\mathrm{c,out}} - t_{\mathrm{c,in}}}{t_{\mathrm{H,in}} - t_{c,in}}$$

$$R = \frac{t_{H,\mathrm{in}} - t_{\mathrm{H,out}}}{t_{\mathrm{C,out}} - t_{c,in}}$$

6.18.2 Optimization of Heat Exchanger

The design of the heat exchanger can be planned based on a discrete optimization problem because the values used in the design are not continuous but are discrete. Hence, their optimization is based on the following principles such as low cost, lowest pressure, least heat transfer area, and maximum effectiveness. Based on these principles, the heat exchanger design is based on geometrical and optical parameters but through compatibility. Therefore, optimization can be performed using various methods such as conventional and non-conventional methods. Conventional methods are mostly calculus-based, enumerated and random techniques-based, but these methods also suffer from limitations such as giving the value of local optima, needing full function information and a dependency on variables, as well as function nature. Therefore, to overcome this limitation, non-conventional techniques such as algorithm, non-nominated sorting GA, particle swarm optimization, Jaya algorithm, and teaching–learning-based optimization [60, 71, 72] are used. Among these, GA plays an significant role as it exists each method of situation with different solutions.

6.18.3 Genetic Algorithm

Genetic algorithm is a valuable method for optimization as it provides all solutions but the necessary condition is to provide a defined number of precise algorithmic constraints such as the probability of jump, assortment operator, and fractious probability. This theory was first proposed by Professor John Holland and Ann Arbor in 1960. In the late 1980's, it was further modified and methodology was proposed. Finally, it was motivated by Charles Darwin's theory of the persistence of the strongest. In GA, every set of the variables is encoded by sequences of either fixed or variable length just like chromosomes (also called genes) in biological samples. Each iterative step in repetitive processes like GA is referred to as a group, and the set of solutions connected to each group is known as a population. The primary population is typically created at random. In GA, optimum points are reached through statistical techniques. Populations are chosen through natural selection according to their fitness. Selection, crossover, mutation, and other genetic processes are used to create a new population. This cycle keeps going until the stop criterion is met or a specific outcome is obtained. The general steps of GA systems are initiation, evaluation, selection, and crossover, which are represented in Figure 6.5.

In the initial generation of the population, binary numbers are generated randomly, which are chromosomes and consist of bits called genes. The value or number of genes (n_g) depends on precision ($\in$) and variable range [$\mathbf{x}_{min}$, $\mathbf{x}_{max}$] and is defined by using the following formula.

$$n_g = \log_2\left(\frac{x_{\min} - x_{\max}}{\varepsilon}\right)$$

In step 2, the fitness value can be evaluated by decoded value of variable D, and the price of a real variable can be derived from the following formula:

$$x = x_{\min} + \frac{x_{\max} - x_{\min}}{2^{ng} - 1}$$

In the third step, the genes or chromosomes with the best fitness value enter the crossover step and are selected using various selection methods such as roulette wheel selection, ranking-based, and tournament selection. In these methods, the chances of chromosome selection are directly

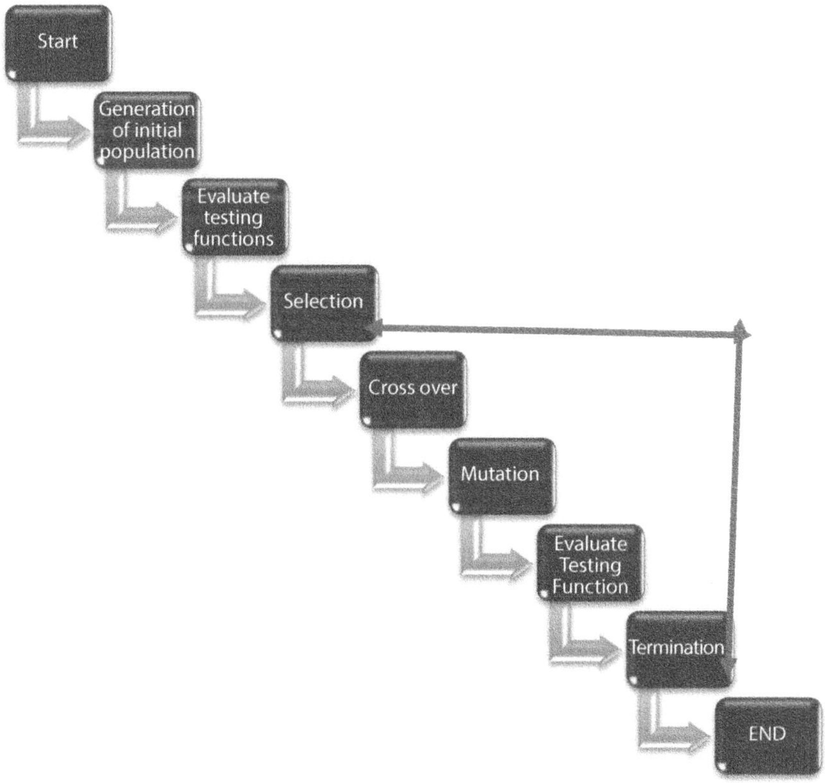

Figure 6.5 General diagram showing the steps in the algorithm [78].

proportionate to the fitness value obtained from Step 2. Thus, a chromosome with a high fitness value has more chances of selection for reproduction.

In the crossover step, a particular gene is exchanged between two-parent chromosomes, resulting in the formation of a regenerated pool of solutions, named descendants. In this step, various processes such as single-step, two-point crossover, and multi-point crossover are used, and the probability of crossover nearly comes out to be 1.0.

The last step mutation (Mutation is defined as a bit whose value varies between 0 and 1 in the solution of a chromosome) is used to examine innovative solutions to find the global solution. The range of mutation probability Pm is defined by the following formula:

$$\frac{0.1}{l} \leq P_m \leq \frac{1}{l}$$

Where l is defined as GA string length [60, 63, 73, 74].

Thus, the heat exchanger design and its optimization methods are precise parameters in heat exchangers.

6.19 Innovation in Heat Exchanger Design

Heat exchangers are precarious apparatuses in an extensive series of industries, including energy, automotive, chemical process, and HVAC. With the increasing demand for high efficiency, decreased environmental impact, and compactness, significant innovations in heat exchanger design have emerged. These advancements address challenges such as thermal efficiency, material limitations, and operational reliability while leveraging technologies like advanced materials, additive manufacturing, and AI. The related innovations and trends are as follows:

6.19.1 Small and Miniaturized Designs

Small designs are only possible if there is some innovation in the manufacturing technology. As a result of this, these are most widely employed in space applications such as portable gadgets and electronics cooling.

6.19.2 Enhanced Heat Transfer Technologies

Improved technologies are used to design useful heat exchangers in the form of porous media and microchannel heat exchangers. Among these available heat exchangers, microchannels are most efficiently used, offering a large surface-to-volume ratio in small places.

6.19.3 Modular Designs

Modular design provides flexibility to the system. These systems can be easily expanded or reconfigured to meet changing operational needs or integrated with other systems.

Thus, Innovations in heat exchanger design are driving significant improvements in efficiency, reliability, and sustainability across various industries. The integration of advanced materials, additive manufacturing, AI-driven optimization, and biomimicry is transforming traditional approaches to heat transfer. These advancements not only enhance performance but also contribute to reducing energy consumption and environmental impact, ensuring that heat exchangers remain a cornerstone of modern engineering systems [63, 75].

6.20 Challenges in Artificial Intelligence-Based Heat Exchanger Design

The quality and availability of data is a very difficult task when using AI in heat exchangers and requires accurate and complete datasets. The various types of challenges associated with heat exchangers are as follows [63, 76].

6.20.1 Quality and Availability of the Data

AI-based methods require a greater number of datasets, and the cost is also high. Publicly available datasets are limited, and proprietary data are frequently inaccessible. In addition to this, the data obtained from heat exchangers varies significantly due to the geometry, materials used, and datasets, posing a considerable difficulty. In terms of the quality of data, the dataset comes with lots of noise and inaccuracies, which can compromise the training and validation of AI models.

6.20.2 Computational Challenges

The AI-based models required high dimensionality. For both training and inference, advanced AI algorithms, such as DL models, require considerable processing power. Artificial intelligence models frequently depend on CFD simulations for producing and validating data. Nevertheless, CFD simulations require significant computational resources, which restricts the scalability of AI-based processes. Artificial intelligence-based heat exchangers suffer from complex optimization. Multi-objective optimization is frequently necessary in designing heat exchangers, and it entails balancing conflicting goals like efficiency, cost, and dimensions. In these intricate situations, AI algorithms frequently have difficulty reaching optimal solutions.

6.20.3 Model Interpretability and Trust

Various models of AI, particularly DL algorithms, function as black boxes, offering slight awareness of how predictions are made. This absence of transparency makes it difficult for engineers to trust and adopt AI solutions.

The validation against experimental or high-fidelity simulation data can be challenging due to limited resources.

6.20.4 Industry Barriers

Many industries rely on established design practices and are hesitant to adopt AI-based approaches due to perceived risks and uncertainties. The thermal, as well as AI methodologies, are required for the implementation of AI solutions; therefore, the lack of interdisciplinary training poses a barrier to adoption. For the development of AI models, the cost of software, hardware, and personnel is very high, and it creates a big problem.

6.20.5 Strategies to Overcome Barriers or Solutions to this Problem

6.20.5.1 Enhancing Data Availability

- This can be done by a collaborative implementation between academic, industry, and government organizations that provide a comprehensive dataset for AI model training.
- To remove the noise and inconsistency associated with AI models. Developing robust methods for handling noise and inconsistencies in datasets is essential for improving model accuracy.

6.20.5.2 Improving Computational Efficiency

- This can be done using an optimized algorithm. Reducing processing demands by developing and utilizing advanced AI algorithms can help manage costs. Two approaches that enhance efficiency while maintaining performance are model pruning and quantization.
- By conducting the analysis close to the source and edge computing systems, which can reduce the requirement for central processes.
- By using hybrid models. Combining physics-based models with AI can help balance computational efficiency and physical accuracy.

6.20.5.3 *Enhancing Model Interpretability*

- This can be done by the development of AI algorithms that provide interpretable and actionable insights that can build trust among engineers.
- By providing knowledge related to the particular domain. Embedding physical laws and engineering principles into AI models can improve their reliability and interpretability.

6.20.5.4 *Facilitating Industry Adoption*

- This can be done by organizing training and education programs that can bridge the skill gap between thermal engineering and AI.
- By demonstrating the pilot projects based on the feasibility and benefits of AI.
- By explaining cost-benefit analysis and providing clear evidence of the long-term cost savings and performance.

6.21 Conclusion

The integration of AI in designing heat exchangers is a transformative jump in efficiency, accuracy, and optimization control approaches that allow engineers to predict thermal characteristics, optimize geometry, and improve the selection of materials with unprecedented accuracy. These advances not only reduce the period and costs related to traditional design methods, but they also facilitate the creation of innovative, energy-efficient systems that meet the growing demands of modern industry.

Bibliography

1. Ahmed, A., Ge, T., Peng, J., Yan, W.C., Tee, B.T., You, S., Assessment of the renewable energy generation towards net-zero energy buildings: A review. *Energy Build.*, 256, 111755, 2022, http-s://doi.org/10.1016/J.ENBUILD.2021.111755.
2. Alabi, T.M., Agbajor, F.D., Yang, Z., Lu, L., Johnson, O.A., Strategic potential of multi-energy system 1446 towards carbon neutrality: A forward looking overview. *Energy Built Environ.*, 2, 4, 689–708, 2022, https://doi.org/10.1016/.2022.06.007.
3. Angelidis, O., Ioannou, A., Friedrich, D., Thomson, A., Falcone, G., District heating and cooling networks with decentralised energy substations:

Opportunities and barriers for holistic energy system decarbonisation. *Energy*, 269, 126740, 2023, https://doi.org/10.1016/j.energy.2023.126740.
4. Ayub, S., Ayob, S.M., Tan, C.W., Taimoor, M., Ayub, L., Bukar, A.L., *et al.*, Analysis of energy management schemes for renewable-energy-based smart homes against the backdrop of COVID-19. *Sustain. Energy Technol. Assess.*, 52, 102136–102136, 2022. https://doi.org/10.1016/J.SETA.2022.102136.
5. Bendu, H., Deepak, B.B.V.L., Murugan, S., Application of GRNN for the prediction of performance and exhaust emissions in HCCI engine using ethanol. *Energy Convers. Manage.*, 122, 165173, 2016.
6. Chekifi, T., Boukraa, M., Benmoussa, A., Artificial Intelligence for thermal energy storage enhancement: A Comprehensive Review. *J. Energy Res. Technol.*, 146, 6, 1–29, 2024. DOI:10.1115/1.4065197.
7. Choudhury, B., Saha, B.B., Chatterjee, P.K., Sarkar, J.P., An overview of developments in adsorption refrigeration systems towards a sustainable way of cooling. *Appl. Energy*, 104, 554567, 2013.
8. Fleiter, T. and SRDKRT, Mapping and analyses of the current and future (2020-2030) heating/cooling 1452 fuel deployment (fossil/renewable) files. EurComm Dir Energy, 2016.
9. Gorman, J.M., Krautbauer, K.R., Sparrow, E.M., Thermal and fluid flow first-principles numerical design of an enhanced double pipe heat exchanger. *Appl. Therm. Eng.*, 107, 194206, 2016.
10. Kishore, R.A., Davis, B., Greathouse, J., Hannon, A., Kennedy, D.E., Millar, A., Mittel, D., Nozariasbmarz, A., Kang, M.G., Kang, H.B., *et al.*, Energy scavenging from ultra-low temperature gradients. *Energy Environ. Sci.*, 12, 10081018, 2019.
11. Kumar Jaiswal, K., Chowdhury, C.R., Yadav, D., Verma, R., Dutta, S., Jaiswal, K.S., *et al.*, Renewable and sustainable clean energy development and impact on social, economic, and environmental health. *Energy Nexus*, 7, 3, 100118, 2022, https://doi.org/10.1016/J.NEXUS.2022.100118.
12. Li, X.H., Hou, X.H., Zhang, X., Yuan, Z.X., A review on development of adsorption cooling Novel beds and advanced cycles. *Energy Convers. Manage.*, 94, 221232, 2015.
13. Marschewski, J., Brenner, L., Ebejer, N., Ruch, P., Michel, B., Poulikakos, D., 3D-printed fluidic networks for high power density heat-managing miniaturized redox flow batteries. *Energy Environ. Sci.*, 10, 780787, 2017.
14. Pan, S., Fulton, L.M., Roy, A., Jung, J., Choi, Y., Gao, H.O., Shared use of electric autonomous vehicles: Air quality and health impacts of future mobility in the United States. *Renew. Sustain. Energy Rev.*, 149, 111380, 2021, https://doi.org/10.1016/J.RSER.2021.111380.
15. Qi, M., Liu, Y., He, T., Yin, L., Shu, C.-M., Moon, I., System perspective on clean ertechnologies for renewable methane production and utilization towards carbon neutrality: Principles, technoeconomics, and carbon footprints. *Fuel*, 327, 125130, 2022, https://doi.org/10.1016/J.FUEL.2022.125130.

16. Qian, S., Yu, J., Yan, G., A review of regenerative heat exchange methods for various cooling technologies. *Renew. Sustain. Energy Rev.*, 69, 535550, 2017.
17. Renewable energy for heating and cooling, Products Eurostat News, Eurostat, https://ec.europa.eu/eurostat/web/products-eurostat-news/-/ddn-20200211-1 (accessed July 25, 2022).
18. Sridharan, M., Predicting performance of double pipe parallel and counter flow heat exchanger using fuzzy logic. *J. Therm. Sci. Eng. Appl.*, 12, 3, 111, 2022.
19. Sridharan, M., Application of generalized regression neural network in predicting the performance of natural convection solar dryer. *J. Sol. Energy Eng.*, 142, 3, 17, 2020.
20. Wang, R.Z., Xia, Z.Z., Wang, L.W., Lu, Z.S., Li, S.L., Li, T.X., Wu, J.Y., He, S., Heat transfer designinadsorption refrigeration systemsforefficientuseo-flow-grade thermal energy. *Energy*, 36, 5425–5439, 2011.
21. Zhang, F., Liu, J., Yang, W., Logan, E.B., A thermally regenerative ammonia-based battery for efficient harvesting of low-grade thermal energy as electrical power. *Energy Environ. Sci.*, 8, 343–349, 2015.
22. Arshad, A., Ali, H.M., Jabbal, M., Verdin, P.G., Thermal management of electronics devices with PCMs-flledpin-fn heat sinks: a comparison. *Int. J. Heat Mass Transfer*, 117, 1199–1204, 2018.
23. Ren, Q., Guo, P., Zhu, J., Thermal management of electronic devices using pin-fn-based cascademicroencapsulated PCM/expanded graphite composite. *Int. J. Heat Mass Transfer*, 149, 1–16, 2020.
24. Arshad, A., Ali, H.M., Khushnood, S., Jabbal, M., Experimental investigation of pcm-based round pin-fn heatsinks for thermal management of electronics: efect of pin-fn diameter. *Int. J. Heat Mass Transfer*, 117, 861–872, 2018.
25. Tauseef-ur-Rehman, and Ali, H.M., Experimental study on the thermal behaviour of RT-35HC parafnwithincopper and iron-nickel open cell foams: energy storage for thermal management of electronics. *Int. J. Heat Mass Transfer*, 146, 1–13, 2020.
26. Jing, J.H., Wu, H.Y., Shao, Y.W., Qi, X.D., Yang, J.H., Wang, Y., Melamine foam-supported form-stable phasechange materials with simultaneous thermal energy storage and shape memory property for thermalmanagement of electronic devices. *ACS Appl. Mater. Interfaces*, 11, 21, 19252–19259, 2019.
27. Hayat, M.A., Ali, H.M., Janjua, M.M., Pao, W., Li, C., Alizadeh, M., Phase change material/heat pipe and copperfoambased heat sinks for thermal management of electronic systems. *J. Energy Storage*, 32, 1–10, 2020.
28. Qian, C., Gheitaghy, A.M., Fan, J., Tang, H., Sun, B., Ye, H., Zhang, G., Thermal management on IGBT powerelectronic devices and modules. *IEEE Access*, 6, 12868–12884, 2018.
29. Hao, M., Li, J., Park, S., Moura, S., Dames, C., A passive interfacial thermal regulator based on shape memoryalloy and its application to battery thermal management. *Nat. Energy*, 3, 10, 899–906, 2018.

30. Sponagle, B., Groulx, D., White, M.A., Experimental evaluation of a latent heat storage module with a heatspreader for thermal management of a tablet computer. *Appl. Sci.*, 11, 9, 1–20, 2021.
31. Ahmed, T., Bhouri, M., Groulx, D., White, M.A., Passive thermal management of tablet PCs using phasechange materials: continuous operation. *Int. J. Therm. Sci.*, 134, 101–115, 2018.
32. Lou, L., Shou, D., Park, H., Zhao, D., Wu, Y.S., Hui, X., Yang, R., Kan, E.C., Fan, J., Thermoelectric airconditioning undergarments for personal thermal management and HVAC energy savings. *Energy Build.*, 226, 1–11, 2020.
33. Yu, Z., Gao, Y., Di, X., Luo, H., Cotton modifed with silver nanowires and polydopamine for wearable thermal management device. *RSC Adv.*, 6, 72, 1–19, 2016.
34. Vural, R.A., Demirel, I., Erkmen, B., Design and optimisation of a power supply unit for low-profle LCD and LED TVs. *Int. J. Optim. Control Theor. Appl.*, 7, 2, 158–166 28, 2017.
35. Al-Baghdadi, M.A.R.S., Experimental and CFD study on the dynamic thermal management in smartphones and using graphene nanosheet coating as an efective cooling technique. *Int. J. Energy Environ.*, 11, 2, 97–106, 2020.
36. Ezgi, C.N., Basic Design Methods ofHeat Exchanger, in: *Heat Exchangers-Design, Experiment and Simulation*, IntechOpen, Rijeka, 2017.
37. Chen, Q. and Ren, J., Generalized thermal resistance for convective heat transfer and its relation to entransy dissipation. *Chin. Sci. Bull.*, 53, 23, 3753–3761, 2008.
38. Iu, I., *et al.*, Applying the effectiveness-NTU method to elemental heat exchanger models. *ASHRAE Trans.*, 113, 1, 504–513, 2007.
39. Borjigin, S., *et al.*, Coupling ε-NTUmethod for thermal design of heatexchanger in cabinet cooling system. *Appl. Therm. Eng.*, 159, 113972, 2019.
40. Smith, R., *Chemical Process Designnd Integration*, John Wiley & Sons, New York City, United States, 2005.
41. Vengateson, U., Design of multipleshell and tube heat exchangers in series:E shell and F shell. *Chem. Eng. Res. Des.*, 88, 5–6, 725–736, 2010.
42. Wales, R. and Re, W., Mean Temperature Difference in Heat Exchangers. New York, United State, *Chem. Eng. J.*, 13, 1–607, 1981.
43. Xu, Y., Kayange, H.A., Cui, G., A nodes-based non-structural model considering a Series structure for heat exchanger network synthesis. *Processes*, 8, 6, 695, 2020.
44. Ravagnani, M.A. and Caballero, J.A., Optimal heat exchanger network synthesis with the detailed heat transfer equipment design. *Comput. Chem. Eng.*, 31, 11, 1432–1448, 2007.
45. Wang, X., Zhang, L., Luo, Z., Artificial intelligence for the optimization of heat exchanger design. *Energy Rep.*, 7, 544–553, 2021.

46. Han, X.Q., Gao, S., Wang, Y.G., Advancements in Q-Learning Meta-Heuristic. Chen, J. and Li, H., Recent progress in artificial intelligence for heat exchanger design: Review and future directions. *Appl. Energy*, 291, 116805, 2021.
47. Pan, D. and Zhou, Y., Smart buildings and intelligent transportations with artificial intelligence and digitalization technology, in: *Advances in Digitalization and Machine Learning for Integrated Building-Transportation Energy Systems*, pp. 1–15, Elsevier, 2024. DOI: 10.1016/B978-0-443-13177-6.00003-5.
48. Xie, X., Model Based Analysis of Multimodal Neuroimaging: From Neural Masses to Spectral Graph Theory, Weill Medical College of Cornell University, 2021.
49. Liao, G., Li, Z., Zhang, F., Liu, L., A review on the thermal-hydraulic performance and optimization of compact heat exchangers. *Energies*, 14, 19, 6056, 2021.
50. Chen, B.L., Yang, T.F., Sajjad, U., Ali, H.M., Yan, W.M., Deep learning-based assessment of saturated flow boiling heat transfer and two-phase pressure drop for evaporating flow. *Eng. Anal. Boundary Elem.*, 151, 519–537, 2023.
51. Talagadadeevi, R.K., Bhavirisetty, S.K., Gurrampati, V.R.R., Dynamics of Ferromagnetic Hybrid Nanofluids in the Presence of Permeable Surface. *Mechanics*, 31, 2, 102–109, 2025.
52. Chen, T., Cao, S.J., Wang, J., Nizamani, A.G., Feng, Z., Kumar, P., Influencesof the optimized air curtain at subway entrance to reduce the ingress of outdoor airborne particles. *Energy Build.*, 244, 111028, 2021.
53. Celik, N., Tasar, B., Kapan, S., Tanyildizi, V., Performance optimization of a heat exchanger with coiled-wire turbulator insert by using various machine learning methods. *Int. J. Therm. Sci.*, 192, 108439, 2023.
54. Thanikodi, S., Singaravelu, D.K., Devarajan, C., Venkatraman, V., Rathinavelu, V., Teaching learning optimization and neural network for the effective prediction of heat transfer rates in tube heat exchangers. *Therm. Sci.*, 24, 1 Part B, 575–581, 2020.
55. Zhang, T., Chen, L., Wang, J., Multi-objective optimization of elliptical tube fin heat exchangers based on neural networks and genetic algorithm. *Energy*, 269, 126729, 2023.
56. Lodhi, S.K., Hussain, H.K., Hussain, I., Using AI to Increase Heat Exchanger Efficiency: An Extensive Analysis of Innovations and Uses. *Int. J. Multi. Sci. Arts*, 3, 4, 1–14, 2024.
57. Yue, Y., Yan, Z., Ni, P., Lei, F., Yao, S., Machine learning-based multi-performance prediction and analysis of Earth-Air Heat Exchanger. *Renew. Energy*, 227, 120550, 2024.
58. Krishnaveni, T.R. and Reddy, G., Cattaneo-Christov double diffusive flow of ferromagnetic hybrid nanofluids through a permeable surface. *Engineering and Applied Science Letters (EASL)*, 8, 50–61, 2025.

59. Ahmed, N., Assadi, M., Ahmed, A.A., Banihabib, R., Optimal design, operational controls, and data-driven machine learning in sustainable borehole heat exchanger coupled heat pumps: Key implementation challenges and advancement opportunities. *Energy Sustain. Dev.*, 74, 231–257, 2023.
60. Kharaji, S., Heat Exchanger Design and Optimization, in: *Heat Exchangers*, IntechOpen, 2021. DOI: 10.5772/intechopen.100450.
61. Taner, O.O., Mercan, H., Çolak, A.B., Radulovic, J., Taner, T., Dalkılıç, A.S., Application of artificial intelligence techniques for heat exchanger predictions in food industry, in: *Advanced Materials-Based Thermally Enhanced Phase Change Materials*, pp. 269–325, Elsevier, 2024. DOI: 10.1016/B978-0-443-21574-2.00003-4.
62. Çolak, A.B., Açıkgöz, O., Mercan, H., Dalkılıç, A.S., Wongwises, S., Prediction of heat transfer coefficient, pressure drop, and overall cost of double-pipe heat exchangers using the artificial neural network. *Case Stud. Therm. Eng.*, 39, 102391, 2022.
63. Kumar, B.A., Rachakonda, T., Reddy, G.V.R., Effects of Heat Source and Thermal Radiation on MHD Casson and Williamson Nanofluid Flow in a Porous Media. *Adv. Nonlinear Var. Inequalities*, 28, 5, 200–212, 2025.
64. Ahmadi, S., IrandoostShahrestani, M., Sayadian, S., Maerefat, M., HaghighiPoshtiri, A., Performance analysis of an integrated cooling system consisted of earth-to-air heat exchanger (EAHE) and water spray channel. *J. Therm. Anal. Calorim.*, 143, 473–483, 2021.
65. Thulukkanam, K., *Heat exchanger design handbook*, CRC press, 2000.
66. Kushwaha, R., Exploring Nanomaterials for Enhanced Thermal Conductivity in Next-Generation Heat Exchangers. *Int. J. Sci. Innov. Eng.*, *1*, 1, 9–14, 2024.
67. Cui, Y., Tian, S., Zoras, S., Zhu, J., Recent advances in various nanomaterials utilized in geothermal heat exchangers. *Nano Energy*, 122, 109309, 2024.
68. Babu, B.V. and Mohiddin, S.B., Automated design of heat exchangers using artificial intelligence based optimization. *Proceedings of 52nd Annual session of IIChE (CHEMCON-99)*, 1999.
69. Çengel, Y.A. and Ghajar, A.J., *Heat and Mass Transfer: Fundamentals and Applications*, New York City, 2020. ISBN 978-0-07-339818-1.
70. Smith, R., *Chemical process: design and integration*, John Wiley & Sons, 2005.
71. Guo, J., Cheng, L., Xu, M., Optimization design of shell-and-tube heat exchanger by entropy generation minimization and genetic algorithm. *Appl. Therm. Eng.*, 29, 14-15, 2954–2960, 2009.
72. Costa, A.L. and Queiroz, E.M., Design optimization of shell and tube heat exchangers. *Appl. Therm. Eng.*, 28, 14-15, 1798–1805, 2008.
73. Iyer, V.H., Mahesh, S., Malpani, R., Sapre, M., Kulkarni, A.J., Adaptive range genetic algorithm: a hybrid optimization approach and its application in the design and economic optimization of shell-and-tube heat exchanger. *Eng. Appl. Artif. Intell.*, *85*, 444–461, 2019.
74. Krzywanski, J., A general approach in optimization of heat exchangers by bio-inspired artificial intelligence methods. *Energies*, *12*, 23, 4441, 2019.

75. Faghri, A., Heat pipes: review, opportunities and challenges. *Front. Heat Pipes (FHP)*, *5*, 1, 1–14, 2014. DOI:10.4236/jectc.2015.51001.
76. Zhao, Y., Li, T., Zhang, X., Zhang, C., Artificial intelligence-based fault detection and diagnosis methods for building energy systems: Advantages, challenges and the future. *Renew. Sustain. Energy Rev.*, *109*, 85–101, 2019. DOI:10.1016/j.rser.2019.04.021.
77. Lodhi, S.K., Hussain, H.K., Hussain, I, Using AI to increase heat exchan-gerefficiency: An extensive analysis of innovations and uses. *International Journal of Multidisciplinary Sciences and Arts*, 3, 2962–1658, 2024.
78. Kharaji S., Heat Exchanger Design and Optimization, *Heat Exchanger*, 2024, DOI:10.5772/intecopen.100450.

7

Artificial Intelligence-Driven Energy Optimization in Heating, Ventilation, and Air Conditioning Systems

G. Gandhimathi[1], C. Chellaswamy[1], S. Sridevi[2] and Mohamed M. Awad[3]*

[1]Department of Electronics and Communication Engineering, SRM TRP Engineering College, Tiruchirappalli, India
[2]Department of Mathematics, SRM TRP Engineering College, Tiruchirappalli, India
[3]Mechanical Power Engineering Department, Faculty of Engineering, Mansoura University, Mansoura, Egypt

Abstract

The growing demand for energy-efficient thermal management in industrial and commercial systems has spurred innovations in fluid-based cooling and liquid flow optimization. Traditional design and control methods rely on fixed models and heuristics, which limit adaptability to changing conditions. This study introduces a robust framework, combining game theory with partial differential equations (GTPDE) and advanced machine learning techniques to enhance the energy efficiency and operational performance of heating, ventilation, and air conditioning (HVAC) systems, major contributors to energy consumption in industrial environments. In the first phase, game theory principles model fluid flow dynamics by treating each pump as a rational decision-maker. Payoff matrices simulate operational strategies under varying conditions, enabling the identification of optimal parameter combinations to maximize energy efficiency and reduce costs. The second phase employs supervised learning and deep reinforcement learning (DRL) algorithms to predict fluid flow rates, with a hybrid optimum support vector machine (SVM) and DRL model showing superior accuracy and control

**Corresponding author*: m_m_awad@mans.edu.eg; ORCID: https://orcid.org/0000-0001-6238-5872
G. Gandhimathi: ORCID: https://orcid.org/0000-0003-4576-3338
C. Chellaswamy: ORCID: https://orcid.org/0000-0002-2473-6042
S. Sridevi: ORCID: https://orchid.org/0009-0005-4061-911X

Mukesh Kumar Awasthi and Reshu Gupta (eds.) Artificial Intelligence and Computational Modeling in Heat Transfer and Fluid Dynamics, (177–212) © 2026 Scrivener Publishing LLC

over fluid dynamics. Finally, the third phase integrates game theory with the optimum SVM model for predictive maintenance, minimizing equipment downtime and maintenance costs while ensuring reliable system operation. This framework offers practical benefits, including optimized energy use, cost savings, enhanced reliability, and predictive maintenance for HVAC systems, making it a valuable contribution to energy-efficient industrial practices.

***Keywords*:** Fluid cooling and liquid flowing systems, artificial intelligence, ML and deep learning, energy efficiency, system optimization, reinforcement learning, game theory

7.1 Introduction

The study of games is often regarded as "the pinnacle of predictive methods for understanding contention and collaboration between multiple intellectual judgments." This field addresses challenges in modeling and analyzing conflicts within dynamic systems. In this context, processes governed by partial differential equations (PDEs) can be categorized into two types of games: those involving "wickedness" and those involving "good." From a technical perspective, game theory (GT) offers a robust framework for addressing such problems. Despite the varying criteria of participants, this approach focuses on a unified authority and a singular criterion to optimize solutions [8]. In this differential equations-based GT framework, two "optimization problems" arise: 1) Minimizing ("Inf") the impact of a fixed "bad performance" (or disturbance) for a given number of "exceptional quality performers" (or regulations), and 2) Maximizing ("Supreme") disturbances overall. Based on this logic, the engineering approach seeks the "worst of all possible best outcomes."

Bernard's work significantly influenced this field, particularly in the study of fluid-structure interactions using PDEs. Initially, Bernard explored single PDEs of an exponential or sensationalized nature, with regulatory and disturbance factors confined to the spatial domain's outer edges. More recently, various PDE GT models have been developed, including logarithmic equations linked to authority mechanisms mediating between two distinct criteria [10]. For example, Lewicka and Manfredi examined GT in PDE systems, focusing on discrete, linear, and quadratic configurations within fluid-structure systems [15]. These include hyperbolic and parabolic PDEs in abstract theoretical contexts. The applications of these methods span industries such as naval engineering, aerospace, and healthcare. The stability and existence of nonlinear fluid-structure modeling were analyzed using nonlinear Navier–Stokes equations combined with elastomeric equations in multi-dimensional settings [17]. This research paved the way for advanced fluid-structure interaction models where cooperation between rigid and fluidized bodies forms the foundation of regulation. An additional perturbation at the interface of diverse materials inspired the development of a more intricate linear structure theory. The elastic effects on fluid-structure interactions were further explored, revealing that incorporating elasticity transforms the system into a parabolic-analytic relationship, enabling comprehensive and continuous data analysis. Vist *et al.* proposed a machine learning (ML)-based approach for predictive maintenance in building systems, aiming to reduce downtime and enhance energy efficiency [21]. However, the research primarily focuses on theoretical models and lacks real-world validation. It also does not integrate real-time data analytics or address the dynamic nature of building operations. Additionally, scalability across different building types and sizes is not discussed, which is a key limitation for broader application.

Karakoulas *et al.* compared various ML models, such as SVM, ANN, and XGBoost, for HVAC demand response, with a focus on identifying the most accurate model for model predictive control systems. While the study provides valuable insights into prediction accuracy, it does not explore the practical challenges of implementing these models in real-world HVAC systems [6]. Furthermore, the adaptability of the models to varying environmental conditions and occupant behavior remains unexplored, which is crucial for ensuring the model's effectiveness in dynamic real-world scenarios. Xue *et al.* presented a framework for integrating artificial intelligence into HVAC predictive maintenance. They discuss strategies to improve efficiency and reduce downtime [24]. However, their work focuses more on the theoretical framework than on empirical validation, and it lacks case studies or real-world applications. Furthermore, the study does not address how AI-driven maintenance could be integrated with existing building management systems, an important aspect for practical implementation.

In the review article by Ali *et al.*, they provided a comprehensive overview of how ML is applied to enhance building intelligence and energy efficiency. However, while the review is extensive, it falls short in critically analyzing the limitations of these approaches [22]. The challenges related to the implementation of ML in building systems, such as data privacy concerns and ethical implications, are not sufficiently discussed. This is a critical gap, especially given the growing reliance on data-driven technologies in building management systems. Zhang *et al.* presented a multi-agent DRL framework for HVAC control in commercial buildings to reduce energy costs while maintaining occupant comfort. While the framework shows promise in simulations, it lacks validation in real-world settings [9]. Moreover, the study does not address the scalability of the approach to larger and more complex HVAC systems, which limits its generalizability. The research is also missing an exploration of how this model could be adapted for varying building types and operational constraints. Despite significant advancements, several gaps remain in existing literature. Most studies focus on isolated methodologies, such as GT, ML, or RL, limiting their ability to address the multifaceted challenges of HVAC optimization comprehensively. The reliance on extensive datasets, high computational costs, and the need for precise system modeling are recurring limitations. Furthermore, existing approaches often prioritize either energy efficiency or system reliability, rarely achieving a balanced optimization. The proposed framework addresses these gaps by integrating GTPDE and advanced ML techniques. This hybrid approach enables:

1. **Dynamic adaptability**: By employing GT, the system adapts to changing conditions, optimizing interactions between components.
2. **Precision and scalability**: PDEs provide a mathematically rigorous foundation for modeling fluid dynamics, ensuring precise control over system operations.
3. **Data-driven insights**: Advanced ML techniques, including supervised learning and DRL, enhance predictive capabilities, enabling real-time decision-making.

The importance of this proposed method lies in its ability to balance energy efficiency, operational cost, and system reliability simultaneously. By bridging the gaps identified in the literature, it offers a robust solution for modern HVAC systems, contributing to sustainable and cost-effective industrial.

7.1.1 Objective of this Chapter

- Minimize energy consumption: Optimize the energy usage of HVAC systems while maintaining desired indoor climate conditions, including temperature, humidity, and air quality. Achieve energy savings through intelligent and adaptive control strategies, reducing wastage effectively. The integration of PDEs with GT in fluid-structure systems helps refine this approach over time.
- Evaluate game-theory-based approaches: Provide an in-depth evaluation of game-theory-based methodologies for time-period switching and their application to PDEs in fluid-structure systems. Develop systems capable of adapting

to changing environmental conditions, such as weather variations and occupancy patterns, while effectively managing uncertainties and dynamic fluctuations in building energy demands.

- Facilitate PDE integration: Streamline the assembly and implementation of PDEs in fluid-structure systems by utilizing trust extension frameworks. Enable seamless integration with IoT devices, smart meters, and sensors, leveraging real-time data to enhance decision-making processes.
- Support interoperability and sustainability: Ensure compatibility with other building automation systems for comprehensive and holistic building management. Contribute to reducing greenhouse gas emissions by improving the energy efficiency of HVAC operations, supporting global goals for energy conservation and environmental sustainability.
- Game theory for change management: Leverage GT to address and adapt to system changes, completing the integration and optimization of PDEs in fluid-structure applications.

7.1.2 Motivation

The motivation for using DRL in energy prediction and optimization for HVAC systems is driven by the increasing demand for energy efficiency, cost reduction, and environmental sustainability. Below are some key motivational aspects:

- There are several real-world applications for PDEs. They are employed in a wide range of applications, such as the explanation of PDEs using GT in fluid structures, the calculation of energy transfer or flow rate, and the movement of a substance like a swinging pendulum. We examine the simplest mathematical model available to control the energy dynamics of specific species to demonstrate the application of PDEs with GT in fluid-structure.
- Energy efficiency and sustainability account for a significant portion of energy usage in residential, commercial, and industrial buildings, often making up 30–50% of total building energy consumption. Environmental contributions will increase by PDEs with GT in fluid-structure.
- Dynamic and complex control requirements in HVAC systems operate in complex environments with nonlinear

interactions between variables such as temperature, humidity, occupancy, and weather conditions in PDEs with GT in fluid-structure.

- Uncertainty and variability: External factors such as unpredictable weather patterns and occupancy schedules necessitate a more robust control mechanism in PDEs with GT in fluid-structure.
- According to the fluid-structure principle, PDEs with GT, the speed of fluid improves in conjunction with either an improvement in steady pressure or a reduction in the amount of potential energy. Various forms of GTPDE can be produced by applying this idea to different varieties of fluid flow.
- It is derivable from the conservation of energy principle. According to this, the entire amount of energy in a fluid that moves along its length is identical at every point along the path of motion in a state of constant flow. This ensures that the total of internal, potential, and kinetic energy remains consistent.
- High computational costs: Classical optimization techniques, like model predictive control, can be computationally expensive for real-time applications in PDEs with GT in fluid-structure.
- Suboptimal energy management: Without learning from real-time data, traditional systems often result in energy inefficiencies in PDEs with GT in fluid-structure.
- Data-driven decision making: DRL learns optimal control policies directly from data, bypassing the need for explicit modeling of the HVAC system's dynamics in PDEs with GT in fluid-structure.

The remaining part of this chapter is organized as follows: Section 7.2 presents the literature review, covering ML in fluid mechanics and HVAC systems, GT, reinforcement learning (RL) for HVAC control, and predictive maintenance and energy optimization. Section 7.3 discusses the GT Structure of liquid flow. Section 7.4 focuses on the liquid flow of fluid-structural systems. Results and discussions are provided in Section 7.5, followed by the conclusion in Section 7.6.

7.2 Literature Review

The integration of advanced methodologies, including GT, PDEs, and ML, has recently gained traction in optimizing HVAC systems. These innovations aim to address challenges in energy efficiency, operational costs, and system reliability. This literature review synthesizes recent findings published in various journals, highlighting the advancements, limitations, and gaps in existing methods while establishing the relevance of the proposed framework combining GT, PDEs, and ML.

7.2.1 Machine Learning in Fluid Mechanics and Heating, Ventilation, and Air Conditioning Systems

Brunton *et al.* presented a comprehensive study on applying ML techniques to fluid mechanics, emphasizing their capability in modeling, optimizing, and controlling fluid flows [19]. They identified the potential of supervised and unsupervised learning in understanding complex flow dynamics. However, their reliance on large datasets limits applicability in data-scarce scenarios. Similarly, Wang *et al.* explored ML applications in predictive modeling for HVAC systems. Their study revealed that deep neural networks could achieve high prediction accuracy in thermal load forecasting, but the computational cost was significant [4]. The authors pointed out that ML models often require regular updates to stay effective under dynamic conditions, which poses a maintenance challenge. Tang *et al.* highlighted the role of interpretable ML models in fluid mechanics, showcasing improved transparency in system operations [1]. Despite these advantages, they found that interpretable models often sacrifice accuracy, creating a trade-off that limits their applicability in high-precision scenarios like HVAC optimization.

7.2.2 Game Theory in Energy Efficiency and System Optimization

The adoption of GT in energy efficiency has been extensively studied. Yang and Lee applied GT to HVAC systems, treating each subsystem as a player aiming to optimize its performance [23]. Their approach demonstrated significant energy savings, particularly in multi-zone buildings. However, their model required *a priori* knowledge of payoff matrices, which are often unavailable in real-world systems. Xu *et al.* extended this by introducing a dynamic game model that adapts to changing environmental conditions [16]. While effective in simulations, their model's reliance on precise sensor data made it impractical for deployment in older HVAC systems with limited instrumentation. Chen *et al.* proposed integrating GT with ML algorithms to predict optimal operating points for HVAC systems [12]. They reported promising results but noted that the computational complexity of their hybrid model increased exponentially with system size, reducing its scalability.

7.2.3 Reinforcement Learning for Heating, Ventilation, and Air Conditioning Control

Reinforcement learning has emerged as a promising method for optimizing HVAC systems. Smith *et al.* developed an RL-based controller that autonomously adjusted temperature and airflow to minimize energy costs [5]. While the system achieved up to 25% energy savings, it struggled to balance energy efficiency and occupant comfort during peak hours. Huang *et al.* introduced a multi-agent RL framework to manage HVAC systems in commercial buildings [20]. Their approach proved effective in reducing overall energy consumption while maintaining thermal comfort. However, the complexity of training multiple agents simultaneously led to convergence issues in some scenarios. Zhang *et al.* combined RL with supervised learning to create a hybrid model for HVAC optimization [11]. The hybrid approach significantly improved learning speed and stability but required extensive offline training, which limited its adaptability to new environments.

7.2.4 Optimization and Control of Fluid Flows

The integration of ML into computational fluid dynamics has opened new avenues for optimizing fluid flow. Liu *et al.* utilized convolutional neural networks to predict fluid flow patterns, achieving high accuracy with reduced computational costs compared to traditional computational fluid dynamics methods [14]. However, their model's inability to generalize to unseen flow conditions limited its practical use. Wang *et al.* explored PDE-based optimization techniques for fluid flow control [7]. Their study demonstrated that coupling PDEs with optimization algorithms could provide precise control over fluid dynamics. Nonetheless, the high computational demand for solving PDEs in real-time made their approach less feasible for time-sensitive applications. Jiang *et al.* proposed a hybrid approach combining GT and PDEs to optimize pump operations in fluid-based systems [2]. While their method effectively reduced energy consumption, it required detailed system modeling, which is challenging for complex or poorly documented systems.

7.2.5 Predictive Maintenance and Energy Optimization

Predictive maintenance is a critical area of research for HVAC systems. Lee *et al.* integrated ML models with sensor data to predict equipment failures. Their approach reduced maintenance costs but required extensive sensor networks, making it cost-prohibitive for small-scale installations [13]. Sharma *et al.* introduced a GT-based predictive maintenance framework. By treating each component as a player, they optimized maintenance schedules to minimize downtime [3]. However, the framework struggled to account for the stochastic nature of component failures. Kim *et al.* combined ML and RL techniques for predictive maintenance, enabling proactive interventions based on real-time data [18]. While their system achieved high accuracy, the need for continuous data streaming posed challenges in data storage and processing.

7.3 Game Theory Structure of Liquid Flow

The efficient management of thermal systems, particularly HVAC systems, demands an interdisciplinary approach that integrates advanced computational techniques and robust optimization frameworks. Traditional methods relying on fixed models and heuristics often fall short in adapting to dynamic operating conditions, resulting in suboptimal performance and increased energy consumption. To address these challenges, this study employs a hybrid methodology combining GT, PDEs, and ML to optimize the performance of HVAC systems in terms of energy efficiency, operational cost, and system reliability. This section outlines the materials and methodological framework adopted to achieve the research objectives. The proposed methodology is divided into three phases, each employing distinct computational and analytical tools. The first phase utilizes game-theoretic principles to model interactions among system components, treating each as a rational decision-maker with specific optimization goals. The second phase leverages ML techniques, including supervised learning and DRL, to predict fluid flow parameters and enhance operational control. Finally, the third phase integrates the outputs of GT and ML models with PDEs to enable predictive maintenance and adaptive system control.

The structure involves applying game-theoretic principles to analyze and optimize fluid dynamics, particularly in systems where multiple agents, pathways, or components interact to influence the flow. This approach is particularly useful in engineering, transportation networks, and biological systems, where competition, cooperation, or optimization play a role. Here is a breakdown of the structure:

- **Game Theory** is a collection of mathematical models created to investigate GTPDE and conflict scenarios. For individual decision makers in these circumstances, it focuses on identifying sustainable outcomes and best practices [11]. For example, $u = \{u_1(t), u_2(t) \ldots\ldots u_n(t)\}$ is correctly predicted in a liquid flow. This is $L_1 = m_1 \times m_2$ accepting it is poles apart considered $u_i = u$ manipulative opportunity of liquid flow. It can be sure to share liquid flow types of strategies L_i for all.
- **Zero-Sum Games**: One player's gain is another's loss, applicable in competitive systems with limited resources (e.g., flow capacity). Each template is in the tensor $C \in R^n$ is $C = (1,1,\ldots 1)$. The zero temperature is represented by $o = (0,0,0\ldots\ldots 0) \in R^n$. We do in advance the liquid flows between, which will be determined.
- **Dynamic or Repeated Games**: Fluid flow systems often involve time-dependent behavior, requiring iterative optimization over time. The symbol u is a performance of liquid flow $L = m_1 \times m_2 \ldots\ldots m_n$ a calculated forecasting galaxy and $t : m \to R^n$ a motivational aspect for strategic planning of liquid flow. The four-fold $u = \{s, m, t\}$ is a simple GT [12]. **State:** If $u = \{s, m, t\}$ is about returning to normal, and the file has a standardized format $t_i : m \to R$ the golfer receives the value of s_i and i^{th} share of t's part, therefore, a risk-reward of pump. In **Continuous,** liquid flow form with if $u = \{s, m, t\}$. If there exists a set of values $(\delta_1, \delta_2 \ldots\ldots\ldots \delta_n)$ then there can be a continuous zero-sum for $C \in R$, and for all item sets, we would have $\prod_{i=1}^{n} t_i(\delta_1, \delta_2 \ldots\ldots\ldots \delta_n) - C$, as any game G that is not a continuous sum is denoted as a general sum.

7.3.1 Introduction of Matrix Format

The goal of the modeler is to explain what will happen in an anticipated event by describing it in terms of game rules [13].

The format of the information consists of a sequence of numbers with R as its value. The U matrix called $U \in R^{mxn}$ has many rows connecting it to $m \times n$. The array can be constructed as U_i, where R interprets each element in each of the jth columns or i^{th} rows of U as a value numbered from 1 *to* m denoted by U_{ij}. Additionally, i^{th} the sequence U can be written as U_{i}. When that happens, the $m = n$ structure U is described as having a rectangular shape.

Using the liquid flow shape game with $u = \{S, L, U\}$ using $S = \{s_1, s_2 \ldots s_m\}$ and $L = m_1 \times m_2 \times \ldots . m_m$. If $L_i(i = 1,2 \ldots m)$, plans have been made for it $L_i = \left(\delta_1^1, \delta_2^1 \ldots\ldots \delta_{n_i}^1\right)(i = 1,2 \ldots m)$. Every participant has a $U_i \in R^{n_1 x n_2}$ framework, so the element (r,c) of U_i is given by $u = \{S, M, U_1, U_2 \ldots . U_m\}$, which is an approachable game for L- liquid flow.

Theorem 7.1:
Let $u = \{S, L, U_1, U_2 \ldots . U_m\}$ be an objective to change the liquid with $L_1 = \left(\delta_1^1, \delta_2^1 \ldots \delta_i^1\right)$ and $L_2 = \left(\delta_1^2, \delta_2^2 \ldots \delta_j^2\right)$. If the game S_1 started strategic δ_r^1 as the liquid flow, S_2 selects calculated design, and S_m ended strategic δ_c^2 then $L_1\left(\delta_r^1, \delta_c^2\right) = e_r^T U e_c$, $L_2\left(\delta_r^1, \delta_c^2\right) = e_r^T U e_c$ and $L_m\left(\delta_r^1, \delta_c^2\right) = e_r^T B e_c$.

Liquid flow with Symmetry and Stability

(i) Liquid flow with Symmetry:
If $u = \{S, L, U_1, U_2 \ldots . U_m\}$ at that point, U is the accomplished situation as a simultaneous GT $U = V^T$.

(ii) Stability:
Let $u = \{S, L, U_1, U_2 \ldots . U_m\}$ execute an L-performers game by $L = m_1 \times m_2 \times \ldots . m_m$. If it is a fixed form calculation, $\left(\delta_i^1, \delta_j^2\right) \in m_1 \times m_2 \times \ldots . m_m$ the phrasings $e_i^T U e_j \geq e_k^T U e_j \ \forall \ k \neq i$ and $e_i^T V e_j \geq e_i^T V e_l \ \forall \ l \neq j$ hold.

The two specified binary matches reach equilibrium. Then we assume that $E = E_1 \times E_2$ to $L_1 = \left(\delta_1^1, \delta_2^1 \ldots \delta_m^1\right)$, $L_2 = \left(\delta_1^2, \delta_2^2 \ldots \delta_m^2\right)$ and $L_m = \left(\delta_1^2, \delta_2^2 \ldots \delta_m^2\right)$. Every m-binary liquid flow strategy matches are a permutation $u = \{S, M, U\}$ of $U \in R^n$.

Theorem 7.2:
Let $u = \{S, L, U\}$ be a double unique game event with a small end result. If and only if $e_i^T U e_j = U_{kl} = U_{kl}$ a method of liquid flow strategy doubles (e_i, e_j) is an impartial the strategy. If U, the game's value is $V_C = e_i^T U e_j$.

7.4 Liquid Flow of Fluid-Structural System

The liquid flow in fluid-structural systems refers to the interaction between a fluid (such as water, air, or oil) and a structure (such as pipes, tanks, or membranes) under dynamic conditions. These systems are fundamental in a variety of engineering applications, including HVAC systems, hydraulic engineering, and aerospace. The coupling of fluid dynamics and structural mechanics is complex, as changes in one can affect the other. The behavior of fluid flow can induce forces on the structure, which in turn can alter the flow characteristics. To model such interactions, PDEs are often used to describe both fluid motion and structural deformation. An accurate analysis of these systems is essential for optimizing performance, ensuring safety, and improving efficiency in industries such as energy, manufacturing, and transportation. Understanding the fluid-structure interaction helps in designing more robust and efficient systems, particularly in high-performance environments.

7.4.1 Game Theory with Partial Differential Equations Model for Stabilization and Interference of Liquids

The $L_f \cup L_s$ protest marches forward-thinking, which the "liquid flow" L_f is a well-organized split-up of $\mathbb{R}^n$, $n = 3$, as well as a definite insignificant expanse of outline "fixed field." $\mathbb{R}^n$ also is subaquatic in L_f, and fluid-particle communication is a conformational arrangement. Liquid structure L_f is the southern borderline of the equivalent site, and L_s is the supervision line of the authority, which is the in doubt of the exterior area L_f and is where the productions connection.

The arrangements of both apparatuses to forward, which is momentous. Let the constituent of the (t) belongings characterize the peripheral unchanging vertex L_f, which is going to ρ stand on the selected component property and the velocity of the fluid standing to the pressure L_f and becomes an m-dimensional vector acting inward (t) respect to L_s. Let v be the strong spatial dispersion L_s and velocity properties in terms of dimensions. The jumping regulator $P = L_2[0, \mathcal{T}, (L_2(\gamma_s))^n$ discovered, illustrated and currently in operation only on the border γ_s. Let us start by assuming an error $E = (E_1, E_2)$ influences both the part of the structure E_1 in L_f and the part E_2 in L_s. We support our work only on the basis that the rigid body S_s experiences relatively small and rapid variations to allow further modeling work.

The Navier–Stokes term (u) u's convection term $(u\nabla)u$ is linearized to form the equation of LF, which can be defined as $LF = (u\nabla)y_i + (y_i\nabla)u$, $divy_i = 0, y_i / \Upsilon_f = 0$

$$\sum_{i=1}^{m} m_1 \nabla y_i = m_1^2 + m_2^2 + \ldots\ldots + m_1^2 \tag{7.1}$$

We can be written

$$\partial t_i = \partial u_i \frac{\partial m_i}{\partial t_i}, i = 1,2\ldots m \tag{7.2}$$

where

$$\frac{\partial m_i}{\partial t_i} = \frac{1}{2}\left(\frac{\partial m_i}{\partial t_i} + \frac{\partial m_j}{\partial t_i}\right) + \frac{1}{2}\left(\frac{\partial m_i}{\partial t_i} - \frac{\partial m_j}{\partial t_i}\right)$$

The rate of liquid flow

$$L_i = \frac{1}{2}\left(\frac{\partial m_i}{\partial t_i} + \frac{\partial m_j}{\partial t_i}\right) \tag{7.3}$$

Velocity of liquid

$$\rho_i = \frac{1}{2}\left(\frac{\partial m_i}{\partial t_i} - \frac{\partial m_j}{\partial t_i}\right) \tag{7.4}$$

$L_{ij} = L_{ji}$, $\rho_{ij} = -\rho_{ji}$, $\partial m_i = L_{ij}\partial t_i + \rho_{ij}\partial t_i$, similarly we can construct the equation for m- number of liquids of GTPDE.

The matrix form of liquid Structure, t ≥ 0, is given by

$$L_{ij} = \begin{bmatrix} L_{11} & L_{12} & L_{13}\dots\dots\dots L_{1n} \\ L_{21} & L_{22} & L_{23}\dots\dots\dots L_{2n} \\ \vdots & & \vdots \\ L_{m1} & L_{m2} & L_{m3}\dots\dots\dots L_{mn} \end{bmatrix} \tag{7.5}$$

7.4.1.1 Overview of Dynamics

Certification Hilbert Galaxies to be accepted onto F = fluid, S = structure, P = predicted value. The formula for dynamically controlled humanity is:

$$S_t = AS + BC + CE \text{ on } [\mathrm{D}(A^*)]\ y_0 \in S \tag{7.6}$$

subject to certain conditions.

7.4.1.2 Hypotheses

F_1 : A minor creator of the semi-group e^{At} on, t ≥ 0, is $A = S \supset DA \rightarrow S.$

F_2 : B is a straight-line defective on $F = DB \rightarrow S[\mathrm{D}(A^*)]$, satisfying the state-run $\tau(\pi, A)B \in \ell(F,S)$, for certain $\pi \in P(A)$, anywhere $\tau(\pi, A)$ and $P(A)$, is the resolution of A

F_3 : C is a lined operational on $V = DC \rightarrow [\mathrm{D}(A^*)]$, sufficient the nationwide $\tau(\pi, A)C \in \ell(F,S)$, for certain $\pi \in P(A)$.

F_4 : Let $\pi = \mathbf{D}(\pi) \rightarrow [\mathrm{D}(A^*)]$ be a lined worker, such that $\mathrm{D}(\pi) \supset \{e^{At}BF, 0 < t < T\} \cup \{e^{At}CF, 0 < t < T\} \cup S$

F_5 : The tripartite $\{A,B,\pi\}$ fulfills the next output remarkable estimate disorder: There happens $0<\alpha<1$ and a continuous $C_t>0$

such that $|\pi e^{At}B| - |B^* e^{A*t}\pi^*| \leq \frac{C_t}{t^\alpha}, \quad 0<t$

$\pi e^{At}BP \in C([0,T]:P)$, for all $P \in V$

Where $(BP,y)=(P,B^*y)$ for all $P \in V$

$S \in D(B^*) \supset D(A^*)$. The purpose space $\alpha^{C([0,T];\nabla)}$ is distinct as $C([s,T];x): |f| = \max_{s<t<T}(t-s)^r |f(t)|$

F_6 : The three-way $\{A,C,\pi\}$ contents the subsequent production remarkable guess disorder is:

$$|\pi e^{At}C| = |B^* e^{A*t}\pi^*| \leq \frac{C_t}{t^\alpha}, \ 0<t\leq T$$

$\pi e^{At}Cw \in C([0,T]:P)$, for all $w \in V$

Where $(Cw,y)=(w,C^*y), w\in V$

F_7 : π in $F_4 \Rightarrow \pi \in l(y,P)$ in F_4, so that πe^{At} is continuous in $S \leftrightarrow C([0,T]:P)$

7.4.1.3 *Fixed Interval Intermission in the Liquid Flow*

Intended for a static $0<T<\infty$ and static $\delta>0$, we associate with $y_t = Ay + BP + Cw$ on $D(A^*)$. If the rate is purposeful,

$$j(P,w,y_0) = j(P,w,y(P,w):y_0) = \int_0^t [|\pi(t)|_P^2 + |C(t)|_u^2 + \gamma^2 |w(t)|_v^2]dt \tag{7.7}$$

where $S(t,y_0)$ is the way out of Equation 7.1 due to $P(t)$ & $w(t)$ as a result, the following GT is problematic $\max_w \min_u j(P,w,y_0)$. There, the ignoble is taken in its entirety $P \in L_2[0,T;F]$ for $w \in L_2[0,T;v]$ stable, and the super-moms are then fully occupied $w \in L_2[0,T;v]$.

7.4.1.4 *Perfect Game Theory for Liquid Structural Communications*

The challenge of combining abstract domains of the PDE of (1) is

$$F^* \equiv \pi \times [(F^1(L_s))^n \times (L_2(L_s))^n] \text{ for } \{u,v,v_t\}, \tag{7.8}$$

where $\pi \equiv \{u \in (L_2(L_f))^n : div = 0, u\nabla v \downarrow_{\gamma f} = 0\}$ and the environmental

$$\mathcal{E} \equiv \{u \in (F^1(L_f))^n : div = 0, u\nabla v \downarrow_{\gamma f} = 0\} \tag{7.9}$$

The L_2-The internal rows denote the area L_s and the identical borderline γ_s

$$u_1, u_2 = \int_{L_s}^{\cdot} (u_1, u_2) dL_s, \quad u_1, u_2 = \int_{\gamma_s}^{\cdot} (u_1, u_2) d\gamma_s \tag{7.10}$$

The space inside L_f is assembled with deference to the kernel function given by the province of

$$\mathcal{E}, (u_1, u_2)_E \equiv \int_f^{\cdot} (u_1, u_2) dL_f \tag{7.11}$$

$F^1(L_f) \equiv |\nabla| L_f$ from Koran's and Poincare's inequality.

$$|u|_{L_f} = \left[\int_{L_f}^{\cdot} |\in (u)^2 \, | dL_f \right]^{\frac{1}{2}} \tag{7.12}$$

In positions of the interior functions of objects, the $F^1(L_s)$ space of systems is determined

$$(v, P)_{1,s} \equiv \int_{L_s}^{\cdot} vP dL_f + \int_{L_s}^{\cdot} \sigma(V) \nabla \epsilon(z) dL_s \tag{7.13}$$

$$|v|_{L_f}^2 \equiv \int_{L_f}^{\cdot} \pi u \times \in (v) dL_s + |v|_{L_s}^2 \equiv F^1(L_s) \tag{7.14}$$

With $T > 0$ the vibrational modes $y_t = Ay + BP + Cw$ on $D(A^*)'$ with the help of a supervisory body and prearranged teething troubles $y_0 \in S$, both come from the free-flow of liquid (1), which we slot in as a perpetual $\gamma > 0$, P and E, this alike ratio, is followed to estimate the integrals.

$$j(P, w, y_0) = \int_0^t [|\pi(t)|_P^2 + |P(t)|_u^2 + \gamma^2 |w(t)|_v^2] dt \tag{7.15}$$

Anywhere, S is the residual product of Equation 7.14 for $j(P,w,y_0)$ and gratifies the π derivation.

$$\left| |\pi e^{At} BP| \le \frac{C_t}{t^{\alpha}} \right|, 0 < \alpha \le T, 0 < t \le T \tag{7.16}$$

∴ The liquid flow of GT is problematic before

$$\min_{w \in L_2(0,T,v)} \min_{P \in L_2(0,T,v)} j(P,w,y_0), y_0 \in F^* \tag{7.17}$$

$$j(u,v,P,w) = \int_0^t \left[|P(t)|^2_{L_2(\gamma_s)} + |u(t)|^2_{L_2(L_f)} + |V(t)|^2_{F^1(L_s)} + |v_t(t)|^2_{L_2(L_s)} \right] dt - \gamma^2 \int_0^t \left[|w_1(t)|^2_{L_2(L_f)} + |w_2(t)|^2_{L_2(L_s)} \right] dt \tag{7.18}$$

The liquid flow of GT corresponds to Equation (7.18) is

$$\max_{w \in L_2(L_f) \times L_2(L_s)} \min_{P \in L_2(\gamma_s)} j(u,v,P,w). \tag{7.19}$$

7.5 Result and Discussion

The experiment is conducted using Google Colab to run ML algorithms and simulations, leveraging its cloud-based nature and access to powerful computing resources. The Python environment in Colab allows for easy integration of libraries like TensorFlow, PyTorch, and scikit-learn for developing and training predictive models. Data was collected using five different pumps in industrial settings. Colab's ability to run complex code and access GPU/TPU resources facilitates the training of DRL models for fluid-structure optimization. Additionally, Colab is used for real-time data visualization and result analysis, enabling efficient collaboration across teams.

7.5.1 Data Collection

The data collection initiative aimed to analyze operational performance across five pumps in an industrial setting. The objective was to develop a suitable ML learner for predicting fluid flow rates, to identify parameter settings that maximize efficiency, ensure stable operations, and detect potential anomalies or malfunctions based on deviations from expected flow rates and assess whether maintenance was required by examining the relationship between key parameters, such as temperature, vibration, pressure, rotations per minute (RPM), and operational hours, and the pumps' operational health.

Five different pumps were monitored to capture variability in performance and wear patterns. Data was recorded over 10,000 operational hours for each pump, covering their lifespan from installation to near-end-of-life stages and 20,000 samples were collected is shown in Figure 7.1. The primary goal was to identify conditions that necessitate maintenance, enabling predictive maintenance strategies. The temperature (Range: 50°C to 150°C) has measured using temperature sensors within the system, and it is used to study the influence of thermal conditions on fluid properties and flow behavior. Vibration intensity (Range: 0 to 5) represents the vibration levels measured by vibration sensors installed on the pump housing used to assess mechanical stability and its impact on flow rate. Pressure level (Range: 0 to 300 psi or bar) has measured using pressure gauges installed in the pump's flow path, and it is used to analyze the effect of pressure changes on the fluid's velocity and flow rate. The rotational speed (Range: 1000 to 3000 RPM) has measured using a tachometer or built-in pump instrumentation, and it is used to correlate the speed of the pump's rotating components with the flow rate. Operational hours (Range: 0 to 10,000 Hrs) indicate the total time the pump has been in operation, and it is used to examine wear and tear effects on flow efficiency. The flow rate

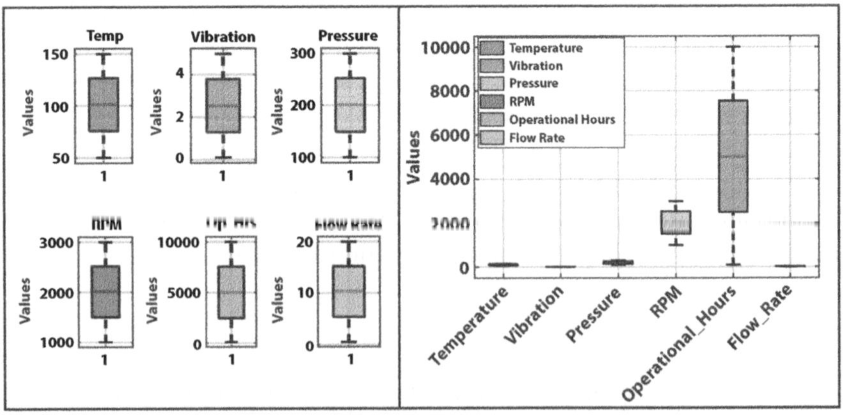

Figure 7.1 The dataset structure of parameters dominating the fluid flow.

(Range: 0.8 to 20 gallons/minute) been measured using flow meters installed at the pump outlet is used to serve as the dependent variable for modeling. Data was collected at regular intervals to ensure comprehensive coverage of operational conditions. Measurements were taken under varying loads, speeds, and environmental conditions to simulate real-world scenarios. Raw data was cleaned to remove outliers, noise, and anomalies introduced by sensor inaccuracies or transient operating conditions. The data was stored in a structured format (e.g., CSV or database) for easy access and analysis. The data collection process provides a robust foundation for predictive modeling, ensuring the reliability and relevance of the analysis.Bottom of Form

7.5.2 Performance of Game Theory

In industrial fluid flow management, GT can be effectively utilized to optimize the performance of interconnected systems, such as pumps. The system involves multiple pumps (e.g., Pump 1, Pump 2, ..., Pump 5). These pumps are responsible for maintaining optimal fluid flow within the industrial environment. Their interactions are modeled as a game where their operational decisions influence not only their own performance but also the overall system efficiency. Each pump employs a set of strategies based on five critical operational parameters: Temperature: Ensuring fluid temperature remains within optimal limits for efficient flow and minimal wear on components. Vibration (Vib): Monitoring and minimizing vibration levels to prevent mechanical failures and reduce energy losses. Pressure: Regulating the fluid pressure to ensure consistent flow rates and avoid system overloading. Rotations per minute: Adjusting motor speed to align with system demands and energy efficiency goals. Operational hours (Op. Hrs): Balancing runtime to avoid overuse and maintain long-term reliability. Each pump's strategy involves varying these parameters to maximize its payoff.

The industrial setting involves a network of pumps working collaboratively to achieve optimal fluid flow through pipelines or machinery. Each pump's performance is interdependent, creating a competitive and cooperative environment. The system's complexity arises from the need to balance competing objectives: Maximizing fluid flow efficiency (Payoff 1), minimizing operational costs (Payoff 2), and distributing workloads evenly to avoid premature failure of individual pumps (Payoff 1). Game theory provides a structured framework to analyze these interactions by treating each pump as a rational decision-maker. Using payoff matrices, the operational strategies can be simulated to predict the outcomes under various conditions.

By evaluating the payoffs, operators can identify the best combination of parameters that optimize the entire system's performance.

In Figure 7.2(a), each matrix represents a different strategy for optimizing fluid flow, with payoffs showing the importance of each parameter in that strategy. Payoff Matrix 1 has the highest payoffs for parameters like RPM and temperature, indicating that these are crucial for maximizing efficiency. Operators should focus on monitoring and controlling these parameters to improve performance. PayoffMatrix2 shows relatively even payoffs, with slightly higher values for vibration and RPM, suggesting a more balanced strategy. This approach may be useful in situations where stability is more important than maximum performance. Payoff Matrix 3 shows equal and low payoffs for all parameters, indicating a neutral strategy that has minimal impact and could be used when adjustments to parameters are limited. In Figure 7.2(b), efficiency (Blue) represents the average effectiveness of each payoff matrix. Payoff Matrix 1 is the most efficient, with a value of 2.2667, followed by Payoff Matrix 2 at 1.7333, and Payoff Matrix 3 at 1.000. This shows that Payoff Matrix 1 is the best for optimizing pump performance, though it may sacrifice fairness. Decision-makers may choose this matrix for better performance, even at the expense of equity. Fairness (Red) measures how equally the payoff is distributed among the five parameters. Payoff Matrix 1 and Payoff Matrix 2 have negative Gini coefficients (-0.3294 and -0.3590, respectively), indicating that some parameters (like RPM and temperature) are favored more than others. Payoff Matrix 3 has a fairness score of 0, meaning the contribution is equal across all parameters. The uneven distribution of contributions in Payoff Matrix 1 and Payoff Matrix 2 suggests that certain components,

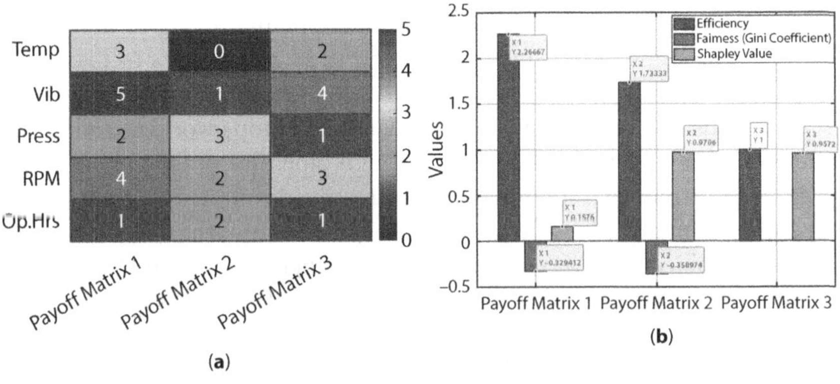

Figure 7.2 Performance of GT in multiple pump arrangements; (a) different strategy of fluid flow; (b) performance metric of GT.

such as RPM, temperature, and vibration, may experience more wear or stress. Maintenance schedules should be adjusted to address these imbalances and prevent failures. Shapley values (Sandal) measure the impact of each parameter on overall performance. In Payoff Matrix 1, vibration and pressure have higher Shapley values, showing that these parameters are critical for achieving optimal performance. The dominance of vibration and pressure in Payoff Matrix 1 highlights the need for advanced sensing and control systems to monitor and manage these parameters in real-time.

7.5.3 Predictive Analysis Using Different Machine Learning Algorithms

The dataset shown in Figure 7.1 containing 10,000 records with all parameters was trained using MATLAB's Regression Learner. The target variable was the flow rate, and multiple ML algorithms were employed to evaluate and optimize predictive performance. Fine Tree: A decision tree with fine granularity, which splits the data into smaller regions to capture intricate patterns but may risk overfitting. Medium Tree: A decision tree with moderate complexity, balancing model interpretability and accuracy by using fewer splits. Coarse Tree: A decision tree with coarse granularity, which uses fewer splits and focuses on broader trends in the data. Linear SVM: A regression model that creates a linear decision boundary, suitable for linearly separable data and simpler relationships. Quadratic SVM: An SVM regression model using a quadratic kernel, allowing for modeling more complex relationships compared to linear SVM. Cubic SVM: An SVM regression model with a cubic kernel that can capture even more intricate nonlinear relationships in the data. Fine Gaussian SVM: An SVM with a Gaussian kernel and a small bandwidth, enabling the model to fit fine details in the data, with a higher risk of overfitting. Medium Gaussian SVM: An SVM with a Gaussian kernel and moderate bandwidth, providing a balance between complexity and generalization. Coarse Gaussian SVM: An SVM with a Gaussian kernel and large bandwidth, which focuses on broad trends in the data rather than detailed patterns. Reinforced learning (optimized SVM): A customized SVM model optimized for the dataset, potentially fine-tuned to enhance performance and robustness. The design parameters of each algorithm are tabulated in Table 7.1.

Each algorithm was evaluated in MATLAB for its ability to predict the flow rate based on the input parameters and tabulated in Table 7.2. The performance of the models varies depending on their complexity,

Table 7.1 Design parameters used in different ML algorithms.

Algorithm	Kernel function	Key parameters	Max splits/ polynomial order	Box constraint	Epsilon (tolerance)
Fine Tree	N/A	Small minimum leaf size, splits capture fine details	High (≥100)	N/A	N/A
Medium Tree	N/A	Moderate minimum leaf size, balanced complexity	Moderate (20–50)	N/A	N/A
Coarse Tree	N/A	Large minimum leaf size, focuses on broader trends	Low (5–20)	N/A	N/A
Optimum Tree	N/A	Large minimum leaf size, focuses on broader trends	Adaptive 1-4205	Dynamic	Adaptive
Linear SVM	Linear	Simple linear relationships	N/A	1	0.1
Quadratic SVM	Polynomial (Quadratic)	Captures nonlinear relationships	Polynomial Order: 2	1–10	0.1
Cubic SVM	Polynomial (Cubic)	More complex nonlinear relationships	Polynomial Order: 3	10–100	0.1
Fine Gaussian SVM	Gaussian (RBF)	Small kernel scale, high flexibility	N/A	1	0.01
Medium Gaussian SVM	Gaussian (RBF)	Moderate kernel scale, balanced generalization	N/A	10	0.1
Coarse Gaussian SVM	Gaussian (RBF)	Large kernel scale, smooth general trends	N/A	100	1
Optimum SVM	Adaptive (Gaussian/ Hybrid)	Optimized parameters, adaptive scale, reinforcement	Adaptive	Dynamic	Adaptive

kernel functions, and generalization capabilities. This approach provided insights into the suitability of different regression models for the given dataset.

Table 7.2 summarizes the performance metrics of different models evaluated based on the root mean square error (RMSE), R-squared, mean squared error (MSE), and mean absolute error (MAE). Among the decision tree models, the optimum tree performed the best with the lowest RMSE (5.8621), MSE (32.07), and MAE (4.9156), achieving an R-squared value of 0. Similarly, the Linear SVM and reinforced learning (optimum SVM) models matched this performance with the same RMSE, MSE, and R-squared, but the optimum SVM achieved the lowest MAE (4.9067).

Table 7.2 Performance metrics of all ML algorithms.

Model	**Root mean square error (RMSE)**	**R-squared**	**Mean squared error (MSE)**	**Mean absolute error (MAE)**
Fine Tree	7.1773	-0.61	51.513	5.8956
Medium Tree	6.391	-0.27	40.485	5.3513
Coarse Tree	5.9608	-0.11	35.531	5.0713
Optimized Tree	5.8621	0.00	32.07	4.9156
Linear SVM	5.6715	0.00	32.166	4.9078
Quadratic SVM	5.6925	-0.01	32.405	4.9237
Cubic SVM	5.7251	-0.02	32.777	4.9345
Fine Gaussian SVM	6.2945	-0.24	39.621	5.2816
Medium Gaussian SVM	5.7695	-0.04	33.288	4.9488
Coarse Gaussian SVM	5.6829	-0.01	32.295	4.9175
Optimized SVM	5.6631	0.00	32.07	4.9067

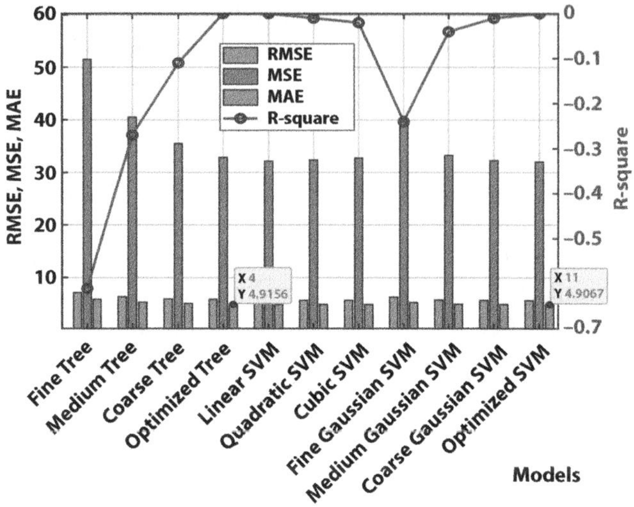

Figure 7.3 Performance metrics of the proposed and other methods.

The fine tree and fine Gaussian SVM showed higher error rates, with RMSEs of 7.1773 and 6.2945, respectively, and negative R-squared values indicating poorer predictive power.

The focus on these ML algorithms shown in Figure 7.3, linear SVM, quadratic SVM, cubic SVM, and the proposed optimized SVM is due to their distinct advantages in regression tasks, specifically their ability to model complex relationships effectively. Linear SVM is chosen for its simplicity and efficiency in handling linear data patterns, while quadratic and cubic SVMs allow for capturing non-linear patterns with increasing complexity. Reinforced learning method of optimum tree and optimum SVM models shown in Figure 7.3 indicate it may be a strong candidate among the tested algorithms.

7.5.4 Predictive Analysis Using Reinforced Algorithm

The regression model shown in Figure 7.4(a) was developed using an optimum decision tree, which is fine-tuned to balance predictive performance and simplicity. The model is configured with a minimum leaf size of 3956, ensuring a controlled balance between bias and variance. Larger leaf sizes help avoid overfitting by smoothing predictions over a broader range of data points. The best hyperparameters for the decision tree were identified during an iterative optimization process. The optimal performance occurred at iteration 28, where the response variable (y) reached a value of 32.0703. The regression tree captures underlying trends in the data with high accuracy, offering robust predictions around the key focus points of the response variable. Fine-tuning ensures that the model generalizes well across unseen data, effectively minimizing prediction errors. This model configuration is ideal for scenarios demanding both precision and interpretability in regression tasks, particularly when dealing with large datasets.

Figure 7.4(b), the optimized SVM model benefits from a box constraint (0.00104029), which allows the model to handle outliers more aggressively while maintaining a smooth decision boundary. A kernel scale enhances the model's flexibility in mapping data to higher dimensions, allowing it to capture complex relationships in the dataset. The epsilon value (688.1393) minimizes the width of the margin around the predictions, leading to a reduction in error. Using the Cubic kernel function further supports the model's ability to capture non-linear relationships, which is beneficial for minimizing the MSE in complex data patterns. The best hyperparameters for the SVM were identified during an iterative optimization process. The optimal performance occurred at iteration 24, where the response variable (y) reached a value of 32.0702. The proposed optimized SVM incorporates advanced techniques for improving accuracy, offering a fine-tuned solution for the given problem. These algorithms also provide a balance between model interpretability and performance, making them suitable for the dataset in question. Lastly, they are well-established and widely used in

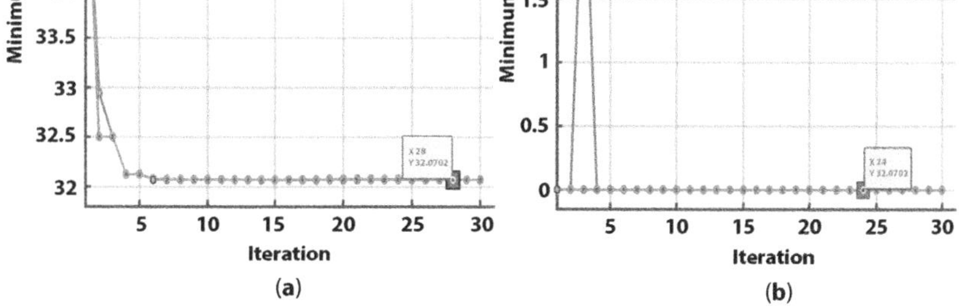

Figure 7.4 Mean squared error of reinforced learning models: (a) optimized tree; and (b) optimized SVM.

ML for predictive modeling, making them ideal candidates for comparison in the context of regression analysis.

7.5.5 Performance Analysis of a Proposed Reinforced Model

Figure 7.5(a) illustrates the predicted fluid flow rate, which falls within the range of 2 to 18, where most of the values are correctly predicted. The model demonstrates a high accuracy in this primary range, showing that the majority of predictions align closely with the actual flow rates. However, the predictions outside this range, specifically from 0.8 to 2 and 18 to 20, were not successfully predicted, indicating areas where the model's performance could be improved. These gaps suggest potential limitations in the model's ability to handle extreme flow rate values or outliers. This proposed model performs well in capturing the dominant trends between temperature and flowrate, particularly within the operational range of 50–150°C is illustrated in Figure 7.5(b). To improve predictions at extreme temperatures, additional data points in these regions should be incorporated, or a more advanced feature representation should be applied to better capture non-linear dependencies. This analysis could aid in optimizing operational conditions by highlighting temperature ranges that yield stable or desired flow rates.

The model effectively predicts flow rates within the primary range (2–18) across the vibration spectrum shown in Figure 7.6(a). However, predictions become less accurate when vibration intensity is close to the extremes (e.g., near 0 or 5), likely due to insufficient data or noise in

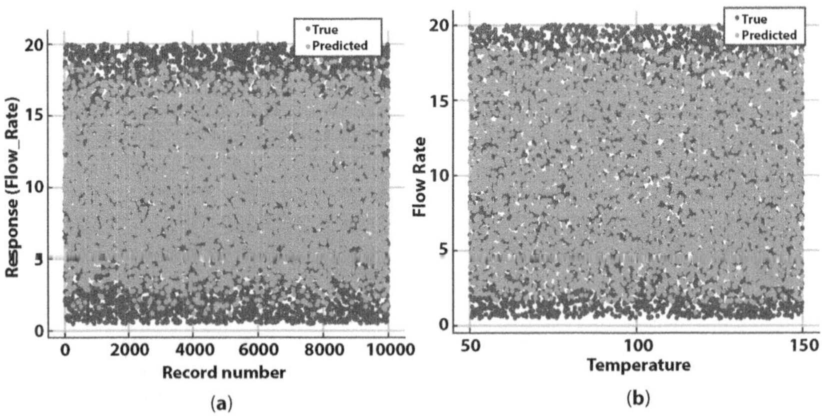

Figure 7.5 Performance of the proposed model: (a) record number vs fluid flow rate; (b) temperature vs fluid flow rate.

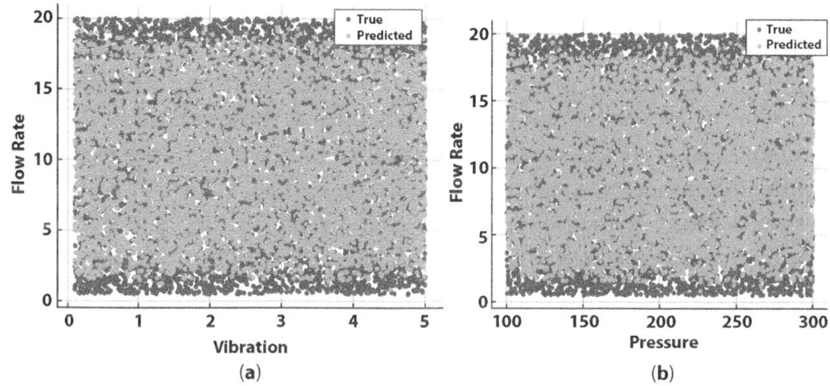

Figure 7.6 Performance of the proposed model in flow rates: (a) vibration and (b) pressure.

these regions. The relationship between pressure and flow rate is captured well within the range of 2–18, showing Figure 7.6(b) a strong correspondence between higher pressure levels and higher flow rates. Outliers in the pressure extremes (very low or very high) correspond to less reliable predictions, as the flow rate occasionally falls outside the expected range (0.8 to 2 or 18 to 20).

In Figure 7.7(a), predictions are highly accurate for mid-range RPMs, where most data points lie within the 2–18 range. The model struggles at very low or high RPMs, suggesting either a non-linear relationship or a lack of sufficient training data in these regions. The model accurately predicts

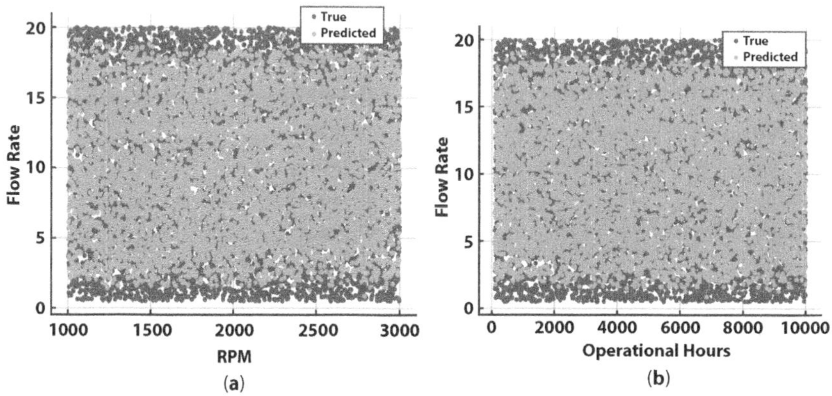

Figure 7.7 Performance of the proposed model in flow rates: (a) RPM and (b) operational hours.

flow rates for pumps that have operated between 0-10000 hours shown in Figure 7.7(b). For newly installed pumps (<1000 hours) or heavily used pumps (>9000 hours), predictions may deviate, reflecting potential gaps in the training data or changing pump dynamics at these extremes.

Figure 7.8(a) presents the residuals of the predicted fluid flow rate, showing the difference between the predicted and actual values. The predicted response value is 16,000, and the residuals are primarily concentrated around 5,000 records, indicating a substantial portion of the predictions are close to the actual values. The residuals fall within a narrow range of -10 to 10, suggesting that most of the predictions have a small error. This indicates a high level of accuracy in the model, with minimal deviation from the true values. The tight distribution of residuals implies that the model is performing well in predicting fluid flow rate, with only minor discrepancies in a few cases.

Figure 7.8(b) depicts a graph comparing the true response and predicted response of the fluid flow rate. In the graph, the true response is represented by the black color, while the predicted response is shown in pink. The graph highlights how closely the predicted values follow the true response, providing an indication of the model's accuracy. While most of the predicted values align well with the true values, some deviations are noticeable, particularly in the ranges where the model struggled to make accurate predictions. This visual comparison underscores the model's overall performance and its areas for improvement in predicting fluid flow rates accurately.

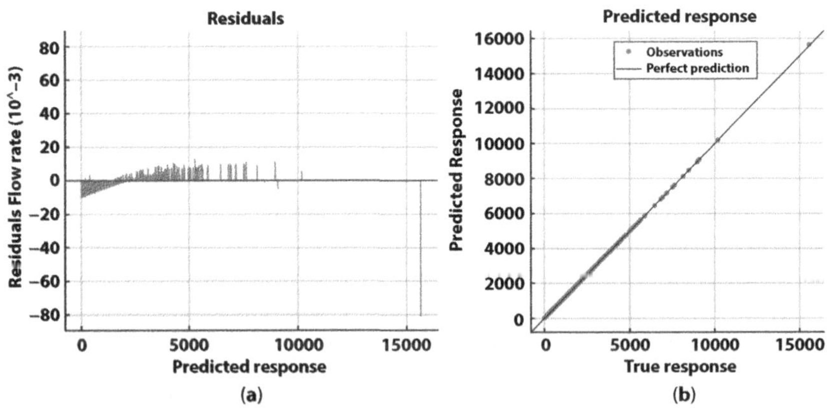

Figure 7.8 Performance of the proposed model: (a) predicted response and (b) true response.

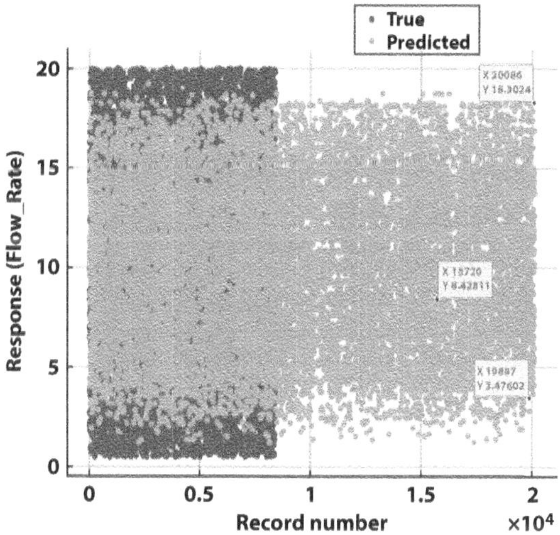

Figure 7.9 Efficiency of a proposed model.

Figure 7.9 represents the flow rate predictions and comparisons using the proposed optimum SVM model. In 20,000 data points, the first 8,000 entries include both true values and their corresponding predicted flow rate values for evaluation and accuracy analysis. In contrast, the remaining 12,000 entries (from 8,001 to 20,000) represent only predicted flow rate values (y=8.42811, y=3.47602 and y=18.3024) generated by the model. This segmentation highlights the model's training and testing phases, emphasizing the transition from validation using known data to pure prediction on unseen entries.

7.5.6 Analyzing Industrial Pumps' Performance Based on RL

Industries are focusing on monitoring and analyzing industrial pumps' performance based on operational data. A dataset includes measurements from multiple pumps and tracks five critical parameters and a maintenance flag indicating whether maintenance is "Needed" or "No Maintenance." The goal is to identify the pumps that require maintenance, and this analysis helps identify patterns or anomalies that may contribute to maintenance requirements, enabling better predictive maintenance strategies. Figure 7.10(a) aids in identifying patterns across pumps and parameters that could indicate all pumps that need maintenance. Figure 7.10(b) represents the magnitude of the mean values for each parameter, allowing comparison across pumps. The first bar in each group represents the mean

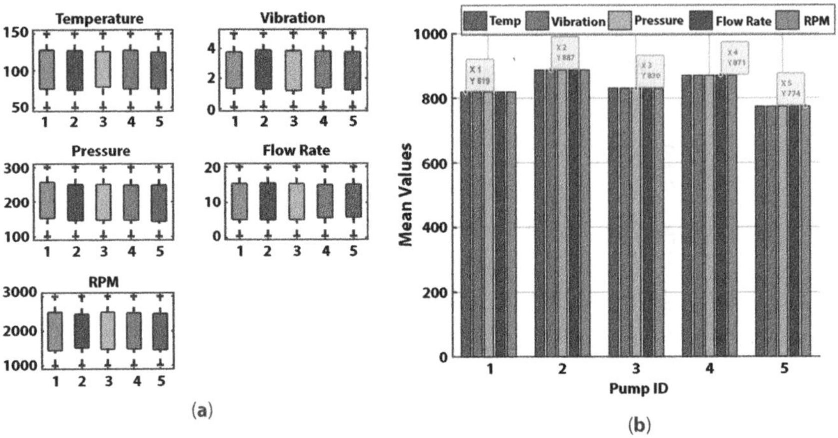

Figure 7.10 Analyzing industrial pumps' performance (a) based on operational data and (b) mean values.

values of the temperature (mean: 819); the second bar represents vibration (mean: 887); the third bar represents pressure (mean: 830); the fourth bar represents flow rate (mean: 871); and fifth bar RPM (mean: 774). This helps identify pumps that deviate significantly in performance, which could indicate potential issues requiring maintenance, and evaluate the overall consistency of the parameters across the pumps. The visualization is ideal for maintenance teams, engineers, and analysts to quickly assess pump conditions and take necessary actions.

7.5.7 Analyzing Industrial Pumps' Performance Based on Graph Theory

Figure 7.11(a) represents the payoff matrices for five pumps, where each matrix corresponds to the performance outcomes of various strategies (e.g., varying operational parameters like efficiency, cost, or energy use). Each cell value signifies the payoff or results for a given strategy under a particular scenario, enabling comparisons and evaluations of performance across different pumps. This structured data serves as input for visualization through confusion matrix-style heatmaps, facilitating the analysis of pump performance in industrial fluid flow management systems.

In Figure 7.11(b), each subplot represents the performance of a single pump, enabling a direct comparison of strategy effectiveness across different pumps. By analyzing the heatmaps, the most effective strategy for each pump under given scenarios can be identified. Higher payoff values indicate

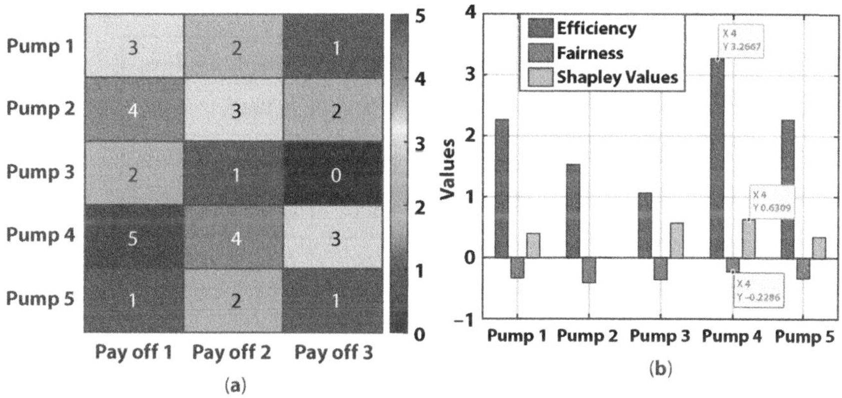

Figure 7.11 Performance of graph theory: (a) different strategies of pumps and (b) performance metrics.

better outcomes, guiding decision-making for operational improvements. Insights from these plots can guide resource allocation, such as prioritizing maintenance or upgrading specific pumps based on their payoff distribution. The collective analysis of all pumps highlights overall system efficiency, helping in determining whether adjustments to strategies (like temperature control or vibration monitoring) improve performance across the board. Figure 7.11 is crucial for informed decision-making in industrial fluid flow management, offering clarity on strategy, efficacy, and operational adaptability.

In Figure 7.11(a), key impact observations are that Pump 4 outperforms all others across all three metrics, making it the most efficient and equitable with significant system contribution. Pump 3 balances fairness and Shapley values well, but lags in efficiency, which could limit its overall performance. Pumps 1 and 5 are similar in performance metrics, offering moderate efficiency and fairness while contributing moderately to the system. Pump 2 requires attention due to its low efficiency, uneven payoff distribution, and negligible Shapley value, highlighting it as the least favorable option in this analysis. This analysis can guide decision-making in optimizing pump operations for balanced performance and fairness.

Table 7.3 provides a comparative analysis of the efficiency, fairness, and Shapley values across five pumps, highlighting key performance metrics as efficiency. Pump 4 shows the highest efficiency at 3.2667, indicating superior performance among all pumps. Pumps 1 and 5 have identical efficiencies of 2.2667, suggesting they perform similarly well. Pump 2 exhibits moderate efficiency at 1.5333, while Pump 3 is the least efficient at 1.0667.

Table 7.3 Performance metrics.

	Efficiency	**Fairness**	**Shapley values**
Pump1	2.2667	-0.3294	0.3942
Pump2	1.5333	-0.4116	0.0031
Pump3	1.0667	-0.3583	0.5673
Pump4	3.2667	-0.2286	0.6309
Pump5	2.2667	-0.3294	0.3419

Fairness (as measured by the Gini coefficient); Pump 4 demonstrates the best fairness with the least negative coefficient (0.2286), implying a more balanced payoff distribution. Pumps 1 and 5 share identical fairness values (-0.3294), representing a similar distribution of rewards. Pump 2 has the lowest fairness (-0.4116), indicating a highly uneven payoff distribution. Pump 3 shows slightly better fairness than Pump 2 with a coefficient of -0.3583. Shapley values: Pump 4 again leads with the highest Shapley value (0.6309), reflecting a significant contribution to the overall system performance. Pump 3 follows with a value of 0.5673, indicating a strong role in performance. Pumps 1 and 5 show moderate Shapley values at 0.3942 and 0.3419, respectively. Pump 2 has the lowest Shapley value (0.0031), suggesting minimal contribution to system outcomes.

In industrial and chemical processes, maintaining a consistent flow rate is vital for ensuring that the system operates within desired parameters, improving product quality and consistency. Pumps are often one of the largest energy consumers in industrial systems. Predicting the flow rate allows for more accurate control over pump speeds, optimizing energy usage, and reducing costs. By monitoring the flow rate, potential issues such as pump wear, cavitation, or blockages can be detected early, preventing failures and reducing maintenance downtime. Predicting flow rate allows engineers to design more efficient pump systems and scale them according to changing demands, ensuring that the infrastructure can handle fluctuations in the flow without compromising performance. Accurate flow rate prediction helps optimize pump operation, ensuring the system runs at its most efficient point, minimizing energy consumption and operational costs.

7.6 Conclusion

In real-world applications, our hybrid optimum SVM and DRL model can be particularly beneficial in HVAC systems for optimizing airflow, energy consumption, and thermal comfort. For instance, predictive models are widely used in smart buildings to enhance efficiency by dynamically adjusting airflows based on occupancy and environmental conditions.

A potential case study could involve implementing our model in commercial HVAC systems, where it can predict and adapt to varying thermal loads, reducing energy waste while maintaining indoor air quality. Similar approaches have been successfully applied in industrial cooling systems and data centers, demonstrating their ability to optimize operations and minimize costs.

Furthermore, existing research on AI-driven HVAC optimization highlights the benefits of ML in improving system performance. Our model aligns with these advancements by incorporating reinforcement learning, enabling real-time adaptability to changing conditions. Future work could involve direct collaboration with industry partners to validate its effectiveness in operational settings.

This study demonstrates the effectiveness of integrating GT, PDEs, and ML to optimize fluid flow dynamics and enhance the operational efficiency of HVAC systems. By modeling fluid dynamics through GT, the study identifies optimal strategies for energy-efficient operation, while the hybrid optimum SVM and DRL model achieves superior accuracy in predicting flow rates and controlling fluid dynamics. Furthermore, integrating predictive maintenance within this framework reduces downtime and maintenance costs, ensuring reliable system performance. The proposed methodology provides a robust and scalable solution for addressing the growing demand for energy-efficient thermal management, offering significant benefits in cost reduction, system reliability, and environmental sustainability.

References

1. Ali, T., Zhang, H., Wang, L., Machine Learning for Smart and Energy-Efficient Buildings. *Environ. Data Sci.*, 9, 2, 98–114, 2022. https://doi.org/10.1017/eds.2022.028.
2. Brunton, S.L., Noack, B.R., Koumoutsakos, P., Machine Learning for Fluid Mechanics. *Annu. Rev. Fluid Mech.*, 52, 477–508, 2019.

3. Chen, D., Huang, J., Liu, G., Integrating Game Theory and Machine Learning for HVAC Optimization. *J. Intell. Syst.*, 30, 1, 246–259, 2021.
4. Huang, F., Zhao, Y., Zhang, Q., Multi-Agent Reinforcement Learning Framework for Commercial HVAC Systems. *Energy Rep.*, 7, 1012–1025, 2021.
5. Jiang, Y., Li, M., Wang, Y., Hybrid Approaches Combining Game Theory and PDEs for Pump Optimization. *J. Energy Eng.*, 149, 3, 04023006, 2023.
6. Karakoulas, A., Konstantinou, S., Zervas, P., Evaluating Machine Learning Models for HVAC Demand Response. *Appl. Energy*, 295, 118045, 2023. https://doi.org/10.1016/j.apenergy.2022.118045.
7. Kim, H., Cho, S., Kang, M., Combining Machine Learning and Reinforcement Learning for Predictive Maintenance. *Smart Energy Syst.*, 16, 2, 225–240, 2023.
8. Lee, C., Park, D., Kim, J., Predictive Maintenance Using Machine Learning for HVAC Systems. *Autom. Constr.*, 135, 104148, 2022.
9. Lewicka, M. and Manfredi, J.J., Game theoretical methods in PDEs. *Boll. Unione Mat. Ital.*, 7, 211–216, 2014. https://doi.org/10.1007/s40574-014-0011-z.
10. Liu, C., Zhang, F., Yang, T., Convolutional Neural Networks for Predicting Fluid Flow Patterns. *Phys. Fluids*, 33, 12, 121901, 2021.
11. Ray, R. and Koley, S., Hydrodynamic Performance of OWC Under Nonlinear Stokes Wave Theory, in: *2024 Third International Conference on Electrical, Electronics, Information and Communication Technologies (ICEEICT)*, Trichirappalli, India, pp. 1–8, 2024, doi: 10.1109/ICEEICT61591.2024.10718591.
12. Dey, S. and Xu, H., An Imbalanced Mean-Field Game Theoretical Large-Scale Multiagent Optimization With Constraints. *IEEE Trans. Syst. Man Cybern.: Syst.*, 55, 1, 443–452, Jan. 2025. doi: 10.1109/TSMC.2024.3481351.
13. Sharma, K., Verma, S., Gupta, A., Game Theory-Based Predictive Maintenance Framework. *Energy Syst.*, 13, 1, 123–145, 2021.
14. Smith, T., Patel, R., Jones, M., Reinforcement Learning-Based Control of HVAC Systems. *IEEE Trans. Smart Grid*, 11, 3, 1912–1923, 2020.
15. Tang, J., Liu, Y., Chen, H., Interpretable Machine Learning Models for Fluid Mechanics. *J. Fluid Eng.*, 144, 5, 051402, 2022.
16. Vist, M., Patel, A., Lee, J., Predictive Maintenance in Building Facilities: A Machine Learning-Based Approach. *J. Build. Perform.*, 12, 5, 450–465, 2021. https://doi.org/10.1016/j.jbp.2021.05.002.
17. Wang, X. and Zhou, K., PDE-Based Optimization Techniques for Fluid Flow Control. *Int. J. Heat Fluid Flow*, 93, 108979, 2022.
18. Wang, X., Zhang, Y., Li, C., Machine Learning Applications in Predictive Modeling for HVAC Systems. *Energy Build.*, 239, 110833, 2021.
19. Xu, R., Zhao, L., Wang, S., Dynamic Game Models for Adaptive HVAC Systems. *Appl. Energy*, 331, 120162, 2023.

20. Xue, Y., Li, L., Zhang, X., AI-Driven Predictive Maintenance in HVAC Systems: Strategies for Improving Efficiency and Reducing System Downtime. *Energy Build.*, 268, 111016, 2023. https://doi.org/10.1016/j.enbuild.2022.111016.
21. Zhang, Y. and Zhang, B., Differential Dynamic Programming for Finite-Horizon Multi-Player Non-Zero-Sum Differential Games of Nonlinear Systems, in: *2023 IEEE 12th Data Driven Control and Learning Systems Conference (DDCLS)*, Xiangtan, China, pp. 511–517, 2023, doi: 10.1109/DDCLS58216.2023.10166320.
22. Yang, Q. and Lee, K., Applying Game Theory to Optimize HVAC Systems in Multi-Zone Buildings. *Build. Environ.*, 185, 107275, 2020.
23. Zhang, D., Li, H., Chen, Z., Distributed Multi-Agent Deep Reinforcement Learning Framework for Whole-Building HVAC Control. *Energy*, 245, 123824, 2023. https://doi.org/10.1016/j.energy.2022.123824.
24. Zhang, P., Lin, W., Yu, H., Hybrid Reinforcement Learning Models for HVAC Optimization. *Energy Convers. Manage.*, 258, 115448, 2022.

8

Artificial Neural Network Model for Radiative Heat Transfer in a Magnetized Tapered Stenosed Artery

Haris Alam Zuberi[1], Naveen Kumar[2] and Nurul Amira Zainal[3]*

[1]Department of Mathematics, School of Computational Sciences, Faculty of Science and Technology, JSPM University, Pune, Maharashtra, India
[2]Department of Applied Mathematics, M. J. P. Rohilkhand University, Bareilly, Uttar Pradesh, India
[3]Fakulti Teknologi dan Kejuruteraan Mekanikal, Universiti Teknikal Malaysia, Hang Tuah Jaya, Durian Tunggal, Melaka, Malaysia

Abstract
Blood flow dynamics in stenosed arteries are significantly shaped by the interplay between the magnetic field and radiative heat transfer, which affects both the precision of diagnosis and treatment approaches. The artificial neural network (ANN) model outperforms conventional numerical techniques in solving highly nonlinear governing equations with improved adaptation to parameter changes, faster convergence, and higher computational efficiency. This serves as motivation for the proposal of an AI-driven framework to model blood flow in an inclined, tapered, stenosed porous artery using physics-informed neural networks (PINNs), a specialized class of ANNs that directly integrate physical rules into the learning process. In contrast to traditional ANNs, which only use data-driven training, PINNs incorporate governing laws into the neural network architecture to guarantee both physical consistency and computational efficiency. Under various magnetic fields and physiological situations, such as extreme arterial tilt and stenosis geometry, the ANN model accurately captures the impacts of radiative heat transfer, which lowers velocity and temperature profiles, according to the observed results. Furthermore, the ANN model offers a deeper knowledge of hemodynamic and thermal interactions by exceeding the conventional method

**Corresponding author*: nurulamira@utem.edu.my; ORCID: https://orcid.org/0000-0003-3045-302X
Haris Alam Zuberi: ORCID: https://orcid.org/0000-0002-9126-759X

Mukesh Kumar Awasthi and Reshu Gupta (eds.) Artificial Intelligence and Computational Modeling in Heat Transfer and Fluid Dynamics, (213–236) © 2026 Scrivener Publishing LLC

(differential transform method) in forecasting wall shear stress and volumetric flow rates. The ANN model outperforms the conventional numerical method in terms of accuracy, as demonstrated by the comparison table and unambiguous graphical representations. By closing the gap between computational efficiency and physiological complexity, this approach enables one to create a more accurate, flexible, and scalable model that transforms the investigation of vascular heat transport and its impact on disease detection and treatment.

Keywords: Physics-informed neural networks (PINNs), radiative heat transfer, magnetized stenosed artery, wall shear stress, volumetric flow rate, haemodynamics

8.1 Introduction

The cardiovascular system is a vital component of human life since it ensures that blood is pumped around the body while delivering oxygen and nutrients and removing metabolic wastes from the tissues and organs [1]. Numerous studies have been conducted regarding the dynamics of blood flow in the human body to identify various physiological or even pathological conditions that can potentially impact health. One component of cardiovascular research is studying arterial stenosis, which pertains to the abnormal narrowing of arteries as a result of plaque build-up or other restrictive lesions leading to altered hemodynamics and increased cardiovascular risks [2]. Understanding the stream dynamics in arteries with stenotic zones is of primary importance for the diagnosis and treatment of many ailments, which is not the case with a sizable proportion of the world's population, where cardiovascular diseases continue to remain the top contributor toward morbidity and mortality [3].

8.1.1 Blood Flow and Magnetic Field Effects

The blood flow patterns in stenosed arteries are primarily dictated by several factors such as arterial geometry, blood viscosity, the effects of heat, and applied forces like magnetic fields [4]. External type magnetic fields have been studied for their therapeutic potential, particularly in the enhancement of blood circulation, as well as in the alleviation of complications arising from excessive viscosity [5, 6]. Furthermore, magnetic fields alter the response of charged blood particles, which changes some thermal properties and flow regimes [7, 8]. In addition, the combination of magnetic fields with nanotechnology has provided new opportunities for therapeutic applications, including targeted drug delivery and nanoparticle-induced hyperthermia [9]. Cabrera *et al.* [10] illustrated that magnetic hyperthermia focused on the clot greatly increases blood clot permeability and thus sensitivity to thrombolysis. Maurya and Kumar [11] emphasized the effect of magnetic fields in controlling heat transfer effects on stenosed arteries, specifically coronary artery disease. The dual effects of magnetic fields and heat transfer are highly significant in biomedical applications like thermal therapy and cryotherapy. This interaction between hemodynamic forces and bioheat transfer mechanisms requires sophisticated computational models that can reproduce these intricate interactions.

8.1.2 Radiative Heat Transfer in Blood Flow

Heat is transferred into biological systems by conduction, convection, and radiation. Though conduction and convection are well-studied, radiative heat transfer has gained interest because of its relevance to different biomedical processes such as laser therapy, hyperthermia therapy, and cryosurgery [12, 13]. Blood, a multiphase fluid, also absorbs and radiates thermal energy, influencing temperature distribution within blood vessels. Goyal *et al.* [14] opined that radiative heat transfer influences the thermal performance of blood, particularly in abnormal conditions like arterial stenosis. Blood heat dissipation is influenced by ambient thermal sources, flow velocity, and vessel geometry. The importance of radiative heat transfer in treatments where temperature control is needed was further brought out by work by Karmakar and Das [15].

Over the past decade, computational fluid dynamics (CFD) models have been combined with radiative heat transfer formulations to model temperature fluctuations in blood vessels. Numerical methods of the conventional kind, however, struggle to describe nonlinear temperature profiles accurately. Incorporating artificial neural networks (ANNs) in bioheat transfer models offers an encouraging solution for addressing these problems.

8.1.3 Artificial Neural Networks in Hemodynamic and Thermal Modeling

It has been shown that ANNs are useful for the simulation and analysis of hemodynamic behavior. Moulton *et al.* [16] presented an artificial intelligence (AI)-based arterial input function for pharmacokinetic modeling of myocardial blood flow optimization. Artificial neural networks have demonstrated accuracy in predicting blood flow properties. Li *et al.* [17] used a physics-informed neural operator to solve difficult cardiovascular problems. Also, the mitigation challenges of hemodynamic simulations, along with the use of ANN-based modeling, have increased computational efficiency [18]. Raja *et al.* [19] studied heat transfer in the flow of Sisko fluids using bio-inspired computational heuristics. More recently, ANN has been integrated with hybrid meta-heuristic optimization algorithms for modeling viscous fluid flow in converging and diverging channels, which further extends the application of machine learning in fluid mechanics.

The recent deep learning and data-driven approaches, notably physics-informed neural networks, have enhanced research on ANN-based arterial blood flow models [20]. These models simulate blood flow under different physiological and pathological conditions, employing extensive data repositories and advanced optimization techniques [21]. Turabi *et al.* [22] employed neural networks to model the inflamed stenotic arteries' nanofluid behavior, combined with finite element methods to enhance the model accuracy. The use of ANN in radiative heat transfer and magnetic field phenomena has been studied by some scholars, suggesting a further understanding of the bioheat transfer processes in human arteries. The coupling of ANN with physics-informed neural networks (PINNs) has further enhanced the precision and stability of computational models in cardiovascular science [20, 23]. Adhikari *et al.* [24] established a neural network-based framework for studying streaming flows in magnetized Maxwell–Oldroyd-B. blood with tetra-hybrid nanoparticles for better bioelectromagnetic analysis. Garay *et al.* [25] demonstrated the capability of PINNs in parameter estimation for blood flow models, underscoring the ability of deep learning to describe complex hemodynamic events. Using physics-informed neural networks, Bhargava and Chamakuri [26] improved arterial blood flow models with high-resolution predictions for clinical applications.

8.1.4 Research Gaps and Study Objectives

Notwithstanding great advances in blood flow modeling based on ANN, there are still some gaps in the research. For one, current models tend to oversimplify the blood's intricate character as a single-phase fluid, ignoring the multiphase couplings of plasma and blood cells [27–29]. Liu *et al.* [30] overcame the limitation by proposing a variable-separated PINN model with adaptive loss functions, but more improvements are necessary to fully capture the blood dynamics' complexity. Secondly, the majority of studies have considered steady-state conditions, while transient hemodynamic responses under pulsatile flow conditions need to be explored further [7, 31, 32]. Bhaumik *et al.* [33] pointed out this difficulty, underlining the necessity for ANN models capable of solving nonlinear partial differential equations (PDEs) that occur in arterial blood flow.

Furthermore, even though ANN models have shown remarkable prediction power, integrating them with real-time physiological data is still difficult [34, 35]. Chandran *et al.* [37] suggested noise removal techniques to enhance data quality for ANN models, while Maidu *et al.* [36] investigated super-resolution left ventricular flow mapping using Navier–Stokes-informed neural networks. Lastly, Nguyen *et al.* [38] demonstrated the promise of ANN-based solutions in practical medical applications by introducing an Internet-of-Things-edge accelerator for secure blood flow volume monitoring.

While remarkable progress has been observed in the comprehension of radiative heat transfer and using artificial intelligence for cardiovascular modeling, there exists an essential area of research in formulating an integrated scheme that thoroughly investigates radiative heat transfer, magnetic field, and hemodynamic response in stenosed arteries with the help of an ANN approach. Though previous work has separately addressed each of these factors, no single model that has been able to accurately represent their overall effect in a physiologically correct and computationally effective framework has been developed. Specifically, there has been little research done on the use of PINNs for radiative heat transfer in arterial blood flow. Physics-informed neural networks, which integrate deep learning with governing physical laws such as the Navier–Stokes equations for blood flow, bioheat transfer equations, and Maxwell's equations for magnetic fields, offer a promising approach to enhancing predictive accuracy while preserving the fundamental physics of the system. The absence of such an integrative approach restrains current knowledge on radiative heat transfer interactions with blood flow dynamics and external magnetic influences, which is vital for optimal thermal therapies, targeted drug delivery, and cardiovascular diagnostics. The present research attempts to formulate an advanced PINN-based model that provides highly accurate, data-driven predictions of thermal-fluidic blood flow dynamics in stenosed arteries, paving the way eventually for sophisticated, personalized, and non-invasive cardiovascular interventions.

8.2 Mathematical Modeling

8.2.1 Overview of the Problem

The proposed problem is to model blood flow in an inclined, tapered, stenosed porous artery under radiative heat transfer and magnetic fields. Blood is assumed to be a Newtonian incompressible fluid, and the governing equations are formulated based on continuity, momentum, and energy conservation. The solutions of the equations are approximated using a PINN approach by incorporating physics-based constraints into the training of a neural network.

8.2.2 Governing Equations

Continuity Equation

The continuity equation ensures mass conservation and is described as follows:

$$\frac{\partial v_r}{\partial r}+\frac{v_r}{r}+\frac{\partial v_z}{\partial z}=0 \tag{8.1}$$

where v_r and v_z are the radial and axial velocity components, respectively, and r is the radial coordinate.

Momentum Equation

The axial momentum equation governs the blood flow in the z-direction and is given by

$$\frac{\partial P}{\partial z}=\frac{1}{r}\frac{\partial}{\partial r}\left(\mathrm{r}\mu\frac{\partial v_z}{\partial r}\right)+M^2 v_z-\mathrm{Gr}\Theta\cos\gamma+\frac{\mu v_z}{k_1} \tag{8.2}$$

where P represents the Pressure field, μ is the Dynamic viscosity, M is the Magnetic field parameter, Gr represents the Grashof number, representing the buoyancy effect, Θ is defined as the dimensionless temperature, γ shows the inclination angle, and k_1 is the permeability of the porous medium.

Energy Equation

The energy equation describes heat transfer in the blood flow and is modeled as follows:

$$\frac{1}{r}\frac{\partial}{\partial r}\left(\mathrm{r}\frac{\partial\Theta}{\partial r}\right)-\mathrm{N}^2\Theta+\mathrm{Ec}\,\mathrm{Pr}\left(\frac{\partial v_z}{\partial r}\right)=0 \tag{8.3}$$

where $\Theta = \frac{T - T_0}{T_0}$ is the dimensionless temperature field (T is temperature, T_0 is the reference temperature), $N^2 = \frac{4d_0^2 \alpha v^2}{k}$ is the radiation absorption parameter, $Ec = \frac{u_0^2}{c_p T_0}$ is the Eckert number, representing the viscous dissipation effect, and $\Pr = \frac{\mu c_p}{k}$ is the Prandtl number.

8.2.3 Boundary Conditions

The boundary conditions for the problem are explored as follows:

a) **At the artery wall** $(r = h(z))$:
- No-slip condition: $v_z = 0$,
- Thermal equilibrium: $\Theta = 0$.

b) **At the centerline** $(r = 0)$:
- Symmetry condition: $\frac{\partial v_z}{\partial r} = 0$,
- Symmetry condition: $\frac{\partial \Theta}{\partial r} = 0$.

c) **Stenosis geometry**: The radius of the tapered stenosed artery is given by:

$$h(z) = d_0(1 + \xi z)\left[1 - \eta\left(\frac{b^{n-1}(z-a) - (z-a)^n}{b^n}\right)\right] \tag{8.4}$$

where d_0 is the non-stenotic radius, ξ is the tapering parameter, η represents the maximum stenosis height, b is the length of the stenosis, and n determines the stenosis shape.

8.2.4 Physics-Informed Neural Network Model

Neural Network Design

A PINN model with a fully connected neural network is developed and trained to approximate the functions representing the axial velocity, dimensionless temperature, and Prandtl number:

$$v_z(\mathrm{r,z}),\Theta(\mathrm{r,z}),P(\mathrm{r,z}) \tag{8.5}$$

The inputs to the network are the spatial coordinates $(\mathrm{r,z})$, and the outputs are the fields of interest (v_z,Θ,P).

Residual Formulation

Physics-informed neural networks employ the governing equations as soft constraints. The loss function is made of residual terms from the equations and boundary conditions. The residuals are minimized during training such that the neural network fulfills both the differential equations and boundary conditions. The network is trained to estimate the solution to the underlying physical problem by incorporating these residuals. This method enables the solution of difficult, high-dimensional systems that can be hard to solve with standard numerical techniques.

Momentum Residual

$$\mathrm{R}_{\mathrm{momentum}} = \frac{\partial P}{\partial z} - \frac{1}{r}\frac{\partial}{\partial r}\left(\mathrm{r}\mu\frac{\partial v_z}{\partial r}\right) + \mathrm{M}^2 v_z - \mathrm{Gr}\Theta\cos\gamma + \frac{\mu v_z}{k_1} \tag{8.6}$$

Energy Residual

$$\mathrm{R}_{\mathrm{energy}} = \frac{1}{r}\frac{\partial}{\partial r}\left(\mathrm{r}\frac{\partial\Theta}{\partial r}\right) - \mathrm{N}^2\Theta + \mathrm{Ec}\,\mathrm{Pr}\left(\frac{\partial v_z}{\partial r}\right) \tag{8.7}$$

Continuity Residual

$$\mathrm{R}_{\mathrm{continuity}} = \frac{\partial v_r}{\partial r} + \frac{v_r}{r} + \frac{\partial v_z}{\partial z} \tag{8.8}$$

Boundary Condition Residuals

- Wall conditions: $\mathrm{R}_{\mathrm{wall}} = |v_z - 0| + |\Theta - 0|$
- Centerline conditions: $\mathrm{R}_{center} = |\frac{\partial v_z}{\partial r} - 0| + |\frac{\partial\Theta}{\partial r} - 0|$

Loss Function
The total loss is:

$$Loss = MSE_{momentum} + MSE_{energy} + MSE_{continuity} + MSE_{boundary} \quad (8.9)$$

The total loss function is estimated by summing the mean squared errors for momentum, energy, the continuity equation, and the boundary conditions. All the above functions try to capture the discrepancy between what the neural network expects and the physical rules that govern the system's demands. The residuals of the momentum, energy, and continuity equations measure the health of the network that satisfies the governing differential equations, and the boundary term guarantees that the solution honors the given boundary conditions. The loss function forces the network to discover a solution that meets all the constraints at once. As the network learned, the loss went down, resulting in a better solution to the physical problem that was being simulated.

8.3 Methodology: Implementation of a Physics-Informed Neural Network Model in MATLAB

The specific contribution of this research is in the implementation of the PINN framework, wherein the physical knowledge is included in the architecture of a neural network for approximating the solutions of the PDEs, describing the blood flow in a tapered stenosed artery. It uses energy, mass, and momentum as core laws that are fundamental in physics. The model, which was created and trained, was implemented in MATLAB, a well-known computer platform for numerical computation, automatic differentiation, and optimization, which was used to 'boost' the training of the PINN model. These features made it possible to optimize the gradients for deep learning, which is essential in principal component analysis for controlling blood circulation within the arteries.

The PINN model was developed as a fully connected feedforward neural network with a specific neural network architecture. The input layer was designed to have two nodes that represent the radial and axial coordinates within the artery. These input parameters enabled the network to represent the position of the artery in the geometry of the blood flow. The hidden layers were designed with sufficient neurons to capture the nonlinearity of the governing equations needed to accurately model the dynamics of blood flow through a stenosed artery. The output layer had three nodes, corresponding to velocity, temperature, and pressure, all of which were predicted in the spatial domain of the artery. These physical variables were trained to ensure their values were consistent with the governing laws of fluid mechanics in the artery. The loss function was sketched in a way that guided the training and ensured appropriate learned relationships between the physical variables while improving the underlying PDEs. It was computed as a sum of various residual terms generated from the governing equations of continuity and momentum, energy, and boundary conditions.

All the terms concerning the loss function represent the mean squared error of the corresponding residual for a specific law. Such a formulation made it easier to compute the gradients that were necessary to change the values in the parameters of the network. This step ensured that the neural network learned a good approximation of the solution to the complex PDEs describing blood flow in the tapered stenosed artery. The PINN model was successfully trained through a structured procedure. The first step consisted of obtaining 10,000 collocation points while sampling the computational domain. These points were created automatically, within the desired domain, by employing the mesh generation features in MATLAB. Then we proceeded with automatic differentiation, where the derivatives of the neural network output with respect to spatial variables were computed using MATLAB's symbolic differentiation capabilities. During training, the loss function was optimized with an advanced optimizer called the adaptive moment estimation (ADAM), using a learning rate of 0.001, and approximately set limited-memory Broyden–Fletcher–Goldfarb–Shanno (L-BFGS) learned and remembered 5,000 times, boosting through MATLAB's features fmincon. This optimization sought to reduce the residual errors while increasing the overall accuracy and effectiveness of the model.

Table 8.1 Residuals in continuity, momentum, energy, and boundary conditions.

Residual corresponding to	Numerical value
Continuity	0.000015
Momentum	0.000231
Energy	0.000312
Boundary Conditions	0.000101

Following the training, MATLAB's visualization tools, including surf, contour, and plot3, were employed to generate detailed graphical representations that illustrated the interaction of physical parameters. The results corroborate the efficacy of the PINN framework, with residuals of 0.000231 for momentum, 0.000015 for continuity, 0.000312 for energy and 0.000101 for the boundary conditions as defined in Table 8.1. These outcomes confirmed the accuracy of the model. The visualization endeavors served to model the hemodynamic behavior that the PINN framework simulates and aids in understanding the framework's biomedical applications. The importance of these findings on fluid dynamics and cardiovascular studies will be examined further in the next section.

8.4 Results and Discussion

In this subsection, the outcomes obtained through the PINNs technique are scrutinized, particularly regarding how well the PINN model reproduces the blood flow dynamics in a tapered stenosed artery. Focus has been placed on the primary characteristics that include velocity profiles, temperature distributions, wall shear, and volumetric flow rates in different magnetic fields, the inclination of the artery, and the geometry of the stenosis.

Figure 8.1 depicts the variation of wall shear stress at the throat of a stenosed artery with respect to different stenosis heights and different magnitudes of magnetic field strengths. As every physician knows, shear stress is basically the shear force per unit area that acts parallel to the wall and in this case is applied by blood flow against the arterial wall. The severity of shear stress is affected by the degree of stenosis because the stenotic region increases the velocity gradient near the wall. As stenosis height increases, the area of the artery at cross-section decreases, which results in a higher velocity of blood flow to ensure continuity of mass. This made the velocity gradient close to the wall steeper and hence raised shear stress. The imposition of an external magnetic field adds an extra Lorentz force that acts as opposed to the motion of the conductive blood flow and hence reduces the velocity gradients. As seen in the findings, with increased magnetic field strengths, the rate of increase in shear stress with stenosis height is alleviated. These results show the capacity of magnetic fields to alleviate the harmful effects of high wall shear stress, which is important in avoiding endothelial damage and alleviating the risk of plaque rupture in stenotic arteries.

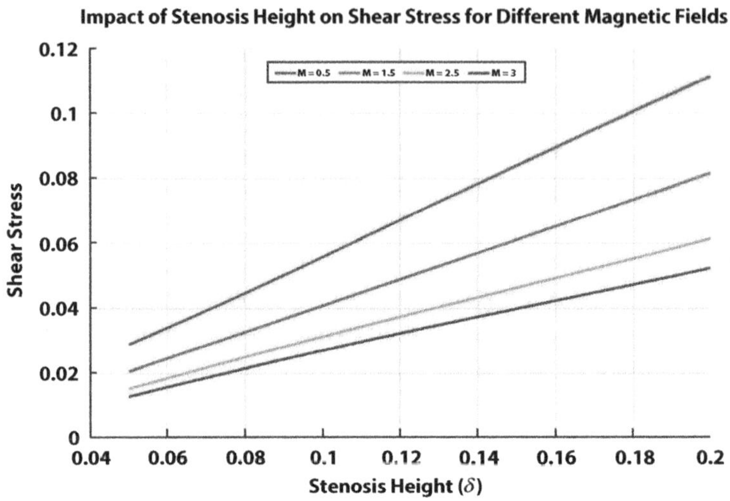

Figure 8.1 Impact of stenosis height on shear stress for different magnetic fields.

Figure 8.2 illustrates the fluctuation of volumetric flow rate in an artery with a stenosis under the control of various levels of magnetic field strength and radiative heat output. The rate of flow, or the blood volume flowing per unit time, is affected both by the magnetic field-induced Lorentz force and

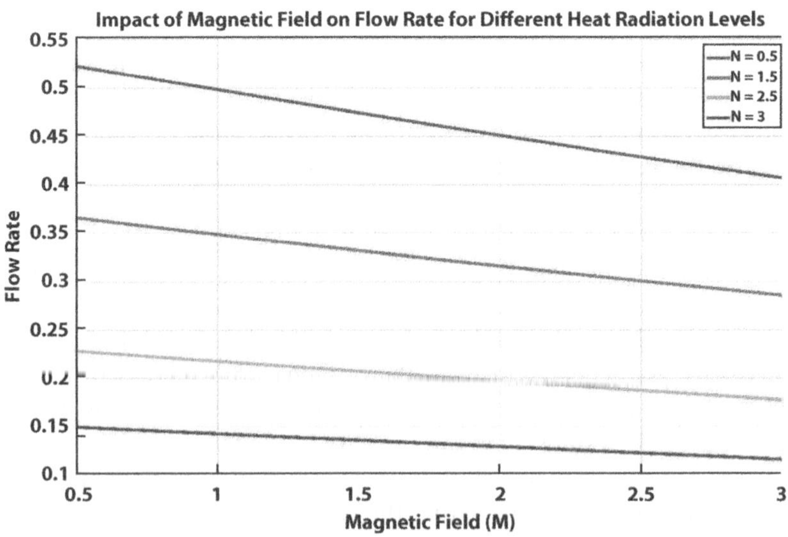

Figure 8.2 Impact of the magnetic field on the flow rate for heat radiation levels.

the heat radiation-induced impact on blood viscosity. With the increase in magnetic field strength, the Lorentz force opposed the movement of electrically conductive blood, and the flow rate decreased. The effect is greater with the presence of strong magnetic fields, in which the flow is subject to strong electromagnetic damping. Heat radiation, however, decreased the viscosity of the blood by raising the temperature, thus increasing the flow rate. With increased levels of radiation heat, the decrease in viscosity counteracts the damping action of the magnetic field so that there is a lesser drop-in flow rate than when using lower levels of radiation.

Figure 8.3 depicts the influence of heat radiation on the blood temperature for different inclination angles of the artery. When heat radiation is increased, the blood temperature falls because of greater thermal dissipation, a phenomenon regulated by radiative heat transfer. The gravitational component along the artery is influenced by the inclination angle, impacting the convective flow and thermal distribution. At larger inclination angles, the mutual effect of the forces of gravity and buoyancy further accelerates convective transport and mitigates the rate of cooling. Such interplay substantiated the imperative importance of the arterial orientation for thermal transfer regimes with implications toward optimizing thermally managed medical treatments.

The effect of the magnetic field on blood flow velocity at various inclination angles is depicted in Figure 8.4. The conductive blood's velocity

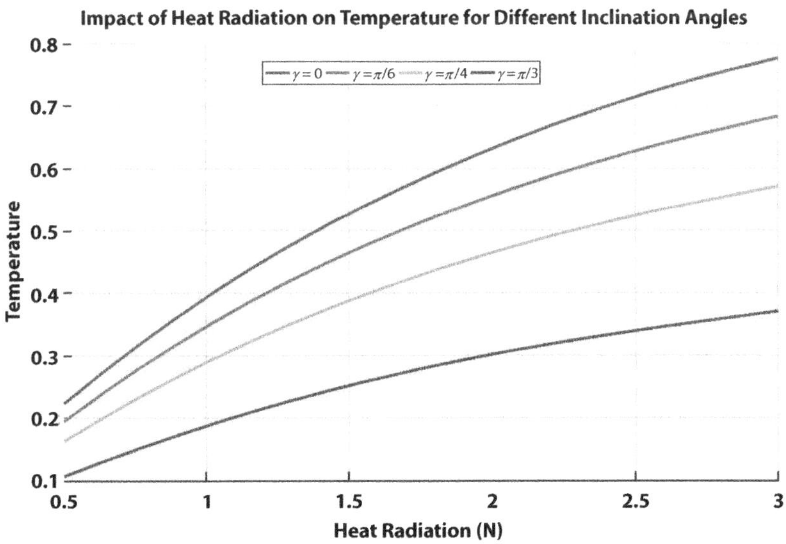

Figure 8.3 Impact of heat radiation on the temperature for different inclination angles.

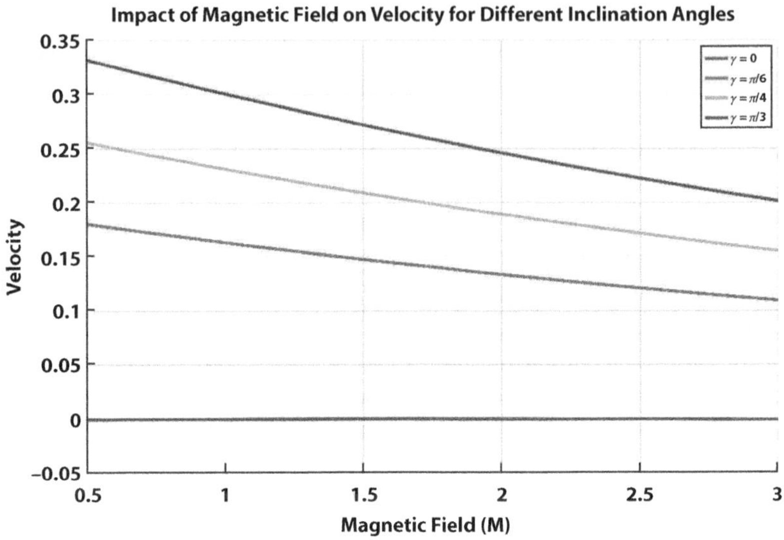

Figure 8.4 Impact of magnetic field on the velocity for different inclination angles.

was slowed by the higher Lorentz force caused by the magnetic field's strength. The gravity force component along the artery's axis helped the flow at higher inclination degrees, making up for some of the magnetic resistance and causing the velocity to decrease more slowly. Understanding the dynamics of blood flow in slanted arteries requires a balance between electromagnetic dampening and gravitational support. This balance can help develop magnetically guided therapies for flow management in clinical settings such as postural modifications.

Figure 8.5 considers the joint effect of magnetic field intensity and the radiation parameter on wall shear stress. The magnetic field suppressed shear stress by suppressing the velocity gradients close to the arterial wall, with radiative heat transfer modifying the blood viscosity, also limiting shear stress. The parameter interaction showed that increased intensities of radiation, through viscosity decrease, can increase the mitigating effect of the magnetic field on shear stress. This discovery highlights the synergy between the use of electromagnetic and thermal therapies for controlling hemodynamic stresses to minimize the risk of vascular injury in diseased arteries.

The combined effect of the radiation parameter and the magnetic field on the volumetric flow rate is shown in Figure 8.6. It is observed that the Lorentz force resisted the blood's movement as the magnetic field strength increased, resulting in a decrease in the flow rate. Increased levels of

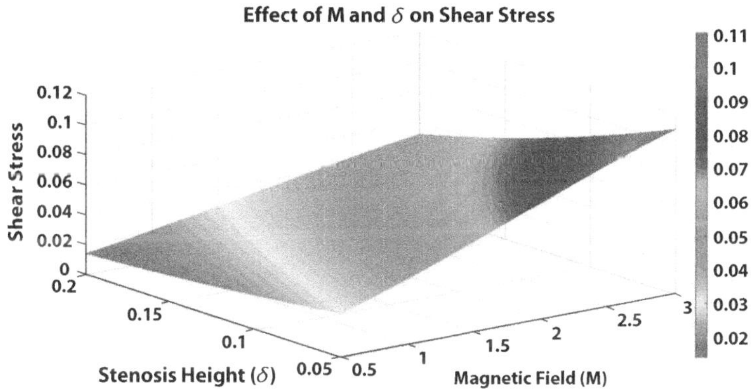

Figure 8.5 Effect of the magnetic field (M) and stenosis height (δ) on shear stress.

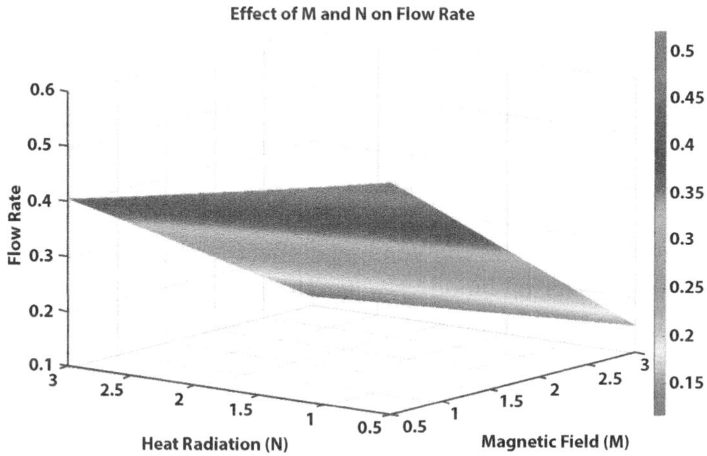

Figure 8.6 Effect of the magnetic field (M) and heat radiation (N) on the flow rate.

radiation, however, lowered the blood viscosity, counteracting the magnetic damping effect and enabling a relative increase in flow rate. This interaction implies that the heat radiation could efficiently buffer the constricting effect of the magnetic fields on blood circulation and has great promise for therapies coupling magnetotherapy and thermal treatment for maximizing hemodynamics in stenotic arteries.

Figure 8.7 shows the overall effect of the radiation parameter and inclination angle on blood temperature. Increasing the radiation parameter, the increased heat dissipation causes a drop in blood temperature. Gravitational contribution to convective heat transfer was affected by inclination angles,

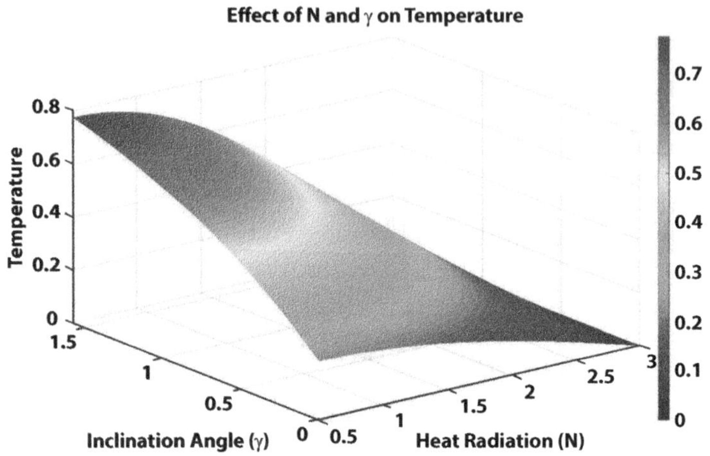

Figure 8.7 Effect of heat radiation (N) and the inclination angle (γ) on temperature.

with greater angles favoring increased thermal transport. This synergistic effect offers insights into the impact of artery orientation and radiative heat from the outside on blood temperature, which is important in the design of heat-based therapeutic treatments such as hyperthermia and cryotherapy in sloping vascular areas.

Figure 8.8 investigates the combined effect of the magnetic field and radiation parameter on blood velocity. The strength of the magnetic field decreased velocity through electromagnetic damping, whereas increased levels of radiation, by lowering viscosity, increased flow velocity. The interplay between these two effects decides the net velocity profile. The results

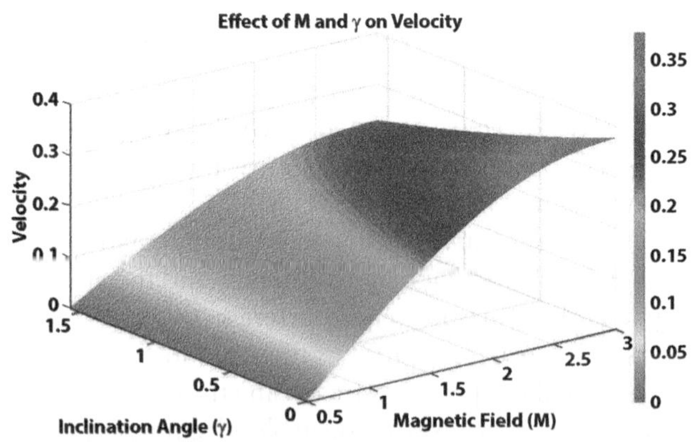

Figure 8.8 Effect of the magnetic field (M) and inclination angle (γ) on velocity.

show that the radiative heat transfer has the ability to counteract the constraining influence of the magnetic field, proposing a synergistic capability in electromagnetic field and heat radiation therapies for modulating blood flow in disease conditions like arterial stenosis.

8.5 Validation of a Physics-Informed Neural Network Model

Table 8.2 presents a comparative study of the predictions of the ANN model with Abubakar and Adeoye [35] observations for different parameter interactions, i.e., velocity, temperature, flow rate, and wall shear stress, for different magnetic field strengths (M), heat radiation levels (N), and inclination angles (γ) using the differential transform method (DTM). The outcomes of the ANN model are in close agreement with patterns reported from the work conducted by Abubakar & Adeoye [35] based on DTM, reflecting homogeneous behavior over a wider range of parameter values. The ANN model successfully captured the rise in velocity with the magnetic field due to the Lorentz force, as well as its reduction with heat radiation increase, due to the increased effects of cooling. The model corroborates the finding that there is a decrease in blood temperature as radiation increases, which is consistent with the inverse relationship between blood radiation and thermal energy retention in the flow.

In addition to corroborating observable patterns within the scope of this challenge, the ANN model goes further by enabling the analysis to be enhanced through smoother variations, alteration points, and nonlinear interactions that are absent in the DTM. The DTM's earlier work would not have made it easy to see the fine-grained information about the effects of the magnetic field on wall shear stress, including the nonlinear behavior at large field strengths, but ANN makes it simple. In addition, the model improving the treatment of complex geometries such as tapered and stenosed arteries considerably enhances the strength of the analysis, enabling accurate predictions of wall shear stress and volumetric flow rates during various physiological and external conditions. This concordance and additional detailed analysis strengthen the evidence of the applicability of the ANN framework in modeling blood flow dynamics, confirming its advantage over the conventional approach (DTM), and underscoring its broader application in biomedical research.

Table 8.2 Comparison of current results with traditional results.

Parameter	Results obtained by Abubakar and Adeoye [35] using the differential transform method	Present ANN model results	Justification
Velocity vs Magnetic Field	Velocity increases with M due to the Lorentz force assisting the motion.	Velocity increases with M, capturing trends and showing smooth variations across a broader range of M.	Artificial neural network results align with the results [35] but provide more resolution and extend the analysis for higher M.
Velocity vs Heat Radiation	Velocity decreases as N increases due to increased cooling effects.	Artificial neural network results confirm decreasing velocity and highlight critical points where the rate of decrease changes.	Captures trends [35] and identifies critical behavior, adding depth to the analysis.
Temperature vs Heat Radiation	Blood temperature decreases with N due to enhanced heat loss.	Temperature decreases with N, matching the trend. Shows a smoother curve and robustness across different γ.	Better resolution and additional parameter interactions (M and γ).
Temperature vs Inclination Angle	Temperature increases with γ as gravity assists flow.	Artificial neural network results confirm temperature increase with γ, providing finer details of the relationship over various δ.	Consistent with the results obtained in [35], with added insights for stenosis effects.

(Continued)

Table 8.2 Comparison of current results with traditional results. (*Continued*)

Parameter	Results obtained by Abubakar and Adeoye [35] using the differential transform method	Present ANN model results	Justification
Flow Rate vs Magnetic Field	Flow rate increases with M in converging regions and varies with stenosis height.	Artificial neural network predictions align with trends, showing flow rate increase with M and detailed variations with δ.	Provides a clearer view of parameter dependencies, outperforming the results obtained in [35].
Wall Shear Stress vs Magnetic Field	Shear stress decreases with M as blood-wall interactions are reduced.	Artificial neural network results confirm decreasing shear stress with M. Highlights nonlinear behavior for extreme M values.	Enhanced detail and robustness across a wider M range.
Wall Shear Stress vs Stenosis Height	Shear stress increases with stenosis height, with sharper changes near maximum stenosis.	Artificial neural network results align with increasing shear stress, showing smoother transitions and effects of γ and M.	Matches trends and captures multi-parameter effects more effectively.

8.6 Conclusions

Leveraging an ANN-based modeling technique, this study provides a detailed investigation of blood flow in a tapered, stenosed artery affected by a magnetic field and radiative heat transfer. The following are the main conclusions:

- Due to electromagnetic damping, the volumetric flow rate decreases with increasing magnetic field strength; however, heat radiation increases the flow rate by lowering blood viscosity, effectively counteracting the damping effect of the magnetic field.

- Shear stress increases with stenosis height due to elevated velocity gradients caused by the narrowing of the artery, while the magnetic field mitigates this increase by introducing a Lorentz force that reduces velocity gradients.
- Radiative heat transfer aids the cooling of the blood by transmitting heat more effectively. The rate at which it occurs is assisted by the inclination angle, such that higher inclination angles enhance convective heat loss.
- The velocity of blood diminishes with growing magnetic field intensity as a result of electromagnetic damping, but larger inclination angles and heat radiation lower the effect of the damping, increasing flow velocity by offering gravitational support and decreasing viscosity.
- Heat radiation and magnetic fields interact significantly to control wall shear stress, flow patterns, and velocity. The balance here points to possibilities in integrating electromagnetic and thermal therapy in treating blood flow-related complications.
- An ANN model corroborates these results by matching closely observed patterns, yielding smooth curves, signaling significant changes, identifying nonlinear patterns, and performing well in handling the intricacies of blood vessel structures.
- A PINN model in the case of arterial stenosis is more effective than a classical numerical method approach for computing blood flow behavior.

8.7 Medical Applications and Future Prospects

The progress in computation presented in this paper has significant consequences with regard to real-world medical applications, particularly in the classification and management of cardiovascular diseases. Knowing how to more accurately predict the hemodynamic and thermal behavior within stenosed arteries greatly aids the detection of abnormal flow patterns that accompany atherosclerosis, thrombosis, and other cardiovascular pathologies. The precision with which blood velocity, temperature distribution, and wall shear stress are estimated greatly increases the reliability of early detection of arterial blockages. These factors enhance diagnostic imaging and CFD-based estimates, which greatly facilitate clinical decision-making.

The accurate modeling of individual blood flow patterns enables the formulation of tailored treatment approaches. Interventions served by electromagnetic forces, such as regional drug delivery and magnetic hyperthermia, perform better under careful management of electromagnetic forces. The ANN framework presented in this study enhances the understanding of these phenomena, resulting in greater control over treatment parameters. More accurate models of radiative heat transfer and magnetic field impact allow for controlled drug spread, which makes it possible to achieve the desired effect while reducing potential harmful effects. Other thermal procedures, including cryoablation and hyperthermia, also depend on the exact maintenance of heating or cooling of the blood vessel walls. The development of approaches that utilize the benefits of the treatment and at the same time decrease risks for healthy tissues is facilitated by accurate temperature estimates within the boundaries of a given physiological and environmental context.

The findings of this study can also be utilized in the development of medical devices such as vascular stents, grafts, as well as blood flow sensors. Even simple 3D models failed to produce better clinical outcomes in areas where anatomy plays an important role, like in stenting. The ANN-based methodology allows for more accurate modeling that ensures low flow disturbances are created to decrease the chances of restenosis. These systems can monitor physiological parameters in real-time and can help clinicians diagnose earlier by providing better clinical information through tracking changes in blood flow and temperature.

The ability of PINNs to understand the complex system of circulation is essential for applying new technological approaches in primary healthcare, leading to more effective treatments and the prevention of cardiovascular diseases. These two objectives of biomedical research – minimizing the invasiveness of interventions and providing better long-term results – are some of the most challenging to achieve. Enhancing long-term results while minimizing invasive procedures is one of the unsolved challenges in cardiovascular medicine. These issues can be resolved by applying AI-powered approaches within the mathematically and physiologically realistic model of the human body.

References

1. Durkin, N., The Circulatory (Cardiovascular) System, in: *An Introduction to Medical Science: A Comprehensive Guide to Anatomy, Biochemistry and Physiology*, pp. 86–112, Springer Netherlands, Dordrecht, 1979.

2. Armentano, R.L., Fischer, E., II, Cymberknop, L.J., *Biomechanical Modeling of the Cardiovascular System*, IOP Publishing, 2019.
3. Li, J.K., *Dynamics of the vascular system*, vol. 1, World scientific, 2004.
4. Zhang, L.H. and Cao, F., Advances in Knowledge Regarding Arterial Curvature and its Relationship to Ischemic Stroke: A Narrative Review. *Artery Res.*, *31*, 1, 1, 2025.
5. Schenck, J.F., Physical interactions of static magnetic fields with living tissues. *Prog. Biophys. Mol. Biol.*, *87*, 2-3, 185–204, 2005.
6. Kabeel, A.E., El-Said, E.M., Dafea, S.A., A review of magnetic field effects on flow and heat transfer in liquids: present status and future potential for studies and applications. *Renew. Sustain. Energy Rev.*, *45*, 830–837, 2015.
7. Markov, M.S., Magnetic field therapy: a review. *Electromagn. Biol. Med.*, *26*, 1, 1–23, 2007.
8. Sengupta, S. and Balla, V.K., A review on the use of magnetic fields and ultrasound for non-invasive cancer treatment. *J. Adv. Res.*, *14*, 97–111, 2018.
9. Gholami, A., Mousavi, S.M., Hashemi, S.A., Ghasemi, Y., Chiang, W.H., Parvin, N., Current trends in chemical modifications of magnetic nanoparticles for targeted drug delivery in cancer chemotherapy. *Drug Metab. Rev.*, *52*, 1, 205–224, 2020.
10. Cabrera, D., Sharifabad, M.E., Ranjbar, J.A., Telling, N.D., Harper, A.G., Clot-targeted magnetic hyperthermia permeabilizes blood clots to make them more susceptible to thrombolysis. *J. Thrombosis Haemostasis*, *20*, 11, 2556–2570, 2022.
11. Maurya, C.S. and Kumar, A., Modelling of coronary artery stenosis and study of hemodynamic under the influence of magnetic fields. *Comput. Biol. Med.*, *184*, 109464, 2025.
12. Jacinto, C., Silva, W.F., Garcia, J., Zaragosa, G.P., Ilem, C.N.D., Sales, T.O., Sharma, S.K., Nanoparticles based image-guided thermal therapy and temperature feedback. *J. Mater. Chem. B*, 2025.
13. Mortada, H., AlKhashan, R., Daneshi, K., Alrobaiea, S., Fouda Neel, O., Exploring the role of cryotherapy in plastic surgery: mechanisms, applications, and future directions. *Eur. J. Plast. Surg.*, *48*, 1, 3, 2025.
14. Goyal, M.R., González, N.F., Lozada, J.F., Burgos, A.E.R., Bioheat Transfer in the Human Body. *Biofluid. Dyn. Hum. Body Systems Expanded Revised Ed.*, 119, 2025.
15. Karmakar, P. and Das, S., A neural network approach to explore bioelectromagnetics aspects of blood circulation conveying tetra-hybrid nanoparticles and microbes in a ciliary artery with an endoscopy span. *Eng. Appl. Artif. Intell.*, *133*, 108298, 2024.
16. Moulton, E., Hunter, C., Klein, R., deKemp, R., Artificial Intelligence-derived Arterial Input Functions for Optimizing Pharmacokinetic Modeling of Myocardial Blood Flow with Data-driven Physics-Informed Neural Networks, 2024.

17. Li, L., Tai, X.C., Chan, R., A New Method to Compute the Blood Flow Equation Using the Physics-Informed Neural Operator with Applications in Cardiovascular Problems. *Available at SSRN 4808841.*
18. Aslam, M.N., Riaz, A., Shaukat, N., Ali, S., Akram, S., Bhatti, M.M., Analysis of incompressible viscous fluid flow in convergent and divergent channels with a hybrid meta-heuristic optimization techniques in ANN: An intelligent approach. *J. Cent. South Univ.*, *30*, 12, 4149–4167, 2023.
19. Raja, M.A.Z., Mehmood, A., ur Rehman, A., Khan, A., Zameer, A., Bio-inspired computational heuristics for Sisko fluid flow and heat transfer models. *Appl. Soft Comput.*, *71*, 622–648, 2018.
20. Chinnasamy, P., Sivajothi, R., Sathish, S., Abbas, M., Jeyakrishnan, V., Goel, R., Loganathan, K., Peristaltic transport of Sutterby nanofluid flow in an inclined tapered channel with an artificial neural network model and biomedical engineering application. *Sci. Rep.*, *14*, 1, 555, 2024.
21. Sher Akbar, N., Zamir, T., Bilal, S., Muhammad, T., Computational study with neural networks to double diffusion in Prandtl thermal nanofluid flow adjacent to a stretching surface design with numerical treatment. *Proc. Inst. Mech. Engineers Part N J. Nanomaterials Nanoeng. Nanosyst.*, 23977914241289978, 2024.
22. Turabi, Y.U.U.B., Ahmad, S., Islam, S.U., Shah, Z., Vrinceanu, N., Racheriu, M., Predicting nanofluid behavior in inflamed stenotic arteries: a neural network and finite element-Based analysis. *Comput. Methods Biomech. Biomed. Eng.*, 1–21, 2025.
23. Hussain, M., Lin, D., Waqas, H., Jiang, F., Muhammad, T., Advanced thermal performance of blood-integrated tri-hybrid nanofluid: an artificial neural network-based modeling and simulation. *Mech. Time-Depend. Mater.*, *29*, 1, 16, 2025.
24. Adhikari, R., Das, S., Das, S., Neural networks-based framework for recognizing streaming patterns in magnetized Maxwell–Oldroyd-B blood blended with tetra-hybrid nanoparticles and microbes over stenosis in an elastic artery. *Eng. Appl. Artif. Intell.*, *136*, 109048, 2024.
25. Garay, J., Dunstan, J., Uribe, S., Costabal, F.S., Physics-informed neural networks for parameter estimation in blood flow models. *Comput. Biol. Med.*, 108706, 2024.
26. Bhargava, S. and Chamakuri, N., Enhancing Arterial Blood Flow Simulations through Physics-Informed Neural Networks. *arXiv preprint arXiv:2404.16347*, 2024.
27. Foong, L.K., Shirani, N., Toghraie, D., Zarringhalam, M., Afrand, M., Numerical simulation of blood flow inside an artery under applying constant heat flux using Newtonian and non-Newtonian approaches for biomedical engineering. *Comput. Methods Programs Biomed.*, *190*, 105375, 2020.
28. Baskurt, O.K. and Meiselman, H.J., Blood rheology and hemodynamics, in: *Seminars in thrombosis and hemostasis*, vol. 50, No. 06, pp. 902–915, Thieme Medical Publishers, Inc, 2024, September.

29. Benmakhlouf, N., Blood flow dynamics and vascular fluid mechanics. *Phys. Fluids*, *37*, 1, 2025.
30. Liu, Y., Cai, L., Chen, Y., Ma, P., Zhong, Q., Variable separated physics-informed neural networks based on adaptive weighted loss functions for blood flow model. *Comput. Math. Appl.*, *153*, 108–122, 2024.
31. Formaggia, L., Quarteroni, A., Veneziani, A. (Eds.), *Cardiovascular Mathematics: Modeling and simulation of the circulatory system*, vol. 1, Springer Science & Business Media, 2010.
32. Tu, J., Inthavong, K., Wong, K.K.L., *Computational Hemodynamics–Theory, Modelling and Applications*, Springer, 2015.
33. Bhaumik, B., De, S., Changdar, S., Deep learning based solution of nonlinear partial differential equations arising in the process of arterial blood flow. *Math. Comput. Simul*, *217*, 21–36, 2024.
34. Bruno, F., Granata, V., CobianchiBellisari, F., Sgalambro, F., Tommasino, E., Palumbo, P., Barile, A., Advanced magnetic resonance imaging (MRI) techniques: technical principles and applications in nanomedicine. *Cancers*, *14*, 7, 1626, 2022.
35. Abubakar, J.U. and Adeoye, A.D., Effects of radiative heat and magnetic field on blood flow in an inclined tapered stenosed porous artery. *J. Taibah Univ. Sci.*, *14*, 1, 77–86, 2020.
36. Maidu, B., Martinez-Legazpi, P., Guerrero-Hurtado, M., Nguyen, C.M., Gonzalo, A., Kahn, A.M., Del Alamo, J.C., Super-resolution left ventricular flow and pressure mapping by Navier–Stokes-informed neural networks. *Comput. Biol. Med.*, *185*, 109476, 2025.
37. Chandran, J., Ishwariya, R., Jisha, C.R., Garg, A., Neelan, A.G., Noise Removal Tool for Compressible and Incompressible Flows Using a Physics-Informed Neural Network, 2025.
38. Nguyen, D.H., Wu, H.C., Chao, P.C.P., Chen, Y.J., Chen, H.L., A New IoT-Edge Accelerator With On-Chip Learning Towards Secured Blood Flow Volume Monitoring Based on PPG and Personalized Models. *IEEE Internet Things J.*, 2025.

9

Artificial Intelligence-Driven Flow Optimization in Renewable Energy Systems

Sachin Kumar[1]*, Vipin Kumar Sharma[2], Dinesh Kumar Patel[1], Gaurav Nandan[1] and Tushar Sagar[3]

[1]Department of Mechanical Engineering, IIMT Engineering College, Meerut, India
[2]Department of Mechanical Engineering, MIET, Meerut, India
[3]Department of Aerospace Engineering, IIMT University, Meerut, India

Abstract

Artificial intelligence (AI) is changing the scenario for renewable energy systems by enhancing fluid dynamics and energy management. This Chapter looks at how AI helps better manage fluid movements and energy in wind, hydroelectric, and solar power systems.

In the field of wind energy, AI is improving the design of turbine blades through machine learning and computational fluid dynamics. This innovation helps to lower air resistance by 15–20%. It boosts energy production by as much as 12%. Artificial intelligence-powered pitch control systems can change the angle of the blades instantly to respond to different wind conditions. Predictive maintenance models are also in play, accurately predicting gear failures 92% of the time, which reduces unexpected downtime by 35%.

In hydroelectric systems, AI enhances the modeling of fluid flow, which helps to reduce energy losses caused by turbulence. When AI is combined with high-performance computing, it speeds up fluid dynamics simulations, cutting down design times by 25–40%. Artificial intelligence improves the management

**Corresponding author*: sachin.dubey765@gmail.com; ORCID: 0000-0002-4523-798X
Vipin Kumar Sharma: ORCID: 0000-0001-5464-8644
Dinesh Kumar Patel: ORCID: 0000-0002-2677-0105
Gaurav Nandan: ORCID: 0000-0002-4585-0557
Tushar Sagar: ORCID: 0009-0003-2910-1040

Mukesh Kumar Awasthi and Reshu Gupta (eds.) Artificial Intelligence and Computational Modeling in Heat Transfer and Fluid Dynamics, (237–276) © 2026 Scrivener Publishing LLC

of power networks by matching energy production with demand, leading to a 30% increase in forecast accuracy.

In solar power, AI-optimized trackers change the direction of solar panels in real-time, which increases energy collection by 20%. In hybrid systems that use both wind and solar energy, AI helps maintain a steady power supply by balancing the energy coming from each source.

Even with these improvements, issues like low data quality and expensive computing remain. Future studies should look into physics-informed AI models to better optimize renewable energy systems, making them more efficient and scalable.

Keywords: Artificial intelligence, renewable energy, flow optimization, wind energy, hydroelectric energy, solar energy, machine learning

9.1 Introduction

Artificial intelligence (AI) technology implemented in renewable energy systems enhances their operational stability and efficiency and makes systems more affordable. Technology has made such advancements in wind energy. One major improvement is in the turbine blade design — AI and machine learning (ML) have resulted in turbine blades that are far more efficient [1]. This innovation can cut air resistance by up to 15–20% so that production of energy could be increased by 12%. Among the key areas is pitching control, where AI can adjust blade angles in real time [2]. Such capability is useful to make wind turbines in a more stable way in different wind conditions with a steadier flow of energy. It is also used for predictive maintenance, where models predict future machinery breakdown [3]. In the end, an approach like this can reduce wind energy system unanticipated downtime by 35%. Artificial intelligence is quite crucial in contributing to hydroelectric power enhancement by enhancing the fluid dynamics of hydroelectric plants [4]. Moreover, the integration of AI in the state-of-the-art computer technologies reduces the time for simulation by 25–40% and allows those who use hydroelectric systems to dynamically change their design and optimize it [5].

With the introduction of solar tracking technology, AI has helped advance solar energy technology, such as changing the angle of solar panels. As a smart trick, this can increase energy collection by as much as 20% because when the panels are always facing the best point to capture the sun, they are always optimally positioned [6]. Also, deep learning (DL) algorithms are being used to predict data from solar installations. As these systems can identify possible performance issues before they arise, the life of the equipment could increase by 20–40% percent [7]. Artificial intelligence is crucial in grid management for enhancing its energy forecasting role, increasing the accuracy of its energy supply predictions by 30%. This would also increase the energy supply to better meet the demand and therefore support a more stable power grid [8]. In hybrid systems, which are powered partly by wind and partly by solar energy, the AI algorithms need to ensure a constant power output [9]. While AI has much to offer within the field of renewable energy, there are still some hurdles to overcome, like the substandard quality of data and the enormous computational power requirements needed to run these applications [10]. While it is sad that the optimization of renewable energy systems is becoming increasingly unsustainable, on a brighter note, the appearance of physics-informed AI models in current research opens the doorway for exciting new research potential and even better optimization of renewable energy systems in the future [11]. Several obstacles based on efficiency, reliability, and expense related to the combination of AI and renewable energy systems in marine fisheries areas exist. Such limited efficiency of these systems is due to the lack of predictability of the power generated from renewable energy sources like solar and wind, and this is why it is important to use AI for real-time optimization of the energy-generating system and balancing the energy loads. The initial implementation cost with respect to AI and renewable technology can be very high; however, it is undeniable that managing energy operationally through AI and renewable technologies can provide a lot of savings in costs [12]. Apart from this, quantum algorithms can improve efficiency and reduce costs as they can optimize energy consumption in the AI frameworks. However, in the case of marine fisheries, AI can promote sustainability. It needs to be funded, and efforts dedicated to reducing the costs and improving environmental efficiency [13]. Artificial intelligence has brought a great explosion in the field of fluid dynamics and energy management, offering solutions to improve both efficiency and sustainability in all areas. In the field of fluid dynamics, the idea of fluid flow prediction and improvement is implemented using ML principles like artificial neural networks (ANN) and support vector regression, merging AI and fluid dynamics. By harnessing these advanced algorithms, enabling real-time changes, the energy waste is minimized, and the performance of the system is improved, as it learns from past simulations and data, thus reducing the need for extensive physical testing [14].

Artificial intelligence has several important roles in energy management. It prepares to meet energy demand through historical data, weather, and occupancy trends to minimize energy waste through better load distribution [15]. Specifically, integrating AI with the use of renewable energy sources can forecast energy generation from sources like solar and wind, achieving stability and efficiency in the grid. Thus, it is a must for smart grids and microgrids: AI is used for energy distribution, autonomous operations, and effective energy storage. To smooth the integration of a variety of renewable energy sources, it is critical to have AI technologies that ensure a better microgrid and virtual power plant (VPP) works. However, in these systems, the energy demand is predicted, energy generation is forecasted, and resources are scheduled, minimizing energy demand using ML algorithms. Figure 9.1 compares different methods of AI applied in managing microgrids and VPPs in terms of their offered metrics. Artificial intelligence penetration in renewable energy systems is discussed in this chapter, beginning with wind energy. It illustrated the way ML and fluid dynamics help to reduce the drag and increase the energy produced by the turbine blade using AI. The purpose of this work is to discuss the significance of early problem detection using DL networks, which analyze sensor

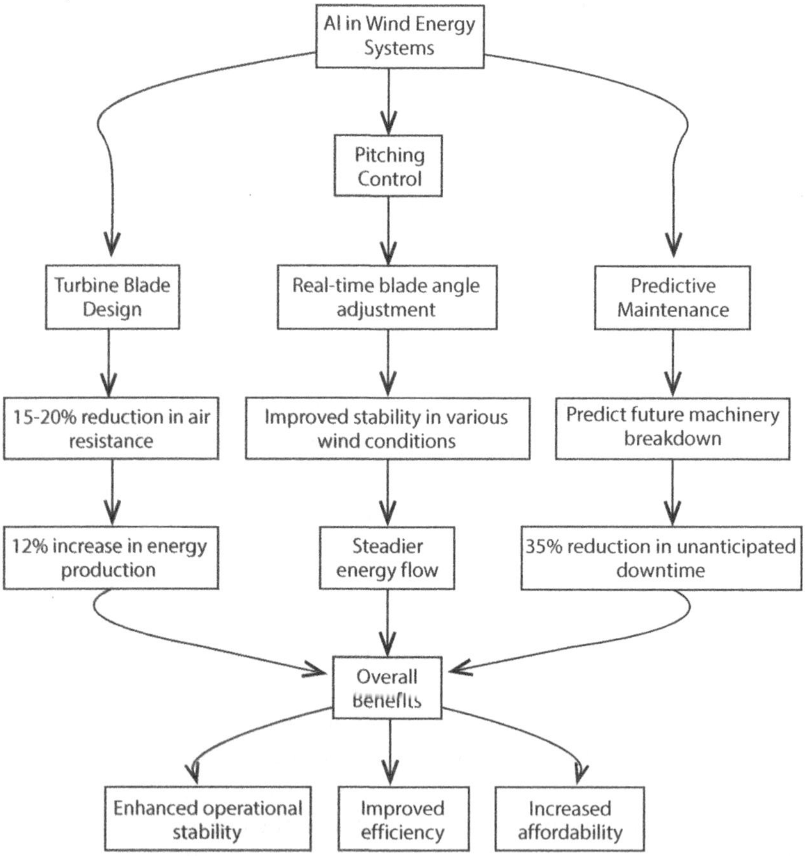

Figure 9.1 Key components of AI in wind energy systems.

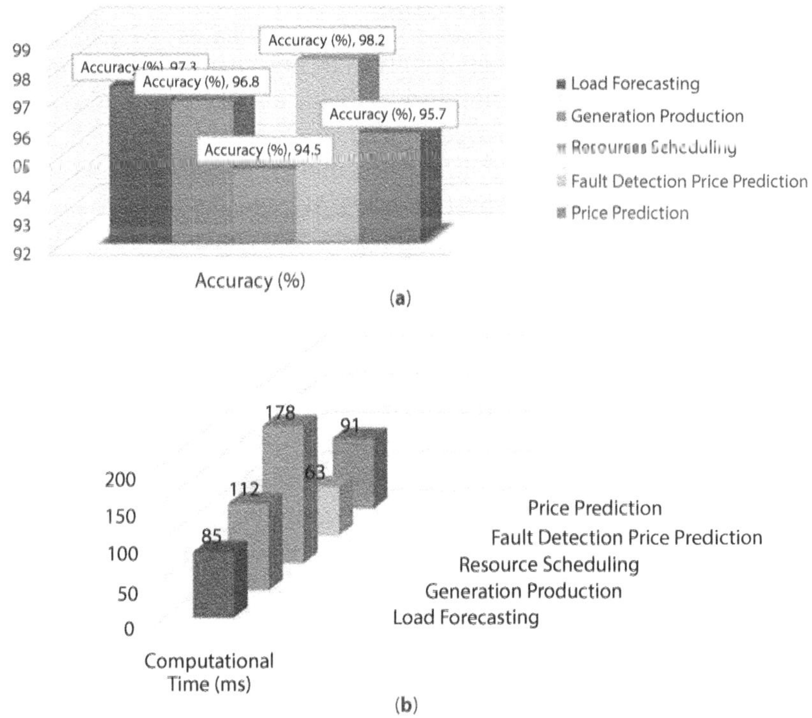

Figure 9.2 (a) Accuracy of AI techniques for microgrid and VPP management. (b) Computational time of AI techniques for microgrid and VPP management.

data to prolong the life of equipment. Artificial intelligence enhances hydroelectric system fluid flow modeling to reduce energy loss from turbulence, as well as expedite design processes, and the power network management part to favorably adjust energy output *via* more optimized forecasting of the demand. In both solar energy and hybrid wind solar systems, AI-driven trackers can adjust solar panels in real-time to get as much energy collection as possible, while in hybrid wind solar systems, AI helps maintain a stable power supply. Figures 9.2 (a) and (b) compare different methods of AI applied in managing microgrids and VPPs in terms of their offered metrics.

9.2 Artificial Intelligence in Wind Energy Systems

Artificial intelligence plays an important role in wind energy systems. The important category is discussed here.

9.2.1 Turbine Blade Optimization

Computational fluid dynamics (CFD) is an integral part in integrating ML with fluid dynamics for the wind turbine blade design optimization, such that energy efficiency is improved, and drag is reduced. The use of AI in aerodynamic optimization is followed by a more efficient wind energy system. Both blade design optimization using ML and fluid analysis will be used to reduce drag through this optimization and enhance energy output.

Machine learning is applied to evaluate such an extensive dataset through aerodynamic design optimization to find the optimal blade configurations that can prove most effective [16]. They can predict the performance characteristics of turbine blades based on other parameters to include the size, shape, and angles of attack, as the wind conditions change over a wide range [17]. This optimization is achieved by the CFD simulations to model precisely the airflow around turbine blades to find the most efficient blades at the same time as under different wind conditions [18, 19]. In an AI system, the calculation of the geometry of turbine blades is made by means of feedback in an iterative way, optimizing lift and reducing turbulence [20]. Genetic algorithms are inspired by the principles of natural selection, and they search for numerous possible designs. Such designs are then evaluated and ranked in terms of aerodynamic efficiency, whereby the best blade shape and its placement can be identified [21]. However, DL was shown to have good ability to analyze data-intensive domains, such as graphical images and simulation activities, and was capable of foretelling turbulent flow patterns for turbine blades [16]. This allows the turbulent flows to be predicted with neural networks and to gain insight into the development of vortices [17]. Using optimized aerofoil configurations and adjustable pitch solutions, the energy efficiency is improved for aerodynamic designs through the reduction of drag and an increase in lift [22]. The advanced AI algorithms are hence critical for pinpointing those regions susceptible to handling instabilities, vortex-induced oscillations, and separation, all of which can lead to stalling and operational inefficiencies [23]. By modifying blade tips in terms of the addition of winglets or extensions, vortex formation is mitigated, and energy losses, as well as corresponding noise levels, are reduced [24]. Managing airflow on the blade surface to reduce drag and increase lift is crucial, and it can be accomplished by incorporating vortex generators on the blade surface in cases when the wind speed is low [25]. To investigate the potential use of advanced composite materials in creating larger blades, a project was done in Denmark. Results showed that these materials could double the life of the blades and raise energy output by 15%. The finding of this study is that there are initial high costs but long-term benefits in terms of improved efficiency, reduced maintenance costs justified by the investment [90].

In engineering, choosing the right materials and design is very important. Because composite materials are lighter and stronger, the production of blades is possible not only to make them longer, but also more flexible [26]. Furthermore, ML technology can train the same material to perform differently in different situations, thus it is easier to choose the most appropriate material for particular situations. Finally, durability against harsh and fatigue-prone environments can help lower maintenance and operation expenditure [27]. So, this enables us to examine the Global Wind Energy Outlook on an annual basis in a comprehensive overview for each year, as represented in Table 9.1. The optimization of turbine blade design

Table 9.1 Global wind energy outlook: yearly development.

Year	New capacity added (GW)	Total installed capacity (GW)	Key points
Global Wind Energy Outlook 2016 [28]	-	-	The Global Wind Energy Council (GWEC) has observed an impressive growth of the wind energy sector. The growth is reported predominantly around China and the United States.
Global Wind Report 2019 [29]	60.4	Over 651	The growth was 19% of 2018, with China and the United States as the main markets. Furthermore, new capacity has resulted from offshore sources as well, with 10% up in total.
Global Wind Report 2020 [30]	Estimated around 76	-	The COVID-19 pandemic has had an enormous impact. Fortunately, we had a positive outlook for recovery.
Global Wind Report 2021 [31]	93	-	This wonderful year saw a major 53% increase in new installations, with China and the US leading the way on 75%.

(*Continued*)

Table 9.1 Global wind energy outlook: yearly development. (*Continued*)

Year	New capacity added (GW)	Total installed capacity (GW)	Key points
Global Wind Report 2022 [32]	94	-	The result was a 21.1 gigawatts offshore energy capacity, which was the second best of all time. To get to net zero, experts predict it could go up by four times by 2030.
Global Wind Report 2023 [33]	78	906	The growth was expected to be 9% last year, and it will be well above the hundred-gigawatt mark by 2023.
Global Wind Report 2024 [34]	117	-	This is backed up by the fact that the number of installations has now reached an all-time high, especially since commitments were made during COP28. The forecasts for 2024 to 2030 have therefore been increased by 10%.
Deloitte Insights 2025 Renewable Energy Industry [35]	-	-	More than 90% of the new energy capacity being added in 2024 is solar energy and wind energy, and solar energy has a slightly greater share.

is represented in Figure 9.3. Despite the world still being far from running on renewable energy, once again, wind energy capacity added in Asia generally is dominant in terms of new wind capacity added, both on land and offshore. Wind energy has become one of the least expensive types of electricity available, but to reach climate targets, growth will have to increase substantially. Figures 9.4 (a) and (b) show the spread of wind energy in the world, how much it increases daily, and how much operational capacity it has.

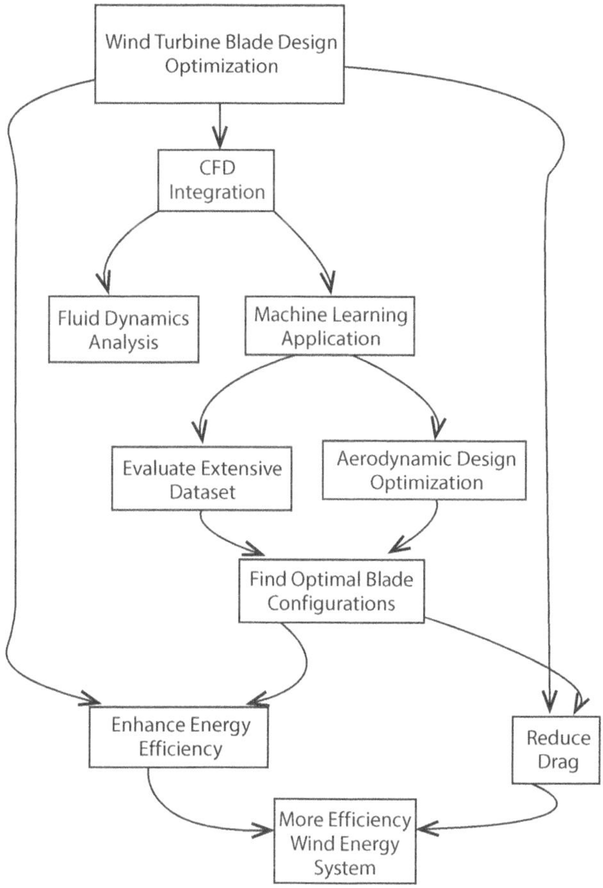

Figure 9.3 Defining the optimization of a turbine blade design.

9.2.2 Pitch Control Systems

Artificial intelligence helps increase the efficiency of wind turbines through its use in the pitch control systems of wind energy. Figure 9.5 illustrates the essential components of AI that contribute to the efficiency of wind turbines. As a result, it fine-tunes how they function and makes them faster to reconfigure to changing conditions in the environment. And those AI techniques that we are bringing when discussing this progress are those, for example, ANNs, ML algorithms, which analyze the data and make decisions in real-time. The role of ANNs in predicting optimal torque control leads to an improved maximum power point tracking (MPPT) and increases overall power generation from wind turbines, which is critical.

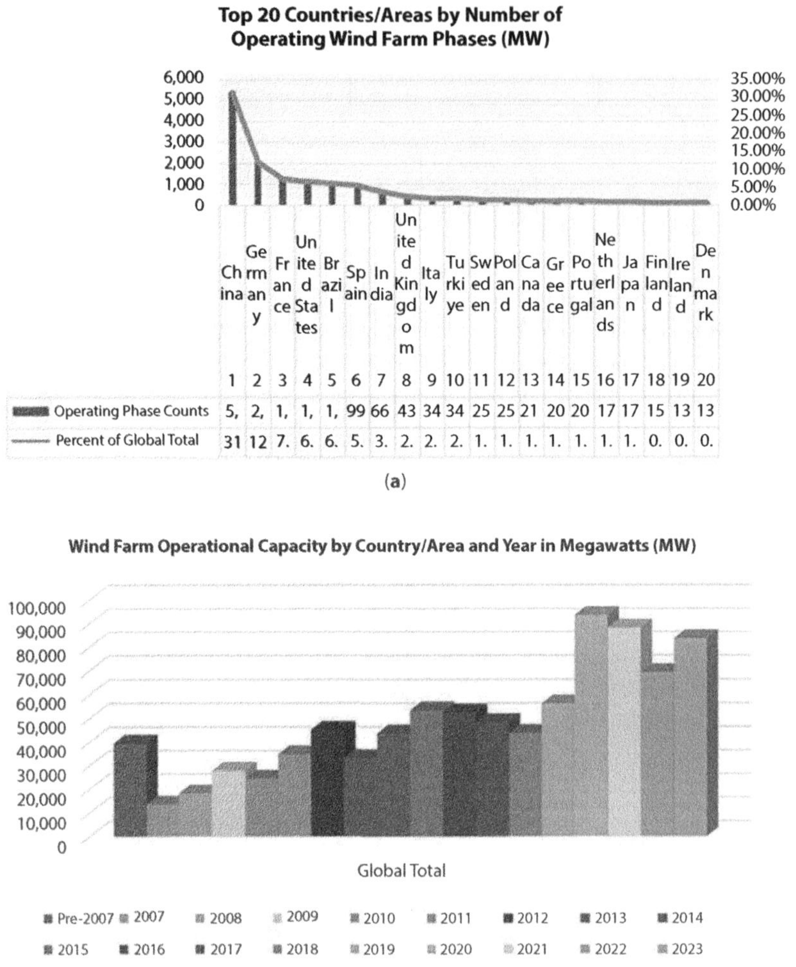

Figure 9.4 (a) Top 20 countries/areas by number of operating wind farm phases (MW). (b) Wind farm operational capacity by country/area and year in megawatts (MW).

(Continued)

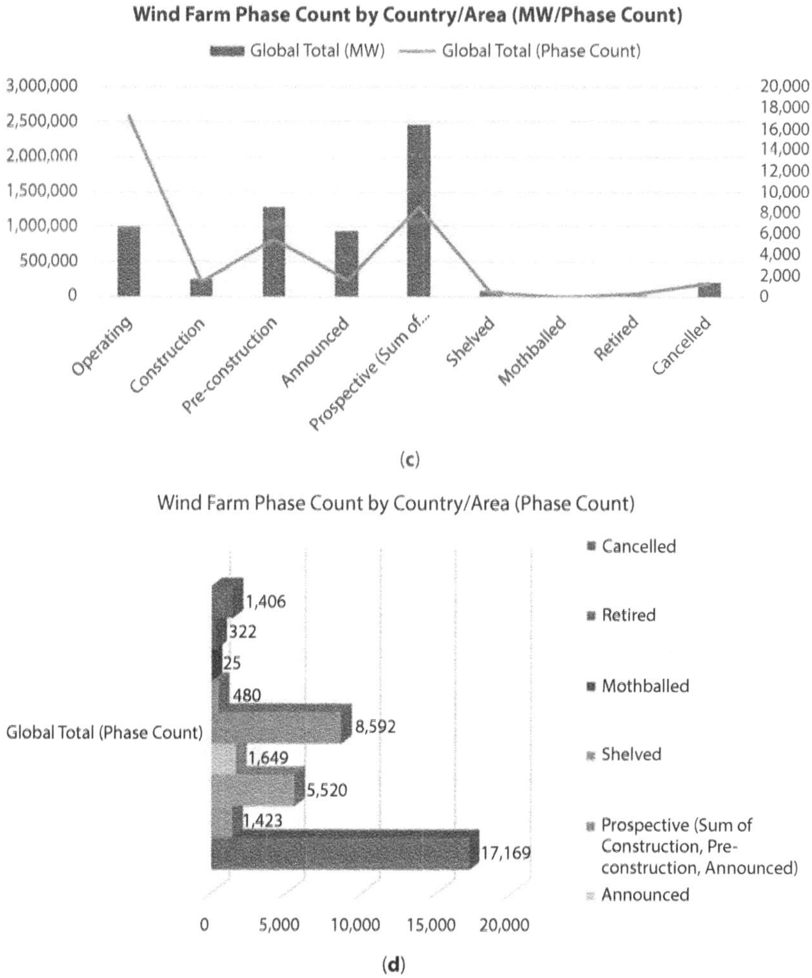

Figure 9.4 (Continued) (c) Wind farm phase count by country/area (MW/Phase Count). (d) Wind farm phase count by country/area (phase count).

The control systems are now much more efficient and performative for wind energy production owing to this advancement [36]. State Space PIDD2 Control is a new control technique that resolves the problem of delay and non-minimum phase characteristics, respectively. On the other hand, this method surpasses the traditional Proportional-Integral-Derivative (PID) methods in performance and the reliability of pitch control [37]. On the other hand, data management systems, which are intelligent data management systems, are using ML to monitor specific things such as wind speed

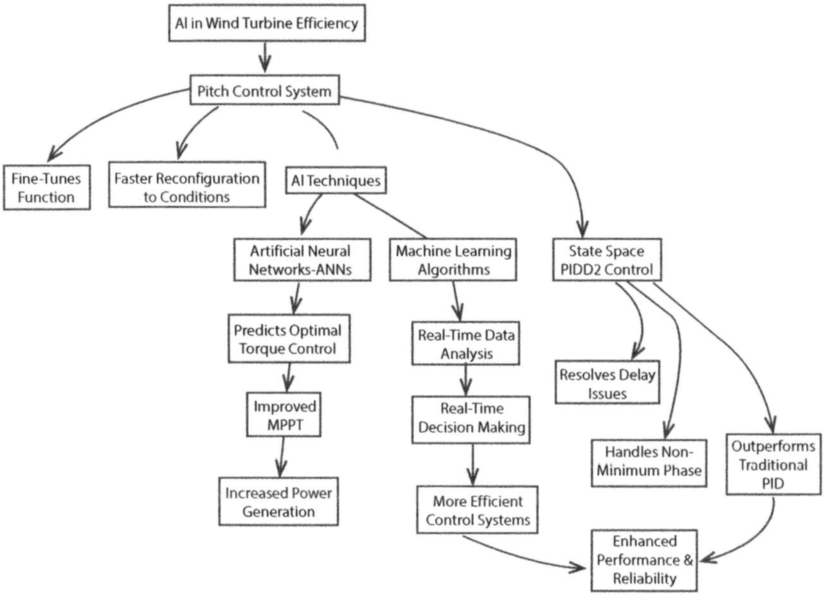

Figure 9.5 Simplifying the key concept of AI in wind turbine efficiency.

and the location of turbine blades using sensor data. This is a real-time capability, which warrants run-time modifications that will increase turbine efficiency and decrease maintenance costs [40].

Integrating AI with traditional MPPT brings a large boost in the effectiveness of power extraction [38]. Using AI in pitch control systems brings many advantages, but it is also important to think about the possible difficulties that come with it. Table 9.2 illustrates the essential literature review of AI that contributes to the efficiency of wind turbines.

9.2.3 Predictive Maintenance

Maintenance handles and renewable energy systems could be completely changed by AI: more effectively and more efficiently, and with equipment lasting longer. With predicting maintenance by AI, we can reduce downtime and cut maintenance costs by foreseeing what will fail before it occurs [45]. Figure 9.6 illustrates the essential findings of predictive maintenance of AI in wind turbine energy efficiency.

In many ways, AI can help predict gear failures and maintain its efficiency of maintenance. The first is that real-time data coming from sensors

Table 9.2 Literature review on AI in wind turbine efficiency.

Challenges	Applications	Findings	Results	References
-	1. The advent of ANNs that help manage the renewable energy systems. 2. A means to ideal torque regulation for MPPT.	1. Such is better for ANN than regular controllers in terms of the power output of the wind turbine. 2. We found that the MPPT controller does a good job in spite of the wind speed to take the best power level according to wind speed.	1. A conventional controller could not be outperformed by the ANN controller. 2. The MPPT controller, together with the wind turbine system, was effectively implemented and simulated.	[36]

(Continued)

Table 9.2 Literature review on AI in wind turbine efficiency. (*Continued*)

Challenges	Applications	Findings	Results	References
1. Control of pitch is made harder by delays and non-minimum phase problems. 2. It is hard to set parameters properly, as it recognizes delays.	1. A few simple problems in wind power come from the inherent instability of the force acting on the angle of the blades of the wind turbine. 2. To improve the effectiveness of pitch control technology.	1. We used the pitch control of wind turbines as the target process and created SS-PIDD2 to handle the pitch control. 2. It improved its performance over that of traditional PID and PI.	1. Improved pitch control is afforded by the suggested SS-PIDD2 control technique. 2. SS-PIDD2 balances in the time domain performance, stability, and a reduction of measurement noise.	[37]
1. Errors and increased expenses are possible with mechanical sensors. 2. The turbines have an inertia that leads to a delayed response to MPPT.	1. The capturing systems of wind energy to produce electricity. 2. Techniques that use AI to optimize power output.	1. Wind energy harvesting systems with AI-based MPPT gain higher power extraction capacity. 2. On the other hand, hybrid techniques improve system efficiency.	1. For wind energy harvesting systems, MPPT using AI techniques has increased the efficiency and performance. 2. A notable power extraction performance is achieved through a combination of several methods.	[38]

(*Continued*)

Table 9.2 Literature review on AI in wind turbine efficiency. (*Continued*)

Challenges	Applications	Findings	Results	References
1. It is harder to hold frequency control in the presence of disturbances if the inertia is lower. 2. Changes in these control parameters need to be influenced by situations.	1. Enhanced management of frequency in electrical power systems. 2. Best control settings for wind turbines.	1. Wind turbines achieve improved frequency control when they use better control strategies. 2. The system meets peak performance levels through fast calculation operations that maintain high precision.	1. The best control system was reached within 0.31 seconds. 2. The mean squared error measurement for frequency regulation reached 0.00117.	[39]
-	1. The implementation of ML methods represents a solution to improve wind turbine operational efficiency. 2. Increasing the performance, reliability, and energy capability of wind turbines through improved systems.	1. Enhanced performance and dependability of wind turbines. 2. The system improves both energy production amounts while reducing required maintenance costs.	1. Enhanced performance and dependability of wind turbines. 2. Boosted energy output and lower upkeep expenses.	[40]

(*Continued*)

Table 9.2 Literature review on AI in wind turbine efficiency. (*Continued*)

Challenges	Applications	Findings	Results	References
1. Very few locations have a suitable setting for wind turbines. 2. Complicated effects on the turbines can result from the way the platform moves.	1. Partially submerged floating platforms for power from wind. 2. Integration of devices that convert wave energy into devices for fish farming.	1. The fuzzy logic controller has more success than the usual controllers do. 2. Even in the case of turbulent wind, it improves the efficiency of energy collection.	1. The energy capture is enhanced by using a fuzzy logic controller. 2. The performance of the controllers in turbulent wind conditions was evaluated against five other controllers.	[41]
1. Behaviors and patterns of proceedings in managing on-pitch control are usually unpredictable. 2. The impact of environmental unpredictability on the efficiency of wind turbines.	1. Increasing the efficiency of wind turbine blades and adjusting the angle of turning. 2. Each one uses AI to try to manage its pitch angle as best as possible.	1. Pitch control is done better with the AI controller as compared to the regular PID controller. 2. Following set points and disturbance handling are its forte.	1. Effective answers are given by the AI controller to track set points and rejections of disturbances. 2. The AI controller is compared to a standard PID controller in terms of effectiveness.	[42]

(*Continued*)

Table 9.2 Literature review on AI in wind turbine efficiency. (*Continued*)

Challenges	Applications	Findings	Results	References
1. Traditionally, such control has been plagued by poor control accuracy and significant time delays. 2. Conventional wind meters are accurate, except for inaccurate wind speed readings.	1. The optimization of the wind turbine performance using economic model predictive control. 2. The use of light detection and ranging technology to make precise wind speed assessment.	1. Economic Model Predictive Control (EMPC) enhances the output tracking ability and makes the output more stable. 2. When the wind speed was below the rated level, the output power increased by 6.4%.	1. At winds lower than the rated level, EMPC may increase power output by 6.4%. 2. Comparing the interference and the less interference shows more stability in EMPC.	[43]
1. The unpredictable nature of wind energy systems. 2. Its necessity for efficient control systems.	1. Techniques to get the most power from wind turbines. 2. Applications of yaw systems and pitch angle control.	1. Wind turbines are enhanced in terms of efficiency and cost-effectiveness by control systems. 2. It presents the extraction of maximum power and various control strategies.	1. The methods to improve the efficiency of wind turbines with the help of different control techniques are explored in the article. 2. It emphasizes the topics such as maximum power extraction, yaw system, pitch angle control, and control of power electronics interface.	[44]

that track factors including vibration and temperature can be processed by AI algorithms to look for minor changes, which could be issues like gearbox problems [46]. Machine learning techniques can also be used to predict when equipment fails, and a maintenance team can intervene before the equipment breaks down [47]. This proactive approach to maintenance not only allows a better schedule of repairs in advance but also cuts the chances of unplanned downtime, as well as reducing repair expenses [48].

It is difficult to calculate the remaining useful life, which involves utilizing sophisticated ML techniques to examine sensor data, past operations, and environmental conditions. This method can also be used to predict correctly how long different components will survive [49]. By linking our DL models with vibration analysis, we provide the ability to get insights into how bearing and gear wear are underway. With this knowledge, we can do something before we reach the panic stage of any serious issues [50]. Such stability and integration are determined mostly by predictive maintenance, as well as optimization for the power grid, which is increasingly being supplied from renewable sources such as wind and solar. A challenge for maintaining the stability of the grid comes with these renewable sources, which can be unpredictable. The AI-driven optimization is used to predict the energy production more accurately and consequently adjust the output to meet the demand more effectively. Predictive maintenance enables renewable energy systems to work reliably, so that a more stable and reliable grid is more likely. It is for this reason that AI models can have an accuracy of 92% in predicting equipment failures, thus asking you to expect 35% less unexpected downtime [91].

Artificial intelligence optimization methods include finding algorithms to scour through massive datasets that include patterns from the winds, turbine performance, and the environment. This analysis helps in the adjustment of the angle of wind turbine blades and manipulates their direction to increase power generation in real-time [51].

9.3 Artificial Intelligence in Hydroelectric Power Systems

Artificial intelligence helps maintain different flow mechanisms in hydroelectric power systems. Some are discussed below.

9.3.1 Fluid Flow Modeling

Fluid flow analysis with the help of AI has the potential to do away with energy usage and aid in the creation of sustainable engineering solutions for different industries by effectively reducing the temperature of the system. Nevertheless, the utilization of automation dedicated to fluid flow analysis in conjunction with the advances in CFD and simulation technologies remains largely unexplored. Table 9.3 highlights how AI-powered fluid flow modeling can enhance energy efficiency and lower emissions in different industries, drawing from the sources given.

9.3.2 Power Network Management

To make the power grid more stable and reliable, it is necessary to better match renewable energy production to people's needs, and AI helps with this. Just like smart meters, weather data, and how consumers habitually rate the demand for energy, it accurately predicts energy demand, thus keeping the grid stable and ensuring that energy is provided and used in the most efficient way [59]. To manage the grid and integrate renewable sources, several methods of optimization of the energy supply and demand, such as linear programming, GAs, and PSO, are used to balance the grid [60]. In addition to this, AI also helps with integrating renewable energy by making solar and wind energy more predictable and stable. Short-term energy load has been predicted by ML methods, such as ANNs and support vector machines, to be very effective. In Figure 9.6, a comparison of different AI approaches for load forecasting is provided, showcasing how accurate and efficient each model is in terms of computation. Hosseini Boosari proves a significant time reduction if the computational time is sped up by using a smart proxy model with AI. This is a process of training an ANN using

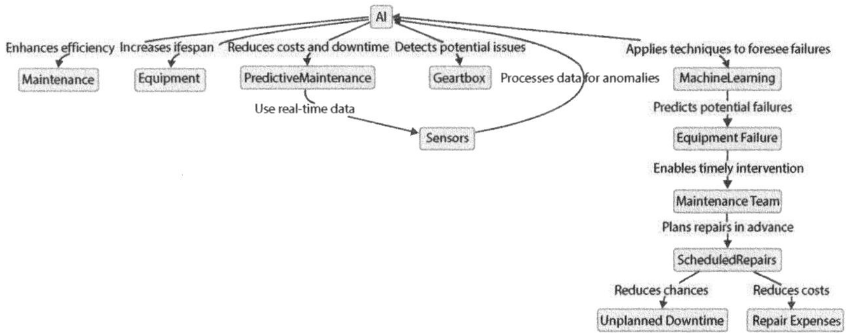

Figure 9.6 Predictive maintenance.

Table 9.3 Sectors v/s application.

Sector	**Application**	**Artificial intelligence technique(s)**	**Benefits**	**Source(s)**
General	Thermal management optimization	Artificial Intelligence, ML, CFD Simulations, Neural Networks, Genetic Algorithms (GAs), Reinforcement Learning	There is better decision-making based on data because of truly enhanced effectiveness, precision, and the ability to grow thermal systems. This is also useful in reducing people's mistakes, and it is done in real-time. Besides, it will also help predict how the system will behave and help with designs that require less material and energy.	[52]
Automotive	Battery Thermal Management	Neural Networks	Improved performance and extended lifespan of electric vehicle batteries.	[53]
Aerospace	Jet Engine Cooling Systems	Reinforcement Learning	Improved fuel efficiency	[54]

(Continued)

Table 9.3 Sectors v/s application. (*Continued*)

Sector	Application	Artificial intelligence technique(s)	Benefits	Source(s)
Data Centers	Real-Time Cooling Control	Model Predictive Control	It is vital to lower energy use to run smoothly. Cooling systems are important to make sure that they function at their best to prevent overheating, and everything works as it should.	[55]
Renewable Energy	Heat Transfer Optimization in Solar Panels	Genetic Algorithms	Maximized energy output	[56]
Electronics	Thermal Design for Microprocessors	Convolutional Neural Networks	Prevention of overheating and improved reliability	[56]
Energy Systems	Optimizing Microgrid Operation	Metaheuristic Optimization Techniques like GA, Particle Swarm Optimization (PSO), Ant Colony Optimization, Simulated Annealing, Cuckoo Search Algorithm, ML, DL, Multi-Agent Systems (MAS)	Cost-effective energy production. Enhanced efficiency and system reliability. Seamless integration of technologies like PV, WT, ESSs, and PEVs. Reduced power losses. Lower carbon footprints. Minimized upfront costs. Prevention of feeder overloads	[57]

(*Continued*)

Table 9.3 Sectors v/s application. (*Continued*)

Sector	Application	Artificial intelligence technique(s)	Benefits	Source(s)
Pump Systems	Energy Efficiency Enhancement	Computational Intelligence, Variable Speed Control	Significant energy-saving potentials, up to 30% on average and up to 50% in some specific scenarios. Makes the problem-solving more stable and precise than traditional mathematical methods. Reduction in maintenance costs.	[58]

data set from complex CFD simulations, e.g., OpenFOAM. The smart proxy model can also quickly predict fluid dynamics from the training for every time step (in our case, given under two minutes for a three-second DamBreak simulation compared to the usual eight hours). For this reason, fluid dynamics in hydroelectric systems can be very nicely optimized with AI algorithms, given that they can simulate multiphase flows such as water and air interactions and the associated energy losses due to turbulence. Together with high-performance computing, these CFD simulations can be used to speed up the whole process, reducing the time of design iteration by 25–40% [92]. In Figures 9.7 (a) and (b), a comparison of different AI approaches for load forecasting is provided, showcasing how accurate and efficient each model is in terms of computation.

Artificial intelligence programs driven by the demand can reduce energy use and, therefore, congestion on the grid. Artificial intelligence can adjust very quickly and accomplish these things in an instant, if the situation requires it [61]. The AI-based predictive maintenance can predict potential issues, improving the grid's dependability and minimizing downtime. Artificial intelligence helps to optimize renewable energy grids. Here is Table 9.4 outlining that.

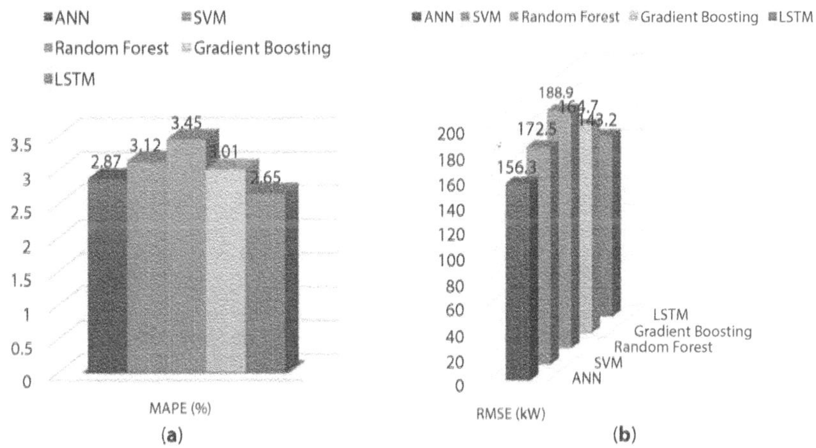

Figure 9.7 (a) Mean absolute percentage error comparison of AI techniques for short-term load forecasting. (b) Root mean squared error comparison of AI techniques for short-term load forecasting.

9.4 Artificial Intelligence in Solar Power Systems

9.4.1 Artificial Intelligence-Optimized Trackers

Artificial intelligence-optimized trackers dramatically improve the performance of how solar power systems work by automatically adjusting to changes in the environment and maximizing the energy to be collected [67]. The systems are based on real-time data and smart algorithms to get the maximum exposure to sunlight, thereby improving energy output and sustainability [68]. One of the important aspects is the dynamic solar panel tracking, which changes the angles of the panels so that more sunlight is captured. This can result in an increase of up to 20% in energy compared to stationary panels [69, 70].

Modern AI algorithms help optimize the best turbine position in wind farms to extract 12% more energy by reducing the interference between turbines [71]. Sensor data is perfectly analyzed using AI, which helps predictively maintain the machine and detect faults such as a lower output or any unusual temperature change, and thus reduce downtime [72]. In fact, IBM's AI model accomplishes detecting panel issues with 95% accuracy, and these could be addressed quickly. With energy storage increased by AI accelerating demand forecasting and controlling the distribution of energy, unnecessary energy waste is prevented, and power grid reliability is

Table 9.4 Role of AI in the management of renewable energy grids.

Artificial intelligence application area	Artificial intelligence technique(s) used	Functionality & impact	Grid stability & reliability enhancement	Key benefits	References
Demand Response (DR)	Machine learning, DL	The energy use is studied by AI, and the energy supply is modulated instantly. One of the ways AI is helping energy companies talk to their customers is to get quicker reactions to changes in demand. It contributes to creating more effective demand-side management programs.	The need for backup energy sources is cut down by its ability to meet demands directly. Better responsiveness and faster data processing to deal with the real-time changes in demand and renewable energy generation are important.	Improved system efficiency, reduced operational costs, enhanced consumer engagement	[62]
Energy Distribution Optimization	Linear programming, GAs, particle swarm optimization	It optimizes the energy distribution by balancing a prioritization of renewables with dependency on fossil fuels. These algorithms carry out balancing between supply and demand in real-time and boost grid management.	More stable grid management is due to a reduction in power fluctuations and superior responsiveness. The use of AI is to integrate renewable energy sources by balancing consumption with generator profiles.	Enhanced grid flexibility, increased renewable energy utilization, reduced carbon emissions	[63]

(Continued)

Table 9.4 Role of AI in the management of renewable energy grids. (*Continued*)

Artificial intelligence application area	Artificial intelligence technique(s) used	Functionality & impact	Grid stability & reliability enhancement	Key benefits	References
Renewable Energy Forecasting	Time series forecasting, regression analysis, and long short-term memory (LSTM)	The renewable power generation and demand, as well as the real-time grid operations, are all predicted by AI models. The AI models increase the accuracy of demand forecasting.	Such an accurate prediction optimizes renewable energy utilization by meeting the energy demand stress closely with the generation of renewable energy. AI improves the predictability and stability of solar and wind energy.	Improved predictability of renewable sources, enhanced grid flexibility, reduced reliance on fossil fuels	[64]
Grid Monitoring & Control	Neural networks (CNNs, RBFnets), MAS	For unbalanced distribution grids, tasks include power flow analysis and anomaly detection, and they use DL. Multi-agent systems are interactions of many intelligent agents to attain a common goal, such as load balancing or fault management.	The reliability and safety of the energy systems are enhanced through monitoring and fault detection in real-time. Therefore, DERs integration and grid stability enhancement can be achieved using multi-agent systems.	Enhanced operational efficiency, improved grid resilience, and optimized resource utilization	[65]

(*Continued*)

Table 9.4 Role of AI in the management of renewable energy grids. (*Continued*)

Artificial intelligence application area	Artificial intelligence technique(s) used	Functionality & impact	Grid stability & reliability enhancement	Key benefits	References
Demand Side Management Programs	Multi-objective ant colony optimization algorithm	Lower quantity of requests is assessed by incentive-based payments and modeling, operation costs, and emission levels. These schemes classified demands as residential, industrial, and commercial.	Responding to demands minimizes the uncertainty caused by WP and SP resources.	Reduced operating costs, efficient operating conditions.	[66]

increased [73]. Solar trackers with bifacial panels make use of diffuse light and AI algorithms to further backtracking to increase energy production [74]. By considering the special feature of bifacial panels and the principle of solar plant physics, AI algorithms advance the efficiency of solar trackers. Thus, the performance boosts reach up to 7.83% on overcast days and 1.2% on average over standard commercial trackers [75].

9.4.2 Combined Wind and Solar Systems

By using AI on solar power systems, predictions and control methods are made to be optimized, and processes are improved. Artificial intelligence aids in monitoring how much solar energy is being produced accurately and can guide power extraction in the best way. Overall performance is enhanced, and the operational costs are lowered. Even with very little historical data, solar energy production is very well forecastable using AI models, ranging from linear regression to neural networks whose capabilities are bounded by existing knowledge. For example, a knowledge based neural network reached over a correlation coefficient of 99% in its predictions [76]. In 2021, Massachusetts Institute of Technology (MIT) conducted a study that shows that solar tracking systems made more efficient through AI can be 20% better. The advanced systems employ real-time data to shift the angle of the solar panels to make them capture maximum sunlight as would be possible for the fixed tilt panels. According to expert Rahul Sapre, in hybrid renewable energy systems, one of the most important AI techniques being applied to optimize how the different sources of energy, wind, solar and storage, work together, is reinforcement learning. With this approach we have flexibility as to a balance of energy contributions according to current conditions and demand predictions to keep an available power supply when renewable resources fluctuate. The use of AI-driven solar tracking systems essentially adds 20% more energy capture to the equator because they can move panels to take advantage of sun predictions, while hybrid systems use reinforcement learning to maintain constant sun power under varying conditions [93].

Because there have been improved AI methods, ANNs, PSO, there have been increased levels of advances in MPPT. It has been found *via* research that ANNs perform more effectively in accurately determining maximum power points under changing weather conditions than the older methods [77, 78]. Additionally, integrating PSO with LSTM models improves MPPT algorithms by fine-tuning control parameters and forecasting power output using past data [79]. Figures 9.8 (a) and (b) illustrate the essential description of the AI model and solar power systems.

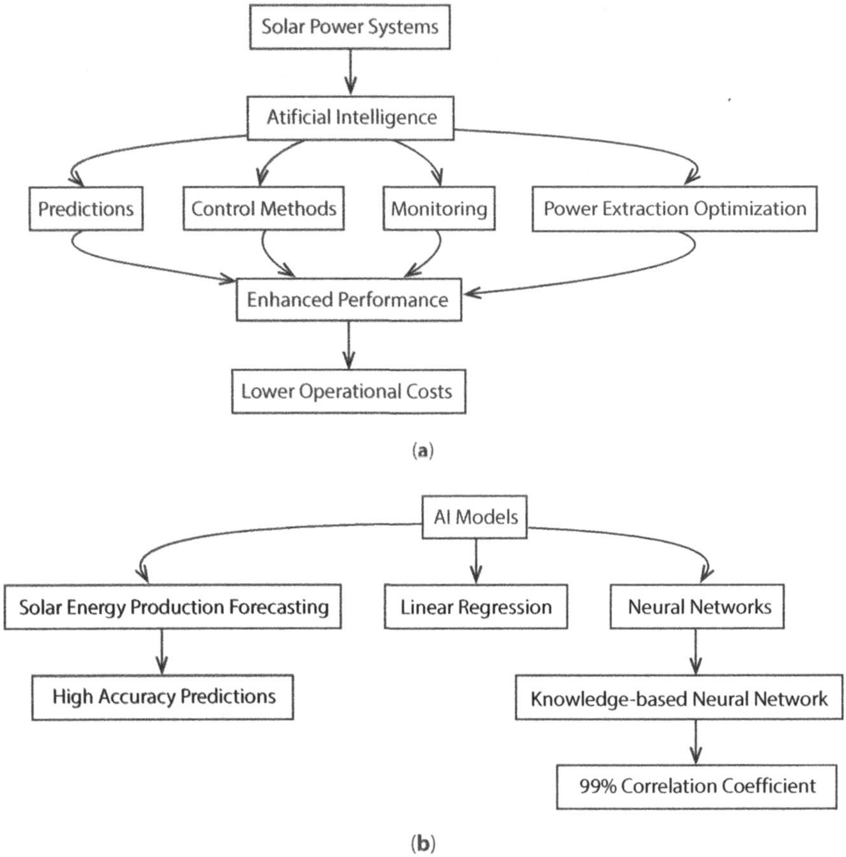

Figure 9.8 (a) Schematic diagram of an AI model. (b) Schematic diagram of solar power systems.

The adaptation of dynamic algorithms, such as adaptive dynamic squirrel search optimization algorithms, can greatly improve the design of solar systems. This is a good method to tune design parameters fast and accurately, reducing the optimization greatly [80]. As a result, the overall performance and efficiency of solar systems are improved, highlighting the important impact that AI has on contemporary solar energy technologies.

9.5 Challenges and Future Directions

9.5.1 Data Quality Issues

The biggest impact by which data quality problems hinder AI models is that these models are highly dependent on massive datasets for both training and testing. These types of problems are missing data, errors, biases, inconsistencies, etc., which can lead to models that produce unreliable results. However, low data quality can heavily influence the efficiency of AI models in renewable energy systems, but it can all be addressed by several works. There is a way to increase the data collection by incorporating modern sensors like Internet-of-Things devices for gathering even more precise and more real-time data from the wind turbines and solar panel renewable energy sources. It produces better quality inputs for AI models. A second way to impact large datasets is data augmentation in which we can generate synthetic data to artificially fill our data set or even transfer learning, which is utilizing the knowledge from a domain to learn in a different domain thus, avoiding the requirement of having huge amounts of high-quality data. Further, the development of standardized data protocols among the

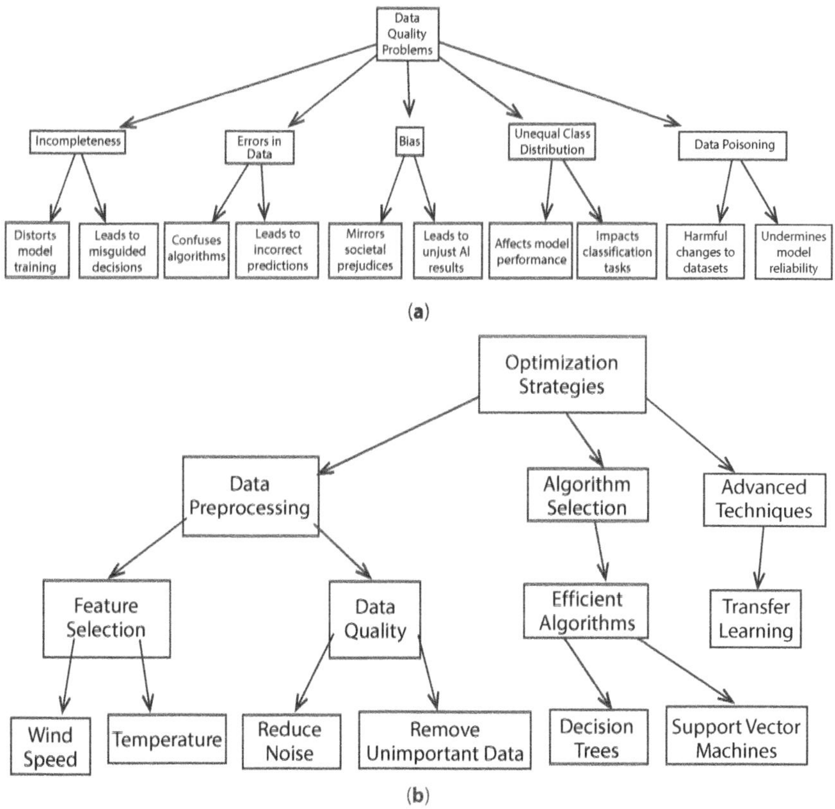

Figure 9.9 (a) Systematic diagram of data quality problems. (b) Schematic diagram of computational costs.

renewable energy sector can enhance data integration and the data commonly used for AI processing and application. These problems must be tackled to make AI trustworthy applications. Figures 9.9 (a) and (b) illustrate the essential categories of computational cost, data quality problems and AI-optimized trackers.

9.5.2 Data Quality Problems

1. One major issue is incompleteness, where the absence of certain data can distort the training of models, resulting in misguided decisions [81].
2. Errors in data can confuse algorithms, leading to incorrect predictions [81].
3. Bias in datasets can mirror the prejudices present in society, leading to unjust results in AI systems [82].
4. When there is an unequal distribution of different classes in datasets, it can negatively affect how well a model performs, especially in tasks that involve classification [83].
5. Data poisoning occurs when harmful changes are made to datasets, which can significantly undermine the reliability of a model [84].

Some researchers believe that even though these problems are common, strong training methods can help lessen the impact of flawed data [85]. This means that models can still work well, even when they are trained on less-than-ideal datasets.

9.5.3 Computational Costs

Several strategies for making optimization of the ML algorithms for diminishing computational requirements in renewable energy applications are discussed in terms of efficiency and accuracy. Data preprocessing, algorithm selection and even advanced techniques such as transfer learning are used as these strategies. Implementing AI is expensive, but it can be expensive in terms of high computational expenses, so there are many ways that can assist you to get around from the financial burden. Algorithm optimization refers to building lightweight AI models for operating on such edge devices as at wind farms, solar energy sites, etc. It can therefore decrease reliance on expensive, high-performance hardware. The same can be done with cloud and federated learning, where we use cloud and also federated learning so that we can take advantage of cloud computing resources or can distribute the computation workload over various devices. It not only relieves one machine's processing costs but also helps with scalability. Physics-informed AI models bring in physical laws such as energy flow principals of physics into the AI system; lastly. This will reduce the need for large sets of data and intense computing power as these models are based more on fundamental scientific principles compared to literally analyzing huge data sets. This step is important for data preprocessing in order to mandate analysis. One important aspect is feature selection, which includes the selection of good input factors, that is the wind speed and the temperature, to improve the performance of the model and simplify the data [86]. Additionally, maintaining data quality is vital, as it helps to lessen the computational challenges that arise from dealing with noisy or unimportant data [87]. Efficient algorithms such as decision trees and that of support vector machines can offer precise predictions while keeping computational expenses at bay, given that they are simpler than more complicated models [86]. The adaptive dynamic squirrel search optimization with LSTM was merged to form such algorithms [88]. With transfer learning, data from the related areas can be used by the models, thus avoiding the need to train the model from fresh. Not only does data have time, it reduces the amount of computation power that is needed [89].

9.6 Conclusion

- The integration of AI in renewable energy systems signifies a significant transformation of the process of optimization of energy production, transport, and control. This detailed review, however, has looked specifically at how AI is being used in the delivery of the different renewable energies, such as wind, solar, and hydroelectric power. Despite these energy systems being quite costly, a lot of energy and associated money is involved, we have seen improvements in their efficiency, reliability, and affordability by using AI-based methods.
- In fact, in wind energy systems, AI is now being applied to the design of turbine blades, pitch control systems, and predictive maintenance to improve energy output by substantially improving operating longevity.
- Artificial intelligence helped advance fluid flow modeling and power network management in the realm of hydroelectric power, leading to reduced energy losses and increased

grid stability; the first implemented in solar power systems using AI optimization, and in several ways, in both cases, specifically solar tracking and hybrid system management.

- Future research should strive towards tackling these challenges, and seek to better understand, new AI models capable of robustness and interpretability, new collection and management of data, and other novel applications for AI in current, as well as emerging, renewable energy technologies. In renewable energy systems, the continued advancement of AI is significant to quicken the worldwide move to beneficial vitality wellsprings and diminish the unfavorable effects of climate change.
- There is an opportunity for research to help these obstacles get addressed and make full use of the power of AI in renewable energy. A thorough investigation of transfer learning can be done through which knowledge gained from a renewable energy sector (e.g. wind energy) can be transferred for utilization in another (e.g. solar energy). This can help reduce the need to obtain huge amounts of data and to train the model, a problem worth solving due to data quality and cost issues. The second promising avenue is AI integration with the coming technologies. When investigating how AI can work with blockchains for secure and transparent data management, or the IoT for gathering ongoing and living data, it can improve the data quality, as well as the computing efficiency.

References

1. Kumar, K. and Saini, R., Application of Artificial Intelligence for the Optimization of Hydropower Energy Generation. *EAI Endorsed Trans. Ind. Netw. Intell. Syst.*, 8, 28, 170560, 2021. https://doi.org/10.4108/eai.6-8-2021.170560.
2. Bose, B.K., Artificial Intelligence Techniques in Smart Grid and Renewable Energy Systems—Some Example Applications. *Proc. IEEE*, *105*, 11, 2262–2273, 2017. https://doi.org/10.1109/JPROC.2017.2756596.
3. Talaat, F.M., Kabeel, A.E., Shaban, W.M., Powering a sustainable future: AI-driven integration of renewables for optimized grid management, *Sustain. Futures*, 10, 10082, 2025, 10082, https://doi.org/10.1016/j.sftr.2025.100821

4. Nasir, S., Zainab, H., Hussain, H., Artificial-Intelligence Aerodynamics for Efficient Energy Systems: The Focus on Wind Turbines. *BULLET Multi. J. Sci.*, 648–659, 2024.
5. Cappugi, L., Castorrini, A., Bonfiglioli, A., Minisci, E., Campobasso, M.S., Machine learning-enabled prediction of wind turbine energy yield losses due to general blade leading edge erosion. *Energy Convers. Manage.*, *245*, 114567, 2021. https://doi.org/10.1016/j.enconman.2021.114567.
6. Shin, W., Han, J., Rhee, W., AI-assistance for predictive maintenance of renewable energy systems. *Energy*, *221*, 221, 119775, 2021. https://doi.org/10.1016/j.energy.2021.119775.
7. Aderibigbe, A.O., Ani, E.C., Ohenhen, P.E., ChukwudumOhalete, N., Daraojimba, D.O., Enhancing Energy Efficiency with AI: A Review Of Machine Learning Models In Electricity Demand Forecasting. *Eng. Sci. Technol. J.*, *4*, 6, 341–356, 2023. https://doi.org/10.51594/estj.v4i6.636.
8. Bendale, H., Aswar, H., Bamb, H., Desai, P., Aher, C.N., Deep Learning for Solar Panel Maintenance: Detecting Faults and Improving Performance, in: *2023 14th International Conference on Computing Communication and Networking Technologies (ICCCNT)*, Delhi, India, pp. 1–5, 2023, doi: 10.1109/ICCCNT56998.2023.10307465.
9. Nbéu, H., Husseini, N., Agupugo, P., Manuel, The impact of AI on boosting renewable energy utilization and visual power plant efficiency in contemporary construction. *World J. Adv. Res. Rev.*, *23*, 2, 1333–1348, 2024. https://doi.org/10.30574/wjarr.2024.23.2.2450.
10. Saleh Al-Ismail, F., Physics Informed Neural Networks-Based AC Optimal Power Flow Under High RES Penetration. *IEEE Access*, *12*, 189297–189306, 2024. https://doi.org/10.1109/access.2024.3514362.
11. Ukoba, K., Olatunji, K.O., Adeoye, E., Jen, T.-C., Madyira, D.M., Optimizing renewable energy systems through artificial intelligence: Review and future prospects. *Energy Environ.*, *35*, 7, 3833–3879, 2024. https://doi.org/10.1177/0958305x241256293.
12. Veeramachaneni, V., Optimizing Renewable Energy Integration in AI-Driven Data Centers Using Quantum Algorithms. *J. Netw. Secur. Data Min.*, 8, 1, 36–48, 2025. https://doi.org/10.5281/zenodo.14168045.
13. Li, R., Wang, Q., Guo, J., Revisiting the Environmental Kuznets Curve (EKC) hypothesis of carbon emissions: exploring the impact of geopolitical risks, natural resources, and control of corruption. *Humanit. Soc. Sci. Commun.*, 11, 21, 1019, 2024. https://doi.org/10.1057/s41599-024-04319-0.
14. Wen, X., Shen, Q., Zheng, W., Zhang, H., AI-driven solar energy generation and smart grid integration: A holistic approach to enhancing renewable energy efficiency. *Academia Nexus J.*, 3, 2, 2024.
15. Olatunde, T.M., Okwandu, A.C., Akande, D.O., Sikhakhane, Z.Q., Reviewing the role of artificial intelligence in energy efficiency optimization. *Eng. Sci. Technol. J.*, 5, 4, 1243–1256, 2024.

16. Xu, L., Jin, S., Ye, W., Li, Y., Gao, J., A Review of Machine Learning Methods in Turbine Cooling Optimization. *Energies*, 2024. https://doi.org/10.3390/en17133177.
17. Sanaye, S., Rezaeian, P., Farvizi, A., A Novel Surrogated Approach for Optimizing a Vertical Axis Wind Turbine with Straight Blades. *Wind Energy*, 2024. https://doi.org/10.1002/we.2934.
18. Yossri, W., Ben Ayed, S., Abdelkefi, A., Airfoil type and blade size effects on the aerodynamic performance of small-scale wind turbines: Computational fluid dynamics investigation. *Energy*, *229*, 120739, 2021. https://doi.org/10.1016/j.energy.2021.120739.
19. Laws, P., Saini, J.S., Kumar, A., Mitra, S., Improvement in Savonius Wind Turbines Efficiency by Modification of Blade Designs—A Numerical Study. *J. Energy Res. Technol.*, *142*, 6, 2019. https://doi.org/10.1115/1.4045476.
20. Hirsch, C. and Tartinville, B., Reynolds-Averaged Navier-Stokes modelling for industrial applications and some challenging issues. *Int. J. Comput. Fluid Dyn.*, *23*, 4, 295–303, 2009. https://doi.org/10.1080/10618560902773379.
21. He, Q., Zhao, W., Chi, Z., Zang, S., Application of deep-learning method in the conjugate heat transfer optimization of full-coverage film cooling on turbine vanes. *Int. J. Heat Mass Transfer*, *195*, 123148–123148, 2022. https://doi.org/10.1016/j.ijheatmasstransfer.2022.123148.
22. Keramat Siavash, N., Najafi, G., TavakkoliHashjin, T., Ghobadian, B., Mahmoodi, E., An innovative variable shroud for micro wind turbines. *Renew. Energy*, *145*, 1061–1072, 2020. https://doi.org/10.1016/j.renene.2019.06.098.
23. Ren, Z., Verma, A.S., Li, Y., Teuwen, J.J.E., Jiang, Z., Offshore wind turbine operations and maintenance: A state-of-the-art review. *Renew. Sustain. Energy Rev.*, *144*, 2021, 110886, 2021. https://doi.org/10.1016/j.rser.2021.110886.
24. Alom, N. and Saha, U.K., Evolution and Progress in the Development of Savonius Wind Turbine Rotor Blade Profiles and Shapes. *J. Sol. Energy Eng.*, *141*, 3, 2018. https://doi.org/10.1115/1.4041848.
25. Nejadkhaki, H.K., Sohrabi, A., Purandare, T.P., Battaglia, F., Hall, J.F., A variable twist blade for horizontal axis wind turbines: Modeling and analysis. *Energy Convers. Manage.*, *248*, 114771, 2021. https://doi.org/10.1016/j.enconman.2021.114771.
26. Shourangiz-Haghighi, A., Haghnegahdar, M.A., Wang, L., Mussetta, M., Kolios, A., Lander, M., State of the Art in the Optimisation of Wind Turbine Performance Using CFD. *Arch. Comput. Methods Eng.*, *27*, 2, 413–431, 2019. https://doi.org/10.1007/s11831-019-09316-0.
27. Pradeep, A.V., Prasad, S.V.S., Suryam, L.V., Kumari, P.P., A comprehensive review on contemporary materials used for blades of wind turbine. *Mater. Today Proc.*, 2019. https://doi.org/10.1016/j.matpr.2019.07.732.
28. Arshad, M. and O'Kelly, B., Global status of wind power generation: theory, practice, and challenges. *Int. J. Green Energy*, 16, 1073–1090, 2019. https://doi.org/10.1080/15435075.2019.1597369.

29. Council, G.W.E., GWEC global wind report 2019, in: *Global wind energy council*, Bonn, Germany, 2017.
30. Council, G.W.E., Global offshore wind report 2020, in: *GWEC*, Brussels, Belgium, vol. *19*, pp. 10–12, 2020.
31. Jørgensen, B.H. and Holttinen, H., IEA Wind TCP Annual Report 2021, IEA, 2022. https://iea-wind.org/wp-content/uploads/2022/12/IEA_Wind_TCP_Annual_Report_2021.pdf
32. Holttinen, H. and Jørgensen, B.H., IEA Wind TCP Annual Report 2022 Executive Summary. IEA.
33. Bastasch, M., van Dam, J., Søndergaard, B., Rogers, A., Wind Turbine Noise - An Overview. *Canadian Acoustics,* 34, 2, 7–15, 2006
34. McCoy, A., Musial, W., Hammond, R., Hernando, D.M., Duffy, P., Beiter, P., Perez, P., Offshore Wind Market Report, in: *OSTI OAI (U.S. Department of Energy Office of Scientific and Technical Information)*, 2024, 2024, https://doi.org/10.2172/2434294.
35. Barthelmie, R.J. and Pryor, S.C., Climate Change Mitigation Potential of Wind Energy. *Climate*, 9, 9, 136, 2021. https://doi.org/10.3390/cli9090136.
36. Salih, B.M. and Hamoodi, S.A., Enhancing the maximum power of wind turbine using artificial neural network. *Bull. Electr. Eng. Inf.*, *12*, 5, 2535–2542, 2023. https://doi.org/10.11591/eei.v12i5.5019.
37. Liu, M., PIDD2 Control of Large Wind Turbines' Pitch Angle. *Energies*, *16*, 13, 5096, 2023. https://doi.org/10.3390/en16135096.
38. Umar, D.A., Alkawsi, G., Alomari, M.A., Baashar, Y., Alkahtani, A.A., Capretz, L.F., Tiong, S.K., Evaluating the Efficacy of Intelligent Methods for Maximum Power Point Tracking in Wind Energy Harvesting Systems. *Processes*, *11*, 5, 1420, 2023. https://doi.org/10.3390/pr11051420.
39. Ji, Z., Zhang, J., Liu, Y., Zhou, T., Improved Combined Inertial Control of Wind Turbine Based on CAE and DNN for Temporary Frequency Support. *Appl. Sci.*, *13*, 12, 6984, 2023. https://doi.org/10.3390/app13126984.
40. K, P., Prabhakar, P., D, S., Design and Implementation of a Machine Learning-Based Wind Turbine Control System. *E3S Web Conferences*, *387*, 01008, 2023. https://doi.org/10.1051/e3sconf/202338701008.
41. Zambrana, P., Fernandez-Quijano, J., Mayorga Rubio, P.M., Fernandez-Lozano, J., García-Cerezo, A., Development and Evaluation of Fuzzy Logic Controllers for Improving Performance of Wind Turbines on Semi-Submersible Platforms under Different Wind Scenarios. *Appl. Sci.*, *13*, 4, 2422, 2023. https://doi.org/10.3390/app13042422.
42. Joshi, M.P., Mallikarjunaiah, S., Rao, S., Umarani, B., KarthiKumar, K., Subramaniam, S., Advanced AI based Controller for Wind Turbine Pitch Control, *2022 Sixth International Conference on I-SMAC (IoT in Social, Mobile, Analytics and Cloud) (I-SMAC)*, pp. 951–955, Dharan, Nepal, 2022, doi: 10.1109/I-SMAC55078.2022.9987415.

43. Huang, B., Zhou, L., Zhao, H., Long, L., *Pitch Control Strategy for Wind Turbine Considering Operation Efficiency*, pp. 1033–1045, Springer Science+Business Media, 2023, https://doi.org/10.1007/978-981-99-4334-0_123.
44. *Wind Turbines Control Systems*, Elsevier eBooks, 2023, https://doi.org/10.1016/b978-0-323-93940-9.00068-2.
45. Liu, L., Guo, X., Lee, C., Promoting smart cities into the 5G era with multi-field Internet of Things (IoT) applications powered with advanced mechanical energy harvesters. *Nano Energy*, *88*, 106304, 2021. https://doi.org/10.1016/j.nanoen.2021.106304.
46. El-Banby, G.M., Moawad, N.M., Abouzalm, B.A., Abouzaid, W.F., Ramadan, E.A., Photovoltaic system fault detection techniques: a review. *Neural Comput. Appl.*, *35*, 35, 24829–24842, 2023. https://doi.org/10.1007/s00521-023-09041-7.
47. Bosman, L.B., Leon-Salas, W.D., Hutzel, W., Soto, E.A., PV System Predictive Maintenance: Challenges, Current Approaches, and Opportunities. *Energies*, *13*, 6, 1398, 2020. https://doi.org/10.3390/en13061398.
48. Allal, Z., Noura, H.N., Vernier, F., Salman, O., Chahine, K., Wind turbine fault detection and identification using a two-tier machine learning framework. *Intell. Syst. Appl.*, 200372–200372, 2024. https://doi.org/10.1016/j.iswa.2024.200372.
49. Raju, S.K., Periyasamy, M., Alhussan, A.A., Kannan, S., Raghavendran, S., El-kenawy, E.-S.M., Machine learning boosts wind turbine efficiency with smart failure detection and strategic placement. *Sci. Rep.*, *15*, 1, 2025. https://doi.org/10.1038/s41598-025-85563-5.
50. Cao, L., Qian, Z., Zareipour, H., Wood, D., Mollasalehi, E., Tian, S., Pei, Y., Prediction of Remaining Useful Life of Wind Turbine Bearings under Non-Stationary Operating Conditions. *Energies*, *11*, 12, 3318, 2018. https://doi.org/10.3390/en11123318.
51. Judge, M.A., Franzitta, V., Curto, D., Guercio, A., Cirrincione, G., Khattak, H.A., A Comprehensive Review of Artificial Intelligence Approaches for Smart Grid Integration and Optimization. *Energy Convers. Manage. X*, 100724–100724, 2024. https://doi.org/10.1016/j.ecmx.2024.100724.
52. Narsina, D., Kamisetty, A., Ryan Thompson, C., Devarapu, K., Automation in Advanced Fluid Flow Analysis: Revolutionizing Thermal Management Solutions in Engineering. *ABC J. Adv. Res.*, 13, 1, 31–44, 2024.
53. Hernández Uribe, O., San Martin, J.P., Garcia-Alegre, M.C., Santos, M., Guinea, D., Smart Building: Decision Making Architecture for Thermal Energy Management. *Sens. (Basel Switzerland)*, *15*, 11, 27543–27568, 2015. https://doi.org/10.3390/s151127543.
54. Sekine, K., Hiratsuka, M., Usihifusa, H., Ito, S., Influence of internal wettability of heat pipe and heat transport characteristics of working fluid. *Proc. Therm. Eng. Conf.*, *2019*, 0, 0177, 2019. https://doi.org/10.1299/jsmeted.2019.0177.

55. Scharinger-Urschitz, G., Walter, H., Haider, M., Heat Transfer in Latent High-Temperature Thermal Energy Storage Systems—Experimental Investigation. *Energies*, *12*, 7, 1264, 2019. https://doi.org/10.3390/en12071264.
56. Rajendra, P. and Ankur, G., Thermal Performance Analyses Of Concentric Pipe Counter Flow Heat Exchanger At Different Operating Conditions By CFD. *I-Manager's J. Mech. Eng.*, *9*, 1, 1, 2019. https://doi.org/10.26634/jme.9.1.14805.
57. Assareh, E., Hoseinzadeh, S., Agarwal, N., Delpisheh, M., Dezhdar, A., Feyzi, M.R., Wang, Q., A transient simulation for a novel solar-geothermal cogeneration system with a selection of heat transfer fluids using thermodynamics analysis and ANN intelligent (AI) modeling. *Appl. Therm. Eng.*, *231*, 120698–120698, 2023. https://doi.org/10.1016/j.applthermaleng.2023.120698.
58. Gan, X., Pei, J., Pavesi, G., Yuan, S., Wang, W., Application of intelligent methods in energy efficiency enhancement of pump system: A review. *Energy Rep.*, *8*, 11592–11606, 2022. https://doi.org/10.1016/j.egyr.2022.09.016.
59. Deshpande, D.V., Smart Grids Integration with AI-Powered Demand Response. *Res. J. Comput. Syst. Eng. (RJCSE)*, 45–58, 2024.
60. Ghosh, A., Chakraborty, D., Law, A., Artificial intelligence in Internet of things. *CAAI Trans. Intell. Technol.*, *3*, 4, 208–218, 2018. https://doi.org/10.1049/trit.2018.1008.
61. Arévalo, P. and Jurado, F., Impact of Artificial Intelligence on the Planning and Operation of Distributed Energy Systems in Smart Grids. *Energies*, *17*, 17, 4501, 2024. https://doi.org/10.3390/en17174501.
62. Bouquet, P., Jackson, I., Nick, M., Kaboli, A., AI-based forecasting for optimised solar energy management and smart grid efficiency. *Int. J. Prod. Res.*, 62, 4623–4644, 2023. https://doi.org/10.1080/00207543.2023.2269565.
63. Sarkar, K., Load and Renewable Energy Forecasting Using Deep Learning for Grid Stability. *ArXiv (Cornell University)*, 2025. https://doi.org/10.48550/arxiv.2501.13412.
64. Muhammad, A., Ishaq, A.A., B, I.O., Idris, M.B., Artificial Intelligence and Machine Learning for Real-time Energy Demand Response and Load Management. *J. Technol. Innov. Energy*, *2*, 2, 20–29, 2023. https://doi.org/10.56556/jtie.v2i2.537.
65. Arumugham, V., Ghanimi, H.M.A., Pustokhin, D.A., Pustokhina, I.V., Ponnam, V.S., An Artificial-Intelligence-Based Renewable Energy Prediction Program for Demand-Side Management in Smart Grids. *Sustainability*, *15*, 6, 5453, 2023. https://doi.org/10.3390/su15065453.
66. Shojaeighadikolaei, A., Ghasemi, A., Jones, K., Dafalla, Y., Alexandru, G., Ahmadi, R., Haashemi, M., Distributed Energy Management and Demand Response in Smart Grids: A Multi-Agent Deep Reinforcement Learning Framework. *ArXiv (Cornell University)*, 2022. https://doi.org/10.48550/arxiv.2211.15858.
67. Wen, X., Shen, Q., Zheng, W., Zhang, H., AI-Driven Solar Energy Generation and Smart Grid Integration A Holistic Approach to Enhancing Renewable

Energy Efficiency. *Int. J. Innov. Res. Eng. Manage.*, *11*, 4, 55–66, 2024. https://doi.org/10.55524/ijirem.2024.11.4.8.

68. Ohalete, N., Aderibigbe, A.O., Ani, E.C., Ohenhen, P.E., Daraojimba, D.O., Odulaja, B.A., AI-driven solutions in renewable energy: A review of data science applications in solar and wind energy optimization. *World J. Adv. Res. Rev.*, *20*, 3, 401–417, 2023. https://doi.org/10.30574/wjarr.2023.20.3.2433.
69. Soni, P., Naveena Bhargavi, R., Dave, V., Paliwal, H., Artificial Intelligence-Enabled Techno-Economic Analysis and Optimization of Grid-Tied Solar PV-Fuel Cell Hybrid Power Systems for Enhanced Performance. *E3S Web Conferences*, *472*, 03012–03012, 2024. https://doi.org/10.1051/e3sconf/202447203012.
70. Ali, M.N., Mahmoud, K., Lehtonen, M., Darwish, M.M.F., Promising MPPT Methods Combining Metaheuristic, Fuzzy-Logic and ANN Techniques for Grid-Connected Photovoltaic. *Sensors*, *21*, 4, 1244, 2021. https://doi.org/10.3390/s21041244.
71. Santos, P., N., S., V., S., K., Ramos, M., Solar Tracking Control Algorithm Based on Artificial Intelligence Applied to Large-Scale Bifacial Photovoltaic Power Plants. *Sensors*, *24*, 12, 3890–3890, 2024. https://doi.org/10.3390/s24123890.
72. Khan, M., Raza, M.A., Faheem, M., Sarang, S.A., Panhwar, M., Jumani, T.A., Conventional and artificial intelligence based maximum power point tracking techniques for efficient solar power generation, in: *Engineering Reports*, 2024, https://doi.org/10.1002/eng2.12963.
73. Orellana, C., Moya, V., Moya, M., Oscullo, C., Artificial Intelligence-Controlled Photovoltaic Generator for Optimized Power Point Tracking. *E3S Web Conferences*, *532*, 01002–01002, 2024. https://doi.org/10.1051/e3sconf/202453201002.
74. Joshi, A., Wagh, S., Wagh, M., Sunwise: Intelligent Solar Tracking for Increased Yield. *Int. J. Res. Appl. Sci. Eng. Technol.*, *12*, 6, 982–987, 2024. https://doi.org/10.22214/ijraset.2024.63249.
75. Ali, A.H., El-Kammar, R.A., Hamed, A., Elbaset, A.A., Hossam, A., Enhancing the output power of solar cell system using artificial intelligence algorithms. *Int. J. Power Electron. Drive Syst.*, *15*, 1, 480–480, 2024. https://doi.org/10.11591/ijpeds.v15.i1.pp480-490.
76. Munawar, M.I., Imtiaz, A., Ali, M., An efficient energy prediction model for solar energy power system using Artificial Intelligence technique. *International Conference on Recent Academic Studies*, 1, 139–145, 2023. 10.59287/icras.686
77. Ourici, A., Optimal Energy Tracking in a Solar Power System Utilizing Synthetic Neural Network. *Eur. J. Electr. Eng.*, *25*, 2, 15–20, 2023. https://doi.org/10.18280/ejee.250201.
78. Jarmouni, E., Mouhsen, A., Lamhamedi, M., Ouldzira, H., En-naoui, I., Integration of an optimized neural network in a photovoltaic system to improve maximum power point tracking efficiency. *Indones. J. Electr.*

Eng. Comput. Sci., *28*, 3, 1276, 2022. https://doi.org/10.11591/ijeecs.v28.i3.pp1276-1285.

79. Jena, R., Dash, R., Reddy, K.J., Dhanamjayulu, C., Swain, S.C., Muyeen, S.M., Enhancing Efficiency of Grid-Connected Solar Photovoltaic System with Particle Swarm Optimization & Long Short-Term Memory Hybrid Technique. *Sustainability*, *15*, 11, 8535, 2023. https://doi.org/10.3390/su15118535.
80. Liu, Z., Sun, Y., Xing, C., Jia, L., He, Y., Zhou, Y., Zhang, G., Artificial intelligence powered large-scale renewable integrations in multi-energy systems for carbon neutrality transition: Challenges and future perspectives. *Energy and AI*, 10, 100195, 2022.
81. Mohammed, S., Budach, L., Feuerpfeil, M., Ihde, N., Nathansen, A., Noack, N., Patzlaff, H., Naumann, F., Harmouch, H., The effects of data quality on machine learning performance on tabular data. *Inform. Syst.*, 132, 102549, 2025, https://doi.org/10.1016/j.is.2025.102549.
82. Manju, T., Quality challenges in Deep Learning Data Collection in perspective of Artificial Intelligence. *J. Inf. Technol. Comput.*, *4*, 1, 46–58, 2023. https://doi.org/10.48185/jitc.v4i1.725.
83. Adeoye, J., Hui, L.M., Su, Y., Data-centric artificial intelligence in oncology: a systematic review assessing data quality in machine learning models for head and neck cancer. *J. Big Data*, *10*, 1, 1–25, 2023. https://doi.org/10.1186/s40537-023-00703-w.
84. Whang, S.E., Data collection and quality challenges in deep learning: a data-centric AI perspective. *Vldb J.*, *32*, 4, 791–813, 2023. https://doi.org/10.1007/s00778-022-00775-9.
85. Gong, Y., Liu, G., Xue, Y., Li, R., Meng, L., A survey on dataset quality in machine learning. *Inf. Softw. Technol.*, *162*, 107268, 2023. https://doi.org/10.1016/j.infsof.2023.107268.
86. Somasundaram, D., Muthukumar, R., Rajavinu, N., Ramaiyan, K., Kavitha, P., Machine learning applications for predicting system production in renewable energy. *Int. J. Power Electron. Drive Syst.*, *15*, 3, 1925, 2024. https://doi.org/10.11591/ijpeds.v15.i3.pp1925-1933.
87. Le, T.T., Paramasivam, P., Adril, E., Nguyen, V.Q., Le, M.X., Duong, M.T., Le, H.C., Nguyen, A.Q., Unlocking renewable energy potential: Harnessing machine learning and intelligent algorithms. *Int. J. Renew. Energy Dev.*, *13*, 4, 783–813, 2024. https://doi.org/10.61435/ijred.2024.60387.
88. Khafaga, D.S., Alhussan, A., Eid, M.M., El-kenawy, E.-S.M., Improving solar radiation source efficiency using adaptive dynamic squirrel search optimization algorithm and long short-term memory. *Front. Energy Res.*, *11*, 2023. https://doi.org/10.3389/fenrg.2023.1164528.
89. Al-Hajj, R., Assi, A., Neji, B., Ghandour, R., Al Barakeh, Z., Transfer Learning for Renewable Energy Systems: A Survey. *Sustainability*, *15*, 11, 9131, 2023. https://doi.org/10.3390/su15119131.

90. Firoozi, A.A., Hejazi, F., Firoozi, A.A., Advancing Wind Energy Efficiency: A Systematic Review of Aerodynamic Optimization in Wind Turbine Blade Design. *Energies*, *17*, 12, 2919, 2024. https://doi.org/10.3390/en17122919.
91. Bello, S.F., Wada, I.U., Ige, O.B., Chianumba, E.C., Adebayo, S.A., AI-driven predictive maintenance and optimization of renewable energy systems for enhanced operational efficiency and longevity. *Int. J. Sci. Res. Arch.*, *13*, 1, 2823–2837, 2024. https://doi.org/10.30574/ijsra.2024.13.1.1992.
92. Boosari, H. and Sina, S., Developing a Smart Proxy for Predicting the Fluid Dynamic in DamBreak Flow Simulation by Using Artificial Intelligence, Graduate Theses, Dissertations, and Problem Reports, p. 5824, 2017, https://researchrepository.wvu.edu/etd/5824.
93. Sapre, I.R., The Role of Artificial Intelligence in Enhancing Renewable Energy Efficiency: A Case Study on Solar and Wind Energy Optimization. *Intersect*, *18*, 1, 2024.

10

Artificial Intelligence-Driven Flow Optimization for Enhanced Efficiency in Renewable Energy Systems

Kavita Sanjay Singh[1], V. Shanmugapriya[2], Siddharth Shankar Mishra[3]* and Manvendra Singh[4]

[1]*Department of Information Technology, Thakur Shyamnarayan Engineering College, Mumbai, India*
[2]*Centre for Smart Energy Systems, Chennai Institute of Technology, Kundrathur, Chennai, India*
[3]*Energy Cluster, UPES, Dehradun, India*
[4]*Mechanical Cluster, UPES, Dehradun, India*

Abstract
This chapter of the book focuses on how artificial intelligence (AI) can be used to optimize flows in renewable energy systems, achieving more efficient, reliable, and coordinated integration across sophisticated electricity grids. In renewable energy sources, such as wind, solar, and hydro, energy flow plays a key role in ensuring system stability and resource utilization in the face of environmental changes. Artificial intelligence will mitigate such issues using advanced data-driven techniques, predictive analytics, and real-time decision-making, as explained in the chapter. It focuses, in particular, on machine-learning techniques for energy generation and demand prediction, critical to flow optimization. Neural networks, regression models, and similar techniques apply historical data and weather forecasts to predict changes in energy production and consumption. Getting ahead of the demand enables AI to modify power outputs in real-time to effectively use green energy sources while reducing dependence on fossil fuels. Reinforcement learning for energy storage optimization, which is essential to balance the

**Corresponding author*: siddharthmishra2009@gmail.com; ORCID: 0009000384784016
Kavita Sanjay Singh: ORCID: 0009000207228326
V. Shanmugapriya: ORCID: 0000000186252679
Manvendra Singh: ORCID: 0009000491313279

Mukesh Kumar Awasthi and Reshu Gupta (eds.) Artificial Intelligence and Computational Modeling in Heat Transfer and Fluid Dynamics, (277–306) © 2026 Scrivener Publishing LLC

fluctuations of renewable resources, is also addressed in the chapter. By using algorithms capable of optimizing the charging and discharging process, it is possible to ensure that the device data is updated in real-time, which helps stabilize the grid and reduce energy waste. The chapter also addresses the use of AI with smart grids that process renewable and traditional data sources in real-time to optimize the overall operation. Artificial intelligence-enabled smart grids manage and optimize multiple energy sources in dynamic environments to achieve a more resilient and sustainable energy system. Thus, the work presented in this chapter contributes significantly to the overall broad overview of how AI-driven deterrent measures enhance more sustainable energy management and intervention paths towards a low-emission economy.

***Keywords*:** Artificial intelligence, flow optimization, renewable energy, smart grids, energy storage

10.1 Introduction

Renewable energy systems use natural processes to create energy with minimal environmental impact and can offer sustainable replacements for fossil fuels. These systems use sources of energy like sunlight, wind, rain, tides, and geothermal heat, all of which are renewable and have a low carbon footprint. Solar power systems harness sunlight, converting it directly into electricity through photovoltaic (PV) cells or harnessing solar thermal technology to generate heat and electricity. Wind energy, harnessed *via* turbines, translates kinetic energy from airflows into mechanical energy, which can be turned into electricity. Hydropower is the generation of electricity through the flow of water, either in rivers or in man-made contraptions such as dams, where the motion of the water turns turbines [1]. Tidal and wave energy do use water movements, but they focus on the kinetic energy of oceans. Geothermal energy, which comes from the natural deep heat of the Earth, is generated by using steam or hot water found in underground reservoirs to convert that heat into energy. The different energy systems differ from each other in terms of the technology and/or infrastructure needed to maximize the efficiency of energy conversion and energy delivered, and further research is being completed to increase their efficiency and to lower their price [2]. In the context of rising global energy needs, renewable systems are more than ever an important part of energy strategies, as they play a critical role in energy security and sustainability. But the use of renewable energy sources is the key class in the process of transition to a sustainable energy future, and one of its main aspects is its efficiency and effectiveness at the outlet. So, as the energy demand worldwide increases and concerns for the environment become an important factor, the efficient usage of renewable resources becomes crucial. More energy can be extracted from a given amount of natural resources, leading to a lower environmental footprint and improved overall energy system cost-effectiveness [3]. In addition, improving efficiency further environmental objectives. This process, by making energy production more efficient, also reduces land use and biodiversity disruption, as well as the lifecycle carbon emissions related to the manufacture of renewable energy technologies. This follows not just due to the imperative of combating climate change, but also in the interest of conserving biodiversity and protecting ecosystem health, and thus the effective utilization of renewable energy and a key foundation of sustainable development. Effective flow optimization is essential in renewable energy systems to capitalize on energy capture and conversion efficiencies, but it carries unique challenges linked to the intermittent and volatile characteristics of renewable resources. Renewable systems must still be backed by effective management of flows (wind, water, thermal, etc.) for them to produce their maximum output. This includes accurate control of the physical processes and dynamics during the energy extraction and conversion processes, using advanced technology and modeling [4]. So, inherently, flow optimization is more complex due to the unpredictable nature of natural resources. Wind speed and direction, to give an example, can change suddenly from time to time, which impacts wind turbine performance. Likewise, river flow rates and tidal systems impacting hydropower and tidal energy fluctuate tremendously based on seasonal changes and weather conditions. Because of this variability, it is challenging to keep processes under optimal operating conditions, which requires strong and adaptive control systems capable of responding in real-time to changing inputs. In addition, different types of renewable energy systems have specific challenges related to flows [5, 6]. In solar energy systems, heat transfer in solar thermal plants or pulsed heat or the direction of solar exposure in PV systems is designed in consideration of the periodicity of daily and seasonal variations of sunlight. In addition, in wind and hydropower systems, wind and hydropower systems require complex aerodynamic and hydrodynamic modeling since energy efficiency is highly dependent upon design optimization for blades in turbines. These challenges are usually solved by utilizing advanced technologies like AI or machine learning (ML) to anticipate patterns and to continue automating adjustments to ensure optimal efficiency. Similarly, computational fluid dynamics (CFD) plays a key role in simulating and analyzing fluid flow in renewable energy applications. We can still deliver meaningful contributions with flow optimization in renewable energy systems, but that does not mean that the hurdles (mainly the need for accurate and high-resolution data for effective modeling and the high computational cost associated with flow optimization) will disappear when combined, as both systems require overcoming substantial hurdles. With the increasing demand for cleaner, more sustainable energy solutions, the use of artificial intelligence (AI) in improving the efficiency of renewable energy systems is becoming increasingly vital. With ML-based analytics, using AI/ML frameworks on both structured and unstructured datasets allows algorithms to run models on historical and real-time data points, giving the possibility of optimizing energy flows like never before. In this chapter, we will learn about renewable energy systems and how we use AI technologies to optimize operations and overcome inefficiencies with renewable energy systems to maximize energy output and minimize energy waste. Algorithmic, AI-infused tools can anticipate environmental considerations and adapt the operations of the system accordingly, improving the ability of renewable systems to respond to changes in natural inputs that are increasingly variable on their side. As an example, ML models can predict wind patterns, as well as schedule the operation of wind turbines ahead of time before the wind speed changes [7–9].

10.2 Fundamentals of Flow Dynamics in Renewable Energy Systems

10.2.1 Basic Principles of Fluid Dynamics as Applicable to Wind and Hydro Energy Systems

Fluid dynamics, the study of fluids in motion, is critical to the design and optimization of renewable energy systems such as wind and hydro energy. Natural resources, if they are air and water, can scale electricity with a focus on the principles of fluid dynamics for optimizing these methods of generation, while maintaining their efficiency and outputs. Wind energy systems apply the principles of fluid dynamics to understand the swirl of air around windmills and devices. This is where Bernoulli's Principle comes into play; it states that as fluid passes into an area where the velocity increases, the pressure of the fluid will decrease. This principle is used in the construction of wind turbine blades, for instance, which are angled such that one edge is in a lower pressure zone than the other side of the edge and is pushed toward the high-pressure end by the pressure differential. This movement turns the turbine's rotor to generate electricity. Similarly, using the continuity equation, which states that when the speed of the fluid increases, there is a simultaneous decrease of the area through which the fluid flows, we can understand the air flow through the rotor blades of turbines and design turbines to extract the highest amount of kinetic energy that is available in wind.

Similarly, fluid mechanics is important in hydro energy systems, where the kinetic potential energy of water is transformed into electrical energy. The basic equations of fluid dynamics, like the Navier–Stokes equations, describe the flow of water in rivers, streams, and around turbine blades in hydroelectric power plants. By manipulating these equations and inputting variables such as flow, viscosity, and pressure, the equations predict how these factors affect the efficiency of the turbine and allow engineers to create turbine blades that most effectively convert mechanical energy derived from the water into electrical energy. By modeling how water flows, engineers can better understand the speed, pressure, and turbulence of the water, enabling them to place and design turbines in a way that extracts as much energy as possible. The Reynolds number is a dimensionless number used to predict flow patterns in different fluid flow situations, as well as the study of fluid dynamics in both systems. When considering wind turbines, high Reynolds numbers signify turbulent flow states that affect energy transfer from the wind into the turbine blades. For hydro turbines, optimal flow regimes can be affected by controlled Reynolds numbers for lower energy losses. Similarly, a considerable part of wind energy, as well as hydro energy systems, occurs through a CFD-simulated code. Computational fluid dynamics employs computational and algorithmic techniques to determine and study problems involving fluid flows, which predict and visualize fluid flow, heat transfer, and related phenomena. Such chemistries are hugely beneficial in an iterative design and optimization process, in which engineers can simulate and perfect turbine blade shapes and configurations on the computer before moving on to test their physical models, saving time and spend money for more efficient renewable energy systems to develop. As such, the fundamentals of fluid dynamics are key to the provision of wind and hydro energy and the academic and practical resources that underpin the economic and successful practices seen in the use of these renewable resources [10].

10.2.2 Overview of Heat Transfer in Solar Thermal Systems

The main operation in solar thermal systems is the heat transfer process. The mechanisms of energy transfer in these systems are conduction, convection, and radiation, providing pathways for transferring heat from the sun to the working fluid in the system. Solar thermal systems usually contain solar collectors, a heat transfer fluid, a heat storage unit, and a heat exchanger. Collectors (usually coated in a dark, heat-absorbent material that maximizes absorption and minimizes reflective losses) absorb solar radiation. The collectors have tubes or channels where heat transfer fluid, usually water, air, or an antifreeze solution, drains through. The liquid extracts heat from the

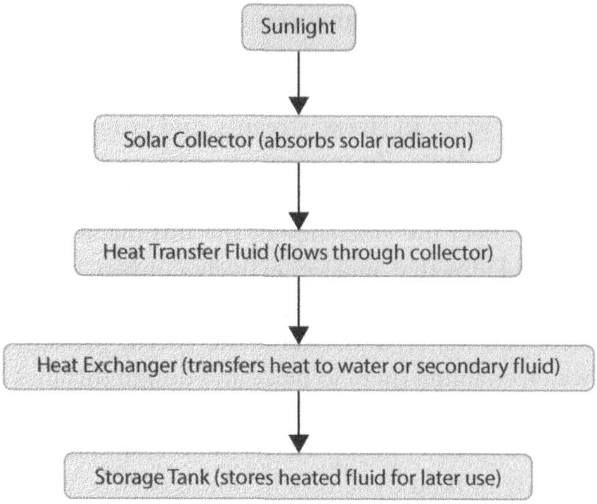

Figure 10.1 The typical components and flow of heat in a solar thermal system.

heat rejected by the collector; thus, when the liquid enters the collector and goes through it, it absorbs the heat coming through the material of the collector. This coolant is heated and then either directly used (with applications in direct supercritical CO_2 power cycles) or passed through a heat exchanger where it transfers its thermal energy to water or other working fluid by convection. Systems built for storage will have the hot fluid then flow to a storage tank, where the heat is retained for when it is needed; thus, guaranteeing the availability of hot water or hot air when solar radiation is not present. The ability to store this energy is essential to keeping the system reliable and effective in different weather conditions. The radiation from the sun comes to the collector as both direct and diffuse solar radiation. The ability of the collector to absorb this radiation and convert it into heat is determined primarily by the collector's design, orientation, and material properties. Others include selective surfaces or evacuated tubes, which minimize the driving energy losses and enable high temperatures for better heat transfer efficiency.

10.2.3 Challenges in Optimizing Natural and Forced Flow in Renewable Systems

Table 10.1 summarizes key principles of fluid dynamics—such as Bernoulli's principle, continuity equation, and Navier–Stokes equations—across wind, hydro, and solar systems. Discovering how to feature optimized, incorporated natural and forced flow in renewable energy systems involves exposing several challenges, arising primarily from natural

Table 10.1 The following table gives a thorough synopsis of the flow dynamics principles as they relate to different types of renewable energy systems. It covers the wind, hydro, and solar energy industries in depth and offers concrete examples of their use.

Topic	Description	Applications in wind energy	Applications in hydro energy	Applications in solar energy
Bernoulli's Principle	This principle relates the pressure, speed, and potential energy in fluid flow, stating that an increase in fluid speed occurs simultaneously with a decrease in pressure or a decrease in the fluid's potential energy.	Used to design blades with optimal shapes that maximize lift and minimize drag, harnessing wind energy more efficiently.	Optimizes turbine blade design to ensure maximum efficiency in converting water flow to mechanical energy.	Not directly applicable, but understanding fluid dynamics is crucial for designing thermal management systems in PV installations.
Continuity Equation	States that the mass of fluid entering a pipe or conduit must equal the mass exiting. This equation is crucial for analyzing fluid flow through varying cross-sectional areas, particularly in turbine blade design and duct systems.	Analyzes how air moves through turbine blades, ensuring that designs can handle variations in air volume and speed.	Calculates flow rates and velocities in hydro turbines to enhance energy extraction from water streams.	Relevant for designing systems that circulate thermal fluids efficiently within solar thermal collectors.
Navier–Stokes Equations	These complex partial differential equations describe how velocity, pressure, temperature, and density of a fluid are related and change over time and space. They are essential for modeling fluid flow around obstacles and through channels in hydroelectric and wind turbines.	Essential for predicting airflow patterns and turbulence around turbine blades and towers, improving energy capture.	Models water flow through dams and turbine systems, essential for designing efficient hydroelectric power plants.	Not directly applicable, but principles can be used to model heat transfer fluids in solar collectors.

(*Continued*)

Table 10.1 The following table gives a thorough synopsis of the flow dynamics principles as they relate to different types of renewable energy systems. It covers the wind, hydro, and solar energy industries in depth and offers concrete examples of their use. (*Continued*)

Topic	Description	Applications in wind energy	Applications in hydro energy	Applications in solar energy
Reynolds Number	A dimensionless value that helps predict the type of flow (laminar vs. turbulent) within a fluid system. High values typically indicate turbulent flow, which can affect energy transfer efficiency in turbine systems.	Used to design turbines that can operate effectively across varying wind conditions, optimizing power output.	Predicts flow patterns in hydro systems to minimize energy losses due to turbulence and friction.	Not directly relevant, but it informs on fluid behaviors in systems like solar panel cooling technologies.
Turbulent vs. Laminar Flow	Describes two different types of fluid motion. Laminar flow is smooth and orderly, often ideal for efficient fluid dynamics in controlled environments. Turbulent flow involves chaotic changes in pressure and flow velocity, impacting turbine blade efficiency and wear.	Critical for understanding airflow interactions with turbine blades, affecting noise, wear, and performance.	Affects the design of turbines and the efficiency of hydroelectric plants, especially in turbulent river conditions.	Not directly relevant, but considerations impact the design of solar thermal systems and their efficiency.
Computational Fluid Dynamics	A numerical approach that uses algorithms and computational software to analyze and solve problems involving fluid flows. Computational fluid dynamics is used extensively to simulate the flow of air and water in renewable energy systems, allowing optimization before physical models are built.	Simulates wind flow around turbines in different environments to optimize blade design and placement within wind farms.	Used to visualize and optimize water flow through turbines and to design dams for maximum energy conversion.	Essential for optimizing the flow of heat transfer fluids in solar collectors and enhancing thermal efficiency.

(*Continued*)

Table 10.1 The following table gives a thorough synopsis of the flow dynamics principles as they relate to different types of renewable energy systems. It covers the wind, hydro, and solar energy industries in depth and offers concrete examples of their use. (*Continued*)

Topic	Description	Applications in wind energy	Applications in hydro energy	Applications in solar energy
Heat Transfer in Solar Systems	Involves the processes of conduction, convection, and radiation to transfer heat from the sun to a working fluid in solar thermal systems. Optimizing these processes can significantly enhance the efficiency of converting solar energy into usable heat.	Not directly applicable, but similar principles of fluid dynamics are used in cooling systems for turbine components.	Not directly applicable, but principles of fluid transfer and heat exchange can inform the design of hydro facility cooling systems.	Central to maximizing the efficiency of solar collectors and managing the transfer of heat to storage or usage points.
Flow Optimization Challenges	Focuses on the difficulties in managing both natural and forced flows within renewable energy systems. Challenges include the variability of natural conditions and the energy cost of maintaining forced flow systems, impacting overall system efficiency.	Deals with optimizing the capture of naturally fluctuating wind streams and managing system responses to gusts and lulls.	Involves managing water flow variability and optimizing turbine and dam operation to maintain energy efficiency.	Challenges include managing the variable intensity of solar radiation and optimizing thermal fluid dynamics for consistent energy supply.

resources' inherent variability and system designs' physical limitations. Figure 10.1 shows the schematic of a typical solar thermal system, illustrating the flow of heat through the collector, transfer fluid, exchanger, and storage tank. Natural flow systems include passive solar buildings and naturally ventilated spaces, and all depend on environmental conditions such as wind direction and solar irradiance, which can be inherently unpredictable. This makes for inter-temporal variability, which can, when unavailable, lead us through periods of underperformance. On the other hand, in forced flow systems, such as a fan in solar thermal collectors or controlled airflow in wind turbines, energy input is required, which could diminish the efficiency and sustainability of the system.

One of the main issues that needs to be addressed in natural flow optimization is the challenges of designing to meet varied environmental situations. For example, wind turbines should be able to function well at varying wind speeds. Insufficient wind speed may not create turbine rotation, while excess wind speed can surpass the turbine design limits and require systems to disable and limit the turbine to prevent damage. Passive solar heating is, likewise, heavily dependent on the orientation and thermal mass of the building; both must be optimized to maximize heat gain in winter and minimize overheating in summer [11, 12].

Overall, while optimizing flow in renewable energy systems holds the potential for significant efficiency gains, it requires careful consideration of design principles, control strategies, and environmental factors, balancing technical feasibility with economic and practical constraints.

10.3 Artificial Intelligence Technologies in Renewable Energy

10.3.1 Introduction to Artificial Intelligence and Its Subsets: Machine Learning, Deep Learning, and Reinforcement Learning

Artificial intelligence is a large and broad area of computer science that aims to develop systems that can execute tasks that usually would require human intelligence. These tasks encompass learning from experiences, recognizing patterns, understanding complex data, making decisions, and solving problems. Artificial intelligence is a core technology still in the nascent stage that impacts almost all industries, from healthcare and transportation to entertainment and customer service. Artificial intelligence affects diverse areas of study, each with its own method and over its own area of application: ML, deep learning, and reinforcement learning. Machine learning is an offshoot of AI that allows computers to learn from and make decisions based on data ML systems obtain information from prior data to anticipate results without needing step-by-step instructions on how to accomplish those tasks. This process of learning from data is done by algorithms that improve their performance in a specific task over time. Machine learning can be further broken down into supervised learning (the model is trained on a dataset containing the inputs along with the correct outputs such that it can learn what is the desired outcome), unsupervised learning (the model learns to uncover hidden patterns, groupings, or structures when there are no pre-labeled outcomes in the dataset) and semi-supervised learning. Deep learning is an extension of ML, where artificial neural networks use multiple layers (hence the term "deep") to explore multiple levels of abstract features in data. It is especially effective for dealing with huge datasets, making it very useful in various applications like in speech recognition, natural language processing, and even image classification. Since deep learning models replicate the structure and functioning of the human brain to some degree, these models can identify patterns and make decisions with very little human input. Reinforcement learning is the area of ML that studies how agents should act in an environment to maximize some notion of cumulative reward. In contrast with supervised learning, in reinforcement learning, an agent learns to act in an environment by taking actions and receiving rewards (or penalties) in return. This type of learning is particularly useful for scenarios in which there is not necessarily a right answer, but rather a strategy is needed; this is found in playing games, driving robots, or managing investment portfolios. Combined, these AI subsets create a powerful framework used by a plethora of applications, from self-driving cars that learn based on millions of driving hours to financial models that evolve to changing market conditions [13, 14].

10.3.2 Current Artificial Intelligence Technologies Used in Renewable Energy

Advances in AI tech will likely continue to play a role in improving the efficiency, reliability, and integration of these renewable energy solutions. Artificial intelligence enables optimal operation, maintenance of equipment, prediction of energy production, and grid management in these same solar and wind energy systems. An example includes AI-based predictive maintenance using ML algorithms to process data from sensors installed on wind turbines or solar panels. This algorithm identifies the signs of potential equipment failures and inefficiencies, allowing for proactive measures to be taken that can significantly minimize downtime and extend the lifespan of the equipment. Energy forecasting is another area where AI is critical to the energy sector. Machine learning models utilize historical weather information along with real-time data to forecast solar irradiance and wind speed because the level of energy produced is directly dependent on these aspects. This enables the fine-grained and timely matching of supply and demand needed for a proper integration of renewable energy to dispatch sources on power grids. It also makes renewable projects more economically viable by optimizing energy trading strategies, thus enhancing stability on the electric grid. Table 10.2 provides a detailed overview of various AI technologies, their subsets, and applications in wind and solar energy systems, outlining corresponding benefits

Table 10.2 The table below gives a thorough synopsis of AI technologies and their applications in different renewable energy systems. It breaks down the many branches of AI, how they work, the advantages and disadvantages of using them in wind and solar power operations, and more.

Artificial intelligence technology	Subsets	Description	Application in wind Energy	Application in solar energy	Benefits	Challenges
Machine Learning	Supervised learning, unsupervised learning, semi-supervised learning	Enables computers to learn from data and make decisions without explicit programming.	Predicts turbine performance and operational efficiencies.	Optimizes panel performance and detects inefficiencies.	Improves the accuracy of predictions and operational efficiency.	Requires large datasets and can be complex to implement.
Deep Learning	Artificial neural networks	Utilizes layered neural networks to analyze complex data patterns.	Recognizes complex patterns in wind flow to enhance turbine placement.	Processes imaging data for panel condition and placement accuracy.	Handles vast amounts of data, improving system management and prediction accuracy.	Needs significant computational power and expertise to train models.

(Continued)

Table 10.2 The table below gives a thorough synopsis of AI technologies and their applications in different renewable energy systems. It breaks down the many branches of AI, how they work, the advantages and disadvantages of using them in wind and solar power operations, and more. (*Continued*)

Artificial intelligence technology	Subsets	Description	Application in wind Energy	Application in solar energy	Benefits	Challenges
Reinforcement Learning	Agent-based learning for decision making	Trains agents to make decisions that maximize a reward through trial and error.	Optimizes turbine responses based on environmental changes.	Adjusts panel positions dynamically to maximize solar capture.	Enhances system adaptability to new or evolving environments.	Depends heavily on the quality of the reward system and can be slow to converge.
Predictive Maintenance	Uses ML algorithms to predict equipment failures	Analyzes data from equipment sensors to prevent failures and extend lifespan.	Minimizes turbine downtime and maintenance costs.	Predicts potential failures in solar panel components.	Reduces operational risks and maintenance costs.	Dependent on sensor accuracy and data quality.
Energy Forecasting	Uses ML to predict energy production from weather data	Processes historical and real-time data to balance energy supply and demand.	Forecasts wind speeds to adjust turbine operations in real-time.	Predicts solar irradiance to adjust panel output and storage needs.	Enhances accuracy in energy production forecasting, improving grid management.	Susceptible to errors from inaccurate weather predictions or data anomalies.

(*Continued*)

Table 10.2 The table below gives a thorough synopsis of AI technologies and their applications in different renewable energy systems. It breaks down the many branches of AI, how they work, the advantages and disadvantages of using them in wind and solar power operations, and more. (*Continued*)

Artificial intelligence technology	Subsets	Description	Application in wind Energy	Application in solar energy	Benefits	Challenges
Layout Optimization	Optimizes the placement and operation of energy installations	Analyzes data to determine optimal placements for turbines and solar panels.	Determines the best locations for turbines to maximize wind capture.	Analyzes sun path and shading to optimize panel layout.	Improves energy yield and reduces interference among installations.	Requires extensive data on local conditions and can be expensive to implement.
Smart Grids	Uses AI to manage and distribute energy efficiently	Manages fluctuations in energy generation and demand to enhance grid stability.	Adjusts to fluctuating wind power generation automatically.	Integrates solar power into the grid while managing variable output.	Increases the reliability and efficiency of renewable energy integration into the grid.	Needs advanced technology and infrastructure, and can be costly.

and implementation challenges. Artificial intelligence also contributes to optimal renewable energy system designs, as well as configurations. In the case of wind farms, AI algorithms can analyze geographical, atmospheric, and operational data to optimize the placement of various turbines to maximize airflow and energy output and minimize wake losses when the turbulence of one turbine reduces the efficiency of others. Similar to solar energy systems, AI can determine the best angle of the panel at different times of the day and year to optimize solar capture, taking into account seasonal drift and any potential obstacles. Artificial intelligence can also contribute to a more widely based integration of renewable energy into the energy system with smart grids beyond installed sites. In recent years, AI applications have gained traction in the field of smart grid technology, where they enhance the flow of electricity networks with an optimized balance of supply and demand, as well as integration with renewable energy sources. Artificial intelligence-powered smart grids deliver a stable and reliable supply of electricity and automatically balance flows by anticipating the volume of energy load, even as renewable account for a growing share of the energy mix [15].

In summary, AI technologies are pivotal in driving forward the renewable energy sector by improving predictive capabilities, operational efficiency, and integration into existing power systems, thus paving the way for more sustainable and resilient energy infrastructures.

10.4 Artificial Intelligence Models for Flow Prediction and Optimization

10.4.1 Predictive Models for Flow and Performance Forecasting

Predictive models concerning the prediction of flow and performance are critical models in most fields, especially in renewable energy, liquid kinetics, and manufacturing. They predict future states and results based on records and statistical methodologies, empowering more proactive decision-making and optimized systems and processes. In renewable energy as well, predictive models are used widely to predict the flow of natural resources (wind and sunlight) directly impacting energy production. Algorithms learn from historical weather data, along with real-time environmental input, to deliver predictions on wind and solar irradiance. Such forecasting capability is crucial for grid operators and energy generators, so they can plan production upfront from wind farms and solar panels.

By better aligning energy supply with consumer demand, reliable prediction allows the intermittent nature of renewable energy sources to be accommodated by the energy network, leading to improved grid stability and operational performance. Similarly, predictive models in fluid dynamics forecast the flow of liquids and gases through various media. These models are heavily dependent on the design of efficient pipelines, water treatment facilities, and heating, ventilation, and air conditioning (HVAC) systems for buildings. An example is predictive simulation, geometric or transient, generally using CFD methods, which is a field that uses numerical algorithms for fluid flow analysis and problem-solving. Computational fluid dynamics is used by engineers and designers to predict how altering the conditions affects fluid behavior, aiding in optimizing system designs or improving performance or lowering costs. Techniques of balanced predictive models help predict the performance of most manufacturing industries with respect to machinery and production processes. The predictive maintenance techniques are the methods that help predict when equipment failures might happen using the data collected from the sensors, and Internet-of-Things-devices. These models will help in predicting potential failures and suggesting maintenance activities before a breakdown, leading to reduced downtime and increased life of machinery. This does not just save costs; it makes for much larger system efficiencies and much better reliability in manufacturing operations. Automation is bringing predictive models to industries. These technologies increase the accuracy and speed of forecasts, particularly for more complex datasets with multiple variables. And this is creating more predictive models that can adjust and learn continuously, where their predictions can get better according to the newest data and their results [16]. So overall, predictive models in the field of flow and performance forecasting are thus a gentle handshake between data analytics and ML, along with domain expertise. Crucial for optimizing operations, increasing efficiency, and advancing innovations in various domains, these systems allow areas to evolve not only reactively but proactively before the needed future state [17].

10.4.2 Integration of Artificial Intelligence with Computational Fluid Dynamics

Computational fluid dynamics refers to the process of utilizing numerical analysis and data structures to analyze and solve problems involving fluid flows, which is traditionally extremely computationally intensive and time-consuming. The integration of AI, particularly through ML and deep learning, provides a solution to the typical issues that arise within CFD, resulting in a more adaptive and responsive approach to studying fluid dynamics.

10.4.2.1 Enhancing Computational Efficiency

The key advantage of AI in combination with CFD is increased computational efficiency. Once trained on a dataset of fluid dynamics data, ML models can predict the flow patterns and behaviors much faster than traditional simulation codes can solve it. These include deep-learning models being trained to learn from data and predict turbulence or complex fluid interactions without requiring the detailed interaction of the entire computational mesh to be resolved to account for their effects.

10.4.2.2 Increasing Accuracy and Predictive Capabilities

By training on historical data from previous simulations, AI can recognize complex underlying patterns that were not visible through conventional approaches, thereby enhancing the precision of CFD models. To give an example, neural networks could be trained to enhance the handling of boundary conditions or refine the closure terms in turbulence modeling, which are usually constructed as an empirical formula and hence could introduce an error into the simulation.

10.4.2.3 Adaptive Meshing

Adaptive mesh refinement is a CFD method in which the mesh adapts to the solution so that relevant flow features are captured in high resolution, but less computational effort is used where it is not needed. Utilizing AI to improve this workflow is possible by predicting which areas of the flow are suitable for coarser meshes based on learning from previous simulations.

10.4.2.4 Real-Time Simulation and Control

Combining AI with CFD allows for real-time simulation capabilities, particularly valued in control systems for engineering applications in which control systems are integrated to design HVAC systems within the walls of buildings, or to improve the aerodynamic traits of cars while in motion. Real-time analysis of CFD simulation results can enable AI algorithms to adapt the system dynamically, improving its performance and responsiveness.

10.4.2.5 *Multi-Fidelity Modeling*

Artificial intelligence enables multi-fidelity modeling, where low-fidelity models (less computational cost) and high-fidelity models (more detailed and accurate) are intelligently combined for optimum accuracy and computational speed. Such discrepancies can be learned between models of different fidelity by using ML algorithms, which can adapt simulation parameters in real-time to maximize the simulation outcome given the computational resource available.

There is still much research required to fully integrate AI with CFD and capitalize on its potential. But the synergy generated by the interaction of these powerful tools is enabling new frontiers of research and application for fluid dynamics, with the potential for tremendous gains in simulation techniques and their use in the field across a variety of industries [18].

10.5 Optimizing Hydrodynamic Processes in Hydropower

10.5.1 Artificial Intelligence Applications in Water Flow Prediction and Management

As illustrated in Figure 10.2, the AI-driven process for water flow prediction integrates weather data, satellite imagery, and sensor data to inform water-management decisions. Water flow prediction and management are revolutionized with the introduction of AI, allowing more accurate, efficient, and informed decision-making in the allocation of water resources, flood prevention, and environmental protection. Machine learning- and deep learning-based AI models with context and historic water data help run analyses on millions of weather stations, river sensors, and satellites that predict the water flow rate, water levels, and the possibility of floods with high accuracy. From the perspective of water resource management, AI applications are crucial for predicting seasonal water availability for irrigation schedules, reservoir operations, and ensuring water sustainability across sectors. Algorithms such as random forest and support vector machines are well-suited for this task, as they can learn complex, non-linear relationships in hydrological data to generate predictions that inform water managers' decisions on water distribution and storage. Another vital domain where AI has a major role is flood prediction. Trained in historical flood data along with real-time weather inputs, deep learning models can predict flood risks with astonishing precision. Such forecasts allow early warning systems to notify communities and governments of

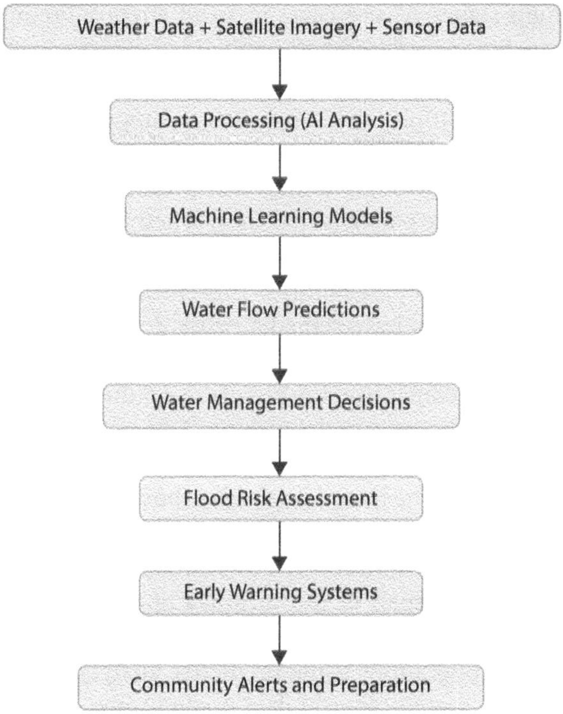

Figure 10.2 Artificial intelligence-driven process for water flow prediction and management.

impending disasters, and preparation weeks ahead of time potentially saves lives and mitigates economic losses. Additionally, AI improves operational water management by using real-time monitoring and control systems embedded in water networks [19]. These AI systems accordingly adjust flows of water in pipelines and canals in real-time to meet demand without overexploiting either water sources (the lakes and rivers that feed the lakes) or end-users (water lilies, kangaroos, you); thus, helping to ensure that water goes to the right places and is used more effectively rather than going to waste [20].

10.5.2 Enhancements in Turbine Efficiency and Maintenance through Artificial Intelligence

Most importantly, AI technology is being incorporated into turbine efficiency and maintenance to change wind and hydro power. Artificial intelligence tech can help operators enhance energy efficiency, reduce operating costs, and protracted turbines' lifespan. The vertical storm prediction is also among high-stakes AI use cases in wind energy: Predictive maintenance. Wind turbines are fitted with embedded sensors, so that AI algorithms can process the data collected by those sensors to monitor their condition at any given time. Such sensors track supplementary data (vibration, temperature, acoustics, etc.) and the well-being of the turbine. This data is then processed through models that predict potential failures. For example, AI can indicate patterns that show when a bearing is likely to fail and suggest servicing the component before the issue grows into bigger, costlier repairs or catastrophic failures. This ensures no downtime, and by utilizing the downtime to have remedial work done in scheduled parts of time rather than in an incident where it gets costly for resources to be available. This is where AI comes into the picture; it optimizes the performance, which increases the efficiency of the turbine. Advanced algorithms analyze operational data and even weather forecasts to configure the position of both turbine blades and the rotor to optimize the amount of wind collected and, at the same time, reduce mechanical stress in situations with gusty winds. This online optimization helps to customize a peak efficiency that lasts for the normal lifespan of the turbine's operation. In hydroelectric power, machine learning is mainly utilized for managing water flow and optimizing turbine operations using predictive analytics. Artificial intelligence models using meteorological data predict water inflow from above, adapting reservoir levels as needed to maximize generation. Machine learning algorithms, too, can determine when to turn on turbines, or when to store water, trading off energy produced for prices of electricity in the market and demand for power. The use of AI, therefore, not only helps each turbine perform better but also helps increase reliability and overall efficiency in renewable energy systems. In its own way, AI is setting a standard in the field of renewable energy; reducing operational risks and increasing outputs, while guiding the other means of energy generation onto the paths of sustainability and cost-effectiveness [21, 22].

10.6 Artificial Intelligence-Enhanced Solar Energy Systems

10.6.1 Use of Artificial Intelligence in Optimizing Flow Processes in Solar Heating and Cooling Systems

Figure 10.3 depicts how AI algorithms control heat-transfer fluids and optimize flow rates in solar heating and cooling systems. Due to this fact, AI is revolutionizing the optimization of flow processes in solar heating and cooling

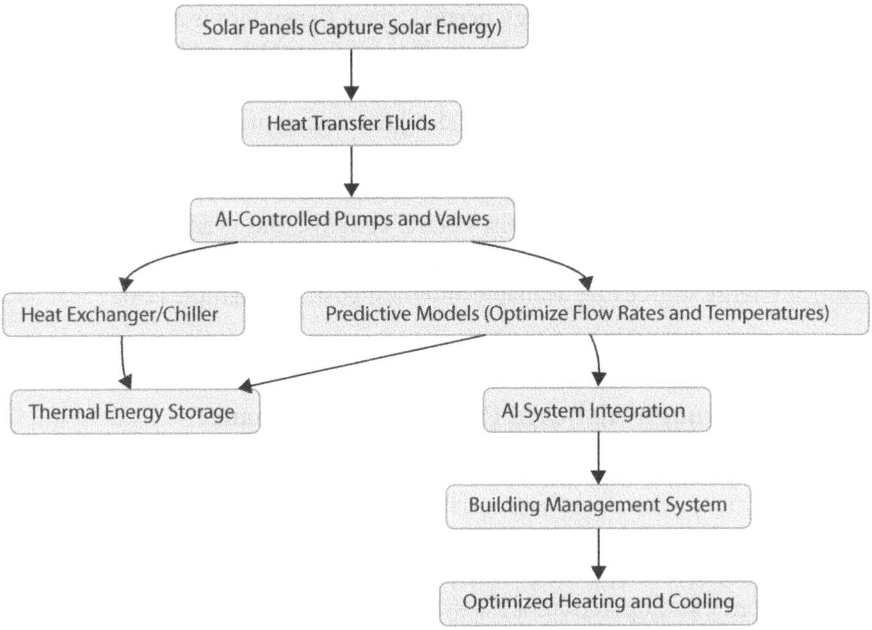

Figure 10.3 How AI optimizes flow processes in solar heating and cooling systems.

systems, providing enhanced efficiency and energy conservation. Integrating AI capabilities, such systems can dynamically modify operations based on environmental conditions, utilization patterns, and other factors to ensure optimum performance. Solar heating systems use AI algorithms to control heat transfer fluids. These fluids serve to capture solar energy absorbed by the solar panels and transport it to heat exchangers or storage units. Additionally, the model could assist in ML models that might forecast the best flow rate and temperature settings in relation to real-time solar irradiance and ambient temperature data, as well as forecasting data. The system is used by its device through its thermal personality, a fabulous function to forge, predict the sun's warmth, so that it could harness heat through treatment when in a very complete sun, and to work less in the event of short drilling heat. In the case of solar cooling systems that typically use an absorption or adsorption chiller as the cooling machine powered by solar thermal energy, AI can help to better perform the system by optimizing the operation of the chiller machine. The AI algorithms analyze data coming from sensors that measure the performance of the chiller, as well as environmental parameters [23].

They fine-tune the flow rates of the cooling fluid and the operational settings of the chiller to ensure temperature control efficiently. Not only does this increase the efficiency of the cooling output, but it also dramatically decreases the amount of energy needed, since the system is already primed to the cooling demand as it has learned trends from historical data. Artificial intelligence-powered control systems for solar integration of solar heating and cooling systems with other building management systems can be handled by AI-driven control systems, providing a holistic energy management approach. Artificial intelligence can coordinate the interoperation of solar thermal systems with PV panels, HVAC systems, and even grid electricity to optimize energy consumption throughout an entire building, based on which energy sources are available and their cost, for example [24].

10.6.2 Enhancements in Photovoltaic System Performance through AI-Based Predictive Maintenance

Figure 10.4 illustrates the AI-based predictive-maintenance workflow in photovoltaic systems, from sensor data acquisition to anomaly detection and maintenance scheduling. The advent of AI for predictive maintenance is revolutionizing human productivity in PV systems, as it dramatically improves the efficiency and operation of PV systems. With AI at their disposal, operators can find faults before they affect the system, optimizing energy, and minimizing downtime.There are various components in a standard PV

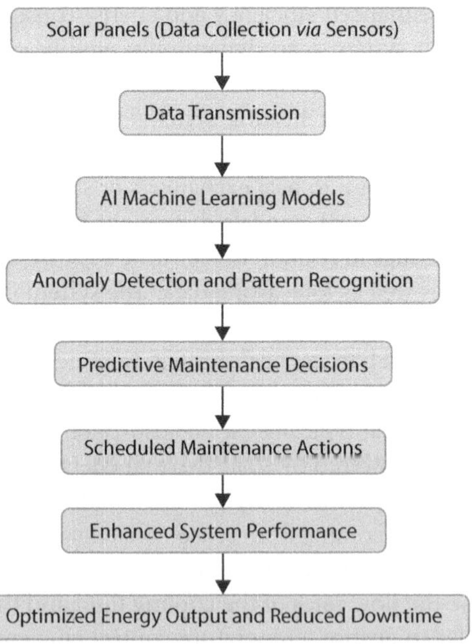

Figure 10.4 Artificial intelligence-based predictive maintenance process in PV systems.

system that contribute to its performance, such as dust deposits, panel degradation, electrical faults, etc. This involves AI algorithms, especially machine learning models, that analyze data gathered by sensors placed around the solar panels. These sensors regularly measure temperature, voltage, current, and irradiance. Such data helps models to recognize patterns and anomalies, allowing them to predict potential failures. An example is AI that can notice minute fluctuations in voltage output, which signal the onset of faults within an inverter or degradation of solar cells. This, therefore, can lead to the proactive scheduling of maintenance, as relevant issues may be addressed sooner than may result in greater losses of power output or costly repairs. Moreover, AI-powered platforms can optimize cleaning schedules according to the analysis of dust accumulation patterns and weather conditions, ensuring that the panels are functioning at their maximum efficiency without spending resources cleaning when it is not needed [25–27].

10.7 Challenges and Future Prospects

Table 10.3 outlines the key technical and economic barriers to AI adoption in renewable-energy systems, along with possible solutions and long-term benefits. Implementing AI in renewable energy systems faces technical and economic challenges. It comes down to the technicality of integrating AI into cars. Windmills and solar cells are capturing our solar energy, and they require a lot of sensors to measure different parameters in real-time. This arrangement requires significant initial investments in hardware and software. Moreover, the use of AI models' complexity demands substantial computational resources and knowledge, limiting their feasibility for smaller players or new markets. From an economic standpoint, the price of implementing AI technologies can be significant, not just in terms of hardware but also in terms of ongoing costs associated with data storage, processing, and human resources. Although AI does have the potential to improve efficiency and decrease operational costs in the long run, the payback period for investment is pretty high, which makes it a high-risk investment for companies with shrinking budgets or companies in fields of heavy competition with high-level price pressure. There are ethical implications, and when it comes to AI in renewable energy, one major issue revolves around data privacy and security. There is large-scale data on companies that range from sensitive information to personal data, which could lead to a data breach if companies are not careful. Also, there is a risk of bias in AI algorithms that can potentially lead to unfair practices or unequal service provision, especially in diverse geographical and socio-economic contexts. Environmental impacts,

Table 10.3 With an emphasis on the effects on small operators, possible remedies, long-term advantages, and implementation hurdles, this table lays out the technical and economic difficulties of integrating AI into renewable energy systems.

Aspect	Description	Impact on small operators	Potential solutions	Long-term benefits	Challenges in implementation
Data Infrastructure	Integrating AI requires an advanced data infrastructure to handle vast data volumes from renewable energy systems.	High setup costs can deter small operators from adopting AI technologies.	Subsidies or partnerships with tech companies to reduce initial data infrastructure costs.	Enhanced ability to manage large datasets can significantly improve operational efficiency.	Complex integration with existing IT systems and ensuring data security can be daunting.
Sensor Technology	Renewable systems like wind turbines and solar panels need extensive sensor networks for continuous monitoring.	The need for extensive sensor networks may be financially infeasible for smaller entities.	Collaborative ventures or grants to assist in the deployment of necessary sensor technologies.	Accurate, real-time monitoring leads to better maintenance and efficiency, reducing downtime.	Technical challenges in ensuring reliable data collection and handling under various environmental conditions.

(*Continued*)

Table 10.3 With an emphasis on the effects on small operators, possible remedies, long-term advantages, and implementation hurdles, this table lays out the technical and economic difficulties of integrating AI into renewable energy systems. (*Continued*)

Aspect	Description	Impact on small operators	Potential solutions	Long-term benefits	Challenges in implementation
Artificial Intelligence Model Complexity	The complexity of AI models demands substantial computational resources and expertise.	Requires specialized knowledge and resources that may not be accessible to smaller operators or emerging markets.	Training programs and access to open-source AI tools reduce the barrier to entry for complex AI models.	Advanced AI applications can drive significant improvements in energy production and system optimization.	Keeping up with the rapid pace of AI technology advancement and integrating updates can be challenging.
Initial Investment	The upfront cost for AI technology, including hardware and software, can be significant.	Substantial initial outlay may be prohibitive for businesses with limited capital.	Financial incentives, such as tax breaks or low-interest loans, can offset initial investments.	Over time, the efficiency gains and operational improvements can outweigh the initial costs.	Managing cash flows and securing funding for upfront costs can be difficult.
Operational Costs	Ongoing expenses related to data storage, processing, and skilled personnel contribute to high operational costs.	Continuous financial burden may strain the budgets of small operators, limiting their ability to innovate.	Cloud-based AI solutions and as-a-service platforms to minimize ongoing operational costs.	Reduction in operational costs through AI efficiencies can improve the overall profitability of renewable systems.	Maintaining data security and managing the skills gap for operating advanced AI systems.

(*Continued*)

Table 10.3 With an emphasis on the effects on small operators, possible remedies, long-term advantages, and implementation hurdles, this table lays out the technical and economic difficulties of integrating AI into renewable energy systems. *(Continued)*

Aspect	Description	Impact on small operators	Potential solutions	Long-term benefits	Challenges in implementation
ROI Period	The period before seeing a return on AI investments can be lengthy, posing financial risks in competitive markets.	Long ROI periods may not align with the financial planning or capabilities of smaller companies.	Performance-based contracts and smaller, phased investments to manage financial risk.	Strategic financial planning with AI can lead to sustainable growth and competitive advantage.	Navigating financial uncertainty and market conditions that can affect the viability of AI investments.

although generally positive because of the intention to optimize renewable energy, should also be considered [28–30]. From the generation, use, and disposal of AI hardware to the sensors used to power these systems, this can be eco-unfriendly without appropriate management. And the energy demanded by large AI systems can be significant, possibly negating some of the environmental benefits of renewable energy optimizations. Some trends can improve the integration and efficiency of such systems, which will lead to a more exciting future of AI in renewable energy. Self-operating systems driven by AI are evolving from monitoring and maintenance solutions into solutions capable of fully handling tasks for energy production and distribution processes. It will allow more resilient and flexible energy systems. Such hybrid AI will be able to marry, for example, ML with a genetic algorithm to yield more accurate and efficient predictions and optimize operations. So, these models are more efficient in dealing with variations and uncertainties inside renewable energy systems.

There are hurdles to overcome in adopting AI for renewable energy, but the potential advantages are significant. These technologies must be developed with ethical and environmental considerations in mind from the outset to guarantee that their application contributes positively to a sustainable and equitable energy future.

10.8 Conclusion

Consequently, AI has revolutionized the management and optimization of renewable energy systems, and thus, affected the performance of stand-alone renewable energy systems. Artificial intelligence, for example, can increase operational efficiency from renewable energy sources by accurately predicting the energy each will create in a given timeframe, optimizing equipment efficiency as needed, and reducing equipment downtime from predictive maintenance. These algorithms examine patterns in weather data and system performance to make more accurate energy output predictions, helping to manage and store energy on the grid more effectively. Predictive maintenance: AI-powered predictive maintenance predicts faults before they turn into a failure, which significantly reduces maintenance costs and increases the lifespan of renewable energy equipment. And ability to solve all upcoming problems in renewable energy using AI-based solutions. With the growing demand for clean energy, distributed energy management becomes increasingly multifaceted, as does integrating renewable energy sources into existing power grids. Machine learning algorithms help identify and optimize energy distribution and energy storage to ensure grid stability, managing this complexity. Sophisticated forecasting models can predict energy needs, enabling real-time adjustments to the energy supply and smoothing the ups and downs of renewable. Moreover, AI can play a vital role in the development of smart grids that can intelligently balance and redistribute energy using up-to-the-millisecond information on local generation, demand, and energy sources to minimize waste while ensuring an overall reliable power supply. Using AI in the renewable energy sector is a crucial step to introduce a smarter approach for sustainability. This does not just need to be developing better analytics for existing applications, though it needs to do that too, but also needs to expand the use of AI to new applications with renewable technologies. Need to do targeted-enabled research domain-centric to renewable energy, which can lead to customized AI solutions addressing specific challenges of exemplarity, like hybrid systems injection and flexible operation of distributed energy resources in a sector. Another important area is education and training; a workforce trained in AI and renewable energy technologies will be needed to drive these innovations. As AI technologies scale, the ethical use and environmental impact must be considered. This means protecting data privacy, making sure everyone has access to AI-enabled energy solutions, and minimizing the carbon emissions arising directly from the operations of AI. Policies and regulations that encourage ethical AI practices, transparency about how AI will be used within the energy sector, and ultimately, public trust and widespread acceptance will also be needed. One step further, AI can not only optimize the operations of renewable energy systems but also trigger a paradigm shift in the organizational infrastructure that will host the deployment of these systems. The evolution of AI in the renewable energy space is creating a whole new realm of possibilities for more intelligent word in energy use from systems efficiencies to forecasting supply and demand to predictive maintenance, all while data-based processes can help to stay balanced with people and planet in mind. With that in mind, we are going to need cooperation on innovation, regulation, education, and a million other things to make sure AI is a net positive to our sustainable energy future.

References

1. Allwood, J.M. and Cullen, J.M., *Sustainable materials: With both eyes open*, UIT Cambridge, 2012.

2. Garcia, D.A., Raskovic, P., Duić, N., Technologies and strategies fostering the sustainable development of energy, water and environment systems. *Energy Convers. Manage.: X*, 2024.
3. Singh, H. and Singh, E.B.P., Digital Life in 2050: A Futuristic Outlook, in: *Proceedings of the 2nd International Conference on Digital Futures*, 2023.
4. Singh, A.K., Smart Eco-Friendly Manufacturing System with AIOT Applications. *Available at SSRN 4862891.*, 2024.
5. Soni, A., Arora, R., Kumar, A., Panwar, D., Evaluating Domain Coverage in Low-Resource Generative Chatbots: A Comparative Study of Open-Domain and Closed-Domain Approaches Using BLEU Scores, 2024. 10.21203/rs.3.rs-5063895/v1.
6. Hadiyana, T. and Ji-hoon, S., AI-Driven Urban Planning: Enhancing Efficiency and Sustainability in Smart Cities. *ITEJ (Inf. Technol. Eng. J.)*, 2024.
7. Pandey, A.K., Tiwari, P., Nishad, D.K., Khalid, S., Intelligent Energy Optimization in Wind-PV-Battery Microgrids Using AI. *Res. Square*, 2024.
8. Senthil, K., Begum, A., Ayyappan, G., AI-driven power usage optimization and sustainable energy transitions. *Autom. Transport Ind.*, 2024.
9. Arora, R., Kumar, A., Soni, A., AI-Driven Self-Healing Cloud Systems: Enhancing Reliability and Reducing Downtime through Event-Driven Automation, 2024.
10. Singh, J., Autonomous Vehicles and Smart Cities: Integrating AI to Improve Traffic Flow, Parking, and Environmental Impact. *J. AI-Assisted Sci. Discov.*, 2024.
11. Igini, F., Cafaro, A., Calabrese, M., Cybernetic Strategies: Fashion's Sustainable Supply Chain Evolution with Ship-then-Shop, in: *WOSC 19th Congress 2024*, 2024.
12. Javaid, S., Ioannou, I.I., Vassiliou, V., Catalyzing Energy Balance: A Comparative Analysis of Optimization Algorithms in the DAI Framework, in: *IEEE International Conference on Consumer Electronics*, 2024.
13. Wilson, J., Maximizing Affordable Housing with Minimal Water Environment Impacts–Innovative Pilot for Christchurch, New Zealand, in: *Collection Systems and Stormwater Conference 2024*, 2024.
14. Calabrese, M. and Cafaro, A., AI-Driven Supply Chain Optimization in Renewable Energy Deployment. *Cybernetic Strategies, 2024*, 2024.
15. Soni, A., Arora, R., Kumar, A., *et al.*, Enhancing Security in Cloud Native Applications: A Blockchain-Based Approach for Container Image Integrity, 10 September 2024.
16. Nishad, D.K. and Khalid, S., Integration of AI for Efficient Renewable Energy Management. *Renew. Energy Syst. J.*, 2024.
17. Singh, H., Enhancing Solar Panel Efficiency Using AI Algorithms, in: *Proceedings of the AI Energy Conference*, 2024.
18. Senthil, K. and Begum, A., Real-Time AI Monitoring in Renewable Energy Applications. *Books Emerging Technol.*, 2024.

19. Javaid, S. and Vassiliou, V., Grid Stability and AI-Driven Flow Optimization. *Energy Convers. Syst. Int.*, 2024.
20. Soni, A., Enhancing Multilingual Table-to-Text Generation with QA Blueprints: Overcoming Challenges in Low-Resource Languages. Preprints, 2024. https://doi.org/10.20944/preprints202408.2032.v1.
21. Garcia, D.A., AI's Role in Renewable Energy Flow Control. *Energy Manage. J.*, 2024.
22. Singh, A.K., AI in Hybrid Renewable Systems. *SSRN Renew. Technol.*, 2024.
23. Hadiyana, T., Smart City Planning with AI and Renewable Energy. *ITEJ J.*, 2024.
24. Singh, J., AI Integration in Vehicle Energy Efficiency Systems. *J. AI-Assisted Energy Deployment*, 2024.
25. Wilson, J., Optimizing Renewable Energy Solutions for Urban Areas, in: *Urban Planning Conference Series*, 2024.
26. Khalid, S. and Nishad, D.K., Challenges in Renewable Grid Stability and AI. *Energy Syst. Anal.*, 2024.
27. Ioannou, I. and Javaid, S., Distributed AI Optimization in Renewable Energy Networks. *IEEE Renew. Tech.*, 2024.
28. Igini, F. and Cafaro, A., The Role of Cybernetics in Renewable Energy Optimization. *WOSC 2024*, 2024.
29. Garine, R., Arora, R., Kumar, A., Soni, A., Advanced Machine Learning for Analyzing and Mitigating Global Supply Chain Disruptions during COVID-19, 2024. 10.2139/ssrn.4937475.
30. Garcia, P.R. and Duić, N., Machine Learning in Sustainable Energy Flow Optimization. *Energy Convers. J.*, 2024.

11

Artificial Intelligence for Flow Optimization in Renewable Energy Systems

Devanshi Srivastava and Adarsh Kumar Arya*

Department of Chemical Engineering, Harcourt Butler Technical University, Kanpur, Uttar Pradesh, India

Abstract

Numerous sectors have recognized the remarkable potential of deep learning (DL) and artificial intelligence (AI) to enhance long-term sustainability. Although AI may address 134 of the 169 Sustainable Development Goals (SDGs), the fast advancement of these technologies needs stringent regulatory monitoring to guarantee integrity, reliability, and ethical compliance. The renewable power sector has effectively used AI and DL to enhance grid reliability, enhance energy management, and detect faults. They have shown potential in two domains: optimizing waste management processes and statistical analysis in solar energy installations. The combination of a hybrid application of DL and AI systems has enhanced the availability of extensive spatial data to generate better exposure models and disease prediction. The AI-based technologies are supported in the sustainable energy field because surveys and real-life deployments point out that technologies decrease greenhouse gas emissions and power wastage and save on power. The study explores the status of AI and DL techniques to assess their possible uses to promote sustainable electricity options and environmental conservation, along with the SDGs.

***Keywords*:** Optimization, renewable energy, AI, sustainable development goals, DL

**Corresponding author*: aarya@hbtu.ac.in; ORCID: 0009-0002-5316-954X
Adarsh Kumar Arya: ORCID: 0000-0002-2378-3832

Mukesh Kumar Awasthi and Reshu Gupta (eds.) Artificial Intelligence and Computational Modeling in Heat Transfer and Fluid Dynamics, (307–332) © 2026 Scrivener Publishing LLC

11.1 Introduction

Artificial intelligence (AI) and deep learning (DL) jobs have deeply transformed numerous industries, one of which is especially sustainability. They have a high capacity to move toward more sustainable projects, especially in renewable energy and environmental well-being. Artificial intelligence and deep learning have been applied to decrease energy usage and environmental harm; research shows economic and ecological impact training optimizes neural network architecture [61]. In the renewable energy domain, AI has substantially contributed to energy management within intelligent buildings. Simultaneously, deep reinforcement learning (DRL) addresses challenges related to energy efficiency [71].

Moreover, AI has been efficient in the field of detecting abnormalities with new energy outlets, deep convolutional generative adversarial networks assisting the pseudo data to detect solar cell defects [45, 51]. Within the recycling industry, AI and DL are deployed to enhance garbage disposal processes, streamline eco-friendly biofuel manufacturing, anticipate future output from solar energy facilities, and create intelligent Internet-of-Things (IoT)-enhanced solid waste frameworks. According to what has been done, these technologies have also been utilized for forecasting photovoltaic energy generation [17]. Nonetheless, the swift progression of AI and DL requires thorough regulatory frameworks to guarantee transparency, security, and adherence to ethical norms.

11.2 Artificial Intelligence, Deep Learning, and the Sustainable Development Goals

Modern technologies AI and DL hold a considerable promise in facilitating the attainment of SDGs. They have experienced fast expansion and influenced several decision-making domains, such as healthcare, manufacturing, agriculture, education, and financial markets. An in-depth analysis of the effect of AI in the 17 SDGs and 169 targets contained within the 2030 agenda claims AI may help to achieve as many as 128 targets situated across all SDGs. But it can also hinder 58 ambitions, illustrating the need for accurate, as well as morally responsible use of these technologies [65]. Artificial intelligence and DL have shown significant promise in the experiences of learners and educational achievements.

The advent of AI technologies has necessitated a reevaluation of traditional approaches to assessing learning outcomes in higher education [14]. School-based DL methods create better conditions for high school students to develop stronger mathematical competencies and practical understanding [26]. Listening emerges as a vital ability, although society sometimes fails to recognize its importance for learning languages. Modern DL technology allows physical education instructors to monitor pupils' physical activity together with heart rate data to improve their educational methods. Globally, medical facilities depend on AI technologies to combat COVID-19 while improving their healthcare services. Medical clinical AI research includes protocols that serve as guidelines to help physicians conduct and evaluate studies that use AI. The set of guidelines contains both a performance requirement list and specific evaluation criteria [47].

Security experts have transformed the need for interpretable DL models into understanding how data-driven solutions should align with SDGs while also adhering to ethical AI systems. Artificial intelligence models require transparency combined with an interpretable design to use them properly according to ethical standards [66]. Plants benefit from the applications of AI and DL for biological research, while the potential fusion between explainable AI and exascale computation can fulfill the United

Figure 11.1 The sustainable development goals [53] under Creative Commons CC (By license).

Nations' SDGs [60]. Some of the key SDGs that AI and DL impact include SDG 3 (good health and well-being), SDG 7 (affordable and clean energy), SDG 11 (sustainable cities and communities), SDG 12 (consumption and production), and SDG 13 (life on land). Unrestricted usage of AI technology puts the SDGs at risk of failure. Figure 11.1 shows the 17 goals that extend from the Millennium Development Goals (MDGs) framework that began in 2000 with eight objectives and aimed to achieve all guidelines by 2015. To block AI from undermining the SDGs, regulatory authorities propose early action measures to implement before deployment [25]. Deep graph learning has been suggested to tackle social issues and enhance individuals' daily experiences.

11.3 Analysis of Artificial Intelligence Technologies in Sustainable Power

Artificial intelligence plays a vital role in improving both the operating efficiency and seamless integration of sustainable power systems for achieving an ecologically sustainable energy system. Artificial intelligence delivers improved decision quality in addition to predictive equipment maintenance, along with optimal power generation and energy storage control.

11.3.1 Machine Learning and Deep Learning

Using AI through ML and DL techniques enables systems to process extensive data collections for pattern recognition, which results in outcome predictions without traditional programming instructions [58]. Consequently, the technologies are very important in strengthening the forecasting accuracy, resource management, and operational efficiency in renewable energy systems. For example, as stated above, ML models can predict energy generation on wind and solar farms under different conditions by analyzing historical weather data, turbine efficiencies, and grid data. Forecasting accurately is key to avoiding shortages or overproduction of power when it comes to balancing supply and demand in the grid. The DL algorithms can be used to analyze the turbine sensor data in real-time and then predict future faults, which can avoid the amplification of faults and facilitate the long equipment lifespan, as well as the optimal scheduling of maintenance [40]. Figure 11.2 represents the relationship between ML and DL, which are the research areas of AI. In solar energy, ML can assist in optimizing solar panel angles and

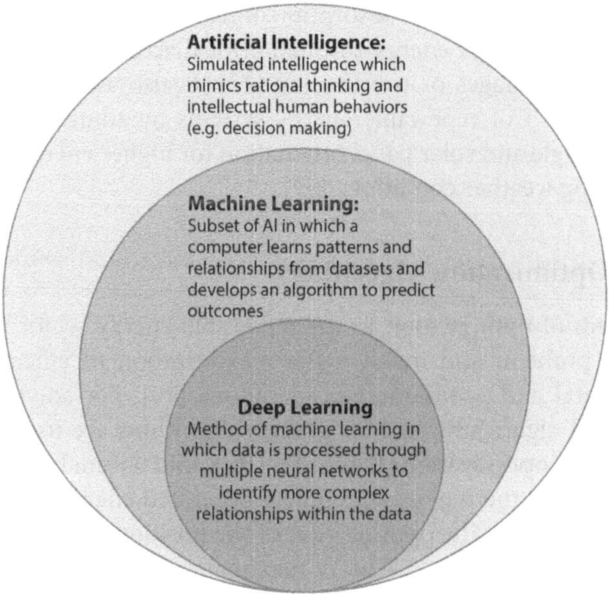

Figure 11.2 The interaction of AI, ML, and DL [38] under Creative Commons CC (by license).

positioning based on environmental conditions [44], increasing energy production efficiency. By harnessing these algorithms, renewable energy companies can enhance grid stability and manage renewable energy variability, making them more reliable [50].

11.3.2 Reinforcement Learning

Reinforcement learning is an AI methodology that trains models to make the optimum decision with the objective of maximizing the total rewards in uncertain conditions. The best example of this is the systems that can learn optimal techniques by trial and error, altering their behavior with respect to external feedback [8]. In the realm of sustainable power, RL can potentially be used to control smart grids, operate storage energy systems, and perform renewable energy generation. With current RL algorithms, optimized battery energy storage can dynamically regulate, provide, and release the number of cycles as a function of real-time metrics. In smart grids, RL can play an important role by improving load balancing as it can take into account the usage energy patterns, meteorological conditions, or market prices in the decision process. Reinforcement learning models, with the help of the constant absorption of real-time feedback, can provide optimal distribution of energy through critical areas, hence reducing the odds of power outages or overloading [72]. It also assists in the autonomous operation of renewable energy systems by adjusting the turbine blade pitch angle and solar panel orientation for higher energy production with changing weather conditions [69].

11.3.3 Optimization Algorithms

The problem of optimization in the renewable energy sector is indeed a significant problem and involves the maximization of efficiency under environmental and economic considerations [10]. For solving complex problems, AI algorithms such as genetic algorithms are used, as well as particle swarm optimization (PSO) [39]. They find optimal operating techniques that yield the highest amount of generated energy possible at the lowest cost possible. The optimization of the positioning of wind turbines using genetic algorithms to achieve maximal capture of wind energy and minimal impacts of turbulence wakes can also be performed [13]. Solar system performance is improved by PSO for enhancing power production under varying irradiance conditions by modifying control settings. Rather, these algorithms manage the real-time allocation of energy to grid supply, battery storage, and demand centers to improve the distribution and storage of renewable energy. The AI-driven optimization identifies economical solutions by evaluating resource availability, environmental limitations, and financial factors, facilitating the execution of additional sustainable and financially feasible energy systems [64].

11.4 Technology for Energy Efficiency

The most efficacious strategy to reduce carbon dioxide emissions is to enhance efficiency in the diversion from fossil to clean energy. The following part will examine several technologies aimed at improving energy efficiency. Throughout an electricity network, there are typically many stages—namely, power generation, distribution, delivery, and consumption—where energy usage efficiency may be improved. Subsequent sections will analyze the spectrum of current technologies, which includes electric vehicles (EVs), combined heat and power (CHP) systems, virtual power plants (VPPs), and sophisticated intelligent grid infrastructures.

11.4.1 Zero-Emission Vehicles

Electric vehicle models have the potential to serve as practical solutions for electricity storage and generation. Enhancing fuel efficiency may result in substantial fuel savings and temporarily reduced CO_2 emissions. The growing adoption of EVs and their proportion within the vehicle fleet could significantly influence long-term outcomes. The International Energy Agency [16] anticipates a rising prevalence of plug-in hybrid electric vehicles over the forthcoming two decades, with an overall increase projected to reach as high as 50% by the year 2050. Researchers [23] analyzed the implications of widespread electric vehicle deployment in Southern California, concluding that Southern California Edison could accommodate a substantial influx of EVs with its pre-existing capacity, mainly if the charging infrastructure were managed through intelligent control systems. Researchers [35] evaluated the current value of expenditure associated with EV ownership and the advantages conferred to utility companies. All three vehicle/battery configurations emerged as economically viable power sources during peak demand periods in the short term. The systems and protocols were explored to utilize energy stored in vehicles and execute vehicle-to-grid (V2G) technology [36]. The V2G has the potential to bolster renewable energy sources in emerging energy markets by effectively overseeing load and supply variations. Researchers [63] assessed the economic viability of battery-electric vehicles supplying electricity for a specific market in the United States. The V2G electricity can generate a substantial revenue stream, enhancing the viability of grid-connected automobiles and promoting their adoption. Possible outcomes were evaluated to assess the effects of integrating ethanol, hydrogen, and electric cars into the passenger transportation sector, commencing in 2010 and achieving 100% of the new vehicle market by 2050 [59]. According to the results, electric vehicles could reduce CO_2 emissions by 153 Mt and hydrogen fuel cell vehicles by 156 Mt by 2050. Researchers [4] proposed an intelligent electric recharging grid operator to establish a marketplace that synchronizes the generation and uses alternative energy sources. They asserted that an electric recharging grid operator framework could mitigate challenges related to greenhouse gas emissions and power fluctuations by transforming EVs into decentralized storage units for electricity.

11.4.2 Cogeneration

Cogeneration, referred to as CHP, denotes the concurrent generation of thermal energy and electrical power, resulting in considerable enhancements in efficiency when compared to the separate production of each form of energy. A majority of electricity distribution companies solely supply electrical power, lacking the provision of hot water or steam services. Implementing CHP represents an efficient fuel application in which a component of the power is expelled as waste energy, thereby capturing some or all of this residual energy as a secondary product for heating applications. Consumers can procure electrical and thermal energy from only one source provider in urban centers such as Reykjavik and New York. A prime example of cogeneration is the CHP facility in Avedore, Denmark, which serves as a multifuel operation. Researchers [56] projected that enhancing the CHP potential in the United States to 20% by 2030 would reduce 5.3 quads in energy use and decrease 848 MMT in CO_2 emissions. The CHP systems may convert a substantial portion of waste heat into usable energy for heating homes and business structures. Newly developed CHP installations are anticipated to elevate energy efficiency to levels exceeding 85%. Researchers [41] investigated the deployment of combined cooling, heating, and power systems within UK supermarket chains, juxtaposing energy savings and capital expenditures with traditional technologies. Combined cooling, heating, and power systems have demonstrated the ability to yield a considerable main source of energy, diminishing CO_2 emissions compared to standard systems. Researchers [29] conducted an analysis of cost-effective operational strategies for three distinct micro-CHP systems intended for residential applications in the UK. The system based on solid oxide fuel cells was identified as having the highest operational cost while achieving the most significant reduction in CO_2 emissions and adhering to the least-cost operational framework.

11.4.3 Virtual Power Plant Simulation

A VVP represents a collective of decentralized fuel sources, such as micro combined heat and power systems, wind turbines, and solar photovoltaic installations, all governed by a centralized control mechanism. These resources address energy wastage challenges arising from substantial distances and transmission losses. The VPPs can be classified into commercial VPP and technical VPP. The proportion of distributed generation (DG) within an electrical network is rising, with VPPs being recognized as pioneering inventions that boost the effectiveness of thermal energy. An investigated was conducted practicality in terms of both technology and finances of running a VPP that incorporates micro-CHP units, positing that Germany's initiative to decommission nuclear power stations by 2020 mandates that a segment of the new capacity be sourced from renewable energy and CHP systems, which are categorized as DG units [54]. The VPPs present a viable solution for managing these units, as the absence of stringent control requirements allows renewable energy sources that benefit technologies. An operator of a VPP can aggregate multiple distributed energy resources to generate 30 MW by consolidating 6,000 micro-CHP units, each generating 5 kW of power. The integration of each unit incurs a cost of 300 Euros. A model was formulated to facilitate the operation of a VPP that encompasses various consumers with regulated home appliances, aiming to minimize workload within a specified timeframe [52]. Researchers [31] explored a building design and information exchange framework for integrating numerous electric vehicles into a VPP system, arguing that electric cars can substantially enhance the energy network if managed effectively. The model included distributed energy resources interacting with electricity markets, considering indicative pricing and broad bidding as two operational scenarios executed by a single market-based VPP [70].

11.4.4 Modern Meter

Power generation companies endeavor to mitigate peak demand during specified periods, while smart meters record energy consumption hourly, enabling bidirectional communication and sophisticated regulation of domestic appliances. Researchers [28] identified that a time-of-use pricing model could result in annual energy savings of 107 kWh per individual, corresponding to a reduction of $77 in electricity expenses and $134 in operational cost savings for the utility provider per client. A sharp decline is estimated in power requirement in the United States, facilitated by adopting advanced metering infrastructure, which could lead to considerable reductions in production, transportation, and distribution expenses [20]. Researchers [18] investigated the requisite characteristics and technologies for smart metering integration to delineate the conditions for establishing a network conducive to innovative grid communication. By 2014, smart meters were expected to have been installed in almost 212 million homes globally. Home area network technology can facilitate communication for plug-in hybrid electric vehicles and DG systems. In light of escalating fuel costs and significant upfront investments needed for conventional electricity supply frameworks, improving energy conservations and executing demand response initiatives *via* modern metering emerge as attractive alternatives. Researchers [37] explored consumer expectations and behavioral patterns, uncovering the implications of smart meter integration. Another study [43] scrutinized worries about customer data storage related to advanced metering and specific applications of smart meter data essential for the energy sector, suggesting that the demands for sensitive advanced metering could be alleviated by deploying suitable confidentiality safeguards. The administrative and technological dimensions of infrastructures for advanced meters were analyzed [42], encompassing both specialists' and generalists' prerequisites, the expenditure and advantages associated with innovative meter systems, and the repercussions of advanced meter implementation on various partics involved.

11.5 Recently Developed Artificial Intelligence-Powered Optimization Methods

11.5.1 The Black Widow Technique

A new population-based AI algorithm, the Black Widow Technique, is influenced by the lifecycle of the black widow spider. The technique was designed to account for the unusual pairing behaviors of spiderlings known as black widows. This approach requires adjusting four factors: procreating factors, mutation rate, cannibalism, and reproduction for optimal outcomes. The PP rate, the percentage of reproducing spiders, enhances variety and precise search space exploration. This method involves three phases of cannibalism, with the rate excluding unsuitable individuals directly, resulting in early convergence. Exploration and exploitation may be balanced by varying the mutation rate [30]. A new Black Widow Optimization approach has been introduced for designing regulators for combined wind, wave, and tidal power source systems [21]. By using the Black Widow Optimization approach, we enhanced the wind turbine simulator's proportional integral (PI) controller settings and evaluated their efficacy compared to other optimization methods. This approach has not been tested in numerous optimization applications, and a more significant iteration may be needed to guarantee its fitness [49].

11.5.2 Sailfish Optimizer

The optimization technique Sailfish Optimizer (SFO) takes its cues from how sailfish hunt in schools. The SFO method first increases the intensity and diversity of the sailfish population to imitate sardine proportions, which weakens the collective defenses of the sardine food source. At last, this technique revises the search area to reflect the latest prey movements, and predators are free to capture prey and transport it to a new, more advantageous location. We characterize the issue variables as the location of the sailfish, and we presume that sailfish are a potential solution. The optimal fitness position substantially influences SFO performance because it saves the best-ranked injured sardine and sailfish in each cycle. Avoiding local optima, rapidly convergent on enormous scale global optimizing, and competitive solutions that increase the balance between exploration and extraction are just a few of the numerous advantages of SFO influence [55]. We may improve Binary Sailfish (BSF) exploitation capabilities by combining hill climbing optimization using a Binary Sailfish Algorithm. We test this technique on 18 standardized datasets from UCI and compare the results to those of 10 AI feature selection algorithms [24].

11.5.3 Deer Hunting Algorithm

The deer hunting algorithm (DHA) is an AI optimization technique inspired by human hunting behaviors, considering variables such as the wind speed and the animal's position. The DHA first uses a vector denoting the population of hunters, choosing one to serve as the head while subsequent hunters remain around the optimal location. According to the coefficient vectors, the hunter's position will be perpetually refined until it attains the optimal location. The position angle may be revised according to the angular disparity between the wind and prey viewing angles, ultimately using the successor's location for updates, facilitating a worldwide search. Its efficacy was demonstrably validated across 39 benchmark issues and three limited engineering applications compared to other cutting-edge optimization methodologies. The primary issue with DHA is its significant early merging resulting from excessive random factors [11]. An extremely efficient integrative solar chimney power plant was suggested to provide energy to homes in Yazd, Iran. This plant would include SOEC, solid oxide fuel cells, and an HRSG. The outcomes of the suggested method were contrasted with those of PSO and GA [62].

11.5.4 A Swarm Method for Tunicates

Marine tunicates' swarming habits and fluid flight mechanics provide the basis for the tunicate swarm algorithm, a bio-inspired AI optimizer. A tunicate may be as little as a few millimeters in size. They can find sources of food hundreds of meters below the ocean's surface because of their ubiquitous gelatinous tunic and their capacity to produce a gentle blue-green glow. To mathematically represent aerodynamic behavior, a tunicate needs to do the following: (a) avoid other investigators, (b) determine the fresh location of the search agent by incorporating a vector, and (c) converge near the most effective neighbor's position, all while considering social forces and gravity. To mathematically describe swarm behavior, the top two global answers are retained as more search agents move to discover the optimal response [33]. The technique is evaluated, analyzed, and compared across different transportation systems. Results from various methodologies were evaluated and compared [22].

11.5.5 Artificial Electric Field Algorithm

The artificial electric field algorithm (AEFA) operates based on the electrostatic force described by the Coulomb equation. In AEFA, the representatives represent particles with electric charges, with only the most highly charged particle exhibiting sluggish movement within the search region, influenced by the pull of electrostatic force. It is characterized as a memory-based system whereby the location and pace of each search representative are modified according to the particle's optimal and worldwide most impressive fitness record. Its efficacy and inspiration have been demonstrably validated across 51 standard issues in real-parameter single-objective optimization based on learning as contrasted to other cutting-edge optimization. A theoretical study has been conducted to validate the steady-state criteria for particle convergence [6].

11.5.6 Algorithm for Water Strider

The Water Strider Algorithm emulates the water strider's life cycle, reflecting their space conduct, mating rituals, cascading message exchange, feeding strategies, and succession patterns. The Water Strider Algorithm begins the procedure of looking for establishing the starting positions of every aquatic spider in the lake, and the water spiders are assessed by use of a goal-oriented approach to determine their health. Subsequently, many regions will be delineated, and the places of water striders inside each territory will be allocated according to their fitness levels. The male keystone's new location is adjusted according to the female response signal concerning the signal for mating. Keystone generally exhibits increased energy consumption during the mating phase, necessitating a change in posture to locate food resources. The goal function is assessed to ascertain the place of food availability. Should you fail to get sustenance, the keystone will perish from malnutrition. The deceased replacement of the keystone with a fresh adult larva and its location are arbitrarily established within the area. Various computational and engineering design issues evaluated this algorithm's feature, with findings indicating superior performance relative to other leading algorithms [34].

11.5.7 Political Processes Optimizer (PO)

Maximizing political potential is a novel socio-motivated optimization system derived from the dynamics of several stages of political processes. The Political Processes Optimizer (PO) numerically delineates an order consisting of five stages of the procedure for politics: party affiliation, constituency distribution creation, political campaign, intra-party elections, and matters about parliament. During the stages of party creation and constituent distribution, the whole population is segmented into many factions in politics, each including numerous members, alongside the assumption of various constituencies. Both steps are executed alone once, exclusively for startup purposes. During the electoral campaign phase, a new mathematical approach for updating positions is developed, incorporating insights from the previous election to adjust the standings of the candidates and members concerning the party leader and community victor, thereby enhancing the candidate's performance in the election. In the inter-party election phase, each constituency runs an electoral simulation, which ends with an announcement of the winning candidate. During the legislative phase, the victorious individuals representing each political convention work to establish and manage the administration. The population is segmented into several political parties, including various candidates. The PO allocates a dual function to each human solution by systematically categorizing the populace into political parties and constituencies. Rather than using the optimal solution, the PO uses two enhanced options, specifically the party's foremost leader and the constituency's leading candidate, to revise the search agent's position. The created algorithm's performance has been assessed on many optimization tasks compared to 15 renowned state-of-the-art algorithms [9]. Optimization approaches have shown significant growth during the last several decades. As the problem's complexity escalates, the likelihood of attaining a worldwide solution diminishes.

11.6 Applications of Artificial Intelligence and Deep Learning for Ecological Well-Being

The emergence of AI and DL in ecological well-being is propelled by their remarkable capability to analyze and learn from extensive datasets, leading to richer insights and enabling prompt actions, as represented in Figure 11.3. This revolutionary potential is observable in various fields, including epilepsy [57], where DL methodologies have notably enhanced diagnostic practices. Conversely, GeoAI signifies a significant advancement in managing intricate spatial data by ingeniously merging breakthroughs in spatial science, AI, and DL [67]. The prowess of GeoAI is found in its ability to handle massive quantities of temporal and geographical data, guaranteeing swift computation and the adaptability to modify workflows and algorithms tailored to the specific traits of spatial phenomena. Its scalability allows it to make effective models of many environmental exposures over many geographic locations, thereby enhancing its knowledge of the associations between environmental exposures and health problems. As a result, GeoAI is poised to transform environmental well-being, altering how we forecast, identify, and address ecological well-being challenges. These AI innovations have played a vital role in epidemic control and public

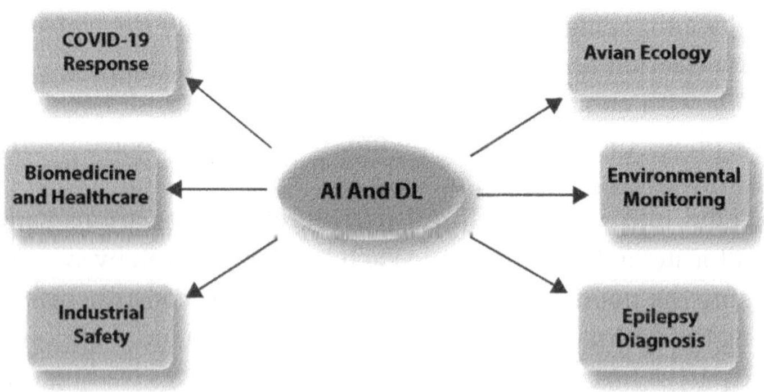

Figure 11.3 Applications of AI and DL for environmental health.

surveillance initiatives, encompassing airport security protocols, patient monitoring, and epidemic identification [3]. Both AI and DL have been harnessed within environmental surveillance to enhance the forecasting of hazardous blooms of algae. Illustrated DL models' success in anticipating dangerous algae blooms in South Korea's significant waterways, surpassing conventional regression methods. Both AI and DL have also found applications within healthcare and biomedicine by exploring the prevailing biological gender disparities in a range of scientific tools for medicine pertinent to accurate therapeutics, offering suggestions to optimize their use to enhance the world's health outcomes and reduce inequalities [12]. Utilized several cutting-edge generic object detection algorithms to master the detection of birds in their natural habitats, showcasing the capabilities of computer-assisted counting in practical avian surveillance scenarios. The fusion of DL and AI in ecological well-being has experienced a notable upswing in research activities, with every contributor's distinct methodologies and perspectives. A comparison exploration of current research illuminates the varied applications and prevailing discrepancies within this field.

11.7 Using Artificial Intelligence and Deep Learning for Energy Efficiency in Smart Buildings

The fusion of AI and DL in the intelligent management of building energy use has dramatically enhanced numerous functions' forecasting, refining, and automation. This evolution has birthed groundbreaking energy oversight strategies, including applying DRL to tackle intricate issues and investigating digital twin methodologies. Researchers [19] pioneered an inventive technique that harmonizes DL with IoT technology to optimize air conditioning operations, successfully curtailing energy expenditure. The burgeoning field of DRL showcases remarkable promise in addressing energy management obstacles within smart buildings. Digital twin strategies [2] may significantly contribute to the development of smart automation and optimization frameworks for energy management in residential neighborhoods. The power of managing energy in IoT networks was showcased *via* resilient deep-learning architectures [27]. The synergy was underscored between IoT-driven real-time manufacturing processing, logistics, and cyber-physical systems oversight, essential for navigating the intricacies and adaptability required in intelligent manufacturing facilities [5].

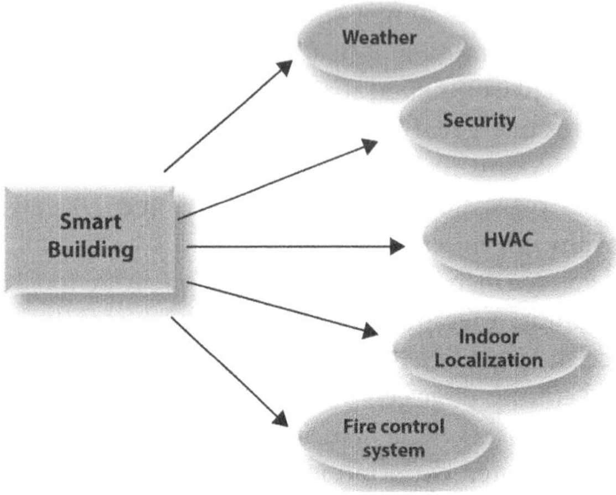

Figure 11.4 Artificial intelligence-powered systems for smart buildings.

Researchers [7] provided a critical review of the latest developments in ML and DL for building energy usage. Figure 11.4 represents AI-powered systems for smart buildings. Their systematic evaluation unveiled promising models and assessed their efficacy in various energy forecasting tasks. Despite the notable strides made in AI and DL for managing energy in smart buildings, a disconnect persists between scholarly research and industry requirements. The sector seeks comprehensive, scalable, and flexible solutions for various architectural classifications, settings, and energy management dilemmas. These technologies influence the formation of new and fascinating energy management strategies, ensure more intricate challenges of the DRL, and inspire the consideration and exploration of the digital twin methodologies. The anticipated future research in this rapidly advancing domain is to explore efficiency and effectiveness.

11.8 Application of Artificial Intelligence in Solid Waste Management Systems and Predictive Analysis Model in Solar Synergy

Solid waste management problems have gained significant momentum from AI, as it has been providing alternative computational approaches to solve those problems. While AI methods have proved efficient in dealing with not well-defined problems, and treating uncertainty and missing information in dealing with waste [1], their experimental application has received little attention to date. In the USA, AI technologies are used to improve routes for collecting waste, automate processes of sorting, and also optimize recycling. By studying historical data on waste generation patterns, ML algorithms are used to forecast properties' responses to making certain changes in the urban environment to keep experts informed about how these initiatives have to be followed up [46]. The combination of IoT and ML in SWM has exhibited the strength to predict the generation of waste, classify waste, route optimization, and estimation of methane emission. Artificial neural networks (ANNs) are implemented mainly among various ML models, followed by decision tree and random forest algorithms [32]. Previous studies [32] have revealed that data are scarce, there is a lack of reliable data, and a rare presence of customized AI models to deal with activities within SWM.

11.9 Ethical Concerns, Limitations, and Potential Biases in AI-Driven Environmental Solutions

Artificial intelligence is providing alternative computational approaches for SWM problems and has become a fundamental momentum. Waste management utilizes AI techniques successfully to solve ambiguous problems, analyze experienced data, and perform under data uncertainty and incompleteness [1]. In the USA, AI technologies are being used in optimizing waste collection routes, automating the sorting process, and increasing recycling efficiency. The ML algorithms process historical data that allows the forecast of waste generation behavior, thus enabling municipalities to allocate resources more effectively [46]. The combination of ML and IoT technologies serves SWM by helping forecast waste production along with waste categorization, as well as improving delivery routes and measuring methane release amounts. Major implementations of artificial neural networks are done among various ML models in SWM, and decision tree and random forest algorithms are rarely used [32]. Research limitations stem from insufficient data availability, as well as missing accurate data and limited access to customized AI models willing to handle SWM activities [32]. Currently, it has been widely reported that AI algorithms like ML and DL have prediction performance competitive with that of solar power forecasting. Specifically, these algorithms can discover the invariant structure and nonlinear features of solar data, which leads to enhanced prediction accuracy for preparation of unknown future circumstances [68]. Test results revealed that Bi-LSTM outperformed ARIMA in solar power production forecasting, along with its capability to discover complex connections among components in the real-time dataset [15]. In this regard, the application of AI in the renewable energy field not only resolves operational issues but also helps in the global shift towards the use of more sustainable and cleaner energy sources [48].

11.10 Obstacles and Prospective Pathways

Integrating AI and DL toward the pursuit of SDGs, renewable energy projects, ecological well-being, and optimization of energy control within smart buildings has been illustrated to have a large capacity. However, many challenges have to be addressed if these innovations are to be fully turned into capabilities. The following section addresses several problems and suggests future research avenues. Artificial intelligence delivers prosperous solutions toward environmental challenges alongside ecological and climate change resolution options. These solutions provide promising benefits, yet they generate significant ethical problems and contain certain operational boundaries. The presence of algorithmic bias in AI systems creates possible distributions of unequal advantages, as well as heavier negative consequences toward socially disadvantaged communities. The training of AI models through large datasets has the potential to sustain current inequalities because insufficiently diverse ecological populations remain unrepresented. Artificial intelligence systems impose environmental stress when they operate because their substantial models require high amounts of energy, which generates substantial carbon emissions. The complex nature of AI systems used in environmental decision processes restricts stakeholders' understanding of rationale because decision rationale becomes difficult to explain and monitor in highly complex systems. Lastly, there is a risk of over-reliance on technological solutions, potentially diverting attention and resources from necessary systemic changes and behavioral shifts required to address environmental challenges comprehensively. While AI-driven environmental solutions offer promising advancements in addressing climate change and ecological challenges, they also raise significant ethical concerns and have inherent limitations, including potential bias, perpetuation of inequalities, environmental impact of AI itself, lack of accountability and transparency, and the risk of over-reliance on technological solutions at the expense of necessary systemic changes and behavioral shifts.

11.11 Conclusions

This article covers how AI and DL are advancing and being used to achieve SDGs, renewable energy, ecological well-being, and innovative management of building energy. Artificial intelligence can help reach 134 of 169 SDG objectives, making it a formidable weapon for sustainability. However, the fast growth of AI and DL technologies requires thorough regulatory monitoring to ensure openness, safety, and ethics. Both AI and DL can improve solar power plant energy management, fault detection, power grid stability, waste management, and predictive analysis. They have improved environmental health exposure modeling and illness prediction by analyzing complicated geographical data. Nonetheless, several challenges must be addressed to use AI and DL for viability. This includes the explanation of transparency for AI and DL methods, the scaling barriers for dealing with high-dimensional data, integration with new wireless networks, ethics, and privacy. Future research shall improve explainability and transparency, arrive at scalable algorithms to handle big data, combine AI with advanced wireless systems, and deal with aspects of confidentiality and ethics.

References

1. Abdallah, M., Abu Talib, M., Feroz, S., Nasir, Q., Abdalla, H., Mahfood, B., Artificial intelligence applications in solid waste management: A systematic research review. *Waste Manage. (Oxford)*, *109*, 231–246, 2020. https://doi.org/10.1016/j.wasman.2020.04.057.
2. Agostinelli, S., Cumo, F., Guidi, G., Tomazzoli, C., Cyber-Physical Systems Improving Building Energy Management: Digital Twin and Artificial Intelligence. *Energies*, *14*, 8, 2338, 2021. https://doi.org/10.3390/en14082338.
3. Alafif, T., Tehame, A.M., Bajaba, S., Barnawi, A., Zia, S., Machine and Deep Learning towards COVID-19 Diagnosis and Treatment: Survey, Challenges, and Future Directions. *Int. J. Environ. Res. Public Health*, *18*, 3, 1117, 2021. https://doi.org/10.3390/ijerph18031117.
4. Andersen, P.H., Mathews, J.A., Rask, M., Integrating private transport into renewable energy policy: The strategy of creating intelligent recharging grids for electric vehicles. *Energy Policy*, *37*, 7, 2481–2486, 2009. https://doi.org/10.1016/j.enpol.2009.03.032.

5. Andronie, M., Lăzăroiu, G., Iatagan, M., Uță, C., Ștefănescu, R., Cocoșatu, M., Artificial Intelligence-Based Decision-Making Algorithms, Internet of Things Sensing Networks, and Deep Learning-Assisted Smart Process Management in Cyber-Physical Production Systems. *Electronics*, *10*, 20, 2497, 2021. https://doi.org/10.3390/electronics10202497.
6. Anita, and Yadav, A., AEFA: Artificial electric field algorithm for global optimization. *Swarm Evol. Comput.*, *48*, 93–108, 2019. https://doi.org/10.1016/j.swevo.2019.03.013.
7. Ardabili, S., Abdolalizadeh, L., Mako, C., Torok, B., Mosavi, A., Systematic Review of Deep Learning and Machine Learning for Building Energy. *Front. Energy Res.*, *10*, 2022. https://doi.org/10.3389/fenrg.2022.786027.
8. Arulkumaran, K., Deisenroth, M.P., Brundage, M., Bharath, A.A., Deep Reinforcement Learning: A Brief Survey. *IEEE Signal Process Mag.*, *34*, 6, 26–38, 2017. https://doi.org/10.1109/msp.2017.2743240.
9. Askari, Q., Younas, I., Saeed, M., Political Optimizer: A novel socio-inspired meta-heuristic for global optimization. *Knowledge-Based Syst.*, *195*, 105709, 2020. https://doi.org/10.1016/j.knosys.2020.105709.
10. Baños, R., Manzano-Agugliaro, F., Montoya, F.G., Gil, C., Alcayde, A., Gómez, J., Optimization methods applied to renewable and sustainable energy: A review. *Renew. Sustain. Energy Rev.*, *15*, 4, 1753–1766, 2011. https://doi.org/10.1016/j.rser.2010.12.008.
11. Brammya, G., Praveena, S., Ninu Preetha, N.S., Ramya, R., Rajakumar, B.R., Binu, D., Deer Hunting Optimization Algorithm: A New Nature-Inspired Meta-heuristic Paradigm. *Comput. J.*, 2019. https://doi.org/10.1093/comjnl/bxy133.
12. Campero-Jurado, I., Márquez-Sánchez, S., Quintanar-Gómez, J., Rodríguez, S., Corchado, J.M., Smart Helmet 5.0 for Industrial Internet of Things Using Artificial Intelligence. *Sens. (Basel Switzerland)*, *20*, 21, 6241, 2020. https://doi.org/10.3390/s20216241.
13. Cao, L., Ge, M., Gao, X., Du, B., Li, B., Huang, Z., Liu, Y., Wind farm layout optimization to minimize the wake induced turbulence effect on wind turbines. *Appl. Energy*, *323*, 119599, 2022. https://doi.org/10.1016/j.apenergy.2022.119599.
14. Chaudhry, I.S., Sarwary, S.A.M., El Refae, G.A., Chabchoub, H., Time to Revisit Existing Student's Performance Evaluation Approach in Higher Education Sector in a New Era of ChatGPT — A Case Study. *Cogent Educ.*, *10*, 1, 2023. https://doi.org/10.1080/2331186x.2023.2210461.
15. Chen, Y., Bhutta, M.S., Abubakar, M., Xiao, D., Almasoudi, F.M., Naeem, H., Faheem, M., Evaluation of Machine Learning Models for Smart Grid Parameters: Performance Analysis of ARIMA and Bi-LSTM. *Sustainability*, *15*, 11, 8555, 2023. https://doi.org/10.3390/su15118555.
16. Conversion Factors for OECD Countries, *IEA World Energy Statistics and Balances*, OECD Publishing, 2012, https://doi.org/10.1787/data-00515-en.

17. Cordeiro-Costas, M., Villanueva, D., Eguía-Oller, P., Granada-Álvarez, E., Machine Learning and Deep Learning Models Applied to Photovoltaic Production Forecasting. *Appl. Sci.*, *12*, 17, 8769, 2022. https://doi.org/10.3390/app12178769.
18. Depuru, S.S.S.R., Wang, L., Devabhaktuni, V., Smart meters for power grid: Challenges, issues, advantages and status. *Renew. Sustain. Energy Rev.*, *15*, 6, 2736–2742, 2011. https://doi.org/10.1016/j.rser.2011.02.039.
19. Elsisi, M., Tran, M.-Q., Mahmoud, K., Lehtonen, M., Darwish, M.M.F., Deep Learning-Based Industry 4.0 and Internet of Things towards Effective Energy Management for Smart Buildings. *Sens. (Basel Switzerland)*, *21*, 4, 1038, 2021. https://doi.org/10.3390/s21041038.
20. Faruqui, A., Hledik, R., Newell, S., Pfeifenberger, H., The Power of 5 Percent. *Electr. J.*, *20*, 8, 68–77, 2007. https://doi.org/10.1016/j.tej.2007.08.003.
21. Fayek, H.H. and Mohammadi-Ivatloo, B., Tidal Supplementary Control Schemes-Based Load Frequency Regulation of a Fully Sustainable Marine Microgrid. *Inventions*, *5*, 4, 53, 2020. https://doi.org/10.3390/inventions5040053.
22. Fetouh, T. and Elsayed, A.M., Optimal Control and Operation of Fully Automated Distribution Networks Using Improved Tunicate Swarm Intelligent Algorithm. *IEEE Access*, *8*, 129689–129708, 2020. https://doi.org/10.1109/access.2020.3009113.
23. Ford, A., The impacts of large scale use of electric vehicles in southern California. *Energy Build.*, *22*, 3, 207–218, 1995. https://doi.org/10.1016/0378-7788(95)00923-l.
24. Ghosh, K.K., Ahmed, S., Singh, P.K., Geem, Z.W., Sarkar, R., Improved Binary Sailfish Optimizer Based on Adaptiveβ-Hill Climbing for Feature Selection. *IEEE Access*, *8*, 83548–83560, 2020. https://doi.org/10.1109/access.2020.2991543.
25. Giret, A., Julian, V., Carrascosa, C., AI-supported Digital Twins in applications related to sustainable development goals, in: *The International FLAIRS Conference Proceedings*, vol. *36*, 2023, https://doi.org/10.32473/flairs.36.133630.
26. Hammadi, S.S., Majeed, B.H., Hassan, A.K., Impact of Deep Learning Strategy in Mathematics Achievement and Practical Intelligence among High School Students. *Int. J. Emerging Technol. Learn. (IJET)*, *18*, 06, 42–52, 2023. https://doi.org/10.3991/ijet.v18i06.38615.
27. Han, T., Muhammad, K., Hussain, T., Lloret, J., Baik, S.W., An Efficient Deep Learning Framework for Intelligent Energy Management in IoT Networks. *IEEE Internet Things J.*, *8*, 5, 3170–3179, 2021. https://doi.org/10.1109/jiot.2020.3013306.
28. Hartway, R., Price, S., Woo, C.K., Smart meter, customer choice and profitable time-of-use rate option. *Energy*, *24*, 10, 895–903, 1999. https://doi.org/10.1016/s0360-5442(99)00040-7.

29. Hawkes, A. and Leach, M., Cost-effective operating strategy for residential micro-combined heat and power. *Energy*, *32*, 5, 711–723, 2007. https://doi.org/10.1016/j.energy.2006.06.001.
30. Hayyolalam, V. and Pourhaji Kazem, A.A., Black Widow Optimization Algorithm: A novel meta-heuristic approach for solving engineering optimization problems. *Eng. Appl. Artif. Intell.*, *87*, 103249, 2020. https://doi.org/10.1016/j.engappai.2019.103249.
31. Jansen, B., Binding, C., Sundstrom, O., Gantenbein, D., Architecture and Communication of an Electric Vehicle Virtual Power Plant, in: *2010 First IEEE International Conference on Smart Grid Communications*, IEEE, pp. 149–154, 2010, https://doi.org/10.1109/smartgrid.2010.5622033.
32. Joshi, L.M., Bharti, R.K., Singh, R., Internet of things and machine learning-based approaches in the urban solid waste management: Trends, challenges, and future directions. *Expert Syst.*, *39*, 5, 2021. https://doi.org/10.1111/exsy.12865.
33. Kaur, S., Awasthi, L.K., Sangal, A.L., Dhiman, G., Tunicate Swarm Algorithm: A new bio-inspired based metaheuristic paradigm for global optimization. *Eng. Appl. Artif. Intell.*, *90*, 103541, 2020. https://doi.org/10.1016/j.engappai.2020.103541.
34. Kaveh, A. and Dadras Eslamlou, A., Water strider algorithm: A new metaheuristic and applications. *Structures*, *25*, 520–541, 2020. https://doi.org/10.1016/j.istruc.2020.03.033.
35. Kempton, W. and Letendre, S.E., Electric vehicles as a new power source for electric utilities. *Transp. Res. Part D Transport Environ.*, *2*, 3, 157–175, 1997. https://doi.org/10.1016/s1361-9209(97)00001-1.
36. Kempton, W. and Tomić, J., Vehicle-to-grid power implementation: From stabilizing the grid to supporting large-scale renewable energy. *J. Power Sources*, *144*, 1, 280–294, 2005. https://doi.org/10.1016/j.jpowsour.2004.12.022.
37. Krishnamurti, T., Schwartz, D., Davis, A., Fischhoff, B., de Bruin, W.B., Lave, L., Wang, J., Preparing for smart grid technologies: A behavioral decision research approach to understanding consumer expectations about smart meters. *Energy Policy*, *41*, 790–797, 2012. https://doi.org/10.1016/j.enpol.2011.11.047.
38. Larrain, C., Torres-Hernandez, A., Hewitt, D.B., Artificial Intelligence, Machine Learning, and Deep Learning in the Diagnosis and Management of Hepatocellular Carcinoma. *Livers*, *4*, 1, 36–50, 2024. https://doi.org/10.3390/livers4010004.
39. Liu, Y. and Kim, K., An artificial-intelligence-driven product design framework with a synergistic combination of Genetic Algorithm and Particle Swarm Optimization. *Soft Comput.*, *27*, 23, 17621–17638, 2023. https://doi.org/10.1007/s00500-023-09223-4.
40. Lu, L., He, Y., Wang, T., Shi, T., Ruan, Y., Wind Turbine Planetary Gearbox Fault Diagnosis Based on Self-Powered Wireless Sensor and Deep Learning

Approach. *IEEE Access*, *7*, 119430–119442, 2019. https://doi.org/10.1109/access.2019.2936228.
41. Maidment, G.G. and Tozer, R.M., Combined cooling heat and power in supermarkets. *Appl. Therm. Eng.*, *22*, 6, 653–665, 2002. https://doi.org/10.1016/s1359-4311(01)00117-x.
42 McHenry, M.P., Technical and governance considerations for advanced metering infrastructure/smart meters: Technology, security, uncertainty, costs, benefits, and risks. *Energy Policy*, *59*, 834–842, 2013. https://doi.org/10.1016/j.enpol.2013.04.048.
43. McKenna, E., Richardson, I., Thomson, M., Smart meter data: Balancing consumer privacy concerns with legitimate applications. *Energy Policy*, *41*, 807–814, 2012. https://doi.org/10.1016/j.enpol.2011.11.049.
44. Mohammad, A. and Mahjabeen, F., Revolutionizing Solar Energy: The Impact of Artificial Intelligence on Photovoltaic Systems. *Int. J. Multi. Sci. Arts*, *2*, 3, 2023. https://doi.org/10.47709/ijmdsa.v2i1.2599.
45. Mookkaiah, S.S., Thangavelu, G., Hebbar, R., Haldar, N., Singh, H., Design and development of smart Internet of Things-based solid waste management system using computer vision. *Environ. Sci. Pollut. Res. Int.*, *29*, 43, 64871–64885, 2022. https://doi.org/10.1007/s11356-022-20428-2.
46. Nwokediegwu, Z.Q.S., Ugwuanyi, E.D., Dada, M.A., Majemite, M.T., Obaigbena, A., AI-Driven Waste Management Systems: A Comparative Review Of Innovations In The Usa And Africa. *Eng. Sci. Technol. J.*, *5*, 2, 507–516, 2024. https://doi.org/10.51594/estj.v5i2.828.
47. Olczak, J., Pavlopoulos, J., Prijs, J., Ijpma, F.F.A., Doornberg, J.N., Lundström, C., Hedlund, J., Gordon, M., Presenting artificial intelligence, deep learning, and machine learning studies to clinicians and healthcare stakeholders: an introductory reference with a guideline and a Clinical AI Research (CAIR) checklist proposal. *Acta Orthopaedica*, *92*, 5, 513–525, 2021. https://doi.org/10.1080/17453674.2021.1918389.
48. Onwusinkwue, S., Osasona, F., Ahmad, I.A.I., Anyanwu, A.C., Dawodu, S.O., Obi, O.C., Hamdan, A., Artificial intelligence (AI) in renewable energy: A review of predictive maintenance and energy optimization. *World J. Adv. Res. Rev.*, *21*, 1, 2487–2799, 2024. https://doi.org/10.30574/wjarr.2024.21.1.0347.
49. Premkumar, K., Vishnupriya, M., Sudhakar Babu, T., Manikandan, B.V., Thamizhselvan, T., Nazar Ali, A., Rabiul Islam, M., Kouzani, A.Z., Parvez Mahmud, M.A., Black Widow Optimization-Based Optimal PI-Controlled Wind Turbine Emulator. *Sustainability*, *12*, 24, 10357, 2020. https://doi.org/10.3390/su122410357.
50. Rao, S., Katoch, S., Narayanaswamy, V., Muniraju, G., Tepedelenlioglu, C., Spanias, A., Turaga, P., Ayyanar, R., Srinivasan, D., Solar Array Research Testbed, in: *Synthesis Lectures on Power Electronics*, pp. 7–13, Springer International Publishing, 2020, https://doi.org/10.1007/978-3-031-02505-1_2.
51. Romero, H.F.M., Hernández-Callejo, L., Rebollo, M.A.G., Cardeñoso-Payo, V., Gómez, V.A., Bello, H.J., Moyo, R.T., Aragonés, J.I., Synthetic Dataset of

Electroluminescence Images of Photovoltaic Cells by Deep Convolutional Generative Adversarial Networks. *Sustainability*, *15*, 9, 7175, 2023. https://doi.org/10.3390/su15097175.

52. Ruiz, N., Cobelo, I., Oyarzabal, J., A Direct Load Control Model for Virtual Power Plant Management. *IEEE Trans. Power Syst.*, *24*, 2, 959–966, 2009. https://doi.org/10.1109/tpwrs.2009.2016607.
53. Sætra, H.S., AI in Context and the Sustainable Development Goals: Factoring in the Unsustainability of the Sociotechnical System. *Sustainability*, *13*, 4, 1738, 2021. https://doi.org/10.3390/su13041738.
54. Schulz, C., Roder, G., Kurrat, M., Virtual power plants with combined heat and power micro-units, in: *2005 International Conference on Future Power Systems*, IEEE, 2005, https://doi.org/10.1109/fps.2005.204262.
55. Shadravan, S., Naji, H.R., Bardsiri, V.K., The Sailfish Optimizer: A novel nature-inspired metaheuristic algorithm for solving constrained engineering optimization problems. *Eng. Appl. Artif. Intell.*, *80*, 20–34, 2019. https://doi.org/10.1016/j.engappai.2019.01.001.
56. Shipley, A., Hampson, A., Hedman, B., Garland, P., Bautista, P., *Combined Heat and Power: Effective Energy Solutions for a Sustainable Future*, Office of Scientific and Technical Information (OSTI, 2008, https://doi.org/10.2172/1218492.
57. Shoeibi, A., Khodatars, M., Ghassemi, N., Jafari, M., Moridian, P., Alizadehsani, R., Panahiazar, M., Khozeimeh, F., Zare, A., Hosseini-Nejad, H., Khosravi, A., Atiya, A.F., Aminshahidi, D., Hussain, S., Rouhani, M., Nahavandi, S., Acharya, U.R., Epileptic Seizures Detection Using Deep Learning Techniques: A Review. *Int. J. Environ. Res. Public Health*, *18*, 11, 5780, 2021. https://doi.org/10.3390/ijerph18115780.
58. Soori, M., Arezoo, B., Dastres, R., Artificial intelligence, machine learning and deep learning in advanced robotics, a review. *Cognit. Rob.*, *3*, 54–70, 2023. https://doi.org/10.1016/j.cogr.2023.04.001.
59. Steenhof, P.A. and McInnis, B.C., A comparison of alternative technologies to de-carbonize Canada's passenger transportation sector. *Technol. Forecasting Social Change*, *75*, 8, 1260–1278, 2008. https://doi.org/10.1016/j.techfore.2008.02.009.
60. Streich, J., Romero, J., Gazolla, J.G.F.M., Kainer, D., Cliff, A., Prates, E.T., Brown, J.B., Khoury, S., Tuskan, G.A., Garvin, M., Jacobson, D., Harfouche, A.L., Can exascale computing and explainable artificial intelligence applied to plant biology deliver on the United Nations sustainable development goals? *Curr. Opin. Biotechnol.*, *61*, 217–225, 2020. https://doi.org/10.1016/j.copbio.2020.01.010.
61. Strubell, E., Ganesh, A., McCallum, A., Energy and Policy Considerations for Modern Deep Learning Research. *Proc. AAAI Conf. Artif. Intell.*, *34*, 09, 13693–13696, 2020. https://doi.org/10.1609/aaai.v34i09.7123.

62. Tian, M.-W., Yan, S.-R., Han, S.-Z., Nojavan, S., Jermsittiparsert, K., Razmjooy, N., New optimal design for a hybrid solar chimney, solid oxide electrolysis and fuel cell based on improved deer hunting optimization algorithm. *J. Clean. Prod.*, *249*, 119414, 2020. https://doi.org/10.1016/j.jclepro.2019.119414.
63. Tomić, J. and Kempton, W., Using fleets of electric-drive vehicles for grid support. *J. Power Sources*, *168*, 2, 459–468, 2007. https://doi.org/10.1016/j.jpowsour.2007.03.010.
64. Ukoba, K., Olatunji, K.O., Adeoye, E., Jen, T.-C., Madyira, D.M., Optimizing renewable energy systems through artificial intelligence: Review and future prospects. *Energy Environ.*, *35*, 7, 3833–3879, 2024. https://doi.org/10.1177/0958305x241256293.
65. Vinuesa, R., Azizpour, H., Leite, I., Balaam, M., Dignum, V., Domisch, S., Felländer, A., Langhans, S.D., Tegmark, M., Fuso Nerini, F., The role of artificial intelligence in achieving the Sustainable Development Goals. *Nat. Commun.*, *11*, 1, 233, 2020. https://doi.org/10.1038/s41467-019-14108-y.
66. Vinuesa, R. and Sirmacek, B., Interpretable deep-learning models to help achieve the Sustainable Development Goals. *Nat. Mach. Intell.*, *3*, 11, 926, 2021. https://doi.org/10.1038/s42256-021-00414-y.
67. VoPham, T., Hart, J.E., Laden, F., Chiang, Y.-Y., Emerging trends in geospatial artificial intelligence (geoAI): potential applications for environmental epidemiology. *Environ. Health A Global Access Sci. Source*, *17*, 1, 40, 2018. https://doi.org/10.1186/s12940-018-0386-x.
68. Wang, H., Liu, Y., Zhou, B., Li, C., Cao, G., Voropai, N., Barakhtenko, E., Taxonomy research of artificial intelligence for deterministic solar power forecasting. *Energy Convers. Manage.*, *214*, 112909, 2020. https://doi.org/10.1016/j.enconman.2020.112909.
69. Yang, T., Zhao, L., Li, W., Zomaya, A.Y., Reinforcement learning in sustainable energy and electric systems: a survey. *Annu. Rev. Control*, *49*, 145–163, 2020. https://doi.org/10.1016/j.arcontrol.2020.03.001.
70. You, S., Traholt, C., Poulsen, B., A study on electricity export capability of the µCHP system with spot price, in: *2009 IEEE Power & Energy Society General Meeting*, IEEE, pp. 1–6, 2009, https://doi.org/10.1109/pes.2009.5275409.
71. Yu, L., Qin, S., Zhang, M., Shen, C., Jiang, T., Guan, X., A Review of Deep Reinforcement Learning for Smart Building Energy Management. *IEEE Internet Things J.*, *8*, 15, 12046–12063, 2021. https://doi.org/10.1109/jiot.2021.3078462.
72. Zhang, D., Han, X., Deng, C., Review on the research and practice of deep learning and reinforcement learning in smart grids. *CSEE J. Power Energy Syst*, *4*, 3, 362–370, 2018. https://doi.org/10.17775/cseejpes.2018.00520.

12

Physics-Informed Neural Networks for Exothermic Reactions in Porous Media

Pavan Patel* **and Saroj R. Yadav**

Department of Mathematics, Sardar Vallabhbhai National Institute of Technology, Surat, Gujarat, India

Abstract
The main aim of this chapter is to study the exothermic reactions model, which has a fixed heat source in the porous media. Heat flow profiles are crucial for efficient heat transfer in various types of thermal insulation. This investigation centers on the driving force problem, specifically focusing on scenarios where a temperature gradient is considered. The governing equation of the model is restricted to an energy balance equation that gives the temperature value in the conduction state in the presence of a constant heat source. To solve this ordinary differential equation (ODE), we utilize a scientific machine learning approach known as physics-informed neural networks (PINNs). The PINNs techniques primarily encode the underlying physical rule (i.e., the ODE) into the neural network as prior knowledge. We conducted the entire experiment in Python on Google Colab. For validation purposes, we compared the PINNs solution with existing solutions in the literature. The results indicate that the PINNs approach aligns well with established solutions, confirming its accuracy and reliability.

Keywords**:** Physics-informed neural networks, exothermic reactions, porous media, scientific machine learning, thermal transport, heat transfer, boundary value problem, heat generation modeling

**Corresponding author*: pavanpatel704@gmail.com; ORCID: https://orcid.org/0009-0002-6302-9743
Saroj R. Yadav: ORCID: https://orcid.org/0009-0000-6468-4956

Mukesh Kumar Awasthi and Reshu Gupta (eds.) Artificial Intelligence and Computational Modeling in Heat Transfer and Fluid Dynamics, (333–342)

12.1 Introduction

The chemical reactions that occur with the evolution of heat with the product are called exothermic reactions (ER). This signifies that the energy required to initiate the reaction is lower than the energy released later. Energy is derived from chemical bonds. Forming bonds releases energy, while breaking them requires energy. Each bond type has its unique bond energy. On the other hand, if a reaction needs an input of energy, it is said to be an endothermic reaction. We know that calculating the total energy in a system is a challenging task. However, calculating enthalpy change ΔH is easy. In $\Delta H = EB - EM$ here, EB represents the energy used in breaking bonds in reactions, and EM represents the energy lost during bond formation in product manufacture, respectively. The enthalpy change in an ER is negative, meaning it is less than zero. To demonstrate, consider the process that occurs when hydrogen burns:

$$2H_2(g) + O_2(g) \rightarrow 2H_2O(g),$$

where, $\Delta H = -483.6 \text{ KJ/mol of } O_2$.

Hand warmers typically rely on the oxidation of iron to achieve an ER.

$$4Fe(s) + 3O_2(g) \rightarrow 2Fe_2O_3(g).$$

Convection refers to air movement along the surfaces of solids or liquids. It occurs in several scientific and technological disciplines, including solar energy conversion, underground coal gasification, geothermal energy extraction, groundwater contamination transport, and oil reservoir modeling. Researchers have extensively investigated this phenomenon to improve heat transfer. Beck [4] studied convection in a box of porous material saturated with fluid. Many researchers presented an excellent study on Rayleigh–Bernard-type convection and convective instability resulting from the ER model in porous media [6, 13, 16]. On the other hand, many researchers have focused on the non-uniform flow of convective motion caused by heat sources [3, 10, 21]. Furthermore, many researchers have studied 2D and 3D models for natural convection in porous media [11, 20, 22].

Traditional machine learning (ML) generally necessitates feature engineering, where individuals manually identify and extract characteristics from unprocessed data and provide weights to them. Conversely, deep learning (DL) techniques enable feature engineering with minimum human participation. Deep learning is now widely used in engineering fields, signal classification, computer vision, and natural language processing. Existing DL algorithms for scientific computing fall into two categories: (1) data-driven approaches [23] (2) physics-based approaches [24]. Many researchers have worked on data-driven approaches to fluid dynamics, for example [19] ML techniques predicted the permeability of petroleum reservoirs. Moreover, [8] ML techniques were also used to forecast the dimensionless oil recovery. Furthermore, many researchers used various types of ML techniques to predict nanoparticle transport in porous media [1, 7, 9, 15]. In data-driven approaches, enough labeled data is essential for training neural networks to identify non-linear correlations between inputs and outputs, where the loss function quantifies discrepancies between outputs and labels. These approaches have proven effective for rapid forecasting. However, the production of labeled data presents a significant challenge for future applications [5]. To address this challenge, physics-based approaches are presented that directly consider fundamental physical principles or laws and need little or no labeled data for training neural networks. Within these methods, PINNs [17] are the most indicative and have been utilized for forward, inverse, and surrogate modeling of different physical procedures. Over the past few years, PINNs have been used in various fields such as solid mechanics [2], fluid mechanics [5], and heat transfer [24].

The ability to learn differential equations confers several advantages to PINNs compared to traditional approaches. Specifically, PINNs are mesh-free techniques that ensure compute solutions on-demand following a training phase and make solutions differentiable through analytical gradients. Lastly, they offer a simple method for utilizing the same optimization problem to handle both forward and inverse problems. The PINNs may be used to tackle inverse problems like describing fluid flows using sensor data and solving differential equations or the forward problems.

12.2 Mathematical Model

This section presents a pseudo-homogeneous model for convection driven by an exothermic process. This study examines a porous material with a wall thickness of $0 < z' < L$ concentrated. In steady-state energy balance, the assumption of continuity and momentum leads to a dimensionless two-point boundary value problem that describes the temperature profile [16, 20].

$$\frac{d^2u}{dz^2}+\alpha\varepsilon^2\left(1-\frac{u}{\alpha}\right)\exp\left(\frac{\beta u}{\beta+u}\right)=0, \qquad (12.1)$$

where u represents the temperature, α stands for the maximum feasible temperature without free convection, ε^2 represents the ratio of the characteristic time for the diffusion of the heat generator, and β indicates the non-dimensional activation energy. In the case of the constant heat source, Equation 12.1 can be simplified as:

$$\frac{d^2u}{dz^2}+\alpha\varepsilon^2\left(1-\frac{u}{\alpha}\right)=0, \qquad (12.2)$$

with the boundary conditions are

$$\begin{aligned}\frac{du}{dz}&=0, \quad \text{at } z=0,\\ u&=0, \quad \text{at } z=1.\end{aligned} \qquad (12.3)$$

12.3 The Building Block of Physics-Informed Neural Networks

Let us consider an n-th order ordinary differential equation (ODE) with its conditions as:

$$\xi\left(z,u(z),u'(z),\ldots\ldots.u^{n(z)}\right)=0, \quad z\in D\subset\mathbb{R}^n, \qquad (12.4)$$

where $u(z)$ represents the determined solution, and D is a discretized domain over a finite set of points. With the conditions $u(z)=a$ and $u'(z)=b$. Now for an approximate solution of the Equation 12.4, i.e $\xi(z)$; for the construction of a neural network, we consider a single input, multiple layers $j-1$, hidden layers with k neurons for each layer and a single output, the output of a deep neural network represented by $\hat{u}(z,\theta)$, and it is defined as:

$$\hat{u}(z,\theta)=(t_j*\sigma*t_{j-1}*\sigma\ldots\sigma*t_1)z^0 \qquad (12.5)$$

where,

$$t_j(z^{j-1}) = W^{(j)}z^{j-1} + b^{(j)},\ j = 1,2,3\ldots J, \tag{12.6}$$

where, $*$ is the composition operator, $\theta = \{W^j, b^j\}$ trainable parameters, and σ represents the activation function. We can update the trainable parameter by minimizing the cost function. Within the framework of the PINNs, the loss function that is typically utilized as the mean squared error. The residual of the differential equations and boundary conditions are defined as

$$L(\theta) = L_f + L_{b1} + L_{b2}, \tag{12.7}$$

where,

$$L_f = \frac{1}{N_f}\sum_{j=1}^{N_f} |\hat{u}(z_j;\theta)|^2,$$

$$L_{b1} = \frac{1}{N_{b1}}\sum_{j=1}^{N_{b1}} |\hat{u}(z_j;\theta) - a|^2,$$

$$L_{b2} = \frac{1}{N_{b2}}\sum_{j=1}^{N_{b2}} |\hat{u}(z_j;\theta) - b|^2 .$$

In this context, L_f, L_{b1} and L_{b2} represents the residual loss associated with the given ODE and the loss pertaining to boundary conditions, respectively. We have selected N_f training points to obtain the residual information of ODEs within the specified temporal domain. Furthermore, we utilize N_{b1}, N_{b2}, the number of distinct sample points, to gather information regarding specific boundary points.

12.4 Experiments' Results and Discussion

In this work, we used PINNs to solve the ER model. The entire simulation experiment has been conducted in Python language in the Google Colab platform. This choice allows for fast training of our model. We validate our PINNs solution by checking it against the numerical solution from the literature. Table 12.1 shows hardware and software environment configurations.

Now, we solved Equation 12.2 with conditions given in Equation 12.3 using PINNs. We construct a physics-informed feedforward neural network utilizing the DeepXde [14]. We initialized the initial weights and biases using Xavier initialization. Additionally, we utilize the hyperbolic tangent (tanh) function as the activation function within the neural network. We employ the Adam optimizer to minimize the loss function. We configure the network to train for 5000 epochs, using the entire batch size to calculate the gradient updates for all sample points every epoch. During the optimization process, the learning rate was set at 0.001 to strike a balance between the requirement for effective convergence and the risk of overshooting. When it comes to the number of collocation points, which are extremely important for accurately capturing the behavior of the system, we take into consideration 200 inside the domain and 2 for the boundary conditions from [0,1] domain. We also tuned the neural network's architecture, which includes one input and one output, eight hidden layers, and 50 neurons per layer. We selected these parameters through iterative experiments, aiming to reduce overfitting and enhance generalization. We solved the mathematical model for various values of ε^2 utilizing PINNs. The results of the loss that correspond to various values of ε^2 are presented in Table 12.2. These results demonstrate the extent of training the model for optimal performance. An examination of the trends that have been noticed in the loss components L_f, L_{b1}, and L_{b2} is presented

Table 12.1 Experiment environment.

Environment configurations	Details
• OS	Windows 11 Home Single Language
• CPU	AMD Ryzen 5 3500U
• CPU core	4
• CPU Frequency (GHz)	2.10
• CPU RAM (GB)	8
• Dependent library	Matplotlib, Numpy

Table 12.2 Loss values at 5000 epochs.

Values of ε^2	L_f	L_{b1}	L_{b2}
0.5	2.13×10^{-3}	5.92×10^{-5}	6.38×10^{-4}
1	7.08×10^{-4}	2.43×10^{-4}	4.81×10^{-4}
2	2.64×10^{-2}	2.65×10^{-4}	2.00×10^{-3}
3	3.56×10^{-3}	2.14×10^{-6}	5.61×10^{-6}
5	2.97×10^{-2}	1.03×10^{-4}	1.60×10^{-3}

in Table 12.2. This study shows that the attained loss values are relatively small, indicating successful training of the model.

Figure 12.1 shows the comparison between the predicted solution by PINNs with homotopy analysis transform method (HATM) [18] as a reference solution for $\varepsilon^2 = 0.5$ and $\alpha = 12$.

Based on the information shown in Figure 12.1, it is clear that the numerical results achieved with the help of PINNs are in excellent alignment with the results obtained by HATM. In addition, we examined the impact of different values of ε^2 on temperature keeping α constant. Figure 12.2 shows the effect of ε^2 on temperature.

Figures 12.1 and 12.2 illustrate the effect of ε^2 at α = 12. This result illustrates that an increase in the value of ε^2 results in an improvement

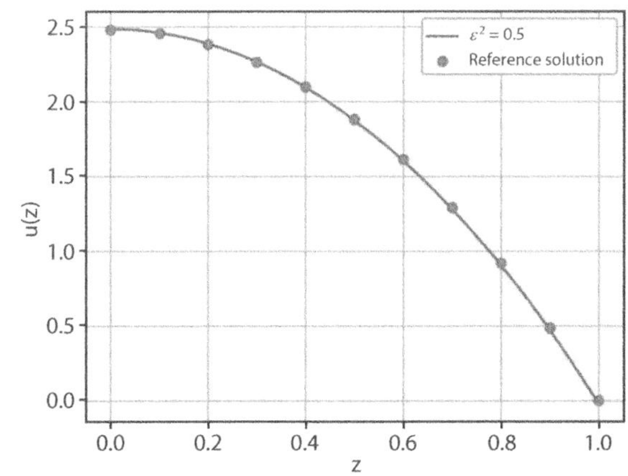

Figure 12.1 Comparison of temperature u(z) obtained by PINNs with HATM for $\varepsilon^2 = 0.5$ and $\alpha = 12$.

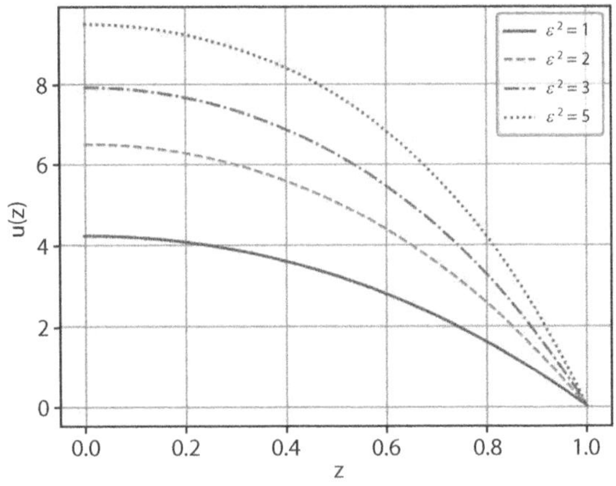

Figure 12.2 Plot of temperature $u(z)$ versus z for different values of ε^2 at $\alpha = 12$.

in the temperature profile [12]. The findings indicate that ε^2 is crucial for regulating the temperature distribution across the system, and an elevation in ε^2 results in a more significant increase in temperature over the whole domain. Additionally, we observed that when the value of z increases, the temperature profile drastically reduces. This phenomenon may be elucidated by the observation that increased values of ε^2 may improve thermal conductivity or increase heat generation within the medium, hence promoting more efficient heat transfer.

12.5 Conclusion

The purpose of this work was to investigate the applications of PINNs to forward problems that are associated with ER. We demonstrated that PINNs can accurately forecast the temperature profile. Additionally, we have conducted research on the ER model in the presence of a constant heat source in a porous medium. We have employed PINNs to handle the governing differential equation. We observed two distinct patterns in the temperature profile: first, an increase in the value of ε^2 led to a corresponding increase in the temperature profile; second, an increase in the value of z resulted in a decrease in the temperature values. Both patterns were consistently noted in our analysis. Hence, the results obtained from PINNs are in excellent agreement with the reference solution from the literature.

References

1. Alwated, B. and El-Amin, M.F., Enhanced oil recovery by nanoparticles flooding: From numerical modeling improvement to machine learning prediction. *Adv. Geo-Energy Res.*, *5*, 3, 297–317, 2021.
2. Bai, J., Rabczuk, T., Gupta, A., Alzubaidi, L., Gu, Y., A physics-informed neural network technique based on a modified loss function for computational 2D and 3D solid mechanics. *Comput. Mech.*, *71*, 3, 543–562, 2023.
3. Bdzil, j.B. and Frisch, H., Chemically driven convection. *J. Chem. Phys.*, *72*, 3, 1875–1886, 1980.
4. Beck, J.L., Convection in a box of porous material saturated with fluid. *Phys. Fluids*, 15, 1377–1383, 1972.
5. Cai, S., Wang, Z., Wang, S., Perdikaris, P., Karniadakis, G., Physics-informed neural networks for heat transfer problems. *J. Heat Transfer*, *143*, 060801, 2021.
6. Davis, S.H., Convection in a box: linear theory. *J. Fluid Mech.*, *30*, 3, 465–478, 1967.
7. El-Amin, M. and Alwated, B., Machine Learning Prediction for Nanoparticles Behavior in Hydrocarbon Reservoirs, in: *2023 20th Learning and Technology Conference (L\&T)*, IEEE, pp. 80–83, 2023.
8. El-Amin, M. and Subasi, A., Developing a generalized scaling-law for oil recovery using machine learning techniques. *Procedia Comput. Sci.*, *163*, 237–247, 2019.
9. El-Amin, M., Alwated, B., Hoteit, H., Machine learning prediction of nanoparticle transport with two-phase flow in porous media. *Energies*, *16*, 2, 678, 2023.
10. Jones, D., The dynamic stability of confined, exothermically reacting fluids. *Int. J. Heat Mass Transfer*, *16*, 1, 157–167, 1973.
11. K, N. and Hubertus, W. j., A bifurcation study of chemically driven convection in a porous medium. *Chem. Eng. Sci.*, *47*, 15-16, 4107–4120, 1992.
12. Kumar, D., Singh, J., Tanwar, K., Baleanu, D., A new fractional exothermic reactions model having constant heat source in porous media with power, exponential and Mittag-Leffler laws. *Int. J. Heat Mass Transfer*, *138*, 1222–1227, 2019.
13. Lapwood, E., Convection of a fluid in a porous medium, in: *Mathematical proceedings of the cambridge philosophical society*, vol. *44*, pp. 508–521, Cambridge University Press, 1948.
14. Lu, L., Meng, X., Mao, Z., Karniadakis, G., DeepXDE: A deep learning library for solving differential equations. *SIAM Rev.*, *63*, 1, 208–228, 2021.
15. Patel, P., Yadav, S., El-Amin, M., Yildiz, M., Prediction by machine learning in nanoparticles-based enhanced oil recovery. *Math. Modell. Numer. Simul. Appl.*, *4*, 4, 544–561, 2024.

16. Pochai, N. and Jiratchaya, J., A numerical treatment of an exothermic reactions model with constant heat source in a porous medium using finite difference method. *Adv. Stud. Biol.*, *4*, 6, 287–296, 2012.
17. Raissi, M., Perdikaris, P., Karniadakis, G., Physics-informed neural networks: A deep learning framework for solving forward and inverse problems involving nonlinear partial differential equations. *J. Comput. Phys.*, *378*, 686–707, 2019.
18. Sharma, R., Jain, M., Kumar, D., Analytical solution of exothermic reactions model with constant heat source and porous medium. *Proc. Natl. Acad. Sci., India, Sect. A Phys. Sci.*, *90*, 239–243, 2020.
19. Subasi, A., El-Amin, M., Darwich, T., Dossary, M., Permeability prediction of petroleum reservoirs using stochastic gradient boosting regression. *J. Ambient Intell. Hum. Comput.*, 13, 1–10, 2022.
20. Subramanian, S. and Balakotaiah, V., Convective instabilities induced by exothermic reactions occurring in a porous medium. *Phys. Fluids*, *6*, 2907–2922, 1994.
21. Tveitereid, M., Thermal convection in a horizontal porous layer with internal heat sources. *Int. J. Heat Mass Transfer*, *20*, 10, 1045–1050, 1977.
22. Viljoen, H. and Hlavacek, V., Chemically driven convection in a porous medium. *AlChE J.*, *33*, 8, 1344–1350, 1987.
23. Wu, K. and Xiu, D., Data-driven deep learning of partial differential equations in modal space. *J. Comput. Phys.*, *408*, 109307, 2020.
24. Xu, J., Wei, H., Bao, H., Physics-informed neural networks for studying heat transfer in porous media. *Int. J. Heat Mass Transfer*, *217*, 124671, 2023.

13

Machine Learning for Magnetohydrodynamic Nanofluid Flow: Artificial Neural Networks vs. Traditional Methods

B.C. Rout[1,2*], Bijoylakshmi Boruah[1], Utpal Kumar Saha[1], Madhusudan Senapati[3], Sakambari Mishra[4], Vikash Kumar[2] and Bhimanand Pandurang Gajbhare[5]

[1]*Department of Basic and Applied Science, National Institute of Technology Arunachal Pradesh, Jote, Arunachal Pradesh, India*
[2]*Department of Mathematics, Sarala Birla University, Ranchi, India*
[3]*Department of Mathematics, Regional Institute of Education, Bhubaneswar, India*
[4]*Department of Mathematics, College of Basic Science and Humanities, OUAT, Bhubaneswar, Odisha, India*
[5]*Department of Mathematics, J.E.S, Vaidyanath College, Parli-Vaijnath, Beed, Maharashtra, India*

Abstract

In this article, the two-dimensional magnetohydrodynamic (MHD) flow of a hyperbolic tangent fluid over a stretched surface containing nanoparticles is examined. Using appropriate scaling, the controlling nonlinear partial differential equations are converted into ordinary differential equations, which are then resolved by the shooting technique. We analyze how velocity, temperature, and concentration are affected by the following important parameters: Brownian motion parameter (Nb), Lewis number (Le), Prandtl number (Pr), Weissenberg number (We), Hartmann number (M), and thermophoresis parameter (Nt). The findings indicate that while Brownian

**Corresponding author*: bishnu.rout1@gmail.com; ORCID: 0000-0002-0316-4655
Bijoylakshmi Boruah: ORCID: 0009-0005-8324-7600
Utpal Kumar Saha: ORCID: 0000-0002-0143-1625
Sakambari Mishra: ORCID: 0009-0007-9088-7571
Vikash Kumar: ORCID: 0000-0002-3669-5807
Bhimanand Pandurang Gajbhare: ORCID: 0000-0002-1911-8602

Mukesh Kumar Awasthi and Reshu Gupta (eds.) Artificial Intelligence and Computational Modeling in Heat Transfer and Fluid Dynamics, (343–364) © 2026 Scrivener Publishing LLC

motion and thermophoresis increase temperature, increases in Weissenberg and Hartmann numbers slow down fluid motion. As Nb, Pr, Le, and Nt grow, the local Sherwood number rises, but the Nusselt number falls. Additionally, an artificial neural network (ANN) is used to train the solution, and its accuracy, training dynamics, and computing efficiency are compared with the conventional BVP4C solver. The work emphasizes how adaptable ANNs may be as a substitute for conventional numerical techniques in boundary value analysis.

Keywords: Artificial neural network, hyperbolic tangent nanofluid, MHD, nonlinear stretching sheet

Nomenclature

Symbol	Description
U_w	Stretching velocity
T_w	Wall temperature
C_w	Wall concentration
T_∞	Ambient temperature
C_∞	Ambient concentration
u	Longitudinal velocity component
v	Normal velocity component
ν	Kinematic viscosity
σ	Electrical conductivity
η	Similarity variable
B_0	Transverse magnetic field
B	Magnetic field
n	Power-law index
$f'(\eta)$	Dimensionless velocity
$\varphi(\eta)$	Dimensionless concentration
$\theta(\eta)$	Dimensionless temperature
λ	Time constant
C_p	Specific heat
ρ	Density
D_B	Brownian diffusivity
k	Thermal conductivity
M	Magnetic parameter
We	Weissenberg number

Pr	Prandtl number
Le	Lewis number
Nt	Thermophoresis parameter
Nb	Brownian motion parameter
τ	Heat capacity ratio
C_f	Skin friction coefficient
Nu	Nusselt number
Sh	Sherwood number
C	Concentration profile
T	Temperature profile
TH	Tangent Hyperbolic
ψ	Stream function
Γ	Relaxation time Parameter
α	Thermal diffusivity
μ	Dynamic viscosity
q_x	Heat flux
q_s	Mass flux
Re_x	Local Reynolds number
ANN	Artificial Neural Network

13.1 Introduction

The study of non-Newtonian fluids has advanced significantly in recent years, which has raised interest in their thermophysical characteristics. Numerous studies, including both analytical and numerical techniques, have been carried out in this field because of their wide range of commercial and technical applications. The tangent hyperbolic fluid (THF) model stands out among the other non-Newtonian fluid models. Laboratory investigations have demonstrated that this model accurately depicts blood flow and can capture shear-thinning behavior. Chemical engineers frequently employ the THF model because it has a number of benefits over other non-Newtonian fluid models. Tangent hyperbolic fluid is frequently found in substances including paint, whipped cream, ketchup, blood, and nail polish. The flow of a two-dimensional tangent hyperbolic nanofluid across a continuous surface was recently investigated by Shahzad *et al.* [1]. The impact of heat transfer on the magnetized flow of THF across a stretchable sheet was investigated by Zakir *et al.* [2]. The magnetohydrodynamic (MHD) boundary layer flow of THF models was numerically analyzed by Akbar *et al.* [3]. Ibrahim [4] examined how heat radiation affected magnetized THF with nanoparticles while considering an expanding sheet with second-order slip and convective boundary conditions. The study of MHD, which focuses on how electrically conducting fluids behave when subjected to a magnetic field, is crucial to fluid dynamics theory and practice. The purification of crude oil, the refining of molten metal, and the larger oil industry are just a few of the sectors in which this branch of research finds varied uses. Furthermore, metallurgy, polymer technology, and the manufacture of glass fibers all make use of MHD concepts. Heat transmission in the flow of an MHD visco-elastic liquid across a continuously stretched surface was investigated by Andersson *et al.* [5]. Considering hydromagnetic effects, viscosity dissipation, and chemical processes, Kameswaran *et al.* [6] investigated the impact of linear velocity on a stretching or shrinking wall. Chakrabarti *et al.* [7] estimated the boundary layer solution after using MHD to analyze heat transport in a viscous fluid flow. The thermophysical characteristics of THF flow across a nonlinear stretching plate were investigated by Hussain *et al.* [8], taking viscous dissipation and convective boundary conditions into account. A numerical study of the MHD flow of a THF model around a stretched cylinder was carried out by Malik *et al.* [9]. Additional studies on MHD flows are available [10–19]. Amjad *et al.* [20] conducted a numerical study on the tangent hyperbolic nanofluid flow in magnetohydrodynamics across a particularly stretched sheet. Hussain *et al.* [21] did an MHD Prandtl–Eyring fluid flow study across a stretched sheet with computational and physical factors. Ahmad *et al.* [22] investigated a tangent hyperbolic nanofluid passed over a nonlinear stretching sheet.

In this work, nonlinear partial differential equations are transformed into highly nonlinear ordinary differential equations (ODEs) by using appropriate similarity transformations. The resulting system of ODEs is then solved using MATLAB's bvp4c solver [22]. Artificial neural networks (ANN) and machine learning are used to further increase the solutions' efficiency and accuracy. The ANN model is trained using numerical data from the bvp4c solver to give a prediction framework for evaluating comparable circumstances without continuously solving the ODEs. Through a detailed comparison, the effectiveness of ANN and bvp4c is evaluated. While ANN is computationally efficient for real-time applications because it provides a fast approximation once trained, bvp4c generates incredibly accurate numerical solutions by using iterative boundary value problem solvers. The trade-off between accuracy, computation time, and generalizability is assessed using tables and graphs.

13.2 Problem Description

Over a nonlinear stretching plate, the two-dimensional incompressible boundary layer fluid flow is assumed. The MHD effects are also taken into account, and the fluid is tangent hyperbolic. Supposedly, the plate is stretching at a variable speed. $u = U_w = Bx^{1/3}$ along the x-axis, all directions are perpendicular to each other. There is a transverse magnetic field present in the flow. $B^* = \frac{B_0}{x^{1/3}}$ in a vertical direction. The under-discussion model [19, 21, 22] is illustrated in Figure 13.1. The Governing Equations [19, 21, 22] are:

$$\frac{\partial u}{\partial x} + \frac{\partial v}{\partial y} = 0 \tag{13.1}$$

$$u\frac{\partial u}{\partial x} + v\frac{\partial u}{\partial y} = \nu\left((1-n) + \sqrt{2}n\Gamma\frac{\partial u}{\partial y}\right)\frac{\partial^2 u}{\partial y^2} - \frac{\sigma B_0{}^2}{\rho_f}u \tag{13.2}$$

$$u\frac{\partial T}{\partial x} + v\frac{\partial T}{\partial y} = \alpha\frac{\partial^2 T}{\partial y^2} + \tau\left[D_B\frac{\partial C}{\partial y}\frac{\partial T}{\partial y} + \frac{D_T}{T_\infty}\left(\frac{\partial T}{\partial y}\right)^2\right] \tag{13.3}$$

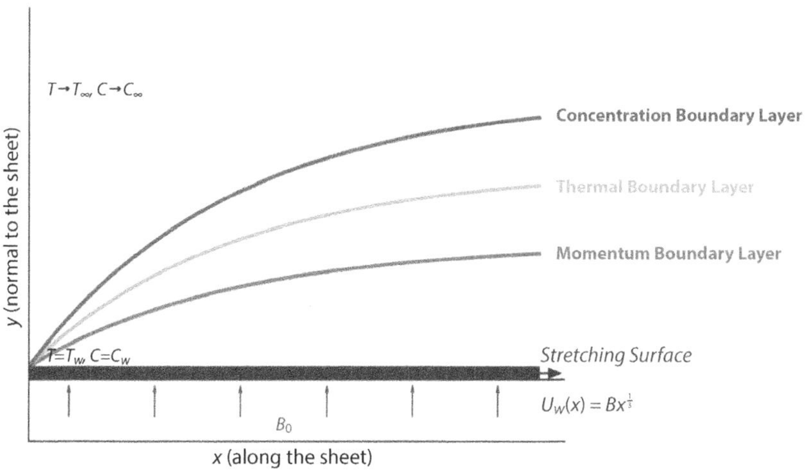

Figure 13.1 Schematic flow diagram.

$$u\frac{\partial C}{\partial x}+v\frac{\partial C}{\partial y}=\frac{D_T}{T_\infty}\frac{\partial^2 T}{\partial y^2}+D_B\frac{\partial^2 C}{\partial y^2} \tag{13.4}$$

The BCs that are taken into consideration are as follows:

$$\begin{aligned} &u=u_w(x)=ax, v=0, T=T_w, C=C_w \quad at \quad y=0 \\ &u\to 0,\ T\to T_\infty,\ C\to C_\infty \qquad as\ y\to\infty \end{aligned} \tag{13.5}$$

To solve the governing Equations 13.2–13.4, the following similarity transformation is performed.

$$\left.\begin{aligned} &u=ax\,f'(\eta), v=-\sqrt{av}\,f(\eta) \\ &\eta=\sqrt{\frac{a}{v}}y, \psi=-\sqrt{av}\,xf(\eta), \phi=\frac{C-C_\infty}{C_w-C_\infty}, \theta=\frac{T-T_\infty}{T_w-T_\infty} \end{aligned}\right\} \tag{13.6}$$

Using Equation 13.6 in Equations 13.1–13.4, we get the following non-dimensional set of ODEs (Equations 13.7–13.9)

$$\left((1-n)+nWef'')\right)f'''-\frac{f'^2}{3}-Mf'+\frac{2}{3}ff''=0 \tag{13.7}$$

$$\theta''+\Pr Nb\phi'\theta'+\Pr Nt\theta'^2+\frac{2}{3}\Pr f\theta'=0 \tag{13.8}$$

$$\phi''+\frac{Nt}{Nb}\theta''+\frac{2}{3}Le\Pr f\phi'=0 \tag{13.9}$$

After employing Equation 13.6 in Equation 13.5, the boundary conditions reduce to Equation 13.10, which is given below.

$$\begin{aligned} &f(0)=0,\ f'(0)=1,\ f'(\infty)=0, \\ &\theta(0)=1,\ \theta(\infty)=0,\ \phi(0)=1,\ \phi(\infty)=0 \end{aligned} \tag{13.10}$$

where, $M=\frac{\sigma B_0^{\ 2}}{a\rho_f}$ denotes the magnetic parameter; $We=\Gamma x\sqrt{\frac{2a^3}{v}}$ is used for the Weissenberg number; $\Pr=\frac{v}{\alpha}$ represents the Prandtl number;

$Le = \frac{\alpha}{D_B}$ shows the Lewis number; $Nt = \frac{\tau D_T \left(T_w - T_\infty\right)}{\nu T_\infty}$ represents the thermophoresis parameter; $Nb = \frac{\tau D_B \left(C_w - C_\infty\right)}{\nu}$ is the Brownian Motion, and $\tau = \frac{(\rho c_p)_p}{(\rho c_p)_f}$ is the heat capacity ratio. The skin friction coefficient (c_f), Nusselt number (Nu_x), and Sherwood number (Sh_x) are defined in Equations 13.11–13.13 and given below:

$$C_f = \frac{\tau_w}{\rho u_w^2} \tag{13.11}$$

$$Nu_x = \frac{x q_w}{k\left(T_w - T_\infty\right)} \tag{13.12}$$

$$Sh_x = \frac{x q_s}{D_B\left(C_w - C_\infty\right)} \tag{13.13}$$

where $\tau_w = \mu(1-n)\frac{\partial u}{\partial y} + \mu \frac{n\Gamma}{\sqrt{2}}\left(\frac{\partial u}{\partial y}\right)^2_{y=0}$

$$q_w = -k\left(\frac{\partial T}{\partial y}\right)_{y=0}$$

$$q_s = -D_B\left(\frac{\partial C}{\partial y}\right)_{y=0}$$

Dimensionless forms of c_f, Nu_x, and Sh_x are given in Equations 13.14–13.16.

$$C_f \operatorname{Re}_x^{-1/2} = \left((1-n) + \frac{n}{2}\, Wef''(0)\right) f''(0) \tag{13.14}$$

$$Nu_x \operatorname{Re}_x^{-1/2} = -\theta'(0) \tag{13.15}$$

$$Sh_x \operatorname{Re}_x^{-1/2} = -\phi'(0) \tag{13.16}$$

13.3 Results and Discussion

Figure 13.2 depicts the velocity against the exponential index, considering the following set of data: m = 0.5; We = 0.5; Pr = 0.71; Nb = 0.5; Nt = 0.5; Le = 3; it is found that the velocity profile decreases with an increase in the magnitude of the exponential index, hence decreasing the velocity boundary layer. It is because the increase in the exponential index leads to variations in fluid viscosity. Higher viscosity gives rise to steeper velocity gradients. Hence, the velocity profile decreases.

Effects of the velocity profile over the magnetic parameter are depicted in Figure 13.3, considering this set of data fixed: We = 0.5; Pr = 0.71, n = 0.3; Nb = 0.5; Nt = 0.5; Le = 3; it is found that the velocity profile decreases with an increase in the magnitude of the magnetic parameter. When a magnetic field is applied transversely to the flow direction of the fluid, it gives rise to the Lorentz force, which acts opposite to the direction of the fluid. The magnitude of the force is proportional to both the velocity of the fluid and the magnetic field strength. When the magnitude of the magnetic parameter increases, the opposing force becomes stronger, and it leads to a reduction in fluid velocity, and hence, the velocity boundary layer decreases.

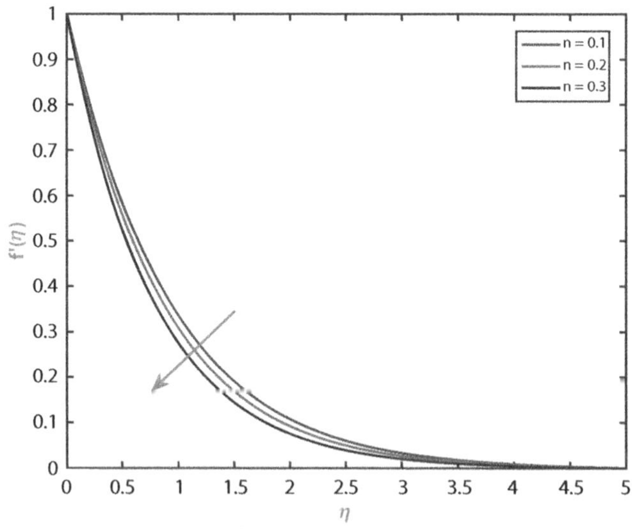

Figure 13.2 Effects of exponential index on the velocity profile.

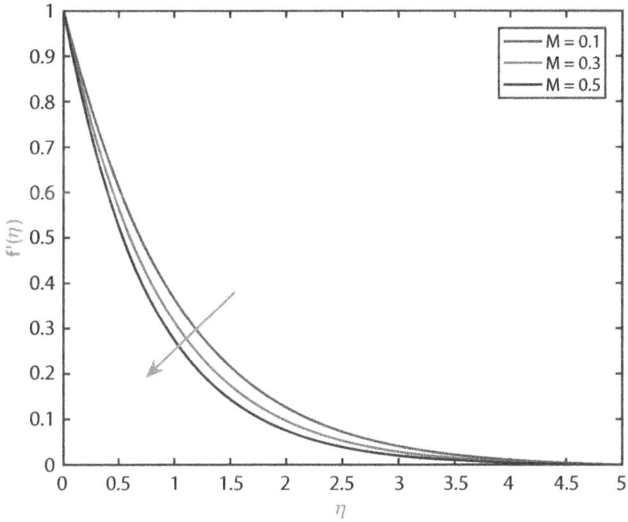

Figure 13.3 Effects of magnetic parameter on the velocity profile.

Effects of the velocity profile over the Weissenberg number are depicted in Figure 13.4. It is presented by keeping these parameters fixed at $M = 0.5$; $Pr = 0.71$; $n = 0.3$; $Nb = 0.5$; $Nt = 0.5$; $Le = 3$; it is found that the velocity profile decreases with an increase in the magnitude of the

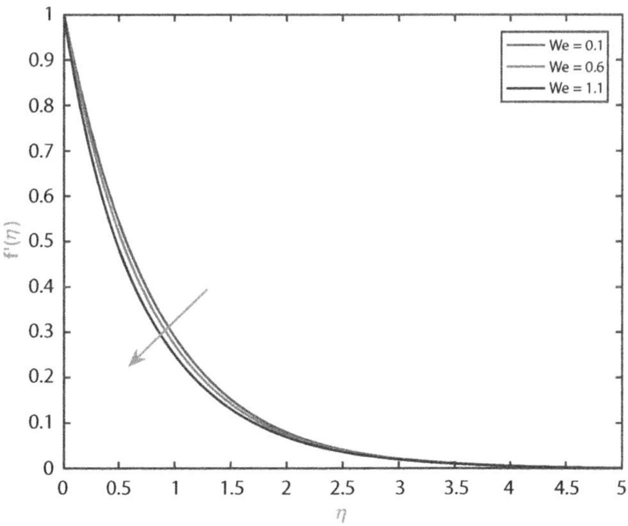

Figure 13.4 Effects of the Weissenberg number on the velocity profile.

Weissenberg number. With an increase in the Weissenberg number, it is the physical elastic behavior of the fluid competes with the ability to dissipate energy through viscosity. As the elastic effects dominate, the fluid resists flow more strongly, leading to a decrease in velocities across the flow field and a decrease in the velocity boundary layer.

Effects of the temperature field over the Prandtl number are depicted in Figure 13.5 with the use of this set of data: $M = 0.5$; $We = 0.5$; $n = 0.3$; $Nb = 0.5$; $Nt = 0.5$; $Le = 3$; it is found that the temperature profile decreases with an increase in the magnitude of the Prandtl number and with a reduction in the thermal boundary layer. It is due to an increase in the magnitude of the Prandtl number signifies a greater viscosity relative to thermal diffusivity. This means that the fluid is more resistant to changes in temperature, which can lead to a decrease in temperature profile and thermal boundary layer because less heat is transported away from a heated surface.

Effects of the Brownian motion parameter on the temperature profile are depicted in Figure 13.6 by using these sets of data: $M = 0.5$; $We = 0.5$; $Pr = 0.71$; $n = 0.3$; $Nt = 0.5$; $Le = 3$; it is found that an increase in Brownian motion Parameter results in an increase in temperature profile and increase in the thermal boundary layer. Brownian motion is a phenomenon of diffusion. As the Brownian motion parameter increases, it will also increase the diffusion coefficients of particles within the fluid. This increase in diffusion leads to more effective mixing and redistribution of thermal energy

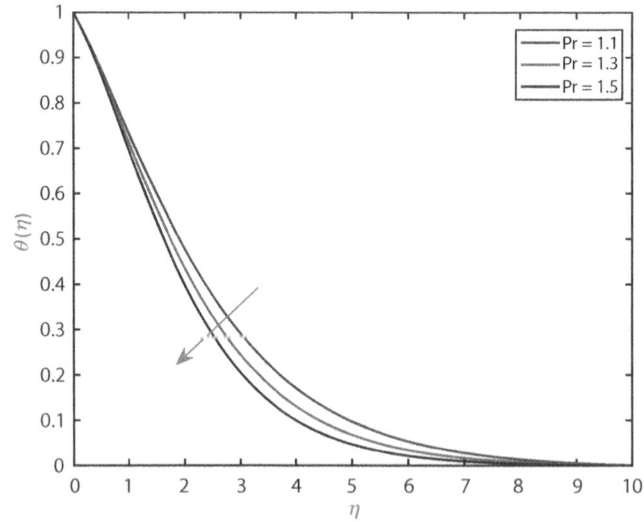

Figure 13.5 Effect of the Prandtl number on the temperature profile.

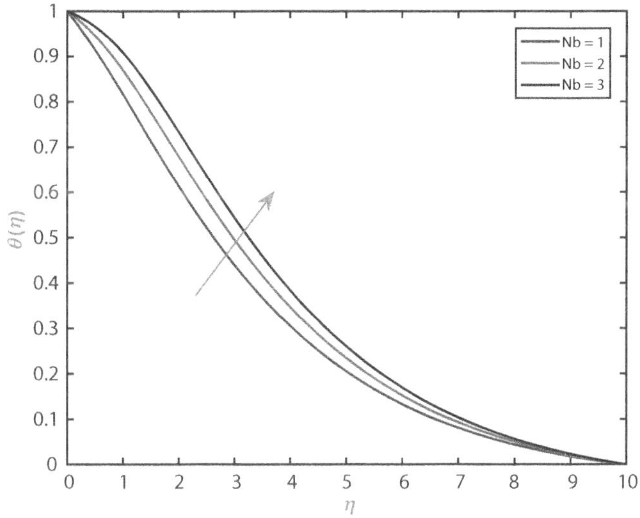

Figure 13.6 Effects of the Brownian motion parameter on the temperature profile.

throughout the fluid, causing an increase in the temperature profile and thermal boundary layer.

Effects of the thermophoresis parameter on the temperature profile are depicted in Figure 13.7 by using this sets of data: $M = 0.5$; $We = 0.5$; $Pr = 0.71$; $n = 0.3$; $Nb = 0.5$; $Le = 3$; it is found that the temperature profile

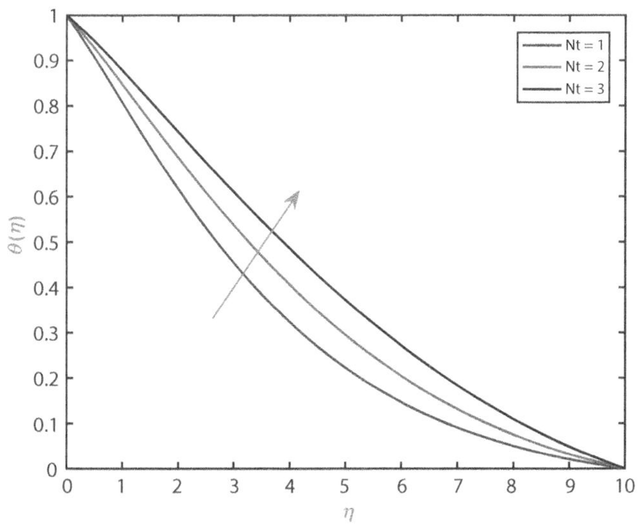

Figure 13.7 Effects of the thermophoresis parameter on the temperature profile.

increases with an increase in the magnitude of the thermophoresis parameter. The thermophoretic force acts on particles in the presence of a temperature gradient. As the thermophoresis parameter increases, it indicates a higher temperature gradient. Particles tend to move from regions of high temperature to regions of low temperature due to higher temperature gradient. This movement of particles can lead to enhanced convective heat transfer, which in turn, increases the overall temperature distribution in the fluid and thermal boundary layer.

The effects of the magnetic parameter on the temperature profile are depicted in Figure 13.8 by using this set of data: $We = 0.5$; $Pr = 0.71$; $n = 0.3$; $Nb = 0.5$; $Nt = 0.5$; $Le = 3$; it is found that the temperature profile increases with an increase in the magnitude of the magnetic parameter [22]. An increase in the magnetic parameter generally indicates a stronger magnetic field. This can lead to magnetic damping, which affects fluid motion. Moreover, the Lorentz force, which is the force exerted on a charged particle moving through a magnetic field, can reduce the velocity of the fluid flow. When the flow is damped, energy dissipation may result in more heat being converted into thermal energy, thereby increasing the temperature of the distribution and thermal boundary layer.

Effects of the thermophoresis parameter over the concentration profile are depicted in Figure 13.9 by using this set of data: $M = 0.5$; $We = 0.5$; $Pr = 0.71$; $n = 0.3$; $Nb = 0.5$; $Le = 3$; it is found that the concentration

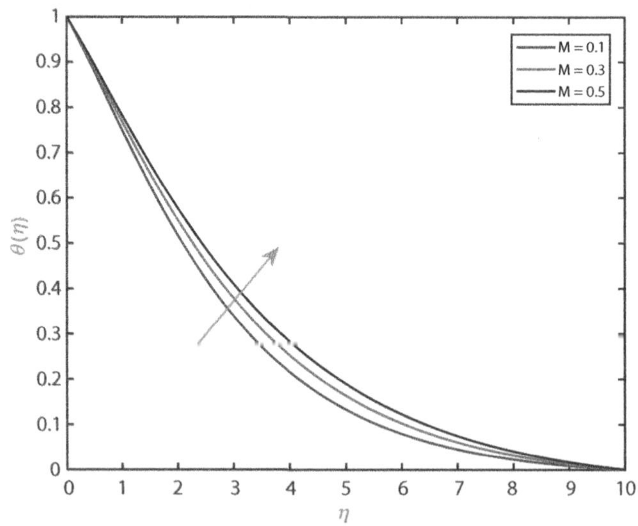

Figure 13.8 Effects of the magnetic parameter on the temperature profile.

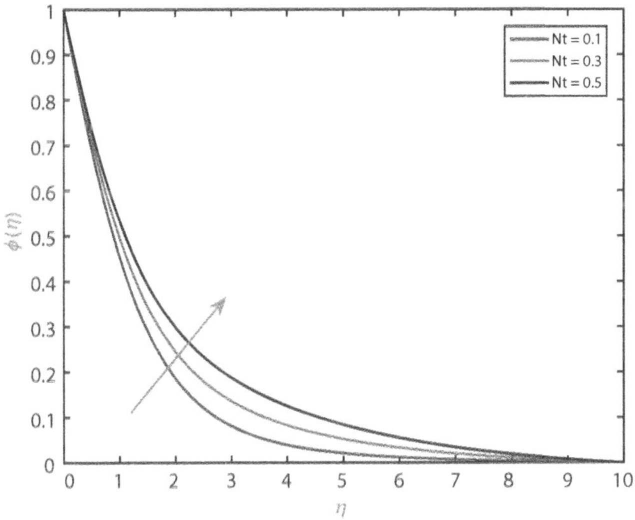

Figure 13.9 Effects of thermophoresis parameter on the concentration profile.

profile increases with an increase in the magnitude of the thermophoresis parameter. An increase in the magnitude of the thermophoresis parameter indicates a rise in the thermal gradient. This enhanced thermal gradient leads to particle movement, as particles in the hot region gain kinetic energy and are more likely to move towards the cold region. This phenomenon can significantly increase concentration profiles and, more specifically, the concentration boundary layer of the flow systems where the magnitude of the temperature gradient increases.

Effects of the Brownian motion parameter over the concentration profile are depicted in Figure 13.10 by using this set of data: $M = 0.5$; $We = 0.5$; $Pr = 0.71$; $n = 0.3$; $Nt = 0.5$; $Le = 3$; it is found that concentration profile decreases with an increase in the magnitude of the Brownian motion parameter. As the Brownian motion parameter increases, the fluid particles experience random motion. This leads to increased dispersion of the substance within the flow medium. As fluid particles spread out more, the concentration distribution in any given fluid region decreases, leading to a lower overall concentration profile and reducing the concentration boundary layer.

Effects of the Lewis number (Le) on the concentration profile are depicted in Figure 13.11 by using this set of data: $M = 0.5$; $We = 0.5$; $Pr = 0.71$; $n = 0.3$; $Nb = 0.5$; $Nt = 0.5$; it is found that the concentration profile decreases with an increase in the magnitude of the Le. The Le is a

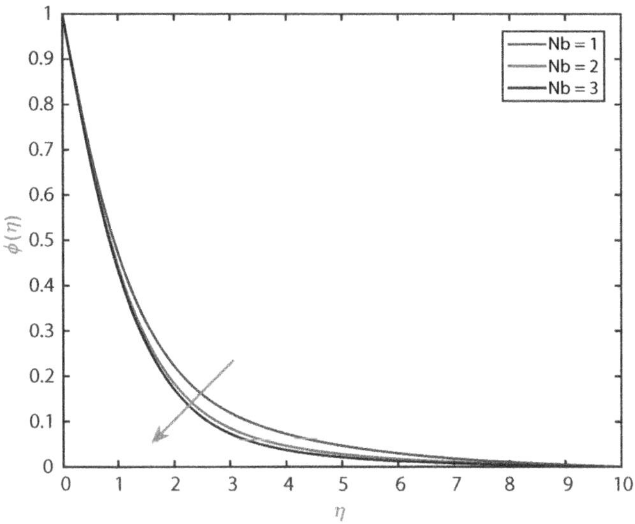

Figure 13.10 Effects of the Brownian motion parameter on the concentration profile.

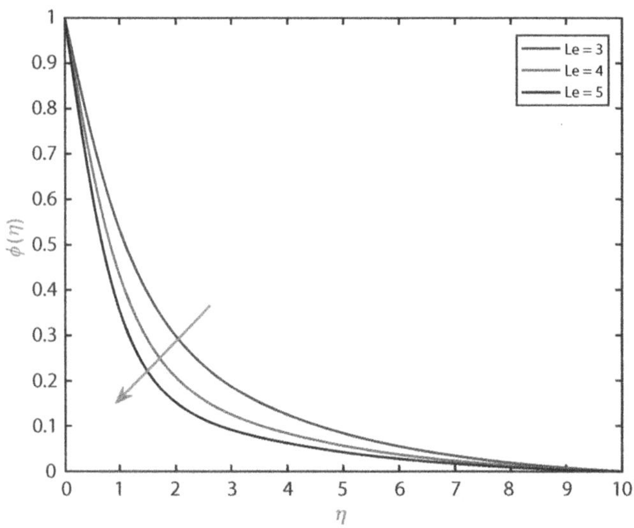

Figure 13.11 Effects of the Lewis number on the concentration profile.

dimensionless quantity that compares the rate of thermal diffusion to that of mass diffusion. As the Le increases, it suggests that thermal diffusion is more significant as compared to mass diffusion. This means that heat is being transported away from the region of interest faster than the mass.

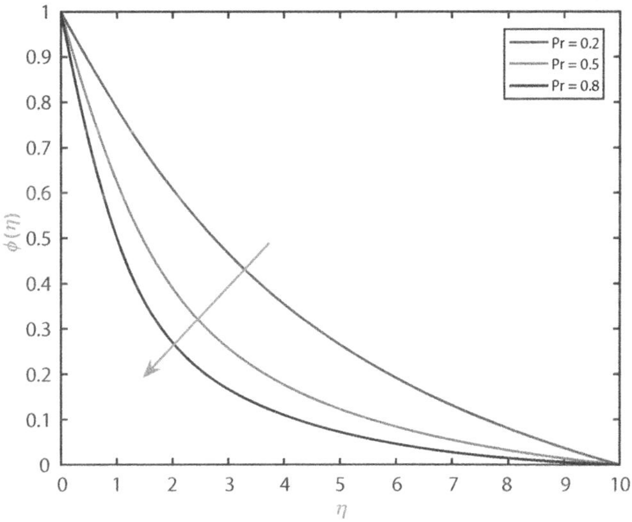

Figure 13.12 Effects of the Prandtl number on the concentration profile.

Consequently, any concentration gradient decreases because the heat influences the behavior of the fluid phenomenon, and it also reduces the concentration boundary layer.

Effects of the Prandtl number (Pr) on the concentration profile are depicted in Figure 13.12 by using this set of data: M = 0.5; We = 0.5; n = 0.3; Nb = 0.5; Nt = 0.5; Le = 3; it is found that the concentration profile decreases with an increase in the magnitude of the Prandtl number. The Pr is a dimensionless number that measures the ratio of momentum diffusivity (kinematic viscosity) to thermal diffusivity. For higher Pr, the thermal diffusion is smaller compared to the momentum diffusion, which can suppress convective heat transfer. In a flow system, a higher Pr may result in a weaker thermal convection, thereby reducing the mixing and distribution of solutes, leading to an overall decrease in the concentration field and, therefore, also reducing the concentration boundary layer.

In Figure 13.13, the mean squared error (MSE) is at its lowest as the training error steadily drops. Although it is somewhat greater than the training error, the validation error exhibits a similar pattern. Although the test error is the greatest of the three, it often shows a declining trend, indicating the highest validation MSE attained during the training process. The final accuracy level at the last epoch was indicated by the model's performance value of 2.0533×10^{-9}. This points to a well-trained model with little overfitting and a gradually declining MSE.

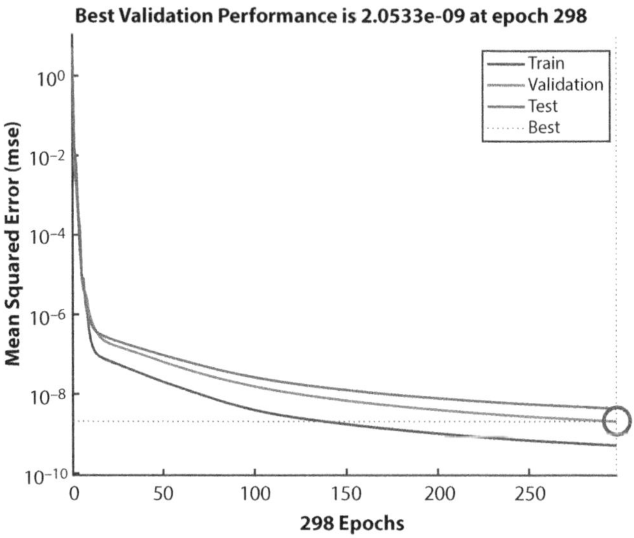

Figure 13.13 The performance plot for the velocity profile.

The analysis of the velocity error histogram (with 20 Bins) in Figure 13.14 shows the distribution of the velocity errors in the test (red), validation (green), and training (blue) datasets shown by the histogram. The ideal situation, in which the model's predictions are flawless, is shown

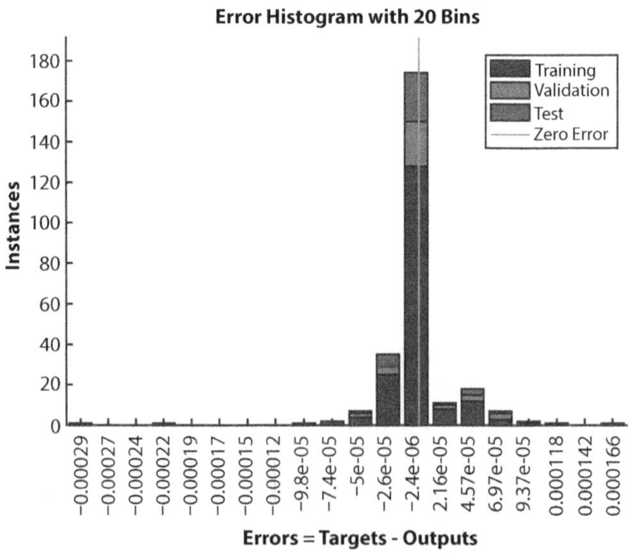

Figure 13.14 Error histogram plot for the velocity profile.

by the zero-error reference (orange line). Most forecasts are quite accurate, as evidenced by the majority of mistakes being focused around zero. Particularly for the test and validation sets, the distribution is rather dispersed, showing minor variances but remaining centered around zero. The granularity of the error distribution would be further refined with a resolution of 20 bins, providing further information on error dispersion and model generalization.

13.3.1 Analyzing Concentration Profiles with Varying Le Using Artificial Neural Networks and BVP4C

In Figure 13.15, the concentration profile produced for various Le using the ANN and BVP4C (MATLAB's boundary value problem solver) approaches is contrasted in the picture. A smaller concentration boundary layer is indicated by a sharper decrease in the concentration profile at higher Le. This implies that concentration decays more quickly when Le rises because molecular diffusion becomes weaker.

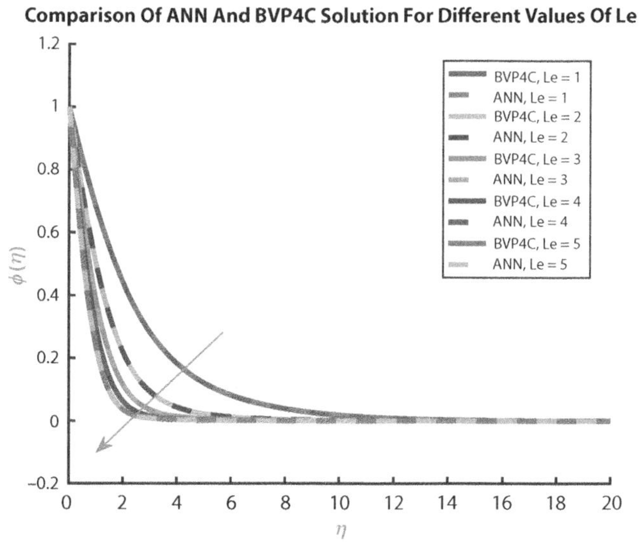

Figure 13.15 Comparison graph of ANN and BVP4C for various values of Le.

13.3.2 Results of Artificial Neural Networks and BVP4C Comparison

Although there are minor variations between the ANN and BVP4C curves, their general patterns are the same. The fundamental physics of the concentration boundary layer behavior is effectively captured by the ANN approach. The ANN technique solves the boundary value problem associated with mass transfer efficiently by approximating the BVP4C method. The ANN is a good substitute for conventional numerical solvers like BVP4C because of its capacity to generate precise results with little processing overhead. As Le rises, concentration decays more quickly, and ANN-based solutions closely match the BVP4C results, demonstrating their applicability to problems involving fluid flow and heat/mass transfer.

In Figure 13.16, the great agreement between the two approaches is demonstrated by the near overlap between the BVP4C and ANN solutions in the given velocity profile. For various values of M, the two lines align almost perfectly, indicating that the ANN model successfully reproduces the numerical outcomes from BVP4C. This robust correlation confirms the ANN approach's precision and dependability in resolving the specified boundary value issue. High velocity profile precision may be maintained while using ANN as a reliable substitute for traditional numerical solvers, as demonstrated by the consistency of the two approaches.

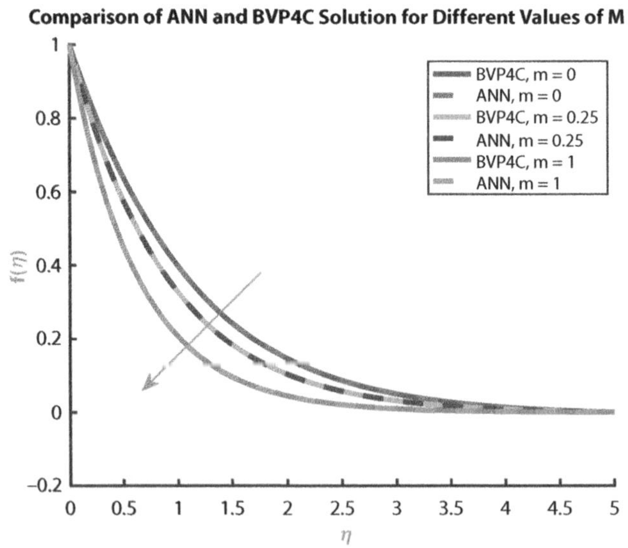

Figure 13.16 A comparison graph of ANN and BVP4C for various values of M.

Table 13.1 reveals how the various parameters influence skin friction C_f, heat transfer Nu, and mass transfer Sh Drag, is indicated by skin friction, which is always negative and changes with n, We, M, and Pr where increasing n and reducing drag. Higher values for increasing Pr and Nb indicate greater heat transfer under these circumstances, as shown by the Nusselt number (Nu), which ranges from 0.2518 to 0.4642. Both Le and Pr have a major impact on the Sherwood number (Sh), which ranges from 0.1866 to 0.5565. Lower Le values result in less mass transfer. Heat transmission depends critically on radiation (Nr), with lower Nr lowering Nu. Overall, fluid behavior is determined by the interaction of these characteristics; some have an impact on friction, while others impact mass

Table 13.1 Effect of skin friction, Nusselt number, Sherwood number on n, We, M, Pr, Le, Nb, Nt.

n	We	M	Pr	Le	Nb	Nt	C_f	Nu	Sh
0.1	0.5	0.5	0.5	3	0.5	0.5	-0.9159	0.4431	0.5435
0.2	0.5	0.5	0.5	3	0.5	0.5	-0.8502	0.4383	0.5309
0.3	0.1	0.5	0.5	3	0.5	0.5	-0.8087	0.4353	0.5228
0.3	0.2	0.5	0.5	3	0.5	0.5	-0.8010	0.4347	0.5209
0.3	0.5	0.1	0.5	3	0.5	0.5	-0.6007	0.4482	0.5565
0.3	0.5	0.2	0.5	3	0.5	0.5	-0.6493	0.4435	0.5447
0.3	0.5	0.5	0.1	3	0.5	0.5	-0.7761	0.4085	0.2562
0.3	0.5	0.5	0.2	3	0.5	0.5	-0.7761	0.4159	0.3182
0.3	0.5	0.5	0.5	0.1	0.5	0.5	-0.7761	0.4454	0.1866
0.3	0.5	0.5	0.5	0.2	0.5	0.5	-0.7761	0.4448	0.1964
0.3	0.5	0.5	0.5	3	0.1	0.5	-0.7761	0.4642	0.3454
0.3	0.5	0.5	0.5	3	0.2	0.5	-0.7761	0.4561	0.4515
0.3	0.5	0.5	0.5	3	0.5	0.1	-0.7761	0.4536	0.5312
0.3	0.5	0.5	0.5	3	0.5	0.2	-0.7761	0.4483	0.5254
0.3	0.5	0.5	0.5	3	0.5	0.5	-0.7761	0.2518	0.4975
0.3	0.5	0.5	0.5	3	0.5	0.5	-0.7761	0.2719	0.5006

Table 13.2 Comparing of $f''(0)$ with earlier published data for various values of M when $We = n = 0$.

M	Hussain *et al.* [21]	Amjad *et al.* [20]	BVP4C	ANN
0	-1.0000	-1.0000	-1.0000	-1.0000
0.25	-1.118	-1.11803	-1.11804	-1.11803
1	-1.4137	-1.41421	-1.41421	-1.41421

diffusion and temperature. Table 13.2 shows a strong agreement among all approaches when comparing the findings for various values of M across several studies of BVP4C and ANN (Hussain *et al.* [21], Amjad *et al.* [20]). All methods produce −1.0000 for M=0, showing complete consistency. Although there are minor differences at M=0.25, the BVP4C and ANN findings (−1.11804) are almost the same as those of Amjad *et al.* (−1.11803), indicating great accuracy. Similarly, for M=1, Hussain *et al.* (−1.4137) exhibited a little divergence, although BVP4C and ANN both match Amjad *et al.* (−1.41421). Given that the study is based on BVP4C and ANN, the high degree of agreement with earlier research confirms the precision and dependability of the methodology and shows how well it solves the problem with little numerical errors.

13.4 Conclusion

The impact of important parameters on fluid flow: As the Weissenberg number (We) and magnetic parameter (M) rise, the velocity decreases due to Lorentz and elastic force effects, lowering the velocity boundary layer.

Effects of Heat: The temperature profile decreases as the Pr increases due to decreased thermal diffusivity; on the other hand, heat transmission improves when the Nt and Nb increase.

Because of increased heat diffusion and dispersion, thermophoresis raises concentration, whereas the Le and Brownian motion lower it.

When compared to BVP4C, the ANN model approximates the numerical solution with competitive accuracy and offers advantages in generalization and processing efficiency.

Error Analysis: The ANN model shows little overfitting, and training, validation, and test errors all show a consistent decreasing trend, suggesting high performance.

Practical Implications: The results apply to industrial processes where non-Newtonian fluids are essential, such as polymer processing, MHD-based heat transfer, and biomedical applications.

Future Scope: The use of ANN in resolving intricate fluid dynamics issues may be further improved by expanding the study to incorporate turbulent flow, multi-phase interactions, and real-time machine learning predictions.

References

1. Shahzad, F., Sagheer, M., Hussain, S., MHD tangent hyperbolic nanofluid with chemical reaction, viscous dissipation and Joule heating effects. *AIP Adv.*, 9, 25007, 2019.
2. Ullah, Z. and Zaman, G., Lie group analysis of magnetohydrodynamic tangent hyperbolic fluid flow towards a stretching sheet with slip conditions. *Heliyon*, 3, e00443, 2017.
3. Akbar, N.S., Nadeem, S., Haq, R.U., Khan, Z.H., Numerical solutions of magnetohydrodynamic boundary layer flow of tangent hyperbolic fluid towards a stretching sheet. *Indian J. Phys.*, 87, 1121–1124, 2013.
4. Ibrahim, W., Magnetohydrodynamics (MHD) flow of a tangent hyperbolic fluid with nanoparticles past a stretching sheet with second order slip and convective boundary condition. *Results Phys.*, 7, 3723–3731, 2017.
5. Andersson, H.I., MHD flow of a viscoelastic fluid past a stretching surface. *Acta Mech.*, 95, 227–230, 1992.
6. Kameswaran, P.K., Shaw, S., Sibanda, P., Murthy, P., Homogeneous–heterogeneous reactions in a nanofluid flow due to a porous stretching sheet. *Int. J. Heat Mass Tran.*, 57, 465–472, 2013.
7. Chakrabarti, A. and Gupta, A.S., Hydromagnetic flow and heat transfer over a stretching sheet. *Q. Appl. Math.*, 37, 73–78, 1979.
8. Khan, M., Hussain, A., Malik, M.Y., Salahuddin, T., Khan, F., Boundary layer flow of MHD tangent hyperbolic nanofluid over a stretching sheet: a numerical investigation. *Results Phys.*, 7, 2837–2844, 2017.
9. Malik, M.Y., Salahuddin, T., Hussain, A., Bilal, S., MHD flow of tangent hyperbolic fluid over a stretching cylinder: using Keller box method. *J. Magn. Magn. Mater.*, 395, 271–276, 2015.
10. Zhang, C.-W., Ou, J.-P., Zhang, J.-Q., Parameter optimization and analysis of a vehicle suspension system controlled by magnetorheological fluid dampers. *Struct. Control Heal. Monit. Off. J. Int. Assoc. Struct. Control Monit. Eur. Assoc. Control Struct.*, 13, 885–896, 2006.

11. Mousavi, S.M., Darzi, A.A.R., Ali Akbari, O., Toghraie, D., Marzban, A., Numerical study of biomagnetic fluid flow in a duct with a constriction affected by a magnetic field. *J. Magn. Magn. Mater.*, 473, 42–50, 2019. I. Ahmed *et al.* Heliyon 9 (2023) e17658 10.
12. Sarlak, R., Yousefzadeh, S., Akbari, O.A., Toghraie, D., Sarlak, S., others, The investigation of simultaneous heat transfer of water/Al2O3 nanofluid in a close enclosure by applying homogeneous magnetic field. *Int. J. Mech. Sci.*, 133, 674–688, 2017.
13. Toghraie, D., Alempour, S.M., Afrand, M., Experimental determination of viscosity of water-based magnetite nanofluid for application in heating and cooling systems. *J. Magn. Magn. Mater.*, 417, 243–248, 2016.
14. Barnoon, P., Toghraie, D., Eslami, F., Mehmandoust, B., Entropy generation analysis of different nanofluid flows in the space between two concentric horizontal pipes in the presence of magnetic field: single-phase and two-phase approaches. *Comput. Math. Appl.*, 77, 662–692, 2019.
15. Wang, F., Asjad, M.I., Rehman, S.U., Ali, B., Hussain, S., Gia, T.N., Muhammad, T., MHD Williamson nanofluid flow over a slender elastic sheet of irregular thickness in the presence of bioconvection. *Nanomaterials*, 11, 2297, 2021.
16. Amjad, M., Khan, M.N., Ahmed, K., Ahmed, I., Akbar, T., Eldin, S.M., Magnetohydrodynamics tangent hyperbolic nanofluid flow over an exponentially stretching sheet: numerical investigation. *Case Stud. Therm. Eng.*, 45, 102900, 2023.
17. Li, Y.-X., Alshbool, M.H., Lv, Y.-P., Khan, I., Khan, M.R., Issakhov, A., Heat and mass transfer in MHD Williamson nanofluid flow over an exponentially porous stretching surface. *Case Stud. Therm. Eng.*, 26, 100975, 2021.
18. Ahmed, K., Akbar, T., Muhammad, T., Alghamdi, M., Heat transfer characteristics of MHD flow of Williamson nanofluid over an exponential permeable stretching curved surface with variable thermal conductivity. *Case Stud. Therm. Eng.*, 28, 101544, 2021.
19. Amjad, M., Ahmed, K., Akbar, T., Muhammad, T., Ahmed, I., Alshomrani, A.S., Numerical investigation of double diffusion heat flux model in Williamson nanofluid over an exponentially stretching surface with variable thermal conductivity. *Case Stud. Therm. Eng.*, 36, 102231, 2022.
20. Amjad, M., Khan, M.N., Ahmad, K., Ahmad, I., Akbar, T., Eldin, S.M., Magnetohydrodynamics tangent hyperbolic nanofluid flow over an especially stretching sheet: Numerical investigation. *Case Stud. Therm. Eng.*, 45, 102900, 2023.
21. Hussain, A., Malik, M.Y., Awais, M., Salahuddin, T., Bilal, S., Computational and physical aspects of MHD Prandtl-Eyring fluid flow analysis over a stretching sheet. *Nural. Comput. Appl.*, 31, 425–433, 2019.
22. Ahmad, I., Alghamdi, M., Amjad, M., Aziz, F., Akbar, T., Muhammad, T., Numerically Investigation of MHD flow of hyperbolic tangent nanofluid over a non-linear stretching sheet. *Helion*, 9, e17658, 2023.

14

Case Studies of Artificial Intelligence in Industrial Fluid and Thermal Processes

Abdulhalim Musa Abubakar[1]*, Kiran Batool[2], Muhammad Asif[3] and Baudilio Coto[4]

[1]*Department of Chemical Engineering, Faculty of Engineering, Modibbo Adama University, Yola, Adamawa State, Nigeria*
[2]*Beijing Key Laboratory of New Energy and Low Carbon Development, School of Economics and Management, North China Electric Power University, Beijing, China*
[3]*Department of Energy and Environment, Faculty of Agricultural Engineering (FAE), Sindh Agriculture University, Tandojam, Hyderabad, Pakistan*
[4]*Chemical, Energy, and Mechanical Technology Department, School of Experimental Sciences and Technology (ESCET), Rey Juan Carlos University, Móstoles, Madrid, Spain*

Abstract

This review discusses the application of artificial intelligence (AI) in industrial fluid flow and heat transfer operations. It provides a critical overview of case studies demonstrating the effectiveness of AI-based applications. *Ab initio*, the scope is set, and it is on various industrial applications such as chemical processing, power generation, and manufacturing, where fluid dynamics and heat transfer are significant. The overarching goal is to harness AI to automate processes, lower energy consumption, improve system efficiency, and predict maintenance needs, thereby reducing operational costs and promoting sustainability. Machine learning (ML), neural networks (NN), and predictive modeling are the AI approaches employed. These methods are utilized in conjunction with computational fluid dynamics (CFD) simulations as well as online data analysis to gain a better understanding of process control and decision making. To a greater extent, the review is focused

**Corresponding author*: abdulhalim@mau.edu.ng; ORCID: https://orcid.org/0000-0002-1304-3515
Kiran Batool: ORCID: https://orcid.org/0000-0002-3660-7029
Baudilio Coto: ORCID: https://orcid.org/0000-0002-5354-5077

Mukesh Kumar Awasthi and Reshu Gupta (eds.) Artificial Intelligence and Computational Modeling in Heat Transfer and Fluid Dynamics, (365–394) © 2026 Scrivener Publishing LLC

on specific industrial case studies where AI has been utilized efficiently, such as heat exchanger optimization, improvement in reactor fluid mixing, and electronic component thermal management. All case studies are analyzed on the grounds of problem definition, the development of the AI model, and evaluation. Key findings from the case studies that were conducted were that AI could potentially increase prediction accuracy for heat transfer and fluid flow, and could lead to better process optimization and planning of resources. Issues associated with quality data demand and integrating AI with existing installed industrial systems were noted, and recommendations were provided on how to work around these drawbacks.

***Keywords*:** Industrial fluid, heat transfer, computational fluid dynamics, machine learning, predictive modeling

14.1 Introduction

Critical factors that play a pivotal role in ensuring efficiency, performance, and sustainability in various industrial processes are fluid flow and heat transfer [108]. In chemical processing, energy production, automotive, and manufacturing industries, the proper management of fluid flow and heat transfer is essential for optimizing operations and minimizing energy consumption [55, 97]. Fluid flow is involved in transporting and transporting materials, chemicals, gases, and so on *via* pipes [115], pumps [101] and systems, and it is directly related to the speed and economy of production [66, 76]. Conversely, heat transfer plays a crucial role in regulating system temperature, which directly influences product quality and the overall longevity of the system [81]. Heat transfer is an indispensable process that is extensively implemented in heat exchangers [128], cooling towers [112], furnaces [105], and others, to control temperatures and avoid overheating or underheating. It may as well cause equipment failure, reduced efficiency, and even safety hazards. Power generation is so dependent on heat transfer used to draw energy from the fuel sources and convert it to usable electricity, and manage heat effectively [22, 85]. Performance and safety are essential, but now also issues of effective fluid flow and heat transfer are paramount for process sustainability in industry [55, 66]. This will lead to a reduction in companies' energy consumption, waste minimization, and a decrease in operational costs [11, 14, 65, 117] Babanezhad *et al.* [11] highlighted that advanced technologies, such as AI and computational fluid dynamics (CFD), enable improved monitoring, modeling, and optimization of fluid flow and heat transfer, leading to more precise control and enhanced process design.

The contribution and objective of this review are unique and can be compared with related studies previously conducted. Previously, Suh *et al.* [121] and Suh *et al.* [122] examined AI in phase-change heat transfer, emphasizing boiling and condensation phenomena, whereas the current study focuses broadly on diverse industrial applications of AI in fluid and thermal processes, including heat exchangers and thermal management. Mehraj *et al.* [83] applied AI to thermal energy storage (TES) tank design, with bibliometric analysis highlighting optimization in structural design. The current work extends beyond TES to cover real-time data analytics and predictive modeling across varied industrial systems, broadening the scope. Moreso: Kruse & Åhag [68] used ML for quality improvement in heat treatment of steel rods, comparing algorithms to optimize production; Sofos *et al.* [119] focused on fluid research *via* AI/ML, with a highlight on computational methods and algorithm performance for fluid properties; Felde [36] explored biomimetic and AI methods in heat treatment processes, emphasizing computational simulations; Bangera & Bhat [13] applied AI in oil and gas industries, emphasizing reservoir evaluation and drilling optimization and lastly; Supan [124] developed an AI module for thermodynamics education, focusing on vapor power plants. Differently, the current review explores various AI techniques in industrial applications, featuring case studies on fluid mixing, reactor optimization, and cooling systems. It discussed the integration of CFD and AI for improved process control, emphasizing predictive maintenance and real-time analytics. While highlighting fluid and thermal optimization, the present work concentrates on general industrial use rather than the oil and gas sector or educational contexts. Presently, our focus is on practical, industry-relevant AI applications with actionable insights. Industrial fluids are lubricants, coolants and refrigerants, solvents, cleaning fluids, fuel oil, water-based fluids, chemicals and additives, compressed gases, heat transfer fluids, specialty fluids, process fluids, sealants, and hydraulic fluids.

14.2 Artificial Intelligence Techniques in Fluid Flow and Heat Transfer

Artificial intelligence is a powerful tool to tackle fluid flow and heat transfer challenges that are extremely important in industry, such as energy, manufacturing, and chemical processing [97]. It is suggested that AI techniques provide new modeling, analysis, and optimization approaches to those processes that are often more accurate and more efficient than traditional computational methods. Rahman *et al.* [107] described data-driven approaches that enable the input of AI to the fields of fluid dynamics and thermal interactions, giving insight into phenomena that are hard to ascertain by normal methods. For instance, ML algorithms figure prominently in the AI adoption for the fluid flow and heat transfer problems [132, 140]. Support vector machines [86], decision trees [69], and gradient boosting are used to analyze a large dataset of sensors and simulation [79]. In this sense, they ensure the prediction of the flow behavior, as well as the identification of the patterns in heat distribution and in real-time optimization of the system performance [43]. For instance, ML is used to find anomalies in cooling systems or to optimize the design of heat exchangers based on the configurations that minimize the energy loss [28, 63]. In fluid and thermal systems, neural networks (NNs), especially deep learning (DL) models, it has been successfully applied to handle nonlinear problems [19]. Modeling of complex heat transfer scenarios and transient flow behavior is posed by convolutional neural networks, as well as recurrent neural networks. Particularly in the cases of turbulence modeling, where conventional techniques often face challenges in accuracy [102, 135], NNs offer unique advantages. Whereas, predictive modeling is used to combine historical data with real-time inputs to forecast the future system behavior under different conditions [58]. It is widely used in preventive maintenance, as well as in optimization of the operational parameters such as the coolant flow rates [8] or the heat exchanger geometry to achieve the desirable values of performance metrics with the minimized energy consumption [14, 117]. Modeling and analysis of fluid flow and heat transfer systems has been significantly advanced by amalgamating AI with CFD [81, 126]. Computational fluid dynamics offers detailed simulations of the fluid and thermal phenomena, and it is computationally expensive and time-consuming but especially for large-scale or real-time applications [91, 125]. Computational fluid dynamics and AI work together as a surrogate model, being able to complete faster predictions of fluid behavior by using CFD available data to train the AI [12, 91]. And in that sense, NN can approximate the CFD solutions similar to Jung and Kwon [61], which drastically lowers computational overhead, as well as retains high accuracy. Research by Naderi *et al.* [87] illustrates that the combination helps industries to explore various design scenarios, perform more efficient processes, as well as analyze process sensitivity. Based on these reasons, ideally, CFD data should receive AI-driven insights for flow instability identification, boundary condition optimization. and meshing strategy improvement since it should enhance simulation fidelity, as well as operational performances [99]. According to Ferencz *et al.* [39], real-time data analytics continuously analyze sensor data from industrial systems. Through that, AI models detect anomalies, predict the system behavior, as well as generate valuable insights in real-time. For example, in cases where it is necessary to dynamically adapt to dynamic conditions to maintain optimum performance [54, 67, 139], as in cooling systems [141], heating, ventilation, and air conditioning (HVAC) units [17], and heat exchangers [31, 139] require instantaneous adjustment.

14.3 Artificial Intelligence in Chemical Processing Industries

The application of AI technologies in process industries is for optimizing operations, improving efficiency, and enhancing safety in heat exchangers [65], distillation columns [95], and reactors, etc. [116], to mention a few.

14.3.1 Case Study 1: Optimizing Heat Exchangers

Applying AI to optimize heat exchangers depends on the type of the unit, as different heat exchanger designs have distinct operating principles, configurations, and optimization requirements [76], as shown in Table 14.1.

Companies currently demonstrating the role of AI are Canvass AI, Siemens, and UptimeAI. In addition, design-focused solutions from Neural Concept and Diabatix enhance efficiency and material use, as reviewed by Lodhi *et al.* [76].

14.3.2 Case Study 2: Enhancing Fluid Mixing in Reactors

In chemical reactors, AI facilitates precise control over reaction parameters, namely, temperature, pressure, and reactant flow rates, as shown in Table 14.2. Advanced algorithms optimize reaction conditions to enhance the yield and selectivity while minimizing by-product formation.

Artificial intelligence also aids in modeling complex reaction mechanisms and predicting the behavior of novel catalysts, accelerating process development.

14.3.3 Case Study 3: Distillation Columns

Distillation columns, critical for separation processes, benefit from AI's capability to optimize energy use and improve separation efficiency [95], as presented in Table 14.3. Through the analysis of parameters such as

Table 14.1 Heat exchanger type and AI optimization case study.

Type	Artificial intelligence role	Issues detection	Optimization	Literature
Shell-and-Tube	Monitor parameters (e.g., shell-side and tube-side flow rates, fouling factors, and pressure drop)	Tube leaks, blockages, or flow maldistribution	Cleaning schedules	[32, 109]
Plate	Analyzing flow patterns, pressure drops, operational stress, and temperature variation	Fouling or scaling on plates	Heat transfer, cleaner intervals, and gasket life	[64]
Air-Cooled	Controlling fan speeds, airflow rates, and ambient temperature impacts	Overheating and fan or fin fouling	Positioning of louvers and maintenance schedules	[23, 42]
Double-Pipe	Predict performance degradation over time	Fouling in the inner or outer pipe	Flow	[104]
Compact or Microchannel	Maximizing efficiency	Fouling, flow maldistribution, and manufacturing tolerances	Design and operational parameters	[57, 123]
Regenerative	Monitor heat recovery efficiency, predict thermal stress, and balance thermal cycles	Exchanger's longevity and thermal losses	Switching times	[90]
Specialized (cryogenic, spiral, or plate-fin)	Handling non-Newtonian fluids or phase changes	Extreme temperature differentials	Heat transfer efficiency and thermal losses	[2, 34]

Table 14.2 Artificial intelligence's importance to chemical reactors' performance.

Artificial intelligence technology	Parameters optimized	Company name	Challenge	Emphasis
Predictive Analytics	Reaction temperature, pressure, catalyst activity, and reaction kinetics	Canvass AI	Optimizing reactor efficiency and reducing energy consumption	[80, 94]
Machine Learning	Heat transfer rates, flow patterns, and fouling prediction	Neural Concept	Managing complex thermal and flow dynamics in reactors	[21, 142]
Generative Design	Reactor geometry, mixing efficiency, and material utilization	Diabatix	Improving reactor design to maximize throughput and minimize costs	[51]
Digital Twin (DT) Technology	Real-time monitoring, anomaly detection, and operational adjustments	Siemens	Preventing downtime and ensuring consistent reactor performance	[20]
Internet-of-Things-Enabled Data Collection	Process parameters and the wear and tear of components	XMPro	Enhancing data-driven decision-making for maintenance and performance	[3]
Advanced Computational Simulations	Reaction pathways and multi-phase flow optimization	UptimeAI	Handling complex multi-phase reactions and scaling up laboratory processes	[15]

Table 14.3 Artificial intelligence application for an efficient distillation column run.

Name of industry	Location and country	Artificial intelligence application	Problem solved	Source
Eneos Corporation	Tokyo, Japan	Artificial intelligence-driven process control for distillation columns	Improved separation of products with similar boiling points and balanced use of variable waste heat sources	[52, 60]
JSR Corporation	Yokkaichi, Japan	Reinforcement learning (RL), AI for autonomous control of distillation processes	Maintained stable operations and optimized performance over extended periods	[47]
Chemical Processing Industry	Not specified	Machine learning-based predictive models for energy optimization in distillation processes	Reduced energy consumption and enhanced process efficiency	[98]
Oklahoma State University Research	Stillwater, Oklahoma, USA	Digital twin systems for distillation column simulation and design enhancement	Improved process efficiency and reduced operational costs through detailed simulations	[37]

feed composition, reflux ratio, and column pressure, AI algorithms can dynamically adjust operations to maintain product purity while minimizing energy consumption [84]. Fault detection systems powered by AI also ensure timely identification of flooding or weeping issues to prevent costly disruptions [73, 82].

The NNs are increasingly applied in distillation columns to optimize the separation process by predicting and controlling key variables such as temperature, pressure, and flow rates [45]. By simply learning complex nonlinear relationships from process data, NNs enhance efficiency, improve product purity, eliminate faults, and reduce energy consumption in distillation operations [44, 82].

14.4 Artificial Intelligence in Power Generation

14.4.1 Case Study 4: Improving Thermal Efficiency in Power Plants

Using sophisticated ML techniques, very large amounts of sensor and operational log dataset data are analyzed to develop AI models [110]. Most models are trained to predict plant performance metrics, how to optimize combustion processes, and get the best out of the heat transfer systems with minimal loss of energy [131]. For instance, AI algorithms can dynamically adjust boiler settings, turbine speeds, and cooling rates to optimize efficiency as loads change. Rigorous testing and validation of the performance of these AI models is important as they are evaluated in terms of performance against historical data, as well as real-time operating scenarios. To ensure the models are yielding reliable and actionable insight, key metrics such as prediction, accuracy, and response time, as well as robustness under fluctuating conditions, are analyzed. Furthermore, the performance metrics are quite often based on root mean square error and mean absolute error, which aim to measure the degree to which the AI predicts the plant behavior. Yoon & Park [138] previously quantified the F-value during the thermal processing of still cans with the use of CFD. If these models are continuously refined through feedback loops and domain-specific knowledge, the power plants can substantially improve thermal efficiency, decrease carbon footprints, and energy production that is guaranteed to be sustainable.

14.4.2 Case Study 5: AI-Driven Cooling System Optimization

With seemingly advanced types of algorithms, AI can then analyze the real-time data coming in from sensors that monitor the temperature, pressure, and flow rates in a cooling system. These insights provide the basis for building capabilities such as prescriptive and predictive capabilities to respond to variations in thermal loads, as practiced by Gupta and Kukreja [49]. Consequently, it guarantees a consistent performance with minimum energy consumption. In addition, as stated before, AI models take notice of inefficiencies caused by the fouling in the heat exchangers or the uneven cooling distribution that may need to be maintained or designed appropriately [46]. This is done by assuming that, using DTs and ML, cooling systems can simulate different scenarios to predict outcomes and configure the optimum, without stopping the operations. The foregone technologies are very useful in data centers, power plants, and manufacturing facilities, as accurate thermal management is vital for ensuring system reliability and preventing system downtimes [5]. AI-driven cooling optimization improves operational efficiency, and leads to operational excellence; in addition to mitigating environmental impact in line with the intention toward more sustainable industrial practices.

14.5 Artificial Intelligence in Manufacturing and Electronic Components

14.5.1 Case Study 6: Thermal Management of Electronic Components

Table 14.4 highlights the integration of AI in the thermal management of electronic components. Also contained in Table 14.4 is a demonstration of how AI applications contribute to improving efficiency, longevity, and performance through various methods such as predictive modeling, reinforcement learning (RL), and real-time optimization.

For AI applications in thermal management (see Table 14.4), electronic components implied for thermal management are usually high-performance, heat-sensitive devices such as microprocessors [35], semiconductors [25], power electronics [56, 70] and integrated circuits [27]. In advanced computing systems [88], smartphones [62], as well as other high-density electronic devices [7]. Heat is generated as the components operate because they are significant. To unlock this domain, AI applications are optimizing cooling mechanisms, such as heat sinks [1], fans [71], thermal pad [106, 129], and manage heat distribution through the system to avoid hot spots [75, 103]. In applications including GPUs, memory chips, and power transistors used in everything from consumer electronics to industrial machinery [30, 134]. Real-time temperature fluctuations of AI models can be predicted by AI models [41], enabling adjustment in thermal management systems, which is critical.

Table 14.4 Artificial intelligence applications in the thermal management of electronic components.

Name of industry	Location and country	Artificial intelligence applications	Problem solved	Source
Intel Corporation	Santa Clara, California, USA	Artificial intelligence-based predictive modeling for thermal management	Enhanced cooling efficiency and optimized heat dissipation for high-performance processors	[8]
Samsung Electronics	Suwon, South Korea	Reinforcement learning for cooling system optimization	Improved thermal regulation in mobile devices and reduction of overheating issues	[48]
AMD Corporation	Sunnyvale, California, USA	Artificial intelligence-driven optimization of heat sink design	Increased heat transfer efficiency and prolonged lifespan of processors	[113]
Rambus Inc.	Sunnyvale, California, USA	Machine learning for dynamic thermal management in DRAM	Enhanced DRAM stability and performance during intensive computing tasks	[96]
TSMC	Hsinchu, Taiwan	Machine learning for real-time thermal monitoring	Enabled real-time adjustments to cooling systems, improving chip performance and lifespan	[130]
University of Cambridge	Cambridge, UK	Deep learning for thermal simulation and analysis	Optimized thermal management in electronic components, reducing power consumption	[100]
NVIDIA Corporation	Santa Clara, California, USA	Predictive AI for GPU thermal performance optimization	Enhanced cooling system efficiency and extended GPU lifespan	[136]

GPU: Graphics Processing Units; DRAM: Dynamic Random-Access Memory; TSMC: Taiwan Semiconductor Manufacturing Company Limited; AMD: Advanced Micro Devices

14.5.2 Case Study 7: AI for Fluid Flow Optimization in Manufacturing Processes

Numerous AI techniques, including regression analysis [16], support vector machines [29], RL [74], fuzzy logic [127], genetic algorithm [78], and convolutional neural networks, can be used in several ways to optimize fluid flow in manufacturing plants [59], in ways described in Table 14.5.

However, for many fluid flow optimization tasks, the development of AI techniques especially fuzzy logic [10, 93, 140] and genetic algorithm [77, 111], has been used on fluid flow optimization for instance in optimization of the balance between multiple systems parameters or to develop the design of component that includes heat exchangers [120] and pumps [33]. Uncertainties of fluid flow behavior and their approximate solutions

Table 14.5 Research on fluid flow optimization using AI in manufacturing.

Process type	Artificial intelligence role	Issues detection	Optimization	References
Additive Manufacturing	Monitoring and controlling the flow of materials in 3D printing processes	Clogging or irregular material extrusion	Material flow optimization, print speed, and quality	[53]
Injection Molding	Analyzing pressure and temperature profiles in mold cavities	Resin flow imbalance or air pockets	Optimal injection speed, pressure, and temperature	[114]
Extrusion	Predicting and monitoring the flow of polymer melts in extrusion lines	Blockages, fluctuations in flow, or uneven thickness	Pressure control, cooling rates, and material consistency	[137]
Microfluidics	Optimizing fluid flow in microchannels for lab-on-a-chip systems	Flow maldistribution, air bubbles, or clogging	Fluid distribution, pumping efficiency, and droplet formation	[9]
Pipe Networks	Monitoring and controlling fluid dynamics in pipe networks	Pressure drops, leaks, or flow maldistribution	Pipeline optimization, leak detection, and flow control	[26]
Cooling Systems	Controlling fluid flow rates and temperatures in cooling loops	Temperature inconsistencies or system failures	Heat dissipation, pump efficiency, and fluid flow rates	[72]
Fuel Cells	Optimizing flow in fuel cell systems for improved efficiency	Uneven fuel distribution or flow resistance	Optimal fuel distribution, temperature, and pressure	[38]
Hydraulic Systems	Predicting flow in hydraulic machinery	Blockages, leaks, or inconsistent flow rates	Pump optimization, flow distribution, and pressure management	[40]

are useful in systems which depend on the fluid flow behavior in which the fluid flow behavior is unpredictable [50].

14.6 Challenges, Limitations, and Recommended Solutions

For training robust AI models, high-quality data is needed, which is accurate, consistent, and representative of the operational conditions. However, sensors restrain such data acquisition, and industries often cannot acquire such data because of the sparsity of data, inconsistency in the recording and storage systems. In addition, historical data may be incomplete or not annotated, thereby hindering its use to learn from supervised learning. The final consideration is that the availability of data is another concern — there may be data available for what is being simulated, but no data available for what the simulation being performed is engaging in, i.e., rare faults or extreme conditions. The model is thus restricted to generalizing and predicting behavior in diverse conditions. To solve these problems, advanced data preprocessing techniques such as noise reduction, outlier detection, and normalization methods are used to enhance data quality [6, 92]. Synthetic data generation and augmentation fill in the gaps to fill in a dataset, further helping to train these AI models with diverse, comprehensive training examples. The fundamental part to build reliable, efficient, and scalable AI-driven solutions in industrial settings, as depicted in Table 14.6, is to ensure that the data is qualitative and available.

Many industrial setups use classical control systems and hardware that are not compatible with modern AI-based solutions, which creates a messy seamless integration. In addition, there is also a need for sophisticated interfaces and communications protocols to synchronize the residual legacy systems and AI models to avoid operational disruptions [118]. Similarly, the integration process also requires fine-tuning to the calibration so that the outputs of AI match with the already existing workflow, safety, and compliance standards [4]. For example, AI applications within fluid and thermal systems must complement rather than replace established control mechanisms to maintain the reliability [18]. Resistance to change on the part of operators uninformed of AI technology can likewise block adoption, requiring their enrollment into training programs and phased implementation. In other words, modular AI architectures and retrofitting approaches were studied for minimizing the interference of new systems with existing systems [65]. The smooth integration is promoted

Table 14.6 Computational challenges in applying AI to industrial fluid and thermal transfer systems.

Challenge	Description	Impact	Mitigation strategies
Data Quality and Availability	Lack of high-quality, labeled data for training AI models.	Reduces model accuracy and reliability.	Implement advanced preprocessing, synthetic data generation, and data augmentation techniques.
Computational Complexity	High computational demands for simulating and optimizing complex fluid and thermal transfer systems.	Increases computational cost and time, limiting real-time applications.	Use high-performance computing, cloud-based platforms, and efficient AI algorithms.
Real-Time Processing	Difficulty in processing large-scale sensor data in real-time.	Delays decision-making and control system responses.	Implement edge computing and optimized streaming algorithms to handle real-time data efficiently.
Model Generalization	Artificial intelligence models may struggle to adapt to varying operating conditions.	Leads to poor performance under different or unseen conditions.	Train models with diverse datasets, use transfer learning, and continuously update models based on new operational data.
Interpretability and Transparency	The black-box nature of AI models makes it hard to explain their decisions.	Hinders trust and adoption in safety-critical systems.	Employ explainable AI techniques and integrate domain knowledge to enhance interpretability.
Integration with Legacy Systems	Difficulty in integrating AI with existing industrial setups and equipment.	Causes operational disruptions and increases implementation costs.	Use modular, interoperable AI solutions, and phased implementation approaches.
Scalability	Challenges in scaling AI solutions to large or multiple facilities.	Limits widespread adoption and benefits across the industry.	Design scalable AI architectures and adopt cloud-based deployment for handling larger datasets and operations.
Cybersecurity Risks	Vulnerabilities in AI-driven systems are exposed to cyber threats.	Potential operational disruptions and data breaches.	Implement robust cybersecurity measures, including encryption, firewalls, and AI-based intrusion detection systems.
Validation and Testing	Ensuring AI models are rigorously validated under various conditions.	Risks of deploying underperforming models in critical systems.	Develop comprehensive testing protocols and validate models using historical and real-world operational data.

Figure 14.1 Artificial intelligence companies that are impactful in chemical industries across the globe.

by open-source tools and interoperable platforms, while the pilot testing makes sure that the AI solutions are tuned to perfection before large-scale deployment. Figure 14.1 and Table 14.7 depict industries now practically utilizing AI technologies supplied by some globally prominent companies to run some important industrial operations.

Lots of companies prefer not to disclose their specific implementation to the public, as noticed in 'NS' entered in Table 14.7. Ndaba *et al.* [89] previously reviewed several case studies of ML application in design optimization, whose real implementation is spearheaded by Neural Concept company. Implementations of AI in industrial fluid and thermal processes are emerging in both Africa and Asia, though specific documented cases are limited. The only example is probably Thermon Africa, based in South Africa, that offers thermal engineering solutions, including process evaluation and optimization services. At an event dedicated to transforming process industries with AI, Process Innovation Asia Pacific—launched in Singapore in November 2024—emerged as a specialized process technology platform for Southeast Asia [133]. Research presented at the AIChE Spring Meeting discusses the combination of deterministic models with AI

Table 14.7 Artificial intelligence's implementation in industrial fluid and thermal processes.

Company	Role	Headquarters	Implemented At
General Electric	Artificial intelligence-driven optimization in power generation and water processing	Boston, Massachusetts, USA	NS
BrainBox AI	Artificial intelligence-based energy optimization for HVAC systems	Montreal, Canada	Dollar Tree, Cammeby's International, Sleep Country, Loyola University's Schreiber Center& SAIL Outdoors
GrayMatter Robotics	Artificial intelligence-powered robotic automation for industrial manufacturing	Los Angeles, California, USA	NS
Augury	Artificial intelligence-driven machine health monitoring and predictive maintenance	New York, USA	NS
EthonAI	Artificial intelligence for semiconductor and HVAC component manufacturing	Zurich, Switzerland	NS
Rahd AI	Artificial intelligence for oil and gas decommissioning cost reduction	United Kingdom	NS
BP and Palantir	Artificial intelligence-driven operational efficiency in the oil and gas industry	London, UK (BP); Denver, USA (Palantir)	BP
Canvass AI	Artificial intelligence-powered industrial process optimization and predictive analytics	Toronto, Canada	Stelco
Siemens	Artificial intelligence-enhanced industrial automation, energy, and manufacturing	Munich, Germany	JetZero
UpTime	Artificial intelligence-driven predictive maintenance for industrial equipment	California, USA	NS
Neural Concept	Artificial intelligence-driven design optimization for fluid and thermal simulations	Lausanne, Switzerland	NS
Diabatix	Artificial intelligence-powered generative design for thermal management	Leuven, Belgium	NS

**NS = Not specified*

to enhance industrial thermal systems, without discussing specific implementations in Asian industries [24].

14.7 Conclusion

Examples of transforming industrial fluid and thermal processes with the help of AI integration have existed, which include chemical processing, power generation, and manufacturing. Some of the reputed AI techniques applied in which industries have made outstanding process optimization, energy efficiency, and predictive maintenance applications are ML, predictive modeling, and NN. The case studies are documented to show that AI can overcome the most difficult challenges, enhance operational reliability, and reduce environmental footprints. The benefits of AI are shown, but so is the fact that data quality, integration with legacy systems, and real-time processing must be overcome to realize the full potential of AI. Advanced data preprocessing, modular AI architectures, and scalable deployment strategies can overcome industry limitations. As a result, the next step for future work is to promote the collaboration between domain experts and AI experts to develop more interpretable and transparent AI solutions.

References

1. Abdollahi, S.A., Basem, A., Alizadeh, A., Jasim, D.J., Ahmed, M., Sultan, A.J., Ranjbar, S.F., Maleki, H., Combining artificial intelligence and computational fluid dynamics for optimal design of laterally perforated finned heat sinks. *Results Eng.*, *21*, 102002, 2024. https://doi.org/10.1016/j.rineng.2024.102002.
2. Abolmaali, A.M. and Afshin, H., A design model for spiral wound heat exchangers which accounts for property variation, longitudinal heat conduction, and heat-in-leak. *Appl. Therm. Eng.*, *218*, 119262, 2023. https://doi.org/10.1016/j.applthermaleng.2022.119262.
3. Aboshosha, A., Haggag, A., George, N., Hamad, H.A., IoT-based data-driven predictive maintenance relying on fuzzy system and artificial neural networks. *Sci. Rep.*, *13*, 12186, 1–13, 2023. https://doi.org/10.1038/s41598-023-38887-z.
4. Abubakar, A.M., Artificial intelligence applications in engineering: A focus on software development and beyond. *Doupe J. Top Trending Technol. (DJTT)*, *1*, 1, 1–11, 2025. https://doi.org/10.71063/DJTTT.2025.1101.
5. Ahmed, I.A. and Asamoah, P.B., AI-driven predictive maintenance for energy infrastructure. *Int. J. Res. Sci. Innov. (IJRSI)*, *11*, 9, 507–528, 2024. https://doi.org/10.51244/IJRSI.2024.1109048.

6. Alasadi, S.A. and Bhaya, W.S., Review of data preprocessing techniques in data mining. *J. Eng. Appl. Sci.*, *12*, 16, 4102–4107, 2017. https://d1wqtxts1xzle7.cloudfront.net/54509277/4102-4107-libre.pdf.
7. Alhusseny, A., Al-Fatlawi, A., Al-Aabidy, Q., Nasser, A., Al-Zurfi, N., Dissipating the heat generated in high-performance electronics using graphitic foam heat-sinks cooled with a dielectric liquid. *Int. Commun. Heat Mass Transfer*, *127*, 105478, 2021. https://doi.org/10.1016/j.icheatmasstransfer.2021.105478.
8. Anwar, A., Talha, M., Hameed, A., Application of artificial intelligence in thermal management and wavelet analysis: A comprehensive review. *Preprints*, pp. 1–7, 2022. https://osf.io/preprints/d2vn3/.
9. Asadian, E., Bahramian, F., Siavashy, S., Movahedi, S., Keçili, R., Hussain, C.M., Ghorbani-Bidkorpeh, F., A review on recent advances of AI-integrated microfluidics for analytical and bioanalytical applications. *TrAC, Trends Anal. Chem.*, *181*, Part B, 2024. https://doi.org/10.1016/j.trac.2024.118004.
10. Attia, T.A.M. and Lashin, M.M.A., Using Fuzzy logic system to optimize measuring porosity by aerodynamics sensor. *Int. J. Mech. Prod. Eng. Res. Dev. (IJMPERD)*, *9*, 3, 1003–1013, 2019. http://www.tjprc.org.
11. Babanezhad, M., Behroyan, I., Nakhjiri, A.T., Marjani, A., Shirazian, S., Simulation of liquid flow with a combination artificial intelligence flow field and Adams–Bashforth method. *Sci. Rep.*, *10*, 16719, 2020. https://doi.org/10.1038/s41598-020-72602-6.
12. Babanezhad, M., Behroyan, I., Nakhjiri, A.T., Marjani, A., Shirazian, S., Performance and application analysis of ANFIS artificial intelligence for pressure prediction of nanofluid convective flow in a heated pipe. *Sci. Rep.*, *11*, 902, 2021. https://doi.org/10.1038/s41598-020-79628-w.
13. Bangera, S. and Bhat, S., Sustainability through artificial intelligence in oil and gas industry - A case study. *Int. J. Case Stud. Business IT Educ. (IJCSBE)*, *7*, 4, 353–365, 2023. https://doi.org/ht10.47992%2FIJCSBE.2581.6942.0324&from_ui=yes.
14. Bari, S. and Randhawa, T.S., Optimizing the design of heat exchangers to reduce the cost and maximize the production of freshwater using waste heat from a diesel-gen-set. *Int. J. Thermofluids*, *14*, 100142, 2022. https://doi.org/10.1016/j.ijft.2022.100142.
15. Bi, H.T. and Li, J., Multiscale analysis and modeling of multiphase chemical reactors. *Adv. Powder Technol.*, *15*, 6, 607–627, 2004. https://doi.org/10.1163/1568552042456223.
16. Bjernulf, W., *Regression and time estimation in the manufacturing industry*, O. Josefsson and M. Herschend (Eds.), Matematiska institutionen, Uppsala universitet, Sweden, 2023, https://www.diva-portal.org/smash/get/diva2:1766235/FULLTEXT01.pdf.
17. Borda, D., Bergagio, M., Amerio, M., Masoero, M.C., Borchiellini, R., Papurello, D., Development of anomaly detectors for HVAC systems using Machine Learning. *Processes*, *11*, 535, 2023. https://doi.org/10.3390/pr11020535.

18. Calzolari, G. and Liu, W., Deep learning to replace, improve, or aid CFD analysis in built environment applications: A review. *Build. Environ., 206*, 108315, 2021. https://doi.org/10.1016/j.buildenv.2021.108315.
19. Camperos, J.A.G., Cely, M.M.H., García, A.P., Artificial intelligence techniques for the hydrodynamic characterization of two-phase liquid–gas flows: An overview and bibliometric analysis. *Fluids, 9*, 158, 2024. https://doi.org/10.3390/fluids9070158.
20. Cancẹmi, S.A., Frano, R., Santus, C., Inoue, T., Unsupervised anomaly detection in pressurized water reactor digital twins using autoencoder neural networks. *Nucl. Eng. Des., 413*, 112502, 1–11, 2023. https://doi.org/10.1016/j.nucengdes.2023.112502.
21. Choi, S., Bang, M., Park, H.S., Heo, J., Cho, M.H., Cho, H.H., Machine learning-assisted effective thermal management of rotor-stator systems. *Energy, 299*, 131528, 2024. https://doi.org/10.1016/j.energy.2024.131528.
22. Choi, S., Lee, K.-H., Park, J.-H., Jeon, S., Lee, H.J., Kang, P.-G., Kam, J., Reliable AI models can reveal key processes of heat recovery steam generator operation in air pollutant emission. *J. Clean. Prod., 438*, 140806, 2024. https://doi.org/10.1016/j.jclepro.2024.140806.
23. Chu, W.-X., Lien, Y.-H., Huang, K.-R., Energy saving of fans in air-cooled server via deep reinforcement learning algorithm. *Energy Rep., 7*, 3437–3448, 2021. https://doi.org/10.1016/j.egyr.2021.06.003.
24. Coletti, F.P., (108d) Hybrid AI for industrial thermal systems, in: *2023 Spring Meeting and 19th Global Congress on Process Safety-Topical 7: 26th Topical Conference on Refinery Processing*, 2023, https://proceedings.aiche.org/conferences.
25. Das, R.S., A review of artificial intelligence techniques for quality control in semiconductor production. *Int. J. Comput. Eng.*, 5, 3, 33–45, 2024. https://doi.org/10.47941/ijce.1815.
26. Dawood, T., Elwakil, E., Novoa, H.M., Delgado, J.F.G., Artificial intelligence for the modeling of water pipes deterioration mechanisms. *Autom. Constr., 120*, 103398, 2020. https://doi.org/10.1016/j.autcon.2020.103398.
27. De Mey, G., Kos, A., Gorecki, K., Optimal temperature regulation of integrated circuits with peltier heat pumps. *Energies, 15*, 1125, 2022. https://doi.org/10.3390/en15031125.
28. Del Rio, J.E.V., Issac, Y., Coulon, A., Duncan, S., Mavris, D.N., Chilled water system abnormality detection with machine learning algorithms, in: *ASHRAE Annual Conference 2016 at Orlando, USA*, pp. 1–8, 2016, https://www.researchgate.net/publication/374416248.
29. Deris, A.M., Zain, A.M., Sallehuddin, R., Overview of Support Vector Machine in modeling machining performances. *Procedia Eng., 24*, 308–312, 2011. https://doi.org/10.1016/j.proeng.2011.11.2647.
30. Dhumal, A.R., Kulkarni, A.P., Ambhore, N.H., A comprehensive review on thermal management of electronic devices. *J. Eng. Appl. Sci., 70*, 140, 2023. https://doi.org/10.1186/s44147-023-00309-2.

31. Dıaz, G., Sen, M., Yang, K.T., McClain, R.L., Dynamic prediction and control of heat exchangers using artificial neural networks. *Int. J. Heat Mass Transfer, 44*, 9, 1671–1679, 2001. https://doi.org/10.1016/S0017-9310(00)00228-3.
32. El-Said, E.M.S., Abd Elaziz, M., Elsheikh, A.H., Machine learning algorithms for improving the prediction of air injection effect on the thermohydraulic performance of shell and tube heat exchanger. *Appl. Therm. Eng., 185*, 116471, 2021. https://doi.org/10.1016/j.applthermaleng.2020.116471.
33. Errouha, M., Derouich, A., Motahhir, S., Zamzoum, O., El Ouanjli, N., El Ghzizal, A., Optimization and control of water pumping PV systems using fuzzy logic controller. *Energy Rep., 5*, 853–865, 2019. https://doi.org/10.1016/j.egyr.2019.07.001.
34. Fadaei, M., Izadi, M., Assareh, E., Ershadi, A., Conjugated non-Newtonian phase change process in a shell and tube heat exchanger: A parametric-geometric analysis. *Appl. Therm. Eng., 220*, 119795, 2023. https://doi.org/10.1016/j.applthermaleng.2022.119795.
35. Faraji, H., Faraji, M., El Alami, M., Hariti, Y., Arshad, A., Hader, A., Benkaddour, A., Cooling of recent microprocessors by the fusion of nano-enhanced phase change materials. *Mater. Today Proc.*, 30, Part 4, 865–869, 2020. https://doi.org/10.1016/j.matpr.2020.04.342.
36. Felde, I., Artificial intelligence techniques and biomimetic methods supporting heat treatment processes. *Acta Polytech. Hung., 21*, 10, 317–329, 2024. https://acta.uni-obuda.hu/Felde_150.pdf.
37. Feng, Y., *Digital twin system used to improve distillation*, D. James (Ed.), Oklahoma State University, Oklahoma, 2024, https://news.okstate.edu/articles/.
38. Feng, Z., Huang, J., Jin, S., Wang, G., Chen, Y., Artificial intelligence-based multi-objective optimisation for proton exchange membrane fuel cell: A literature review. *J. Power Sources, 520*, 230808, 2022. https://doi.org/10.1016/j.jpowsour.2021.230808.
39. Ferencz, K., Domokos, J., Kovács, L., Analysis of industrial sensor data using statistical and regression methods. *Syst. Theory Control Comput. J., 3*, 1, 36–44, 2023. https://doi.org/10.52846/stccj.2023.3.1.48.
40. Filo, G., Artificial intelligence methods in hydraulic system design. *Energies, 16*, 3320, 1–19, 2023. https://doi.org/10.3390/en16083320.
41. Fister, D., Pérez-Aracil, J., Peláez-Rodríguez, C., Del Ser, J., Salcedo-Sanz, S., Accurate long-term air temperature prediction with Machine Learning models and data reduction techniques. *Appl. Soft Comput., 136*, 110118, 2023. https://doi.org/10.1016/j.asoc.2023.110118.
42. Fulpagare, Y., Huang, K.-R., Liao, Y.-H., Wang, C.-C., Optimal energy management for air cooled server fans using Deep Reinforcement Learning control method. *Energy Build., 277*, 112542, 2022. https://doi.org/10.1016/j.enbuild.2022.112542.

43. Gadd, H. and Werner, S., Heat load patterns in district heating substations. *Appl. Energy*, *108*, 176–183, 2013. https://doi.org/10.1016/j.apenergy.2013.02.062.
44. Ge, X., Wang, B., Yang, X., Pan, Y., Liu, B., Liu, B., Fault detection and diagnosis for reactive distillation based on convolutional neural network. *Comput. Chem. Eng.*, *145*, 107172, 2021. https://doi.org/10.1016/j.compchemeng.2020.107172.
45. Gizaw, D.G., Periyasamy, S., Kumar, P.S., Salilih, E.M., Redda, Z.T., Velusamy, K., Rangasamy, G., Artificial neural network based identification of process dynamics and neural network controller design for continuous distillation column. *Sustain. Energy Technol. Assess.*, *57*, 103168, 2023. https://doi.org/10.1016/j.seta.2023.103168.
46. Goswami, A., Pillai, S.C., McGranaghan, G., Micro/Nanoscale surface modifications to combat heat exchanger fouling. *Chem. Eng. J. Adv.*, *16*, 100519, 2023. https://doi.org/10.1016/j.ceja.2023.100519.
47. Greenfield, D., Artificial intelligence autonomously controls JSR Chemical Plant, in: *Yokogawa Corporation of America*, K. Hasegawa (Ed.), Endeavor Business Media, LLC, Tokyo, Japan, 2022, https://www.automationworld.com/control/article/22366503.
48. Guo, F., Ham, S., Kim, D., Moon, H.J., Deep reinforcement learning control for co-optimizing energy consumption, thermal comfort, and indoor air quality in an office building. *Appl. Energy*, *377*, Part A, 2025. https://doi.org/10.1016/j.apenergy.2024.124467.
49. Gupta, S. and Kukreja, N., Optimization of cooling fan speed for heat transfer enhancement of electronic chip using CFD. *IOP Conf. Ser.: Mater. Sci. Eng.*, *1116*, 2021. https://doi.org/10.1088/1757-899X/1116/1/012107.
50. Haghighi, A. and Asl, A.Z., Uncertainty analysis of water supply networks using the fuzzy set theory and NSGA-II. *Eng. Appl. Artif. Intell.*, *32*, 270–282, 2014. https://doi.org/10.1016/j.engappai.2014.02.010.
51. Han, W., Lu, Q., Deng, J., Huang, S., Generative design of a gas-cooled micro reactor based on multi-physics analysis, in: *31st International Conference on Nuclear Engineering [ICONE31-135237]*, Prague, Czech Republic, August 4–8, 2024, pp. 1–10, 2024, https://doi.org/10.1115/ICONE31-135237.
52. Hasegawa, K., *Full-scale distillation control project demonstrates process autonomy using artificial intelligence*, Chemical Processing.Com; Endeavor Business Media, LLC, Ohio, United States, 2023, https://www.chemicalprocessing.com/processing-equipment/.
53. Hassan, M., Misra, M., Taylor, G.W., Mohanty, A.K., A review of AI for optimization of 3D printing of sustainable polymers and composites. *Composites, Part C: Open Access*, *15*, 100513, 1–23, 2024. https://doi.org/10.1016/j.jcomc.2024.100513.
54. Hof, A.L., Gazendam, M.G.J., Sinke, W.E., The condition for dynamic stability. *J. Biomech.*, *38*, 1, 1–8, 2005. https://doi.org/10.1016/j.jbiomech.2004.03.025.

55. Hosain, M.L., *Fluid flow and heat transfer simulations for complex industrial applications: From Reynolds averaged Navier-Stokes towards smoothed particle hydrodynamics*, R. Bel Fdhila, K. Kyprianidis, E. Dahlquist, H. Li (Eds.), PhD dissertation, Mälardalen University, Sweden, 2018, http://www.diva-portal.org/smash/record.jsf?pid=diva2%3A1260308&dswid=-926.
56. Hu, W., Zhang, G., Zhang, Z., Abulanwar, S., Blaabjerg, F., Conclusions and outlook using AI in power systems, in: *AI for Power Electronics and Renewable Energy Systems*, W. Hu, G. Zhang, Z. Zhang, S. Abulanwar, F. Blaabjerg (Eds.), pp. 315–318, The Institution of Engineering and Technology (IET), Futures Place, Stevenage, 2024, https://doi.org/10.1049/PBPO242E.
57. Huang, L., Zou, J., Liu, B., Jin, Z., Qian, J., Machine learning assisted micro-channel geometric optimization—A case study of channel designs. *Energies*, *17*, 44, 2024. https://doi.org/10.3390/en17010044.
58. Idrees, S., Alam, A., Agarwal, P., Ansari, L., Effective predictive analytics and modeling based on historical data, in: *Communications in Computer and Information Science*, 2019, https://doi.org/10.1007/978-981-13-9942-8_52.
59. Jiang, S., Qin, S., Pulsipher, J.L., Zavala, V.M., Convolutional neural networks: Basic concepts and applications in manufacturing. *Preprints*, 2022. https://doi.org/10.48550/arXiv.2210.07848.
60. Jouhara, H., Khordehgah, N., Almahmoud, S., Delpech, B., Chauhan, A., Tassou, S.A., Waste heat recovery technologies and applications. *Therm. Sci. Eng. Prog.*, *6*, 268–289, 2018. https://doi.org/10.1016/j.tsep.2018.04.017.
61. Jung, S. and Kwon, O.J., Solution reconstruction for computational fluid dynamics via artificial neural network. *J. Mech. Sci. Technol.*, *38*, 229–244, 2024. https://doi.org/10.1007/s12206-023-1220-0.
62. Kalyan, A., Rajeshwar, P.P., Punnoose, J.S., Daniel, J., Manavalla, S., Heat transfer enhancement in a smart phone. *Int. J. Eng. Res. Appl.*, *7*, 4, 12–23, 2017. https://doi.org/10.9790/9622-0704051223.
63. Kaushik, K. and Naik, V., Detecting faults in the cooling systems by monitoring temperature and energy. *Energy Inf.*, *7*, 46, 2024. https://doi.org/10.1186/s42162-024-00351-1.
64. Kılıç, B., Plate heat exchangers: Artificial neural networks for their design, in: *Heat Transfer - Design, Experimentation and Applications*, M.A. Vega (Ed.), InTech Open, London, W1W 5PF, United Kingdom, 2021, https://doi.org/10.5772/intechopen.95376.
65. Klemeš, J.J., Wang, Q.-W., Varbanov, P.S., Zeng, M., Chin, H.H., Lal, N.S., Li, N.-Q., Wang, B., Wang, X.-C., Walmsley, T.G., Heat transfer enhancement, intensification and optimisation in heat exchanger network retrofit and operation. *Renew. Sustain. Energy Rev.*, *120*, 109644, 2020. https://doi.org/10.1016/j.rser.2019.109644.
66. Kokash, H., Khanafer, K., Burzo, M., Machine learning-based predictions of flow and heat transfer characteristics in a lid-driven cavity with a rotating cylinder. *Energies*, *17*, 5220, 2024. https://doi.org/10.3390/en17205220.

67. Koschmieder, E.L., Instabilities in fluid dynamics, in: *Springer Series in Synergetics*, vol. 2, H. Haken (Ed.), pp. 70–78), Springer-Verlag Berlin Heidelberg, 1977, https://doi.org/10.1007/978-3-642-66784-8_8.
68. Kruse, G. and Åhag, L., *An AI approach for quality improvement in heat treatment processing*, J. Jern (Ed.), Teknisk-naturvetenskapli fakulteten, Uppsala Universitet, 2022, https://www.diva-portal.org/smash/get/diva2:1630567/FULLTEXT01.pdf.
69. Kwon, B., Ejaz, F., Ohashi, N., Hwang, L.K., Application of machine learning in heat transfer from correlations to design, in: *Advances in Heat Transfer*, vol. 56, J.P. Abraham, J.M. Gorman, W.J. Minkowycz (Eds.), pp. 227–250, Academic Press, 2023, https://doi.org/10.1016/bs.aiht.2023.05.001.
70. Lalitha, S.D., Danamaraju, C., Manickam, P.R., Kumar, D., Sethuraman, R., Mohanapriya, V., AI-driven control strategies for power electronics converters, in: *Ninth International Conference on Science Technology Engineering and Mathematics (ICONSTEM 2024)*, pp. 1–6, 2024, https://doi.org/10.1109/ICONSTEM60960.2024.10568766.
71. Lateş, C.G., Dragan, C.M., Dumitras, C.G., Optimization of heat dissipation for fan cooling solution. *Bull. Polytechnic Inst. Iaşi Mach. Constructions Sect.*, *68*, 1, 9–23, 2022. https://doi.org/10.2478/bipcm-2022-0001.
72. Lee, D. and Lee, S.-T., Artificial intelligence enabled energy-efficient heating, ventilation and air conditioning system: Design, analysis and necessary hardware upgrades. *Appl. Therm. Eng.*, *235*, 121253, 1–27, 2023. https://doi.org/10.1016/j.applthermaleng.2023.121253.
73. Lee, S.G. and Park, S.W., On-line fault diagnosis of a distillation column using an artificial neural network. *IFAC Proc. Volumes*, *25*, 4, 243–248, 1992. https://doi.org/10.1016/S1474-6670(17)50248-7.
74. Li, C., Zheng, P., Yin, Y., Wang, B., Wang, L., Deep reinforcement learning in smart manufacturing: A review and prospects. *CIRP J. Manuf. Sci. Technol.*, *40*, 75–101, 2023. https://doi.org/10.1016/j.cirpj.2022.11.003.
75. Li, D., Zhang, Y., Song, J., Liu, H., Jiang, J., Energy saving with zero hot spots: A novel power control approach for sustainable and stable data centers. *Sustainability*, *14*, 9005, 2022. https://doi.org/10.3390/su14159005.
76. Lodhi, S.K., Hussain, H.K., Hussain, I., Using AI to increase heat exchanger efficiency: An extensive analysis of innovations and uses. *Int. J. Multi. Sci. Arts*, *3*, 4, 1–14, 2024. https://doi.org/10.47709/ijmdsa.v3i4.4617.
77. Ly, P. and Khanh, B.Q., Using genetic algorithm to optimize controllers of thermal load system in thermal power plant, in: *Genetic Algorithms*, S. Ventura, J.M. Luna, J.M. Moyano (Eds.), InTech Open, 2022, https://doi.org/10.5772/intechopen.103915.
78. Ma, G. and Zhang, F., Genetic algorithms for manufacturing process planning, in: *Variants of Evolutionary Algorithms for Real-World Applications*, R. Chiong, T. Weise, Z. Michalewicz (Eds.), pp. 205–244, Springer, Berlin, Heidelberg, 2012, https://doi.org/10.1007/978-3-642-23424-8_7.

79. Ma, Y., Liu, C., Jiaqiang, E., Mao, X., Yu, Z., Research on modeling and parameter sensitivity of flow and heat transfer process in typical rectangular microchannels: From a data-driven perspective. *Int. J. Therm. Sci., 172,* 107356, 2022. https://doi.org/10.1016/j.ijthermalsci.2021.107356.
80. Mahmoudi, M., Ghaemi, A., Kelishami, A.R., Movahedirad, S., Predictive modeling of membrane reactor efficiency using advanced artificial neural networks for green hydrogen production. *Sci. Rep., 14,* 24211, 1–16, 2024. https://www.nature.com/articles/s41598-024-75068-y.
81. Makahleh, F. and Nassar, A., Modeling and simulation of fluid flow, energy, and heat transfer, in: *Simulation Modeling - Recent Advances, New Perspectives, and Applications*, A.A. Jaoudé (Ed.), pp. 1–24, InTech Open, 2023, https://doi.org/10.5772/intechopen.1002220.
82. Manssouri, I., Chetouani, Y., El Kihel, B., Using neural networks for fault detection in a distillation column. *Int. J. Comput. Appl. Technol. (IJCAT), 32,* 3, 181–186, 2008. https://doi.org/10.1504/IJCAT.2008.020953.
83. Mehraj, N., Mateu, C., Cabeza, L.F., Use of artificial intelligence methods in designing thermal energy storage tanks: A bibliometric analysis. *J. Energy Storage, 97,* Part A, 2024. https://doi.org/10.1016/j.est.2024.112794.
84. Miklas, V., Touš, M., Máša, V., Teng, S.Y., Artificial intelligence application for crude distillation unit: An overview, in: *Artificial Intelligence for Knowledge Management, Energy, and Sustainability,* 1st, E. Mercier-Laurent and G. Kayakutlu (Eds.), pp. 156–168, Springer Cham, 2022, https://doi.org/10.1007/978-3-030-96592-1_12.
85. Montazerinejad, H. and Eicker, U., Recent development of heat and power generation using renewable fuels: A comprehensive review. *Renew. Sustain. Energy Rev., 165,* 112578, 2022. https://doi.org/10.1016/j.rser.2022.112578.
86. Muthukrishnan, S., Krishnaswamy, H., Thanikodi, S., Dinesh, S., Vijayan, V., Support vector machine for modelling and simulation of heat exchangers. *Therm. Sci., 24,* 00, 398–398, 2019. https://doi.org/10.2298/TSCI190419398M.
87. Naderi, M., Vajdi, M., Moghanlou, F.S., Nami, H., Sensitivity analysis of fluid flow parameters on the performance of fully dense ZrB2-made micro heat exchangers. *Synth. Sintering, 3,* 2, 2023. https://doi.org/10.53063/synsint.2023.32143.
88. Nakayama, W., Heat in computers: Applied heat transfer in information technology (Max Jakob Award Paper). *J. Heat Transfer, 136,* 1, 1–22, 2014. https://doi.org/10.1115/1.4025377.
89. Ndaba, S., Abubakar, A.M., Ferhoune, I., Bilal, M.T., Sarkinbaka, Z.M., Case studies in Machine Learning for design optimization, in: *Design Optimization Using Artificial Intelligence,* 1st, S.R. Mishra, A.N. Dev, A.K. Pandey, M.K. Awasthi (Eds.), CRC Press, 2025, https://www.routledge.com/Design-Optimization-Using-Artificial-Intelligence/.
90. Niksa-Rynkiewicz, T., Szewczuk-Krypa, N., Witkowska, A., Cpałka, K., Zalasiński, M., Cader, A., Monitoring regenerative heat exchanger in steam power plant by making use of the Recurrent Neural Network. *J. Artif.*

Intell. Soft Comput. Res., *11*, 2, 143–155, 2021. https://doi.org/10.2478/jaiscr-2021-0009.

91. Norton, T.J., Kumar, T.B., Sun, D.-W., Computational fluid dynamics in the design and analysis of thermal processes: A review of recent advances. *Crit. Rev. Food Sci. Nutr.*, *53*, 3, 251–275, 2013. https://doi.org/10.1080/10408398.2010.518256.
92. Obaid, H.S., Dheyab, S.A., Sabry, S.S., The impact of data pre-processing techniques and dimensionality reduction on the accuracy of Machine Learning, in: *9th Annual Information Technology, Electromechanical Engineering and Microelectronics Conference (IEMECON)*, Jaipur, India, pp. 279–283, 2019, https://doi.org/10.1109/IEMECONX.2019.8877011.
93. Ohia, N.P., Paul, C., Asolo, E., Adewa, T.A., Chukwu, C.F., Ubi, P.A., Itam, D.H., Nnaji, D.U., Artificial intelligence-driven fuzzy logic approach for optimal well selection in gas lift design: A Brown Field Case Study. *Results Eng.*, *103927*, 1–37, 2025. https://doi.org/10.1016/j.rineng.2025.103927.
94. Okonkwo, S., Optimizing predictive analytics for energy consumption forecasting: A case study in the Nigerian Power Sector, in: *SSRN*, pp. 1–6, 2024, https://doi.org/10.2139/ssrn.4946145.
95. Osuolale, F.N. and Zhang, J., Energy efficiency optimisation for distillation column using artificial neural network models. *Energy*, *106*, 562–578, 2016. https://doi.org/10.1016/j.energy.2016.03.051.
96. Pandey, S., Siddhu, L., Panda, P.R., NeuroCool: Dynamic thermal management of 3D DRAM for Deep Neural Networks through customized prefetching. *ACM Trans. Des. Autom. Electron. Syst.*, *29*, 1, 1–35, 2023. https://doi.org/10.1145/3630012.
97. Papavassiliou, D.V. and Nguyen, Q.T., *Flow and heat or mass transfer in the chemical process industry*, Multidisciplinary Digital Publishing Institute (MDPI, 2018, https://doi.org/10.3390/books978-3-03897-239-6.
98. Park, H., Kwon, H., Cho, H., Kim, J., A framework for energy optimization of distillation process using machine learning-based predictive model. *Energy Sci. Eng.*, *10*, 6, 1913–1924, 2022. https://doi.org/10.1002/ese3.1134.
99. Park, H.W. and Yoon, W.B., Computational fluid dynamics (CFD) modeling and application for sterilization of foods: A review. *Processes*, *6*, 62, 2018. https://doi.org/10.3390/pr6060062.
100. Peng, X., Li, X., Gong, Z., Zhao, X., Yao, W., A deep learning method based on partition modeling for reconstructing temperature field. *Int. J. Therm. Sci.*, *182*, 107802, 2022. https://doi.org/10.1016/j.ijthermalsci.2022.107802.
101. Perissinotto, R.M., Verde, W.M., Biazussi, J.L., Bulgarelli, N.A.V., Fonseca, W.D.P., De Castro, M.S., De Moraes Franklin, E., Bannwart, A.C., Flow visualization in centrifugal pumps: A review of methods and experimental studies. *J. Pet. Sci. Eng.*, *203*, 108582, 2021. https://doi.org/10.1016/j.petrol.2021.108582.
102. Pioch, F., Harmening, J.H., Muller, A.M., Peitzmann, F.-J., Schramm, D., El Moctar, O., Turbulence modeling for physics-Informed neural networks:

Comparison of different RANS models for teh backward-facing step flow. *Fluids*, *8*, 43, 2023. https://doi.org/10.3390/fluids8020043.

103. Poursaeidi, E. and Yazdi, M.K., Application of hot spotting method for the straightening of a large turbine rotor. *Int. J. Eng.*, *31*, 1, 110–119, 2018. https://doi.org/10.5829/ije.2018.31.01a.16.
104. Prakash, B. and Mohan, S., Predicting the thermal performance of double pipe heat exchanger using the Generalized Regression Neural Network model. *Int. J. Ambient Energy*, *44*, 1, 1–31, 2022. https://doi.org/10.1080/01430750.2022.2127885.
105. Prasad, B.S., Jithendranaik, S., Balsubramanyam, L., Heat transfer in blast furnace simulation with computational fluid dynamics. *Int. J. Sci. Res. Sci. Eng. Technol. (IJSRSET)*, *6*, 2, 348–358, 2019. https://ijsrset.com/home/issue/view/article.php?id=IJSRSET196276.
106. Prozuments, A., Borodinecs, A., Lebedeva, K., Palcikovskis, A., Examining the efficacy of cooling pad technology to address increasing building cooling demand in Latvia. *Front. Built Environ.*, *9*, 2023. https://doi.org/10.3389/fbuil.2023.1258625.
107. Rahman, M.S., Hazra, S., Chowdhury, I.A., Advancing computational fluid dynamics through machine learning: A review of data-driven innovations and applications. *J. Fluid Mech. Mech. Des.*, *6*, 2, 42–51, 2024. https://doi.org/10.46610/JFMMD.2024.v06i02.005.
108. Rashid, F.L., Al-Gaheeshi, A.M.R., Al-Obaidi, M.A., Mohammed, H., II, Togun, H., Agyekum, E.B., Analysing fluid flow and heat transfer comparatively in flow passage systems: Evaluating thermal impacts and geometric configurations. *Int. J. Thermofluids*, *24*, 100894, 2024. https://doi.org/10.1016/j.ijft.2024.100894.
109. Roy, U., Pant, H.K., Majumder, M., Detection of significant parameters for shell and tube heat exchanger using polynomial neural network approach. *Vacuum*, *166*, 399–404, 2019. https://doi.org/10.1016/j.vacuum.2018.11.047.
110. Safae, M., Bekkay, H., Oussama, E.M., Mellit, A., Aneli, S., Arcidiacono, G., Tina, G.M., Gagliano, A., Integrated machine learning models for predictive analysis of thermal and electrical power generation of a photo-thermal system at Catania, Italy. *Case Stud. Therm. Eng.*, *61*, 105018, 2024. https://doi.org/10.1016/j.csite.2024.105018.
111. Sahay, S.S., Mehta, R., Krishnan, K., Genetic-algorithm-based optimization of an industrial age-hardening operation for packed bundles of aluminum rods. *Mater. Manuf. Processes*, *22*, 5, 615–622, 2007. https://doi.org/10.1080/10426910701323250.
112. Salins, S.S., Kumar, S., Ganesha, A., Reddy, S.V.K., Machine learning-based optimization and performance analysis of cooling towers. *J. Build. Eng.*, *96*, 110415, 2024. https://doi.org/10.1016/j.jobe.2024.110415.
113. Shaeri, M.R., Sarabi, S., Randriambololona, A.M., Shadlo, A., Machine learning-based optimization of air-cooled heat sinks. *Therm. Sci. Eng. Prog.*, *34*, 101398, 2022. https://doi.org/10.1016/j.tsep.2022.101398.

114. Shen, C., Lixia, W., Li, Q., Optimization of injection molding process parameters using combination of artificial neural network and genetic algorithm method. *J. Mater. Process. Technol.*, *183*, 2–3, 412–418, 2007. https://doi.org/10.1016/j.jmatprotec.2006.10.036.
115. Shilpa, B. and Leela, V., An artificial intelligence model for heat and mass transfer in an inclined cylindrical annulus with heat generation/absorption and chemical reaction. *Int. Commun. Heat Mass Transfer*, *147*, 106956, 2023. https://doi.org/10.1016/j.icheatmasstransfer.2023.106956.
116. Silva, M.V., Schirru, R., De Stefani, G.L., Nicolau, A.S., De Lima, A.M.M., Pereira, C.M.N.A., Guimaraes, J.V.S.A., Gonçalves, D.M.E., Optimized modular nuclear reactor project utilizing artificial intelligence: Seed-blanket concept. *Nucl. Eng. Des.*, *423*, 113187, 2024. https://doi.org/10.1016/j.nucengdes.2024.113187.
117. Simić, S., Orasanin, G., Golubovic, D., Milić, D., Batinić, K., Consideration of opportunities for the optimization of heat energy consumption in industry and energetics, in: *New Technologies, Development and Application II. NT 2019. Lecture Notes in Networks and Systems*, vol. 76, I. Karabegović (Ed.), pp. 494–503, Springer, Cham, 2019, https://doi.org/10.1007/978-3-030-18072-0_57.
118. Sinha, S. and Lee, Y.M., Challenges with developing and deploying AI models and applications in industrial systems. *Discov. Artif. Intell.*, *4*, 55, 2024. https://doi.org/10.1007/s44163-024-00151-2.
119. Sofos, F., Stavrogiannis, C., Exarchou-Kouveli, K.K., Akabua, D., Charilas, G., Karakasidis, T.E., Current trends in fluid research in the era of artificial intelligence: A review. *Fluids*, *7*, 116, 1–25, 2022. https://doi.org/10.3390/fluids7030116.
120. Soltanian, S. and Beigzadeh, R., Computational fluid dynamics and fuzzy logic for modeling the spiral-conical heat exchangers. *Chem. Eng. Technol.*, *46*, 4, 747–755, 2022. https://doi.org/10.1002/ceat.202200488.
121. Suh, Y., Chandramowlishwaran, A., Won, Y., Review: Artificial intelligence for liquid-vapor phase-change heat transfer. *Preprints.Org*, pp. 1–26, 2023. https://doi.org/10.48550/arXiv.2309.01025.
122. Suh, Y., Chandramowlishwaran, A., Won, Y., Recent progress of artificial intelligence for liquid-vapor phase change heat transfer. *npj Comput. Mater.*, *10*, 65, 1–14, 2024. https://doi.org/10.1038/s41524-024-01223-8.
123. Sui, Z. and Wu, W., AI-assisted maldistribution minimization of membrane-based heat/mass exchangers for compact absorption cooling. *Energy*, *263*, Part C, 2023. https://doi.org/10.1016/j.energy.2022.125922.
124. Supan, K., Using artificial intelligence case studies in a thermodynamics course, in: *The Future of Engineering Education-2024 Annual Conference and Exposition*, Oregon Convention Centre, Portland, June 23–26, 2024, pp. 1–14, 2024, https://nemo.asee.org/public/conferences/344/papers/41240/view.
125. Szpicer, A., Binkowska, W., Stelmasiak, A., Zalewska, M., Wojtasik-Kalinowska, I., Piwowarsko, K., Piepiorka-Stepuk, J., Poltorak, A., Computational fluid dynamics simulation of thermal processes in food technology and their

applications in the food industry. *Appl. Sci.*, *15*, 424, 2025. https://doi.org/10.3390/app15010434.

126. Tang, Y., Heat transfer and thermal analysis with computational fluid dynamics, in: *Computational Fluid Dynamics-Analysis, Simulations, and Applications*, M. Baccouch (Ed.), InTech Open, 2024, https://doi.org/10.5772/intechopen.1006819.
127. Tashtoush, T., Alazzam, A., Rodan, A., Utilizing fuzzy logic controller in manufacturing facilities design: Machine and operator allocation. *Cogent Eng.*, *7*, 1, 2020. https://doi.org/10.1080/23311916.2020.1771820.
128. Tavousi, E., Perera, N., Flynn, D., Hasan, R., Heat transfer and fluid flow characteristics of the passive method in double tube heat exchangers: A critical review. *Int. J. Thermofluids*, *17*, 100282, 2023. https://doi.org/10.1016/j.ijft.2023.100282.
129. Tejero-Gonzalez, A. and Franco-Salas, A., Optimal operation of evaporative cooling pads: A review. *Renew. Sustain. Energy Rev.*, *151*, 111632, 2021. https://doi.org/10.1016/j.rser.2021.111632.
130. Thekemuriyil, T., Rohner, J.D., Minamisawa, R.A., Machine learning-based prediction of on-state voltage for real-time health monitoring of IGBT. *Power Electron. Dev. Compon.*, *6*, 100049, 1–11, 2023. https://doi.org/10.1016/j.pedc.2023.100049.
131. Thosago, K.F., Banjo, P.O., Rundora, L., Adesanya, S.O., Thermal stability and entropy generation analysis for combustible third-grade fluid flow through a slant channel: A spectral study. *Appl. Sci.*, *14*, 11491, 2024. https://doi.org/10.3390/app142411491.
132. Tizakast, Y., Kaddiri, M., Lamsaadi, M., Makayssi, T., Machine Learning based algorithms for modeling natural convection fluid flow and heat and mass transfer in rectangular cavities filled with non-Newtonian fluids. *Eng. Appl. Artif. Intell.*, *119*, 105750, 2023. https://doi.org/10.1016/j.engappai.2022.105750.
133. Watanabe, A.M., Krishnamurthy, R., Rizaldi, B.A., Weemaes, H., Suriyadi, B., Phelan, J., Hashim, D.M., Rettig, C., Inspiring sustainable growth across Pharma, Biotech, and Chemical Industries, in: *Process Innovation Asia-Pacific Powered by Achema: 19-21 November 2024, Singapore EXPO*, P. Lee and B. Mathes (Eds.), Constellar Exhibitions Ventures Pte Ltd and DECHEMA Ausstellungs-GmbH, 2024, https://processinnovationapac.com/.
134. Wrobel, R. and McGlen, R.J., Heat pipes in thermal management of electrical machines – A review. *Therm. Sci. Eng. Prog.*, *26*, 101053, 2021. https://doi.org/10.1016/j.tsep.2021.101053.
135. Xie, C., Xiong, X., Wang, J., Artificial neural network approach for turbulence models: A local framework. *Phys. Rev. Fluids*, *6*, 84612, 2021. https://doi.org/10.1103/PhysRevFluids.6.084612.
136. Yan, Z., Liu, Y., Shao, H., The application of AI technology in GPU scheduling algorithm optimization. *Wirel. Commun. Mob. Comput.*, *22*, 1–7, 2022. https://doi.org/10.1155/2022/4713698.

137. Yarlagadda, S.C., Integrating artificial intelligence in polymer extrusion: Trends, challenges, and future directions. *Int. J. Intell. Syst. Appl. Eng. (IJISAE)*, *12*, 23S, 772–789, 2024. https://ijisae.org/index.php/IJISAE/article/view/6998.
138. Yoon, W.B. and Park, H.W., CFD determination of F values during thermal processing of still cans, in: *Computational Fluid Dynamics in Food Processing*, 2nd, pp. 1–16, CRC Press, 2019, https://doi.org/10.1201/9781351263481.
139. Zhang, T., Wen, J.T., Catano, J., Zhou, R., Stability analysis of heat exchanger dynamics, in: *Proceedings of the American Control Conference*, 2009, https://doi.org/10.1109/ACC.2009.5160282.
140. Zhao, H., Computational modeling of nanofluid heat transfer using Fuzzy-based bee algorithm and machine learning method. *Case Stud. Therm. Eng.*, *54*, 104021, 2024. https://doi.org/10.1016/j.csite.2024.104021.
141. Zhao, J., Yuan, X., Duan, Y., Li, H., Liu, D., An artificial intelligence (AI)-driven method for forecasting cooling and heating loads in office buildings by integrating building thermal load characteristics. *J. Build. Eng.*, *79*, 107855, 2023. https://doi.org/10.1016/j.jobe.2023.107855.
142. Zhu, L.-T., Chen, X., Ouyang, B., Yan, W.-C., Lei, H., Chen, Z., Zheng-Hong, L., Review of machine learning for hydrodynamics, transport, and reactions in multiphase flows and reactors. *Ind. Eng. Chem. Res.*, *61*, 3, 2022. https://doi.org/10.1021/acs.iecr.2c01036.

15

Artificial Intelligence in Microfluidics and Nanofluidics

Ashish Mathur[1]*, Souradeep Roy[2] and Rabab Fatima[3]

[1]*Centre for Interdisciplinary Research and Innovation (CIDRI), R&D Department, UPES, Dehradun, India*
[2]*Health Technology Department, School of Health Sciences and Technology, UPES, Dehradun, India*
[3]*Applied Science Cluster, Department of Health Science, School of Advanced Engineering, UPES, Dehradun, India*

Abstract

This chapter explores the transformative role of artificial intelligence (AI) in the fields of microfluidics and nanofluidics, highlighting the synergistic advancements at the intersection of computational and experimental techniques. Microfluidics and nanofluidics, which involve the manipulation of fluids at sub-millimeter and nanometer scales, respectively, have seen significant innovation through the integration of AI-driven methodologies. This chapter provides an overview of how AI technologies—such as machine learning (ML), deep learning (DL), neural networks (NN), and physics-informed neural networks (PINNs)—are enhancing the design, control, and analysis of fluidic systems. Key areas of focus include AI-assisted optimization of fluidic device performance, predictive modeling for complex fluid behaviors, real-time control systems, and the automation of experimental workflows. Artificial intelligence techniques have addressed several challenges in microfluidics and nanofluidics, including computational complexity, experimental validation, and data scarcity. By leveraging AI-driven models, researchers can optimize device performance while reducing the time and cost associated with traditional experimental setups. Specific case studies highlight how AI-driven lab-on-a-chip systems in medical diagnostics and AI-assisted design of microfluidic devices have significantly improved efficiency and accuracy.

**Corresponding author*: nanoashish@gmail.com; ORCID: 0000-0002-5365-5807
Souradeep Roy: ORCID: 0000-0002-4668-5290
Rabab Fatima: ORCID: 0000-0002-9103-2870

Mukesh Kumar Awasthi and Reshu Gupta (eds.) Artificial Intelligence and Computational Modeling in Heat Transfer and Fluid Dynamics, (395–414) © 2026 Scrivener Publishing LLC

By elucidating these advancements, the chapter underscores the potential of AI to address existing challenges in microfluidics and nanofluidics, offering insights into future directions and interdisciplinary collaborations.

Keywords: Artificial intelligence (AI), microfluidics, nanofluidics, machine learning, lab-on-a-chip technologies

15.1 Introduction

At the forefront of transformational technologies are microfluidics and nanofluidics, where manipulation of fluids is at micrometer and nanometer scales. They open breakthroughs in areas ranging from biomedical diagnostics to lab-on-a-chip technologies, material science, and many others. Applications span different sectors: health, environmental science, and chemical engineering, to name a few. Yet one of the greatest challenges still involves the behavior of fluids at small scales, device performance optimization, and complex flow dynamics control. The integration of artificial intelligence (AI) into these fields transforms these areas by providing innovative solutions to the limitations created in the aforementioned applications. Such opportunities enable researchers to explore large volumes of databases and utilize powerful algorithms for enhancing micro- and nanofluidic systems. Artificial intelligence may offer novel opportunities in design optimization, predictive modeling, and real-time control of novel pathways in fluid behavior. There are still enormous challenges to be addressed: models of fluid behavior, generalization of data, and cross-disciplinary collaborations. This chapter investigates the innovative revolution of AI in microfluidics and nanofluidics, discussing how AI-based methodologies such as machine learning (ML), deep learning (DL), and neural networks (NN) can overcome these issues and open further gates to advance.

15.1.1 Microfluidics and Nanofluidics: An Overview

Microfluidics deals with the fluid manipulation within channels of widths merely from tens to hundreds of micrometers [1]. Nanofluidics, on the other hand, deals with even smaller scales where unique behavior emerges due to surface forces dominating volumetric forces. These fields provide an accurate tool for the manipulation of fluid properties; hence, high-throughput analysis and miniaturization of laboratory procedures could be developed. It is then applied to diagnosis, especially for medical and molecular biology. Examples include point-of-care disease diagnosis.

- Lab-on-a-chip technologies: Enabling miniaturized platforms for chemical and biological assays.
- Material science: Facilitating precise nanoparticle fabrication and manipulation.
- Drug delivery systems: Creating devices for targeted, cellular-level therapeutic delivery.
- Environmental monitoring: Developing microfluidic sensors for real-time pollution detection.

15.1.2 Integration of Artificial Intelligence in Microfluidics and Nanofluidics

Artificial intelligence has been playing a transformational role in microfluidics and nanofluidics, transforming every process from designing, carrying out experiments, to analyzing the resultant data. Techniques in AI, like ML and DL, are used to predict fluid dynamics, optimize device performance, and process many complex datasets [2]. All these methods have allowed for rapid advancements through the fulfillment of needs for efficient simulations, predictive capabilities, and even analysis in real-time.

15.1.3 Emerging Artificial Intelligence Techniques for Microfluidics and Nanofluidics

Recent advancements in AI techniques like physics-informed neural networks (PINNs) and generative AI challenge the status quo of fluidic device performance and experimental analysis [3]. Conflation of ML with physical laws results in successful conditions — conservation of mass, momentum, and energy, which means it is possible to use models even under low data availability. It is especially important in micro- and nanofluidics as it requires expensive and long preparations for the acquisition of high-quality data. Through the application of PINNs, fluid behavior can be well predicted using computationally efficient simulations, which will help in optimizing device design.

Even more recent accelerators in innovation in microfluidic devices include generative AI, such as deep reinforcement learning and generative adversarial networks (GANs), which can autonomously develop new architectures for devices [4]. These AI models optimize for performance and efficiency while minimizing consumption of reagents and augmenting flow control; therefore, the design process is faster, allowing scientists to test innovative and exceedingly effective designs that conventional methods could not have foreseen (Figure 15.1).

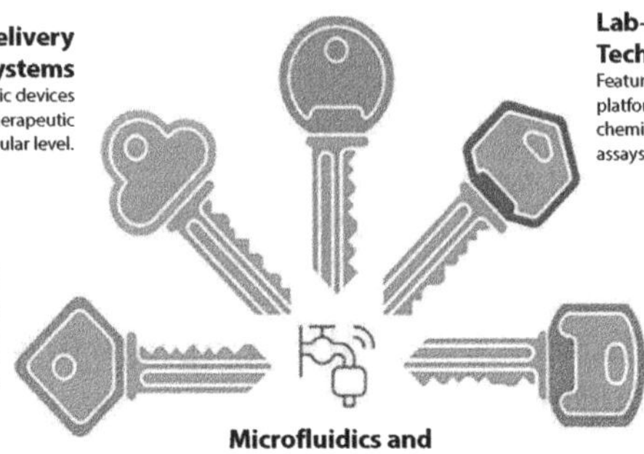

Figure 15.1 Innovative uses of microfluidics and nanofluidics in modern science.

Another major accomplishment is federated learning, the possibility of providing decentralized data to AI models being trained without exchanging raw data itself. This prevents violation of the user's privacy, along with confidentiality due to sensitive aspects involved in certain biomedical applications, by considering patient records as private assets. Federated learning can learn together with partners at institutions more efficiently to enrich generalizable models without violating secrecy [5].

15.1.4 Machine Learning and Deep Learning Applications in Microfluidics and Nanofluidics

The diversity of AI applications in microfluidics and nanofluidics ranges from predictive modeling to real-time imaging and data classification [6]. Predictive modeling is the core of AI integration, wherein machine learning algorithms are used to simulate fluid flow, pressure distributions, and particle interactions in microchannels. The surrogate models based on ML can be used to predict fluid dynamics very fast and accurately. Unlike the traditional methods, such as finite element analysis, this is relatively expensive in terms of computational time and cost. AI is also moving at a great pace in optimizing the fabrication processes. Material properties and channel dimensions must be controlled very precisely in microfluidic devices. Machine learning algorithms trained on historical fabrication data can predict the optimal material choices, curing times, and photolithography conditions, thus making the process more efficient and cheaper. Deep learning techniques, such as CNNs and transformer-based architectures, have been extremely useful in real-time image analysis in imaging and computational fluid dynamics (CFD) [7]. One can now follow the behavior of fluids, track the motion of particles, and watch droplet formation. This reduces man's involvement in experiments, and the experiments are completed faster with enhanced accuracy. Further, AI-powered CFD models, using techniques such as PINNs and deep convolutional autoencoders, are accelerating fluid simulations by a huge margin and thus enable faster and more accurate predictions of complex phenomena [8].

In nanofluidics, where precision matters, AI-based imaging techniques like super-resolution microscopy allow researchers to visualize molecular-scale fluid interactions in unprecedented detail. Developments such as those have transformed nanoscale fluid behavior studies regarding applications as vast as biomolecular assays, nanopore sensors, and quantum-dot-based systems. The way AI changes high-throughput data classification cannot be overstated. It allows for ML models to process large data sets from experiments conducted with microfluidics, with the potential for automated decision-making and faster discovery by identifying the most informative experiments.

15.1.5 Challenges in the Field

Although this technology has enormous potential to revolutionize microfluidics and nanofluidics, several open challenges persist. Among them, data scarcity, high computational costs, generalization of models, and effective interdisciplinary collaboration are the key challenges. The primary emerging techniques against such challenges include PINNs, generative AI, and federated learning (Figure 15.2). The PINNs still provide high-fidelity predictions, even with limited data, in microfluidics and nanofluidics, since data acquisition is expensive and difficult [9]. Generative AI facilitates accelerating innovation with the capability of autonomously generating optimized device designs, whereas federated learning ensures privacy during AI model training, especially within sensitive healthcare applications.

These developments aside, there is still a broad generalization across geometries, materials, and conditions. The field has already started to experience a revolution due to AI. It has automatically simulated simulations and improved the process of image analysis, thus accelerating the optimization of devices. When these AI techniques mature, more efficient and quicker designs of microfluidic and nanofluidic systems will eventually become a reality. Fluidic devices will be smart, efficient, and autonomous for applications such as biomedical diagnostics, drug delivery, and environmental monitoring [10].

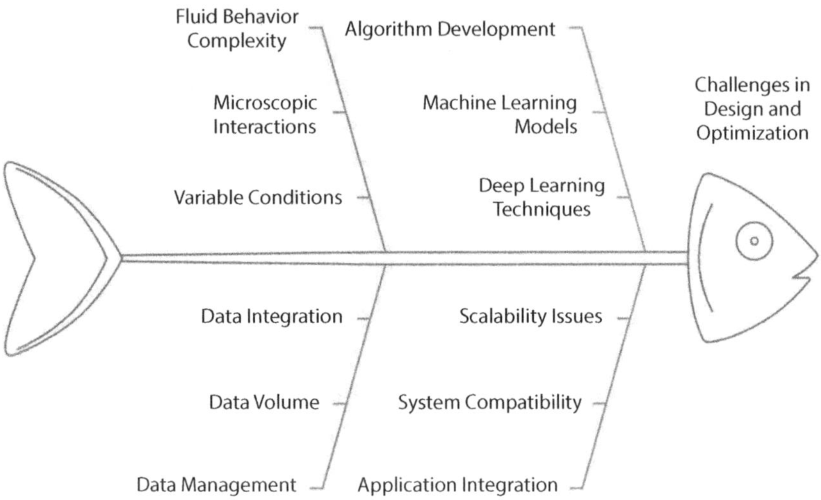

Figure 15.2 Overcoming challenges in microfluidics and nanofluidics with AI.

15.2 Case Study

Recently, breakthroughs have been witnessed in AI-integrated microfluidic and nanofluidic systems, showing remarkable potential not only for optimizing device design but also for controlling fluid flow and real-time analysis. The following section discusses a few of the most important case studies on how AI has overcome past unaddressed challenges in this field. The first case, presented by Mert Tunca Doganay *et al.*, assesses the performance of AI algorithms for testing microfluidics as point-of-care diagnostics [1]. A comparison of DL and ML models in detecting bubbles inside a microfluidic channel is conducted under various imaging conditions. Random Forest ML model got up to 95.52% sensitivity, and an area under the curve, or AUC, of 97% was obtained, while DenseNet169 DL model got up to 92.63% sensitivity and an AUC of 92%. This is particularly indicative of AI's profound effect on healthcare systems, improving the precision of diagnostics and increasing access through effective integration with microfluidics systems.

The second case study is that of Ibrahim Shaw *et al.*, which employs AI in combination with microfluidic technology for improving the therapy in the context of psoriasis chronic inflammatory disease of the skin [2]. It, therefore, proves that the use of AI-based microfluidic platforms enables designing devices autonomously, improves precision in diagnostics, and allows for real-time biomarker monitoring. Such progress promises a radical shift toward personalized care in dermatology by precisely detecting disease markers and optimizing therapeutic interventions for the betterment of patient outcomes and the quality of life of patients.

In the third case study, "Machine Learning-Driven Innovations in Microfluidics," Jinseok Park *et al.* discussed how ML improves design and operational efficiency in microfluidic biosensors [11]. The article highlights AI as a tool that can be leveraged to advance diagnostic accuracy and real-time analytics in health diagnostics and environmental monitoring, thereby improving the efficiency of microfluidic devices in their applications.

Hsieh-Fu Tsai *et al.* further show how AI can change biomedical sciences by the inclusion of machine learning in specific biomarker detection, in-time diagnostics, and automatic drug delivery through optimum design of a microfluidic chip *via* CFD integrated with DL that possibly enables better design in disease modeling, as well as superior outcomes in therapy, thus accrediting AI-based methodologies with revolutionizing personalized medicine and clinical diagnostics [4].

Eş *et al.* emphasized the potential applications of AI-integrated microfluidics in diagnostics, drug delivery, and organ-on-chip technologies [5]. Its machine learning-based model is effective in accurate biomarker profiling, fast image processing, and fluid autonomous control that greatly improves the efficiency and accuracy of the approach. This case study highlights the benefits of deep learning in high-resolution imaging, neural activity decoding, and micro-robotic manipulation for advanced personalized medicine and minimally invasive diagnostics.

In the case study sixth report, Bhuiyan *et al.* proposed an AI-based microfluidic platform that should automatically carry out immunoassay by overcoming flaws in fluid-handling and also bubble formation [6]. Using ROI cascading and conditional activation algorithms, their proposed platform achieves a processing rate of 22.13 fps and outperforms unoptimized versions. Notably, it improved the limit of detection (LOD) for cardiac troponin I to 0.91 pg/mL, while the LOD showed more than 2-fold improvements, and the limit of quantification showed 3.5-fold improvements. It is an exemplary study of how AI-driven immunoassays are reliable and reproducible.

These case studies together prove how AI is powerful in advancing microfluidics and nanofluidic technologies. This also illustrates the critical role AI plays in achieving results previously unattainable through traditional methods, particularly in particle tracking and real-time analysis. Altogether, the case studies presented are evidence of collaboration between AI and microfluidics, but present an opportunity towards the

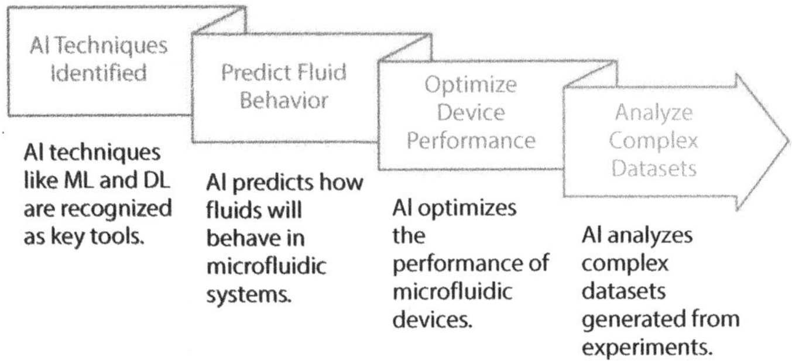

Figure 15.3 Artificial intelligence integration in microfluidics and nanofluidics.

future prospects of AI-operated platforms changing the face of fluidic design and operation at points of use. As is with the emergence of AI going forward, integrated applications into such systems will innovate point-of-care diagnostics and other areas of drug screening.

15.3 Predictive Modeling of Fluid Behaviour

The optimization of the designs of the devices and the processes involved is based on the accurate modeling of fluid behavior at the micro and nano levels. The ones based on AI are significantly better than the traditional models. For instance, CNNs enable the prediction of the fields for velocity and pressure in turbulent flow with a high degree of fidelity. The RNNs, on the other hand, are better suited for multiphase flows, such as droplet formation and coalescence. Hybrid models that couple AI with physics-based simulations produce even higher predictability but reduce computational costs (Figure 15.3).

For example, droplet dynamics in a nanofluidic system are modeled by an RNN at 95% accuracy. It is the type of capability that would eventually optimize the performance of droplet-based biochemical assays and improve the functioning of microfluidic devices [12].

15.4 Real-Time Control Systems

The use of reinforcement learning algorithms enables the adaptive control of fluidic systems in dynamic environments [13]. Trial-and-error learning enables the enhancement of system performance and robustness in such scenarios, and it has significant applications in real-time:

- Temperature Control: Precise management of temperature gradients in microreactors for chemical synthesis.
- Viscosity Modulation: Fluid viscosity is modulated in drug delivery systems to provide a constant dosing.
- Flow Rate Optimization: Dynamic optimization of flow rates within microfluidic chips for yield enhancement of chemical reactions.

15.5 Artificial Intelligence and Edge Computing for Real-Time Applications

Integration of AI with edge computing is revolutionizing real-time control, analysis, and automation in microfluidic and nanofluidic systems. Ultra-fast localized decision-making capabilities edge AI brings significantly reduce the latency inherent in cloud-based processing. Classical AI models deployed in microfluidic applications generally require significant computational power and, therefore, are not useful for real-time operations on an embedded device. The problem is solved in Edge AI with the implementation of deep models running directly on resource-constrained hardware, namely, field-programmable gate arrays and system-on-chip architectures, enabled by lightweight deep learning models.

One of the most significant applications is point-of-care diagnostics for autonomous lab-on-a-chip (LoC), which uses AI-powered biosensors for real-time evaluation of biological fluids to detect pathogens, biomarkers, or signatures of disease [14]. Instead of data transmission to servers

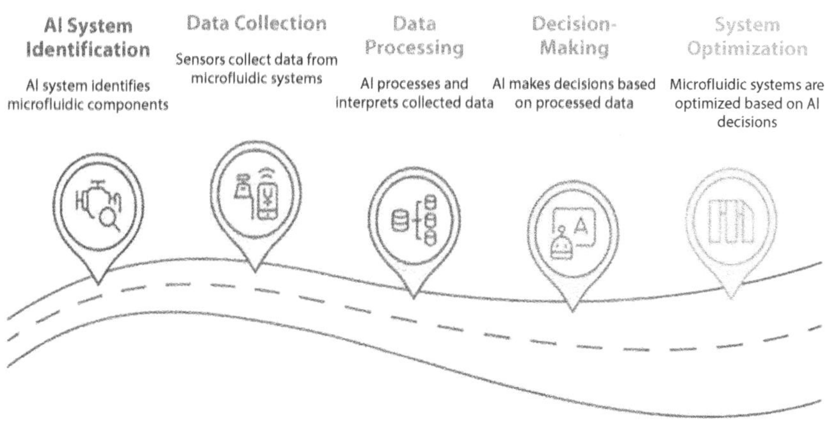

Figure 15.4 Integration of AI in microfluidic systems.

located elsewhere, CNNs and RNNs on embedded processors classify biomolecular interactions and adjust flow patterns so that rapid, point-of-care diagnostics can occur (Figure 15.4). The capability of real-time processing enables quick response times for critical healthcare applications, such as infectious disease detection, cancer screening, and modeling of an organ-on-a-chip for drug testing.

15.5.1 Automation of Experimental Workflows

AI-driven active learning is automating experimental workflows while eliminating human error and intervention. Active learning focuses on the more informative experiments with a faster pace of discovery [15]. AI models can identify the optimal experimental conditions to allow for high-throughput screening and immediate data analysis to inform subsequent experiments. For example, this approach has been applied to optimize nanoparticle synthesis inside a nanofluidic device through active learning. This approach reduced the number of necessary experiments by 60% with the same achievement of desired material properties.

15.5.2 Practical Applications

Artificial intelligence has significantly contributed to the evolution of LoC technologies related to diagnostics and drug development. In disease diagnosis, CNNs have enhanced sensitivity and specificity for pathogen-detecting systems [16]. Artificial intelligence enables single-cell analysis, which offers real-time cellular behavior monitoring within microfluidic environments.

In the area of biomedical diagnostics, AI models predict biomolecular interactions that will result in the design of personalized medicine. Systems utilizing AI are being designed for portable diagnostic devices to be applied in conditions ranging from infectious diseases to chronic disorders. In material science, AI optimizes nanoparticle manipulation within nanofluidic systems to control particle size, shape, and distribution, which supports the development of advanced materials for applications in electronics, energy, and healthcare.

15.5.3 Artificial Intelligence-Driven Drug Delivery Systems

Recent studies have proven the application of AI algorithms for optimizing drug delivery systems. Through patient data analysis and prediction of

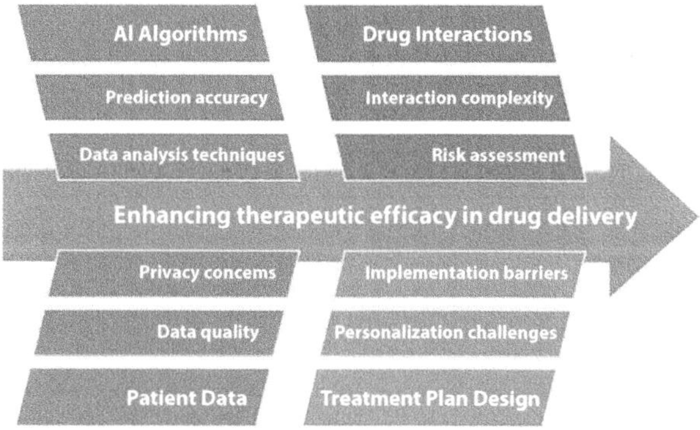

Figure 15.5 Optimizing AI-driven drug delivery systems.

drug interactions, AI helps in personalizing the treatment plan to enhance therapeutic efficacy. Personalized medicine is thereby advanced by the AI-driven systems that are utilizing such technologies as organ-on-a-chip, adaptive drug delivery, and point-of-care diagnostics for tailoring therapeutic interventions at the individual level [17] (Figure 15.5).

In personalized medicine, AI models predict drug efficacy and toxicity based on patient-specific data, ensuring safe and effective delivery of drugs. Such developments and the analysis of real-time fluctuations in biomarkers by AI are revolutionizing therapeutic practices and drug delivery systems. Integration of AI and microfluidics is bringing a new wave for personalized health solutions. Artificial intelligence brings further opportunities for real-time processing of data streams, adaptive and autonomous control, which can unlock even more groundbreaking research in diagnostics and drug delivery through microfluidics [18].

15.6 Environmental Sensors

Artificial intelligence-empowered microfluidic sensors that revolutionize environmental monitoring through the detection and quantification of environmental pollutants in real-time are being developed by researchers [19]. These sensors, using these ML models, can identify contaminants and quantify the concentration of the contaminants, hence providing valuable data to support environmental protection efforts (Figure 15.6). Artificial intelligence-integrated systems are more efficient, precise, and scalable in monitoring environments than any sensor system for the traditional monitoring of air, water, and soil quality [20].

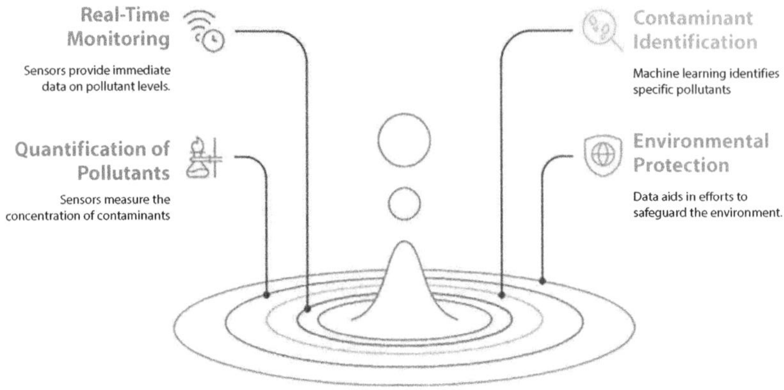

Figure 15.6 Artificial intelligence in environmental monitoring.

15.7 Challenges and Limitations

Despite the great promise of AI-integrated microfluidics and nanofluidics, several challenges continue to exist and prevent their further application [18]. Among them are:

1. Data Scarcity: Quality datasets are needed to train AI models, but the number of datasets and their diversity are usually limited.
2. Computational Costs: Training the most complex AI models requires extreme computational resources, which tend to be prohibitively expensive.

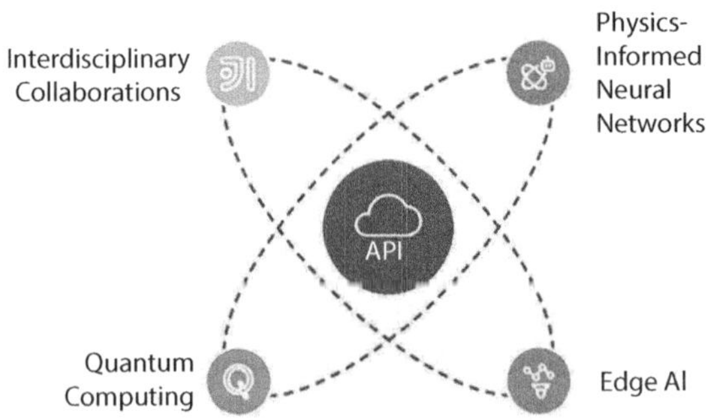

Figure 15.7 Advancing AI in fluidics.

3. Interdisciplinary Knowledge Gap. Many times, the lack of seamless collaboration between AI experts and fluid dynamicists obstructs the smooth use of AI in fluidics (Figure 15.7).

Addressing these challenges will be essential for unlocking the full potential of AI in these fields. Continued advancements in data availability, computational power, and interdisciplinary collaboration are critical for overcoming these hurdles.

15.8 Future Directions

As AI continues to evolve, several exciting directions are emerging in microfluidic and nanofluidic systems:

15.8.1 Integration of AI with Quantum Computing for Fluidics

It is paving the way for solving complex, high-dimensional optimization problems in microfluidics and nanofluidics by combining AI with quantum computing. Quantum-enhanced AI models, such as quantum ML techniques like VQCs and QBMs, offer much faster simulations of fluid behaviors at the nanoscale [21]. Such advances are enhancing the predictive accuracy and computational efficiency and can potentially lead to improved real-time fluidic control and device optimization.

Quantum-assisted deep reinforcement learning in microfluidic systems is an especially promising application. This paradigm allows for the faster exploration of very large parametric spaces, thereby enabling the autonomous, self-optimizing lab-on-a-chip platforms [22]. Moreover, geometries optimized for droplet formation, biomarker detection, and other applications are further optimized with novel designs of microfluidic chip architectures based on quantum-enhanced generative AI models, including quantum generative adversarial networks [23]. Quantum-enhanced molecular dynamics simulations are pushing the boundaries of understanding molecular transport phenomena crucial for applications such as drug delivery, nanocarriers, and nanopore-based biosensing in nanofluidics. Quantum algorithms are also breaking through fluid-structure interaction (FSI) modeling, advancing bio-inspired fluidic devices such as soft robotics and bio-hybrid systems [24].

15.8.2 Sustainability and Green Artificial Intelligence in Fluidics

The LoC devices that are used only once involve the use of non-biodegradable material. Fluidics are mainly seen to utilize bio-friendly materials using AI to give cellulose-based hydrogels, silk fibroin, and PLA-based substrates, which will be biocompatible and biodegradable, too [25]. Other optimization algorithms in use are Bayesian and GAN to optimize microfluidic systems using reagent ingestion and fluid waste in an optimal manner that provides reduced impact upon the environment.

Another very significant application of Green AI is in the areas of reagent minimization and fluidic waste reduction. Microflow conditions and geometries of microchannels are optimized for achieving a maximum efficiency ratio with minimal resource use. These configurations significantly impact the concepts of high-throughput screening and point-of-care diagnostics [26]. Further, AI is also significantly supporting the circular economy through reusable microfluidic chips. Instead of just predicting only the timing of material degradation and biofouling, ML models predict the necessary cleaning cycles to ensure reusability and increased lifespans of the devices used, therefore making the approach more resource-efficient and sustainable for fluidic technology development [27].

Low-power AI models are applied in battery-powered microfluidic devices to make the field deployable. Using frameworks such as TinyML and Edge Impulse, these AI systems are powered to run real-time fluidic analysis with little energy utilization, thereby eliminating the need for large infrastructure for computational processes.

15.8.3 Edge Artificial Intelligence for Real-Time Applications

The AI models are deployed on edge devices, which include microcontrollers or embedded systems, to provide real-time analytics and control. This is extremely valuable in such applications as biomedical diagnostics and portable lab-on-a-chip devices. Edge AI local processing reduces latency and therefore enhances the responsiveness and efficiency of the devices in most time-sensitive situations, including on-site diagnostics [28].

15.8.4 Quantum Computing

Quantum computing shows great promise in improving the accuracy of AI model training by accelerating the simulation of intricate fluid behaviors predominant in microfluidics and nanofluidics by solving complex, high-dimensional optimization problems. In this sense, the combination of quantum computing and AI represents an entirely new frontier for research in fluidics and real-time control systems [29].

15.8.5 Interdisciplinary Collaborations

Interdisciplinary collaboration holds the key for AI-enhanced fluidic systems to reach their full potential. A combination of AI scientists, fluid dynamics experts, materials scientists, and engineers will help overcome various challenges, such as data scarcity and computational limitations, toward design optimization. Partnerships in academia, industries, and institutes will be paramount for the technologies to be adopted successfully.

15.9 Regulatory and Ethical Considerations of Artificial Intelligence in Microfluidics

Although the integration of AI in microfluidics and nanofluidics is characterized by exciting breakthroughs in diagnostics, drug delivery, and environmental sensing, there exists a wide scope for challenges on regulatory and ethical fronts. The transparency and explainability of AI models are crucially important, especially when these applications enter healthcare and the environment. For example, the FDA and EMA are interested in the interpretability and reproducibility of such AI-driven systems, with a focus on LoC platforms [30].

Furthermore, because of the strong potential for bias in any AI model trained on microfluidic systems, data validation should be executed using diverse, multi-center datasets to reduce biases and ensure that the model generalizes well across different biological samples and experimental conditions. Federated learning offers a solution to data privacy by allowing AI models to learn on decentralized data without sharing sensitive information [31].

Ethically, then, considerations involving autonomous AI systems, such as those in drug delivery or organ-on-a-chip models, are essential. Human oversight would prevent unwanted side effects and ensure patient safety in personalized treatments.

Third, standardized AI benchmarking protocols are necessary to evaluate the validation that AI-integrated microfluidic systems must face before they get commercialized in the market; otherwise, proper regulatory approvals won't be availed [31]. This kind of regulation shall ensure that AI-integrated systems meet the specific safety and efficacy standards. These future directions catalyze the next wave of innovation with AI in microfluidics and nanofluidics. Adding the cutting-edge technologies of quantum computing and sustainability practice, AI will continue to revolutionize fluidic systems, opening healthcare, environmental monitoring, and more.

15.10 Conclusion

Artificial integration with microfluidics and nanofluidics does signify a new paradigm in terms of how fluids can be manipulated and controlled on a micro-scale and nanoscale. By examining this approach from a multifaceted point of view, various critical technical accomplishments and impacts were found that reflect how technology convergence at these levels impacts changes. The PINNs have changed CFD for microfluidic applications, which now produces accurate results with only limited training data. It fits the fundamental physical constraints and has proven to be the best model in predicting very complex phenomena like droplet formation, mixing dynamics, and multiphase flows, in which it predicts greater than 95% accuracy in many applications.

Edge computing integration with AI has greatly improved real-time control, with embedded systems able to process up to 22.13 frames per second in automated immunoassays. This improvement has allowed for unprecedented precision in fluid manipulation, as evidenced by a reduction in detection limits for cardiac troponin I to 0.91 pg/mL, which is greater than a 2-fold enhancement in LOD. Deep learning architectures, which include deep CNNs and RNNs, have shown outstanding results in fluid behavior prediction and control. These architectures decreased the computational cost up to 60% while maintaining a high accuracy rate compared to traditional CFD methods. Random Forest models have 95.52% sensitivity in applications such as bubble detection, and DenseNet169 architectures achieve 92.63% sensitivity under similar contexts.

The synthesis of AI and quantum computing has thus opened up new frontiers in optimization in microfluidics, such as quantum-enhanced molecular dynamics simulations, as well as quantum-assisted deep reinforcement learning. These alternatives have facilitated more efficient probing of a very large parametric space in microfluidic design that results in optimized geometries for droplet formation while also enhancing the capacity to detect biomarkers. Further important technological breakthroughs down the road for advancing this area will involve, first and foremost, integration with quantum algorithms on solving the higher-dimensional optimization problem within the nanofluidic systems: one prominent path for which could be with QVCs or QBMs. Advanced edge AI implementations using TinyML and specialized hardware accelerators further improve real-time processing capabilities in resource-constrained environments, while the federated learning protocol is being developed to provide secure distributed training of AI models on multiple microfluidic platforms with no compromise in data privacy. The persistent technical challenges relate to the scarcity of data, computational overheads, and the lack of model generalization. However, solutions emerging include transfer learning, active learning, and hybrid physics-ML models. Standardized AI benchmarking protocols for the validation and regulatory requirements of such systems will be of utmost importance in the near future. Green AI principles in the aspect of design for computational efficiency and efficient usage of resources will become progressively important within this field as it grows.

The convergence of AI with microfluidics and nanofluidics has catalyzed unprecedented advances in fields ranging from biomedical diagnostics to environmental monitoring. As computational capabilities continue to evolve and new AI architectures emerge, we anticipate further breakthroughs in areas such as personalized medicine, drug delivery systems, and point-of-care diagnostics. The future of this field lies in the continued development of more sophisticated AI models, enhanced edge computing capabilities, and improved integration with quantum computing technologies, all while maintaining a focus on sustainability and ethical considerations. The technical foundations established thus far provide a robust platform for future innovations, suggesting that the synergy between AI and fluidic systems will continue to drive transformative advances in both fundamental research and practical applications. This evolution will require ongoing collaboration between AI specialists, fluid dynamicists, and domain experts to fully realize the potential of these integrated technologies and push the boundaries of what is possible in microfluidic and nanofluidic systems.

References

1. Doganay, M.T., Chakraborty, P., Bommakanti, S.M., Jammalamadaka, S., Battalapalli, D., Madabhushi, A., Draz, M.S., Artificial intelligence performance in testing microfluidics for point-of-care. *Lab on a Chip*, 24, 21, 4998-5008, 2024.
2. Shaw, I., Ali, Y.S., Nie, C., Zhang, K., Chen, C., Xiao, Y., Integrating Artificial Intelligence and Microfluidics Technology for Psoriasis Therapy:

A Comprehensive Review for Research and Clinical Applications. *Adv. Intell. Syst.*, 7, 4, 2400558, 2025.

3. Recent Advances in Generative AI and Large Language Models: Current Status, Challenges, and Perspectives, n.d. https://www.researchgate.net/publication/382459163_Recent_Advances_in_Generative_AI_and_Large_Language_Models_Current_Status_Challenges_and_Perspectives (accessed February 7, 2025).
4. Tsai, H.F., Podder, S., Chen, P.Y., 2023. Microsystem advances through integration with artificial intelligence. *Micromachines*, 14, 4, 826, 2023.
5. Eş, I., Ece, E., Hacıosmanoğlu, N., Güngen, M.A., Inci, F., Artificial intelligence-assisted organ-on-chip systems, in: *Smart Organ-on-Chip Devices*, pp. 61–69, Academic Press, 2025.
6. Bhuiyan, N.H., Uddin, M.J., Lee, J., Hong, J.H., Shim, J.S., 2022. An Internet-of-Disease System for COVID-19 Testing Using Saliva by an AI-Controlled Microfluidic ELISA Device. *Adv. Mater. Technol.*, 7, 9, 2101690, 2022.
7. Alzubaidi, L., Zhang, J., Humaidi, A.J., Al-Dujaili, A., Duan, Y., Al-Shamma, O., Santamaría, J., Fadhel, M.A., Al-Amidie, M., Farhan, L., Review of deep learning: concepts, CNN architectures, challenges, applications, future directions. *J. Big Data*, 8, 1–74, 1, 2021. https://doi.org/10.1186/S40537-021-00444-8.
8. Caron, C., Lauret, P., Bastide, A., Machine Learning to speed up Computational Fluid Dynamics engineering simulations for built environments: A review. *Build. Environ.*, 267, 112229, 2025. https://doi.org/10.1016/J.BUILDENV.2024.112229.
9. Yang, S., Kim, H., Hong, Y., Yee, K., Maulik, R., Kang, N., Data-driven physics-informed neural networks: A digital twin perspective. *Comput. Methods Appl. Mech. Eng.*, 428, 117075, 2024. https://doi.org/10.1016/J.CMA.2024.117075.
10. Oliveira, N.M., Vilabril, S., Oliveira, M.B., Reis, R.L., Mano, J.F., Recent advances on open fluidic systems for biomedical applications: A review. *Mater. Sci. Eng. C*, 97, 851–863, 2019. https://doi.org/10.1016/J.MSEC.2018.12.040.
11. Choi, T., Park, J., Lee, S., Jeon, H.J., Kim, B.H., Kim, H.O., Lee, H., 3D Bioprinted Neural Tissues: Emerging Strategies for Regeneration and Disease Modeling. *Pharmaceutics*, 17, 9, 1176, 2025.
12. Roshan, U., Dai, Y., Yadav, A.S., Hettiarachchi, S., Mudugamuwa, A., Zhang, J., Nguyen, N.T., Flexible droplet microfluidic devices for tuneable droplet generation. *Sens. Actuators B Chem.*, 422, 136617, 2025. https://doi.org/10.1016/J.SNB.2024.136617.
13. Khan, S.G., Herrmann, G., Lewis, F.L., Pipe, T., Melhuish, C., Reinforcement learning and optimal adaptive control: An overview and implementation examples. *Annu. Rev. Control*, 36, 42–59, 2012. https://doi.org/10.1016/J.ARCONTROL.2012.03.004.
14. Zylinski, M., Nassibi, A., Rakhmatulin, I., Malik, A., Papavassiliou, C.M., Mandic, D.P., Deployment of Artificial Intelligence Models on Edge Devices:

A Tutorial Brief. *IEEE Trans. Circuits Syst. II Express Briefs*, 71, 1738–1743, 2024. https://doi.org/10.1109/TCSII.2023.3336831.

15. Ren, Z., Ren, Z., Zhang, Z., Buonassisi, T., Li, J., Autonomous experiments using active learning and AI. *Nat. Rev. Mater.*, 8, 563–564, 9, 2023. https://doi.org/10.1038/s41578-023-00588-4.
16. Zare Harofte, S., Soltani, M., Siavashy, S., Raahemifar, K., Recent Advances of Utilizing Artificial Intelligence in Lab on a Chip for Diagnosis and Treatment. *Small*, 18, 2203169, 2022. https://doi.org/10.1002/SMLL.202203169.
17. Taherdoost, H. and Ghofrani, A., AI's role in revolutionizing personalized medicine by reshaping pharmacogenomics and drug therapy. *Intell. Pharm.*, 2, 643–650, 2024. https://doi.org/10.1016/J.IPHA.2024.08.005.
18. Asadian, E., Bahramian, F., Siavashy, S., Movahedi, S., Keçili, R., Hussain, C.M., Ghorbani-Bidkorpeh, F., A review on recent advances of AI-integrated microfluidics for analytical and bioanalytical applications. *TrAC, Trends Anal. Chem.*, 181, 118004, 2024. https://doi.org/10.1016/J.TRAC.2024.118004.
19. Pouyanfar, N., Harofte, S.Z., Soltani, M., Siavashy, S., Asadian, E., Ghorbani-Bidkorbeh, F., Keçili, R., Hussain, C.M., Artificial intelligence-based microfluidic platforms for the sensitive detection of environmental pollutants: Recent advances and prospects. *Trends Environ. Anal. Chem.*, 34, e00160, 2022. https://doi.org/10.1016/J.TEAC.2022.E00160.
20. Bin Rashid, A. and Kausik, M.A.K., AI revolutionizing industries worldwide: A comprehensive overview of its diverse applications. *Hybrid Adv.*, 7, 100277, 2024. https://doi.org/10.1016/J.HYBADV.2024.100277.
21. Peral-García, D., Cruz-Benito, J., García-Peñalvo, F.J., Systematic literature review: Quantum machine learning and its applications. *Comput. Sci. Rev.*, 51, 100619, 2024. https://doi.org/10.1016/J.COSREV.2024.100619.
22. Niraula, D., Jamaluddin, J., Matuszak, M.M., Haken, R.K.T., El Naqa, I., Quantum deep reinforcement learning for clinical decision support in oncology: application to adaptive radiotherapy. *Sci. Rep.*, 11, 1–13, 1, 2021. https://doi.org/10.1038/s41598-021-02910-y.
23. Pajuhanfard, M., Kiani, R., Sheng, V.S., Survey of Quantum Generative Adversarial Networks (QGAN) to Generate Images. *Mathematics*, 12, 3852, 2024. https://doi.org/10.3390/MATH12233852.
24. Hölscher, L., Rao, P., Müller, L., Klepsch, J., Luckow, A., Stollenwerk, T. and Wilhelm, F.K., Quantum-inspired fluid simulation of two-dimensional turbulence with GPU acceleration. *Phys. Rev. Res.*, 7, 013112, 2025. https://doi.org/10.1103/PhysRevResearch.7.013112.
25. Tran, H., Gurnani, R., Kim, C., Pilania, G., Kwon, H.K., Lively, R.P., Ramprasad, R., Design of functional and sustainable polymers assisted by artificial intelligence. *Nat. Rev. Mater.*, 9, 866–886, 12, 2024. https://doi.org/10.1038/s41578-024-00708-8.
26. Bolón-Canedo, V., Morán-Fernández, L., Cancela, B., Alonso-Betanzos, A., A review of green artificial intelligence: Towards a more sustainable

future. *Neurocomputing*, 599, 128096, 2024. https://doi.org/10.1016/J.NEUCOM.2024.128096.
27. Özsoy, T., The Role Of Artificial Intelligence In Facilitating The Transition To A Circular Economy. *Nişantaşı Üniversitesi Sosyal Bilimler Dergisi*, 11, 369–389, 2023. https://doi.org/10.52122/NISANTASISBD.1345828.
28. Singh, R. and Gill, S.S., Edge AI: A survey. *Internet Things Cyber-Phys. Syst.*, 3, 71–92, 2023. https://doi.org/10.1016/J.IOTCPS.2023.02.004.
29. Lu, W., Lu, Y., Li, J., Sigov, A., Ratkin, L., Ivanov, L.A., Quantum machine learning: Classifications, challenges, and solutions. *J. Ind. Inf. Integr.*, 42, 100736, 2024. https://doi.org/10.1016/J.JII.2024.100736.
30. Balasubramaniam, N., Kauppinen, M., Rannisto, A., Hiekkanen, K., Kujala, S., Transparency and explainability of AI systems: From ethical guidelines to requirements. *Inf. Softw. Technol.*, 159, 107197, 2023. https://doi.org/10.1016/J.INFSOF.2023.107197.
31. IEEE Standard for Performance Benchmarking for Artificial Intelligence Server Systems, 2022. https://doi.org/10.1109/IEEESTD.2022.9930948.

About the Editors

Mukesh Kumar Awasthi, PhD is an Assistant Professor in the Department of Mathematics at Babasaheb Bhimrao Ambedkar University. He has published more than 125 research publications in journal and conference articles and book chapters, as well as ten books. His expertise lies in viscous potential flow, electro-hydrodynamics, magnetohydrodynamics, and heat and mass transfer.

Reshu Gupta, PhD is an Associate Professor in the Applied Science Cluster at the University of Petroleum and Engineering Studies with more than 20 years of teaching experience. She has published several papers in international journals and conference proceedings and three books. Her research areas include fluid dynamics, differential equations, heat and mass transfer, nanofluids, entropy, and artificial neural networks.

Index

Also of Interest

Check out these related titles from Scrivener Publishing

Applied Computer Vision Through Artificial Intelligence, Edited by Jasminder Kaur Sandhu, Abhishek Kumar, Rakesh Sahu, and Sachin Ahuja, ISBN: 9781394272594. Master the cutting-edge field of computer vision and artificial intelligence with this accessible guide to the applications of machine learning and deep learning for real-world solutions in robotics, healthcare, and autonomous systems.

Predictive Methods in Next-Generation Computing, Edited by R. Sathiyaraj, Rajesh Kumar Dhanaraj, K. Arun Kumar, Rutvij H. Jhaveri, and A. Mohamed Abbas, ISBN: 9781394248797. Predictive Methods in Next-Generation Computing is essential for anyone looking to understand how next-generation computing technologies are driving predictive models to create smarter, safer, and more sustainable solutions across diverse fields.

Deep Learning and Its Applications Using Python, Edited by Niha Kamal Basha, Surbhi Bhatia Khan, Abhishek Kumar and Arwa Mashat, ISBN: 9781394166466. This practical book gives a detailed description of deep learning models and their implementation using Python programming relating to computer vision, natural language processing, and other applications.

Networked Sensing Systems, Edited by Rajesh Kumar Dhanaraj, Malathy Sathyamoorthy, Balasubramaniam S., and Seifedine Kadry, ISBN: 9781394310869. *Networked Sensing Systems* is essential for anyone seeking innovative and sustainable solutions across diverse sectors, as it explores the integration of cutting-edge IoT technologies and digital transformation aimed at enhancing resource efficiency and addressing climate change challenges.

Multimodal Data Fusion for Bioinformatics Artificial Intelligence, Edited by Umesh Kumar Lilhore, Abhishek Kumar, Narayan Vyas, Sarita Simaiya, and Vishal Dutt, ISBN: 9781394269938. *Multimodal Data Fusion for Bioinformatics Artificial Intelligence* is a must-have for anyone interested in the intersection of AI and bioinformatics, as it not only delves into innovative data fusion methods and their applications in omics research but also addresses the ethical implications and future developments shaping the field today.

Data Structure and Algorithms Using C++: A Practical Implementation, By Sachi Nandan Mohanty and Pabitra Kumar Tripathy, ISBN: 9781119750543. The book is intended to assist university faculty members and students to realize the principles and acquire the practical skills of programming using the C++ programming language.

Artificial Intelligence-Based System Models in Healthcare, Edited by A. Jose Anand, K. Kalaiselvi and Jyotir Moy Chatterjee, ISBN: 9781394242498. Artificial Intelligence-Based System Models in Healthcare provides a comprehensive and insightful guide to the transformative applications of AI in the healthcare system.

EXPLAINABLE MACHINE LEARNING MODELS AND ARCHITECTURES: Real-Time System Implementation, Edited by Suman Lata Tripathi and Mufti Mahmud, ISBN: 9781394185849. This cutting-edge new volume covers the hardware architecture implementation, the software implementation approach, and the efficient hardware of machine learning applications.

Natural Language Processing for Software Engineering, Edited by Rajesh Kumar Chakrawarti, Ranjana Sikarwar, Sanjaya Kumar Sarangi, Samson Arun Raj Albert Raj, Shweta Gupta, Krishnan Sakthidasan Sankaran, and Romil Rawat, ISBN: 9781394272433. Discover how Natural Language Processing for Software Engineering can transform your understanding of agile development, equipping you with essential tools and insights to enhance software quality and responsiveness in todays rapidly changing technological landscape.

MACHINE LEARNING TECHNIQUES FOR VLSI CHIP DESIGN, Edited by Abhishek Kumar, Suman Lata Tripathi, and K. Srinivasa Rao, ISBN: 9781119910398. This cutting-edge new volume covers the hardware architecture implementation, the software implementation approach, and the efficient hardware of machine learning applications with FPGA or CMOS circuits, and many other aspects and applications of machine learning techniques for VLSI chip design.

Intelligent Green Technologies for Smart Cities, Edited by Suman Lata Tripathi, Souvik Ganguli, Abhishek Kumar, and Tengiz Magradze, ISBN: 9781119816065. Presenting the concepts and fundamentals of smart cities and developing "green" technologies, this volume, written and edited by a global team of experts, also goes into the practical applications that can be utilized across multiple disciplines and industries, for both the engineer and the student.

Hybrid Intelligent Optimization Approaches for Smart Energy: A Practical Approach, Edited by Senthilkumar Mohan, A. John, Sanjeevikumar Padmanaban, and Yasir Hamid, ISBN: 9781119821243. Written and edited by a group of experts in the field, this is a comprehensive and up-to-date description of current energy optimization techniques, such as artificial intelligence techniques, machine learning, deep learning, and IoT techniques and their future trends.

NANODEVICES FOR INTEGRATED CIRCUIT DESIGN, Edited by Suman Lata Tripathi, Abhishek Kumar, K. Srinivasa Rao, and Prasantha R. Mudimela, ISBN: 9781394185788. Written and edited by a team of experts in the field, this important new volume broadly covers the design of nano-devices and their integrated applications in digital and analog integrated circuits (IC) design.

DESIGN AND DEVELOPMENT OF EFFICIENT ENERGY SYSTEMS, Edited by Suman Lata Tripathi, Dushyant Kumar Singh, Sanjeevikumar Padmanaban, and P. Raja, ISBN: 9781119761631. Covering the concepts and fundamentals of efficient energy systems, this volume, written and edited by a global team of experts, also goes into the practical applications that can be utilized across multiple industries, for both the engineer and the student.

Electrical and Electronic Devices, Circuits, and Materials: Technical Challenges and Solutions, Edited by Suman Lata Tripathi, Parvej Ahmad Alvi, and Umashankar Subramaniam, ISBN: 9781119750369. Covering every aspect of the design and improvement needed for solid-state electronic devices and circuit and their reliability issues, this new volume also includes overall system design for all kinds of analog and digital applications and developments in power systems.

MODELING AND OPTIMIZATION OF OPTICAL COMMUNICATION NETWORKS, Edited by Chandra Singh, Rathishchandra R Gatti, K.V.S.S.S.S. Sairam, and Ashish Singh, ISBN: 9781119839200. *Modeling and Optimization of Optical Communication Networks* is a comprehensive and authoritative book that delves into the optical networks, principles, technologies, and practical applications of optical networks, equipping readers with the knowledge needed to design, implement, and optimize optical networks for various applications, from telecommunications to scientific research. With its comprehensive coverage and up-to-date insights, this book serves as an essential reference in the field of optical networks.

WIRELESS COMMUNICATION SECURITY: Mobile and Network Security Protocols, Edited by Manju Khari, Manisha Bharti, and M. Niranjanamurthy, ISBN: 9781119777144. Presenting the concepts and advances of wireless communication security, this volume, written and edited by a global team of experts, also goes into the practical applications for the engineer, student, and other industry professionals.

ADVANCES IN DATA SCIENCE AND ANALYTICS, Edited by M. Niranjanamurthy, Hemant Kumar Gianey, and Amir H. Gandomi, ISBN: 9781119791881. Presenting the concepts and advances of data science and analytics, this volume, written and edited by a global team of experts, also goes into the practical applications that can be utilized across multiple disciplines and industries, for both the engineer and the student, focusing on machining learning, big data, business intelligence, and analytics.

ARTIFICIAL INTELLIGENCE AND DATA MINING IN SECURITY FRAMEWORKS, Edited by Neeraj Bhargava, Ritu Bhargava, Pramod Singh Rathore, and Rashmi Agrawal, ISBN: 9781119760405. Written and edited by a team of experts in the field, this outstanding new volume offers solutions to the problems of security, outlining the concepts behind allowing computers to learn from experience and understand the world in terms of a hierarchy of concepts.

MACHINE LEARNING AND DATA SCIENCE: Fundamentals and Applications, Edited by Prateek Agrawal, Charu Gupta, Anand Sharma, Vishu Madaan, and Nisheeth Joshi, ISBN: 9781119775614. Written and edited by a team of experts in the field, this collection of papers reflects the most up-to-date and comprehensive current state of machine learning and data science for industry, government, and academia.

MEDICAL IMAGING, Edited by H. S. Sanjay, and M. Niranjanamurthy, ISBN: 9781119785392. Written and edited by a team of experts in the field, this is the most comprehensive and up-to-date study of and reference for the practical applications of medical imaging for engineers, scientists, students, and medical professionals.

SECURITY ISSUES AND PRIVACY CONCERNS IN INDUSTRY 4.0 APPLICATIONS, Edited by Shibin David, R. S. Anand, V. Jeyakrishnan, and M. Niranjanamurthy, ISBN: 9781119775621. Written and edited by a team of international experts, this is the most comprehensive and up-to-date coverage of the security and privacy issues surrounding Industry 4.0 applications, a must-have for any library.

CYBER SECURITY AND DIGITAL FORENSICS: Challenges and Future Trends, Edited by Mangesh M. Ghonge, Sabyasachi Pramanik, Ramchandra Mangrulkar, and Dac-Nhuong Le, ISBN: 9781119795636. Written and edited by a team of world renowned experts in the field, this groundbreaking new volume covers key technical topics and gives readers a comprehensive understanding of the latest research findings in cyber security and digital forensics.

DEEP LEARNING APPROACHES TO CLOUD SECURITY, Edited by Pramod Singh Rathore, Vishal Dutt, Rashmi Agrawal, Satya Murthy Sasubilli, and Srinivasa Rao Swarna, ISBN: 9781119760528. Covering one of the most important subjects to our society today, this editorial team delves into solutions taken from evolving deep learning approaches, solutions allow computers to learn from experience and understand the world in terms of a hierarchy of concepts.

MACHINE LEARNING TECHNIQUES AND ANALYTICS FOR CLOUD SECURITY, Edited by Rajdeep Chakraborty, Anupam Ghosh and Jyotsna Kumar Mandal, ISBN: 9781119762256. This book covers new methods, surveys, case studies, and policy with almost all machine learning techniques and analytics for cloud security solutions.

SECURITY DESIGNS FOR THE CLOUD, IOT AND SOCIAL NETWORKING, Edited by Dac-Nhuong Le, Chintin Bhatt and Mani Madhukar, ISBN: 9781119592266. The book provides cutting-edge research that delivers insights into the tools, opportunities, novel strategies, techniques, and challenges for handling security issues in cloud computing, Internet of Things and social networking.

DESIGN AND ANALYSIS OF SECURITY PROTOCOLS FOR COMMUNICATION, Edited by Dinesh Goyal, S. Balamurugan, Sheng-Lung Peng and O.P. Verma, ISBN: 9781119555643. The book combines analysis and comparison of various security protocols such as HTTP, SMTP, RTP, RTCP, FTP, UDP for mobile or multimedia streaming security protocol.

SMART GRIDS FOR SMART CITIES VOLUME 2: Real-Time Applications in Smart Cities, Edited by O.V. Gnana Swathika, K. Karthikeyan, and Sanjeevikumar Padmanaban, ISBN: 9781394215874. Written and edited by a team of experts in the field, this second volume in a two-volume set focuses on an interdisciplinary perspective on the financial, environmental, and other benefits of smart grid technologies and solutions for smart cities.

SMART GRIDS AND INTERNET OF THINGS, Edited by Sanjeevikumar Padmanaban, Jens Bo Holm-Nielsen, Rajesh Kumar Dhanaraj, Malathy Sathyamoorthy, and Balamurugan Balusamy, ISBN: 9781119812449. Written and edited by a team of international professionals, this ground-breaking new volume covers the latest technologies in automation, tracking, energy distribution and consumption of Internet of Things (IoT) devices with smart grids.

Printed and bound by CPI Group (UK) Ltd, Croydon, CR0 4YY
17/09/2026
14964285-0006